THE KING IN EXILE

THE KING IN EXILE

The Fall of the Royal Family of Burma

Sudha Shah

With 32 pages of photographs/illustrations

HarperCollins *Publishers* India
a joint venture with

THE INDIA TODAY GROUP

New Delhi

First published in India in 2012 by
HarperCollins *Publishers* India
a joint venture with
The India Today Group

Copyright © Sudha Shah 2012

ISBN: 978-93-5029-226-6

2 4 6 8 10 9 7 5 3 1

Sudha Shah asserts the moral right to be identified as
the author of this work.

Layout of image inserts: Gita Simoes
Scanning, restoration and toning of images: Mazda Imaging Pvt. Ltd, Mumbai

HarperCollins *Publishers*
A-53, Sector 57, Noida, Uttar Pradesh 201301, India
77-85 Fulham Palace Road, London W6 8JB, United Kingdom
Hazelton Lanes, 55 Avenue Road, Suite 2900, Toronto, Ontario M5R 3L2
and 1995 Markham Road, Scarborough, Ontario M1B 5M8, Canada
25 Ryde Road, Pymble, Sydney, NSW 2073, Australia
31 View Road, Glenfield, Auckland 10, New Zealand
10 East 53rd Street, New York NY 10022, USA

Typeset in 12.5/15 Venetian301 BT at
SÜRYA

Printed and bound at
Thomson Press (India) Ltd

For my parents, Sheila and Janak Malkani

In memory of Ashin Hteik Su Myat Phaya Gyi, the First Princess

In deep appreciation for all the help, support and warmth given to me by Prince Taw Phaya Galae (Prince Frederick), also known as U Aung Zae, and affectionately called Taw Taw. A nationalist, an entrepreneur, a writer, a history researcher, an English teacher, he was a man of quiet dignity and great charm. In spite of his failing health, he generously helped me with my research. Over phone conversations and in emails, he commented that he hoped to live to read my book. This was not to be—sadly, he passed away on 18 June 2006.

Prince Taw Phaya Galae was the grandson of the last king of Burma, King Thibaw, and his wife, Queen Supayalat, and the son of the Fourth Princess, Ashin Hteik Su Myat Phaya Galae, and her husband, Ko Ko Naing.

Picture taken by author on 27 February 2005 at Prince Taw Phaya Galae's home in Yangon

CONTENTS

PART III: AFTER THE EXILE

Preface

Thibaw, the last king of Burma, belonged to the Konbaung dynasty, a line of rulers known as 'Kings who rule the Universe' and treated as demi-gods by their subjects. His wife, Queen Supayalat, had great influence over him and is said to have been the true ruler of the kingdom during their seven-year reign.

In late 1885, after defeat in a war against Britain, King Thibaw, the heavily pregnant Queen Supayalat, their two very young daughters, and the king's junior queen, Supayagalae, were exiled to India. Here, in the culturally alien and remote town of Ratnagiri, they lived for over thirty years.

The First, Second, Third and Fourth Princesses, so called for the sake of brevity by the various British officers in charge of the family during their exile (the princesses, as per custom, were known by lengthy titles and not common names), were brought up in Ratnagiri by parents mourning their loss and nursing their wounds. Like their parents, the princesses were not allowed to interact freely with the residents of Ratnagiri. There was no question of them enrolling at a local school or playing with the town children; even if the British had permitted it, it is unlikely their parents would have. So they lived, attended to by an army of servants and assistants, until the princesses

were all in their thirties. By this time, two of them had fallen in love
with 'highly unsuitable' men, and all four of them had been endowed
with a deep awareness of their ancestry, a sense of entitlement, and a
feeling of bereavement. None of them had received the kind of
exposure or education necessary to adequately equip them for life in
the outside world.

King Thibaw died in 1916 without ever setting foot on his homeland
again. His junior queen had died a few years before him. Both were
entombed in Ratnagiri, where their mortal remains lie to this day. In
1919, not long after World War I (1914–18) concluded, Queen
Supayalat and the princesses were permitted to return to British-
occupied Rangoon.

This book tells the story of King Thibaw, his wives, his daughters
and his grandchildren. It has not been written as a work of fiction—I
found the actual story too captivating to add any embellishments.
(The bizarre twists and turns their lives sometimes took were truly
stranger than any credible fiction could ever have been!) The raison
d'être of the book is to provide an insight into, first, how an all-
powerful and very wealthy family coped with forced isolation and
separation from all that they had once known and cherished; and,
second, how the family lived once the exile ended. When I first started
researching for this book, I thought I would end with the death of the
Third Princess, that is, on 21 July 1962. But the more I delved, the
more I realized that for a sense of completion and closure one needed
to examine the lives of the princesses' children as well, for the
children's lives were inextricably intertwined with those of their
mothers, and they too were impacted by the deposition, the exile, and
their lineage.

Part I depicts the life of the king and queen during their reign. I felt
this background was essential to put into context the royal family's
life during and after the exile. My sources for Part I include two well-
researched, fictionalized accounts of historical events which, I believe,
accurately represent the essence of what actually happened. The
authors of both these books (*The Lacquer Lady* and *Thibaw's Queen*)
interviewed (inter alia) maid(s) of honour who served under Queen
Supayalat. Conversations and facts reproduced from these sources

have been clearly identified in the endnotes (as have all my other sources).

Parts II and III—the heart of my research and of my book—details the family's life during and after the exile. No fictionalized source has been used for these parts (except for an unpublished manuscript by James Halliday aka David Symington who was collector of Ratnagiri about ten years after the departure of the royal family from Ratnagiri. Two brief bits of information have been used from this source—the first is regarding Mr Tennant's infatuation with the Fourth Princess, and the second is about the notice put up at the Royal Residence after the king's death). However, I have depended much—particularly for Part III—on peoples' memories (on their verbal and written accounts), and memories, as we know, are informed by the perceptions of the narrator. When differing, and sometimes even contradictory, versions of the same occurrence have been narrated, the version that has seemed the most credible to me has been worked into the book. Ever so often, however, it has been impossible to sift actual facts from those based on peoples' assumptions, extrapolations and imagination. Since so much of what happened was not documented, and since many of the protagonists of this story lived long ago, I have often had to depend on just one source for a piece of information.

Vikram Seth wrote in his book *Two Lives*: 'Every even-handed biography of a completed life has to deal with private matters and to present its subject as fully as possible, even if the subject, when alive, might have preferred to keep these matters obscured—or at least not open to the world.' While writing this book, I have had to occasionally mentally wrestle with whether or not to include certain facts (particularly for Parts II and III). It is apparent that family descendants I interviewed sometimes have had a similar conflict—what to divulge to me and how much, what to gloss over or totally conceal. There are certain matters the family would perhaps have preferred not revealed, but by not including them would this biography have been at all meaningful? In making a decision, I have tried to consider whether the matter would add something consequential to either our understanding of the people involved or the events that occurred. If the answer is yes, I have included it, but with as much sensitivity as I could.

Certainly I have tried to be 'even-handed' in this book, but after so many years of research and interaction, fondness for and empathy with many members of the family may have sometimes clouded my judgement. What I do know for sure, however, is that the profound effect of the deposition and exile echoed forever in the lives of not just the king and his queens, but in that of all the four princesses, and each of their children.

LIST OF PEOPLE

Allbon: Police officer in charge of the king during his exile—1888 to 1894. The king took a hearty dislike to this officer and petitioned to have him removed.

Andreino: The Italian consul general during King Thibaw's rule; Andreino also represented the interests of the Bombay-Burma Trading Company in the kingdom.

Ashin Hteik Su Myat Phaya Gyi: King Thibaw and Queen Supayalat's eldest daughter. Aka the First Princess. Born in Mandalay on 5 September 1880. Gopal Bhaurao Sawant was her companion from 1905/1906. Died in Ratnagiri on 3 June 1947. One daughter, Tu Tu.

Ashin Hteik Su Myat Phaya Galae: King Thibaw and Queen Supayalat's youngest daughter. Aka the Fourth Princess. Born in Ratnagiri on 25 April 1887. Married Ko Ko Naing in 1920. Died in Moulmein on 3 March 1936. Two daughters, Princess Hteik Su Phaya Gyi and Princess Hteik Su Phaya Htwe, and four sons, Prince Taw Phaya Gyi, Prince Taw Phaya, Prince Taw Phaya Nge and Prince Taw Phaya Galae.

Ashin Hteik Su Myat Phaya Lat: King Thibaw and Queen Supayalat's second daughter. Aka the Second Princess. Born in Mandalay on

11 August 1881. Married Latthakin in 1917. Died in Calcutta on 4 April 1956. One son, Maung Lu Gyi.

Ashin Hteik Su Myat Phaya: King Thibaw and Queen Supayalat's third daughter. Aka the Third Princess. In Burma she was sometimes known as Madras Supaya as she was born in Madras. Born on 7 March 1886. Married Prince Hteik Tin Kodaw Gyi in 1921. Divorced him in 1930. Married U Mya U in 1931. Died in Maymyo on 21 July 1962. One daughter, Princess Rita.

Attlee, Clement: Prime minister of Britain from 1945 to 1951.

Aung San (Bogyoke or General): A leading nationalist, often called the father of modern Burma. Assassinated on 19 July 1947. Father of Aung San Suu Kyi.

Barber: Police officer in charge of the king during his exile—1894 to 1895.

Bernard: The chief commissioner of British Lower Burma at the time of the Third Anglo-Burmese war.

Bonvillian: Mattie Calogreedy's lover, whom she considered to be her husband (according to prevailing Burmese custom).

Brander: Collector of Ratnagiri. In 1911, and again, 1916 to mid-1918.

Brendon: Collector of Ratnagiri. From mid-1818 till the time of the royal family's departure from Ratnagiri.

Browne (Major): A member of the British Burma Expeditionary Force, he later wrote a memoir detailing his experiences.

Butler, Harcourt (Sir): Governor of Burma from 1923 to 1927.

Calogreedy, Mattie: One of Queen Supayalat's European maids of honour and confidantes, she supposedly betrayed the queen in 1885 by passing on confidential French agreements.

Chandu: One of Tu Tu's sons, his full name is Chandrakant Shankar Pawar.

Chun Taung Princess: One of King Mindon's daughters. Acted, in Mandalay, on behalf of the royal family during their exile.

Comber: Police officer in charge of the king during his exile—1903 to 1910.

Cox (Colonel): First police officer in charge of the king during his exile—during the king's stay in Madras.

Devi Thant Cin: Prince Taw Phaya Galae's daughter. Born on 2 January 1947.

Dinshaw, Mary: A Eurasian girl whose father was a Frenchman and mother a Burmese. She was 'adopted' by Queen Supayagalae during the exile. She went on to become the royal family's housekeeper.

Edgelow, Frederick: A solicitor hired by King Thibaw in 1892 to help him make representations to the government.

Fanshawe: Police officer in charge of the king during his exile—1886 to 1888.

First Princess: See Ashin Hteik Su Myat Phaya Gyi.

Fourth Princess: See Ashin Hteik Su Myat Phaya Galae.

Gopal Babu: Aka Gopal. A friend of Latthakin's. At some stage, he worked (in Kalimpong) as Latthakin's manager.

Gopal: Royal Residence gatekeeper and driver; the First Princess's companion; Tu Tu's father. Married to Laxmibai, one son Chandrakant. His full name was Gopal Bhaurao Sawant, aka Shivrekar. Date of birth not known. Died on 7 September 1972.

Gulabi: Aka Kamal Chandarana. Daughter of Jaiman and Satyamaya; although not adopted by the Second Princess (as her brother Maung Lu Gyi was) she grew up in the Second Princess's home. Born on 15 March 1937.

Head: Political officer in charge of the royal family during their exile, 1915–17.

Hmanthagyi Ywasar: Mother of Kin Maung Lat or Latthakin. One of Queen Supayalat's trusted maids of honour.

Holland: The district superintendent of police, Ratnagiri, who accompanied the royal family back to Burma in 1919.

Inmam: Police officer in charge of the king during his exile—for a few months in 1910.

Jaiman: Father of Maung Lu Gyi and Gulabi. He was of Nepali origin. He and his family stayed with the Second Princess in Kalimpong.

Kanaung Prince: King Mindon's brother whom he had named as his successor and who was assassinated shortly thereafter (1866); commonly known as the crown prince.

Khin May: Prince Taw Phaya Galae's wife. Born on 3 November 1927.

Kin Maung Lat: King Thibaw's secretary; the Second Princess's husband; later known as Latthakin. Born on 9 September 1887. Died on 10 January 1955.

King Mindon: King of Burma from 1853 to 1878. Father of King Thibaw, Supayagyi, Queen Supayalat and Queen Supayagalae. Son of King Tharrawaddy.

King Thibaw: The last king of Burma. Married three sisters—Supayagyi, Supayalat and Supayagalae. Ruled from 1878 to 1885 and was deposed by the British in the end of November 1885. Born on 1 January 1859 in Mandalay. Died in Ratnagiri on 16 December 1916. Four daughters, Ashin Hteik Su Myat Phaya Gyi, Ashin Hteik Su Myat Phaya Lat, Ashin Hteik Su Myat Phaya, Ashin Hteik Su Myat Phaya Galae. (One son and two daughters died in infancy.)

Kinwun Mingyi: The chief minister during King Mindon and King Thibaw's reigns.

Ko Ba Shin: An honorary magistrate in Rangoon deeply loyal to the royal family. He supplied the family (at cost) with whatever they needed from Burma during their exile.

Ko Ko Naing: The Fourth Princess's husband. Born on 22 July 1890 in Shapinhla (Magwe district). Died on 2 September 1959 in Rangoon.

Latthakin: See Kin Maung Lat.

Laungshe Queen: A Shan princess who became one of King Mindon's wives. King Thibaw's mother.

Laxmibai: Gopal Bhaurao Sawant's wife. Died in 1957.

Lord Dufferin: Viceroy and governor general of India (under whose jurisdiction Burma came) from 1884 to 1889.

Ludu Daw Ahmar: A highly respected Burmese journalist and writer. Died in 2008.

Madanlal: A lawyer and a friend of Latthakin's. Aka Madanlal Pradhan and Madan Kumar Babu.

Malti: One of Tu Tu's daughters. Her full name is Malti Madhukar More.

Mama Gyi: Prince Hteik Tin Kodaw Gyi's wife, after his divorce from the Third Princess.

Manook, Hosannah: One of Queen Supayalat's European maids of honour; sometimes known as Selah.

Marks, John (Dr): A missionary in Burma. As children, Thibaw and Supayalat attended his school in Mandalay for a while.

Maung Lu Gyi: Adopted son of the Second Princess and Latthakin; aka Premlall Jan. Born on 28 January 1932 in Kalimpong. Died in Calcutta on 18 December 2008. Birth parents: Jaiman and Satyamaya. Married Bina Devi. No children.

Maung Maung Khin: Princess Hteik Su Phaya Gyi's husband. Died in 1984.

Maung San Shwe: Secretary to King Thibaw in Ratnagiri from late 1909/early 1910 to late 1912. Husband of the Pinya Princess.

Meik Hti Lar Princess: King Thibaw's full sister.

Mekkhara Prince: One of King Mindon's sons. A strong contender as successor to the throne. Killed during the 1879 massacre of royals.

Mi Khingyi: Also known as Daing Khin Khin. A young woman with whom King Thibaw was briefly infatuated. He planned to make her a queen. She was executed in April 1882.

Myint Myint Aye: Prince Richard's junior wife. He married her in 1993.

Myngun Prince: One of King Mindon's sons whom Sinbyumashin had in mind for marriage with her youngest daughter Supayagalae. The Myngun Prince had tried to assassinate King Mindon in 1866.

Ne Win (General): From 1958 to 1960 he headed a caretaker government in Burma. Staged a military coup on 2 March 1962. Burma has been a military dictatorship since then to 2011.

Nyaungok Prince: One of King Mindon's sons. The Nyaungyan Prince's brother. Ran away from the palace in 1878—a few months before the massacre of royals.

Nyaungyan Prince: One of King Mindon's sons. Was the strongest contender as successor to the throne. Ran away from the palace in 1878—a few months before the massacre of royals. Died in 1885.

Paw Tun (Sir): Briefly made prime minister of British Burma in 1942. In 1945, as home minister, he approached Prince Taw Phaya Gyi with an offer to make him king designate.

Pawar, Shankar Yeshwant: Worked in the Royal Residence in Ratnagiri. One of the servants who travelled to Burma with the family at the end of their exile. He later became Tu Tu's husband (1930). Date of birth 1902 (?). Died in 1976.

Pinya Prince: Served Queen Supayalat faithfully in Mandalay, then in Ratnagiri for a few years, and then again in Rangoon for some months. Wife of Maung San Shwe.

Prendergast (General): Led the British Burma Expeditionary Force into Burma to defeat and depose King Thibaw.

Prince Hteik Tin Kodaw Gyi: The Third Princess's first husband. Prince Kanaung's grandson through his daughter, Princess Hteik Khaung Tin Aye. Date of birth 1904 (?). Died on 11 November 1954 in Mandalay.

Prince Richard: Prince Taw Phaya and Princess Rita's son. Aka Prince Taw Phaya Myat Gyi and Tun Kyaw. Born on 14 May 1945. Married Princess Hteik Su Phaya Htwe (daughter of the Fourth Princess) in 1962. Married Myint Myint Aye in 1993.

Prince Taw Phaya Galae: The Fourth Princess's fifth child and youngest son. Aka Prince Frederick and U Aung Zae; affectionately called Taw Taw. Born on 30 July 1926 in Rangoon. Married Khin May in 1945. Died on 18 June 2006 in Rangoon. One daughter, Devi Thant Cin.

Prince Taw Phaya Gyi: The Fourth Princess's eldest child, also known as Prince George. Born on 6 May 1922 in Rangoon. Married Susan in 1945. Killed on 12 April 1948 outside the town of Pyinmana. Two sons, Soe Win and Myint Thein.

Prince Taw Phaya Nge: The Fourth Princess's fourth child; aka Prince Terence. Born on 17 July 1925 in Rangoon. Married Ma Khin Su in 1955. Divorced her in 1962 or 1963. Married Ma Khin Zaw in 1964 (?). Died near Moulmein on 21 April 1995. Three daughters, Ma Akeyi, Ma Kalaya and Ma Thitra, and one son, Maung Min Thu Aung.

Prince Taw Phaya: The Fourth Princess's third child; aka Prince Edward and U Tun Aung. Born on 20 March 1924 in Rangoon. Married Princess Rita (daughter of the Third Princess) in 1944. Two daughters, Ann-Marie (Princess Su Phaya Lay) and Rose Marie (Princess Su Phaya Naing), and four sons, Richard (Prince Taw Phaya Myat Gyi), David (Prince Taw Phaya Myat), Joseph (Prince Taw Phaya Myat Aye) and Paul (Prince Taw Phaya Myat Thike).

Princess Hteik Su Phaya Gyi: The Fourth Princess's second child and eldest daughter; aka Princess Tessie and Su Su Khin. Born on 5 April 1923 in Rangoon. Married Maung Maung Khin in 1943. Two daughters, Cho Cho Khin and Devi Khin, and three sons, Win Khin, Kyaw Khin and Aung Khin.

Princess Hteik Su Phaya Htwe: The Fourth Princess's youngest child; aka Princess Margaret. Born on 20 August 1927 in Rangoon. Married Prince Richard (son of Prince Taw Phaya and Princess Rita) in 1962. Died on 21 June 2003 in Rangoon. One son, Maung Aung Khine.

Princess Rita: Aka Hteik Su Gyi Phaya. Daughter of the Third Princess and Prince Hteik Tin Kodaw Gyi. Born on 20 May 1924. Married Prince Taw Phaya (son of the Fourth Princess) in 1944. Died on 27 November 2002. Six children (for names, see under Prince Taw Phaya).

Queen Mae Nu: Sinbyumashin's mother. King Bagyidaw's wife.

Queen Supayagalae: King Thibaw's junior wife and queen. She had no children. Queen Supayalat's younger sister. Daughter of Sinbyumashin and King Mindon. Born in 1862 in Mandalay. Died in 1912 in Ratnagiri.

Queen Supayalat: King Thibaw's favourite wife and chief queen. Daughter of Sinbyumashin and King Mindon. Born on 13 December 1859 in Mandalay. Died on 24 November 1925 in Rangoon. Mother of the First, Second, Third and Fourth Princesses. (She also had one son and two more daughters who died in infancy.)

Sakhalakar: Huzur deputy collector, Ratnagiri, who took over the responsibility of the royal family in 1917 till they departed for Burma (in place of the political officer).

Sangharakshita: An English Buddhist monk who lived in Kalimpong for some years and knew the Second Princess and Latthakin well.

Sao Shwe Thaik: Nephew of the old Sawbwa of Nyaungshwe (an ardent supporter and confidant of Queen Supayalat), whose title he inherited when his uncle died; Sao Shwe Thaik was the first president of independent Burma.

Satyamaya: Mother of Maung Lu Gyi and Gulabi; of Nepali origin she married Jaiman and stayed with the Second Princess.

Sawbwa of Nyaungshwe: A Shan chief who was very close to the royal family—as a young boy he had been 'adopted' by King Mindon and had been brought up in the Golden Palace. He was an ardent supporter and confidant of Queen Supayalat. After the exile ended, he visited her often in Rangoon.

Sayadaw U Ottama: A highly revered Burmese monk imprisoned by the British, and on whose behalf the Second Princess made an appeal.

Second Princess: See Ashin Hteik Su Myat Phaya Lat.

Shakuntaladevi: Gopal Bhaurao Sawant and Laxmibai's daughter-in-law; wife of their son, Chandrakant.

Sinbyumashin: One of King Mindon's sixty-three wives; a senior queen and mother of Supayagyi, Supayalat and Supayagalae. Daughter of Queen Mae Nu and King Bagyidaw. Died on 27 February 1900 in Rangoon.

Sladen, Edward (Colonel): British Resident in Mandalay, 1865–69 (during King Mindon's reign). Accompanied British Burma Expeditionary Force to Mandalay for deposition of King Thibaw in November 1885.

Supayagyi: Queen Supayalat's eldest sister who was supposed to be King Thibaw's chief wife and queen, but was displaced and discarded. Daughter of Sinbyumashin and King Mindon. Born in 1854. Died before her mother (who died in 1900).

Susan: Aka Ma Khin Kyi. The beautiful daughter of a district session judge, she married the Fourth Princess's eldest son, Prince Taw Phaya Gyi. Died in 1995.

Taingda Mingyi: A very influential minister during King Thibaw's rule.

Tandawzin: An old Burmese gentleman in the employ of Queen Supayalat (in Ratnagiri). He looked after King Thibaw's and Queen Supayagalae's coffins and wrote the queen's letters. He knew only Burmese.

Tara: One of Tu Tu's adopted daughters. Also known as Sulabha Gijbale.

Thahgaya Prince: A Konbaung prince on whom Supayalat had a teenage crush. Killed in 1879 during the massacre of royals.

Thakin Kodaw Hmaing/Maung Lun: A highly respected Burmese poet, journalist, playwright, historian, intellectual, nationalist and peace activist. As a young boy, he had seen the royal family being taken away from Mandalay. He revered Queen Supayalat and was a frequent visitor to her home after her exile. He died in 1964.

Third Princess: See Ashin Hteik Su Myat Phaya.

Thonze Prince: One of King Mindon's sons, he was a strong contender as successor to the throne. Killed in 1879 during the massacre of royals.

Trewby (Miss): English lady companion to the Fourth Princess in Ratnagiri (there were two Miss Trewbys—two sisters—who joined the services of the Fourth Princess one after the other).

Tu Tu: The First Princess and Gopal's daughter. Born on 26 November 1906 in Ratnagiri. Married Shankar Yeshwant Pawar in 1930. Known after her marriage as Baisubai Shankar Pawar. Died on 24 October 2000 in Ratnagiri. Four daughters, Pramila, Malti, Chandra and Tara, and seven sons, Digambar, Srikant, Narayan, Suresh, Chandrakant (Chandu), Babloo and Rajkumar.

U Mya U: The Third Princess's second husband. Married her in 1931. Born in 1867(?). Died in July 1943 in Sagaing.

U Nu: Burma's first prime minister after her independence.

U Than Swe: A well-respected Burmese writer on the Konbaung dynasty.

Curzon, George: Viceroy of India, 1899–1905.

Vickery (Mrs): English lady companion to the Fourth Princess during a few years of the exile.

Vilas: Gopal Bhaurao Sawant and Laxmibai's grandson. Chandrakant and Shankuntaladevi's son. Married to Manali.

Wet-masoot Wundauk: A junior minister during King Thibaw's rule. He worked under the Kinwun Mingyi and was one of the two officials who had been entrusted to carry King Thibaw's letter requesting for armistice to General Prendergast towards the end of the Third Anglo-Burmese war. He continued to support the royal family after the king's deposition, exile and death.

Willingdon (Lady): Wife of the governor of Bombay (Lord Willingdon was the governor of Bombay from 1913 to 1919).

Yanaung: A close friend of King Thibaw's and therefore a man with considerable influence in the kingdom. Fell out of favour and was murdered in 1882.

Ywasargyi Sein Beida: A talented musician whom Queen Supayalat was fond of. He travelled to Ratnagiri and performed at the royal family's housewarming ceremony. He also played for the queen after the exile, in her home in Rangoon.

PART I

BEFORE THE EXILE

1

THIBAW AND SUPAYALAT

Even as a young girl Supayalat must have known that she was very privileged. Born on 13 December 1859, she was a princess of pure royal blood. Her father, King Mindon, was an absolute monarch with the power of life and death over his subjects. Her mother, Sinbyumashin, was one of King Mindon's sixty-three wives and also his first cousin; during this period, Burmese kings were encouraged to marry close blood relatives, including half-sisters, to continue the purity of the Konbaung dynasty. Although Sinbyumashin was not King Mindon's chief queen, she was one of his four senior queens. An intelligent, ambitious and domineering woman, she wielded enormous clout in the Golden Palace.

King Mindon ruled the Kingdom of Ava (also known as Upper Burma) from the sprawling Golden Palace in Mandalay. Towering over the palace was a gilded seven-tiered wooden spire or *pyatthat*, grandly said to mark the centre of the universe. The palace was right in the middle of the Royal Golden City. The royal family lived in the palace; ministers, nobility and various other people who were part of the court stayed in the Royal Golden City. Vast fortified walls surrounded the square-shaped city, and a wide moat, covered almost year round with pink–red lotuses, encircled these walls. The actual town of Mandalay, where the general population lived, lay beyond the moat. Supayalat's world was within the Golden Palace grounds, in a warren of ornate buildings and carefully laid-out gardens. Her huge extended family comprised a vibrant community and it is unlikely she ever felt the need to venture beyond.

Supayalat had no dearth of playmates—there were numerous princesses, young girls from noble families and maids to choose from. Wilful, imperious and high in the pecking order of princesses, she could pick and choose upon whom to bestow her favour.

When Supayalat experienced a teenage crush she defied custom by dressing up as a boy and going to the Northern gardens—a male section of the palace forbidden to the opposite sex—in search of the object of her affection, her half-brother, Thahgaya. Unable to find him, she asked another half-brother, Thibaw, for his help. Thibaw hesitated, for he did not immediately recognize her in the male attire she had donned for the occasion. Impatient at his slowness, she smacked him on the head and moved on. Quickly but thoroughly she searched, but Thahgaya was nowhere to be found. Disappointed, she returned to the female section of the palace, leaving behind, quite unknown to her, a smitten Thibaw. Word of her daughter's misadventure soon reached Sinbyumashin, for the palace was full of eavesdroppers and talebearers anxious to curry favour with the powerful queen. Supayalat was immediately confined to her rooms, and the queen resolved to marry off her errant daughter as quickly as possible. But a good alliance was hard to arrange when she was in disgrace, so Supayalat was eventually released under strict supervision.[1]

Thibaw, in the meanwhile, was nearing the completion of his education. In his younger days he and many of his siblings, including Supayalat, had studied at a missionary school started in Mandalay by Reverend Dr John Marks. (The arrival of Thibaw and the other princes on the first day of school was remarkably dramatic: each on the back of a richly decorated elephant, two golden umbrellas shading every prince, accompanied by a veritable army of attendants carrying the required royal paraphernalia such as gold gem-encrusted betel-nut boxes and spittoons. As soon as the princes entered school all the students slipped off their desks onto the ground in the deeply respectful *sheiko* position that was traditionally adopted in the presence of royalty. Dr Marks had to rush around the classroom pulling up each boy, only to have him sink again the moment he let go. After much reassurance, the boys were persuaded to sit at their desks in the presence of the princes. [2])

At the missionary school Thibaw learnt, among other things, some English and cricket.[3] He also got some piano lessons; in the palace, Burmese classical music was taught to all the princes as they were expected to be accomplished in eighteen arts including archery, horsemanship and fencing by the time they were sixteen.[4] Dr Marks remembers Thibaw in his memoirs as

> a quiet, inoffensive, docile lad, without any particular vice or virtue to distinguish him from the other boys of his age. He was obedient and orderly and gave but little trouble. He never presumed for one moment on his position to expect any preferential treatment . . . [He] was of a modest and trustful disposition, easily influenced for good or for evil. Unfortunately he was not long enough with us to strengthen the good points of his character.[5]

After a couple of years at the missionary school Thibaw donned the yellow robes of a *pongyi* or Buddhist monk as a novice. This was a custom that all Burmese Buddhist boys followed, for a short period at least, after which they could disrobe and revert to their normal lives. Thibaw spent three years at the Royal Golden monastery, studying the Three Baskets of the Buddhist Law. He did extremely well in the examination that followed, much to the delight of his deeply devout father. Thibaw, a son who had earlier not made much of an impression on King Mindon (he was a reticent, shy boy, and the son of an out-of-favour Shan queen—the Laungshe Queen—who had been dispatched to a nunnery as she had been 'unpardonably intimate' with a pongyi),[6] became a prince of some importance. The king wistfully even imagined that this son might be the next Buddha![7] A grand ceremony honouring Thibaw was held and he was now entitled to use four golden umbrellas.[8] The king, and only the king, could use eight white umbrellas.

Before he took the exam, not long after his encounter with Supayalat, Thibaw penned a love poem for her, which he sent through one of her trusted old maids:

> You ought to be my queen,
> We will always be together till death do us part.
> Now I'm learning to become a *Patamagyo*,
> Upon hearing the beatings of time-signal drum of the Palace,
> I feel so lonely.
> The face of Su Su appears in my mind's eye,
> I just see your face and that hinders my studies.[9]

A flattered but cautious Supayalat pretended that she was annoyed at Thibaw's overture, and scolded her maid for having consented to be the courier. A few days later, still feigning annoyance, she told the maid to return Thibaw's letter to him. In fact, the letter she gave her maid was not Thibaw's letter at all, but a poem she had written herself:

> I have been waiting to win your love and affection
> Since the time I was wearing a quarter yard length of hair
> Hoping you should one day be a king.
> Only that you should be faithful to me,
> On my part, I, Su will always keep you in my heart
> Just as Princess Yashodhara pays respect to Prince Siddhartha
> I obediently pay my respect to you.[10]

The maid of honour, unaware of the deception, wrapped the letter in a scarf and took it to Thibaw, and according to U Than Swe (a reputed Burmese writer on the Konbaung dynasty) an exchange like the one below purportedly took place:

'Is this a reply?' demanded Thibaw.

   'No, my lord,' the maid answered, 'she scolded me and is very angry and has returned your letter.'

   Thibaw, visibly upset, asked, 'She didn't even *read* my letter?' He then proceeded to open the scarf and when he couldn't stop smiling the old maid realized she had been tricked. Thibaw hurriedly wrote his reply; the maid returned to Supayalat and paid homage.

'Old lady, have you been to Thibaw?' asked Supayalat.

'Yes,' replied the maid, 'I said, she is so angry she asked me to give your letter back. And oh! He is so sad, he threw the letter in the fire.'

'*What*, didn't he *read* it?' an indignant Supayalat asked.

'Nooooo . . .' said the maid, then, seeing Supayalat's crestfallen expression, she relented, 'You are like a daughter to me, don't lie to me in future. Here is his reply.'[11]

Supayalat immediately rewarded her maid of honour with a big diamond hairpin that had been given to her by her mother. The maid, very pleased, impulsively tucked it into her hair right away.[12]

Correspondence between the couple now flourished. Thibaw's love letters, artistically and painstakingly written in gold on special pink paper, were smuggled to Supayalat. A very pleased Supayalat read these letters over and over again and showed some of them to her friend, Mattie Calogreedy (a girl of Greek and Burmese descent who was to later become one of her European maids of honour).[13] Not surprisingly, in a palace full of spies, word of this exchange soon reached Sinbyumashin. But she was far from displeased. She was an ambitious woman and in Thibaw she saw the means to an end. As mother of three daughters and no sons she knew she could never be the mother of a king. But she could be the king's mother-in-law.

In the Kingdom of Ava, there was no strict law of succession. It was up to the king to choose his heir. It was, however, stated that the first-born son of the king would be the heir apparent unless the king wanted otherwise. If this son died, there was no order of selection prescribed. King Mindon had chosen his brother, the Kanaung Prince, as his successor. Displeased with this choice, two of King Mindon's sons had staged a rebellion in 1866 during which the Kanaung Prince was killed. King Mindon's first-born son, the Malun Prince, had also been killed in the same rebellion.[14] The king had had forty-eight sons but some had died, a couple had rebelled, and now there were twenty-two sons from which to choose his successor.[15] Speculation was that one of the following three would be selected: the Thonze Prince, who was the eldest; the Mekkhara Prince, a brave and able warrior; or the Nyaungyan Prince, a pious man and the king's favourite son.[16] The Nyaungyan Prince had the support of most people.[17]

It is said that King Mindon, although very pleased with his forty-first son, Thibaw, never seriously considered him as a possible heir to the throne. In fact, he is supposed to have commented that should Thibaw become king, the kingdom would cease to be independent![18] But in September 1878, when King Mindon became seriously ill with dysentery and lay dying, Sinbyumashin skilfully persuaded (some say with the help of '50 viss of gold'[19]) her husband's chief minister, the Kinwun Mingyi, and other ministers to support her choice of Thibaw as the next king.[20] They supported her because they saw Thibaw, as Sinbyumashin and the rest of the palace saw him—laid back and easy to influence. In other words, a puppet to be manipulated by them.[21]

Sinbyumashin had not forgotten what had happened not so long ago when the Kanaung Prince had been selected as King Mindon's successor. Therefore, before approaching the king for his approval of Thibaw, she and her coterie wanted to ensure history would not repeat itself. Without the king's knowledge, she had his sons summoned to his bedside. They all rushed quickly and unsuspectingly—all except the Nyaungyan and the Nyaungok Princes, who, very suspicious that all the princes had been called together, fled the palace. As soon as the other princes assembled outside the king's chamber, they were apprehended and led away to be imprisoned.[22]

King Mindon, though very frail and weak by now, noticed the absence of his sons. He repeatedly asked for them, especially for the Nyaungyan Prince who used to regularly read religious passages to him.[23] This prompted some of his queens and ladies of the palace, who had been frightened into silence by dire threats, to tell the king what had happened. The king promptly ordered that his sons be released and brought before him. When they came (all expect the Nyaungyan and Nyaungok Princes who had by now taken refuge with the British Resident in Mandalay), he told them that it was his wish that the Kingdom of Ava be divided into three provinces.[24] The Thonze Prince, the Mekkhara Prince and the Nyaungyan Prince were appointed as regents and each of them was assigned one of these provinces. The other princes were told that they were free to align themselves with any one of the selected three. King Mindon then bade his sons a fond farewell and asked them to use his royal steamers to hastily sail away. A loving father, King Mindon well understood how bloody politics in the palace could get.[25]

Unknown to King Mindon his orders were ignored. The Kinwun Mingyi strongly objected to the kingdom being carved into three parts. He felt that such a division would lead to public unrest[26] and adversely affect trade in the kingdom, thus giving the British, who had been making threatening noises from time to time, the excuse they needed to appropriate it.[27] He and Sinbyumashin therefore jointly decided not to allow the princes to get away, and before the princes could leave the palace grounds they were re-captured and re-incarcerated. Their desperate relatives were now prevented from going anywhere near the king.[28]

Now all that was left for Sinbyumashin to do was to persuade King Mindon to make Thibaw the *eingshe-min* or heir apparent. There are so many versions of what happened next that it is impossible to know for sure how actively the king participated in this decision. This can only be a matter of conjecture. One credible version is that Sinbyumashin went to see King Mindon with a *parabeik* (a tablet made of dried palm-leaf that was used for writing on) that had written on it the names of four princes—Thonze, Mekkhara, Nyaungyan and Thibaw. Against Thibaw's name there were two marks that she claimed the ministers had made to indicate their choice. She reminded King Mindon that he had already selected the Thonze, Mekkhara and Nyaungyan Princes as regents and had sent them away to take charge of their respective territories. She suggested that in their absence it was best if Thibaw was made eingshe-min. Not waiting for any response, she put a stearite pencil in the king's hand, placed her hand firmly over his, and made a large and prominent cross against Thibaw's name.[29] Thibaw was officially made crown prince on 15 September 1878. A few days later, King Mindon's health improved temporarily, and although conscious of the fact that Thibaw had been made eingshe-min, he did not raise any objection, or try to make a change.[30]

King Mindon died on 1 October 1878. For six days, his body lay in state on a special couch in front of the Bee Throne in the Glass Palace, one of the most elaborate and ornate buildings in the palace complex. On either side of him knelt mourning queens and princesses, clad in white, waving peacock feather fans. As was the custom, he was wrapped in white cloth and his face, feet and hands were covered with gold leaf. A small heart-shaped piece of gold was hung over him, in which his *leip-bya* or 'butterfly spirit' was thought to temporarily reside. The public paid their last respects by filing past the body and making a sheiko, which brought them on their knees and elbows before their dead king.[31] The people were genuinely sad. King Mindon had been wise and kind and had done much for them. Fear and uncertainty was palpable because the past had taught them that bloodshed generally accompanied any Konbaung king's succession.

King Mindon's funeral was held on 7 October 1878. Reverend Colbeck, the British missionary who had replaced Dr Marks, attended the funeral and recalls it in interesting detail: Around fifty princesses led King Mindon's funeral procession holding in their hands a long, thick white rope which created the illusion that they were pulling the king's coffin. King Mindon's body was shaded with eight white umbrellas and surrounded by queens. Thibaw came to his father's funeral on an ornate throne-like palanquin carried by numerous hefty men. At each corner of the palanquin, crouched in the sheiko position on her elbows and knees, was a young girl. Ministers and guards surrounded the palanquin. Thibaw attended the funeral not in the mourning colour of white as everybody else, but in magnificent golden clothes, with the crown on his head.[32]

When King Thibaw arrived at the funeral, everyone silently fell to the ground. A royal herald crawled forward, and read out a petition requesting the new king to authorize the commencement of his father's funeral ceremonies. 'Let it be done duly and well'—King Thibaw is purported to have answered, before immediately retreating with his entourage into the palace. The reason for the hasty departure was fear of rebellion and assassination. It was Sinbyumashin who personally supervised King Mindon's entombment; it had been his wish not to be cremated, as was the custom, but to be entombed within the palace grounds.[33]

On 11 October 1878 an 'oath of allegiance to the king' ceremony was held during which people of the kingdom were exhorted to:

Take me and me alone as your Lord.
  Don't behave like the palm of your hand; stay like the palm of your foot [that cannot change sides].

Use the best of your ability to get things to turn out well in the affairs of province, capital city and the religion.

Do not avoid your duty by giving excuses.

Never do anything not in the least bit to discredit the [Buddha's] religion, your province and your capital city.

If you know anyone who would do any act of sabotage . . . stop him if possible; if not report.[34]

A long and imaginative list of ghastly curses was enumerated for those who did not follow the oath, and all kinds of rewards and happiness was wished for those who did.[35]

King Thibaw was now known by a plethora of colourfully descriptive titles including 'ruler of the sea and land, lord of the rising sun . . . king of all the umbrella bearing chiefs, lord of the mines of gold, silver, rubies, amber . . . Master of many white elephants, the supporter of religion, owner of the *sekya* [the Hindu god Lord Indra's weapon], the sun descended monarch, sovereign of the power of life and death, great chief of righteousness, king of kings, possessor of boundless dominions and supreme wisdom, the arbiter of existence'.[36] Born on 1 January 1859, Thibaw was under twenty when he became the bearer of all these titles and the king of Ava. His transition from a monk to a king had happened almost overnight, and he knew absolutely nothing about affairs of state. He had no training or experience in governing, and was completely dependent on the advice of those around him.[37] And this suited Sinbyumashin and the ministers who had put Thibaw on the throne just fine.

Even as these solemn ceremonies were taking place, Sinbyumashin remained constantly alert for any possibility of a rebellion or attempt on the throne. She wasted no time in imprisoning various queens and princesses—mothers, sisters, wives and daughters of princes who had any chance to the throne. She also confiscated their jewellery. A few days after King Mindon's funeral, Sinbyumashin, Supayalat and her friend Mattie sat together looking at this jewellery piled in a glittering heap before them. Supayalat is said to have picked out a diamond necklace, held it against her neck, turned to Mattie and asked if it didn't make her look like a queen. Sinbyumashin reacted swiftly and furiously; she roughly snatched back the necklace, and shouted, 'There is only one queen at present.'[38] In a palace full of intrigues, Sinbyumashin must have known that she would not be the only powerful queen forever. However, it is unlikely that she, at this stage, had even a hint as to who would usurp her position and how quickly. She had no inkling that Supayalat's ambition and ingenuity eclipsed her own.

There were many princesses, including numerous half-sisters of King Thibaw, who were eligible to become one of his four senior queens. Most importantly, there was the Salin Princess who had been declared the *tabindaing* princess by King Mindon, which meant he had selected her to be the next king's chief queen. (King Mindon was very partial to this daughter since he believed her to be the reincarnation of his late mother.[39]) Also, Supayagyi, as Supayalat's older sister, was higher in the hierarchy than Supayalat to be one of King Thibaw's senior queens. When Thibaw became king, the Salin Princess, aware of his love for Supayalat, shaved off her head and became a nun.[40] But there were other princesses who were not quite so considerate.

Supayalat realized she had to act quickly to ensure King Thibaw's continued interest in her. She, who had loved him when he had been just a monk, certainly did not want to lose him now. She knew there would be many suddenly interested in him; not only was he king but he was also very good looking.[41] In order to hold on to him she felt she had to be physically near him—not a simple matter in a segregated palace. So Supayalat sent King Thibaw a highly unconventional and brazen message. She asked that he order her to come and stay with him, under the pretext of wanting her to dress his hair for him. And she added that he was 'to give the answer I want before the sun has set this evening'![42]

While history has very unfortunately not recorded King Thibaw's reaction to this extraordinary request, we do know that he sent for Supayalat and installed her in his own apartments. Something like this had never happened before. The palace, with its elaborate protocols and rules of conduct, was a deeply traditional environment. Supayalat, a princess of pure royal blood, was now actually living with a man, albeit the king, without having been given to him as his queen. The risk Supayalat took in doing this was tremendous. Had the king tired of her, or decided not to make her a queen, she would have been unfit for marriage to any other prince. The audacity of the arrangement set the palace abuzz, and an outraged Sinbyumashin ordered Supayalat to return immediately to her apartments. Supayalat, basking in the all-powerful king's support, ignored her mother's directive. And her mother—the woman who had made Thibaw king—could do absolutely nothing about it. [43]

This arrangement continued despite persistent and desperate efforts by Sinbyumashin and King Thibaw's ministers to dislodge Supayalat. To their great discomfort, her influence over the king increased each day. Whenever they protested that her presence in his apartments was highly inappropriate, he is purported to have gazed into her eyes and said that the decision was entirely hers, but if she chose to stay, 'then shall she stay with me forever'.[44] One of Thibaw's ministers (the Taingda Mingyi) advised King Thibaw that kingly pride should compel him to immediately take eight wives (an old tradition[45]). This could be followed, at a later date, by the many more wives he was entitled to. The Kinwun Mingyi advised the same, for multiple wives would necessarily divert and divide the king's attention, which was right now so disconcertingly focused on just one woman—a woman the Kinwun Mingyi increasingly distrusted. But Supayalat's 'hairdressing' gamble paid off handsomely: King Thibaw declared that Supayalat, and no other, was to be his queen. However, even a king sometimes has to bow to custom and general sentiment. King Thibaw, one suspects with Supayalat's blessings, agreed to also marry Supayalat's older sister Supayagyi in a joint ceremony. Although Supayalat would naturally have preferred the king all to herself, she did not perceive her 'plain, nun-like' older sister a significant threat for the king's affection.[46] While she was not classically beautiful, Supayalat groomed herself carefully and carried herself well. Short and petite, she had considerable charm and an electric presence, and it is said women much more beautiful than her were not noticed in her company.[47]

In Burma there was no need for a formal wedding ceremony. A man and woman were considered married once they had eaten 'rice and curry out of the same dish'[48] and had started living together. However, various ceremonies and investiture rituals were held for Supayagyi and

Supayalat to make them King Thibaw's wives and senior queens. The king was entitled to four senior queens—the Southern Palace Queen or chief queen, followed in seniority by the Northern Palace Queen, the Middle Palace Queen and the Western Palace Queen. Since Supayagyi was the older sister, she would be the chief queen and Supayalat, the Myauknandaw Mibaya or the Northern Palace Queen.[49]

Three temporary gold-leafed structures were constructed where the two to-be-queens had their hair ceremonially washed (the head was considered 'the noblest part of the body' and therefore had to be cleaned for important occasions[50]), dressed in formal and elaborate brocade clothes and waited for the auspicious moment to present themselves. At the selected time, in the late afternoon (in November 1878), the two women put on their crowns and walked into the Glass Palace with King Thibaw in the centre holding a hand of each. All three of them then sat on the Bee Throne. Priests pronounced blessings, and the Royal Messenger read out three poems. It is said that Supayalat looked truly dazzling that day, the depth of her emotions reflected in her expressive large brown eyes.[51]

On the night of her investiture as queen, Queen Supayagyi slept in the chief queen's apartments that had been readied for her. But she slept alone. The king slept in his own apartments with Queen Supayalat. Defying protocol yet again, Queen Supayalat did not shift to her newly allotted apartments in the Northern Palace on that day, or on any other day. And every day and night after this it was the same: Queen Supayagyi may have nominally been the king's chief queen, but Queen Supayalat was always by the king's side.[52]

King Thibaw's coronation ceremony took place in early June 1879, after the investiture of his queens.[53] Now all the five important emblems of Konbaung regalia—a white ceremonial umbrella, a crested headdress (his crown), a whisk (for fanning) made of yak tail hair, a four-edged dagger (called *Than Lyet* which had at one time been owned by the founder of the Konbaung dynasty, Alaungpaya) and royal footwear[54]—were officially his.

2

FIRST YEAR OF THE REIGN

The kings of Ava had such absolute power that not only the country but also its people were assumed to be their personal possessions, their slaves.[1] Much of Burma, including all its seaports together with Rangoon, had been lost to the British during two previous wars fought during 1824–26 and 1852–53, and now the Kingdom of Ava had been reduced to Upper Burma. The Kinwun Mingyi, one of the 'great burden bearers' (as the four top ministers or *wungyi*s in the kingdom were called)[2], and one of the most influential ministers of the Hluttaw or Council of State, wanted to preserve the independence of what was left of the kingdom. To try and ensure this he felt radical administrative and infrastructure reforms (based on what he had observed in the West), coupled with revised policies to meet some of the demands made by the British (including the enabling of easier trade), were necessary. Right after King Thibaw's ascension to the throne, the Kinwun Mingyi set about forming new ministries. A newly appointed minister of finance was to approve all expenses, including those of the royal family (which, of course, included the king). And it was decided that all important policy matters were to be decided collectively by the full cabinet, not individually by the king.[3] In other words, the Kinwun Mingyi envisaged a constitutional monarchy, which meant the king's power would be significantly reduced.[4]

To pre-empt any objections from the royal family while the new government established itself, the Kinwun Mingyi suggested that the king take an extended vacation abroad. He hoped this trip would also broaden the king's horizon, and he would come back not only worldly wise and enlightened, but also appreciative of the need for the changes that the Kinwun Mingyi had in mind. To aid this process, the new minister of finance had prepared extensive literature entitled 'Treatise on the Compassionate Disposition of Righteous Government' for the king to read during his travels. King Thibaw eagerly agreed to go; he had hardly ever left the palace grounds in the past, and had never left Mandalay. But Queen Supayalat thought otherwise. While she did not voice any objection to the Kinwun Mingyi's various other reforms, she took deep offence at the curtailment of the king's powers. She, with the support of her mother and Yanaung (a close friend of the king), advised King Thibaw not to undertake an extended trip at this critical juncture. Listening to their counsel, he backed out.[5]

Queen Supayalat now set about consolidating her position. She accused her older sister Queen Supayagyi of witchcraft, and Sinbyumashin, fearing for her daughter's safety, had her vacate the chief queen's apartments and move back in with her.[6] It is said that King Thibaw and Queen Supayagyi never again had anything to do with each other.[7] Queen Supayalat was now effectively King Thibaw's only queen, and much to her mother's chagrin, arrogated to herself the chief queen's title and authority.[8]

She soon influenced the king to dismiss several ministers of the new government. Not surprisingly, the minister of finance was one of them, and with his removal all checks on royal spending disappeared. She also started undermining the respected Kinwun Mingyi's authority, and leaning more on the Taingda Mingyi for advice.[9] The Taingda Mingyi and his supporters either did not believe in a weakened king, or opposed the Kinwun Mingyi for personal benefit. Whatever their reasons, it was the Taingda Mingyi and 'a clique of . . . middle-level ministers and military men' that were a constant impediment to the Kinwun Mingyi.[10] (The Kinwun Mingyi was a learned man; the Taingda Mingyi had no such pretensions, and derived his power from the brute strength of his well-armed supporters.[11] The Kinwun Mingyi was known for his view that British interests needed to be accommodated; the Taingda Mingyi was known for his total opposition to the British.) Queen Supayalat, with the Taingda Mingyi firmly behind her, encouraged the king to publicly contradict the Kinwun Mingyi, and it did not take her long to have the authority shifted from the ministers to the king—and to her.[12] The ministers were to continue to govern, but with curtailed power and autonomy, especially in matters of direct interest to the royal family.

When King Thibaw had become king, Dr Marks—his teacher from the missionary school he had attended in his younger days—wrote him a congratulatory letter. Aware of the history of massacres at the beginning of almost all Konbaung reigns he said, 'The Priest wishes that like your royal father, your Majesty may be famous for your mercy and kindness to all your subjects, and especially he would ask your royal kindness and clemency for the princes, your royal brothers and schoolfellows . . .'[13] But this was not to be.

For three days starting on 15 February 1879, about eighty members of the royal family—princes, queens and princesses—were killed, including Prince Thahgaya (on whom Supayalat had had a teenage crush) and the Thonze and Mekkhara Princes.[14] (Apparently, the Mekkhara Prince was overheard saying to his half-brother, the Thonze Prince, who was pleading for mercy, 'My brother, it is not becoming to beg for life; we must die, for it is the custom. Had you been made King, you would have given the same order.'[15]). Only sons of King Mindon who were either very young, or who had previously run away, survived the pogrom.[16] The royal relatives were killed in the traditional manner: princes bludgeoned to death by blows on the back of their neck, and queens and princesses by blows on their throat. Rumour has it that while these executions were being effected, to drown out the bloodcurdling screams and to distract members of the royal family not being executed, pwes or traditional Burmese dramas were loudly staged.[17]

Before the massacre there had been increasing rumours that various princes, with the help of their supporters, were plotting to overthrow King Thibaw and seize the throne.[18] Although there has been much debate as to whether it was Sinbyumashin or Queen Supayalat who ordered the massacre, in all probability it was Sinbyumashin. These were still early days of King Thibaw's reign; she was still a force to contend with; and she was still keen to secure King Thibaw's position. She was an old hand at palace intrigues, and knew princes could lead revolts from behind prison walls, and from places of refuge, however distant. She also knew if King Thibaw was now overthrown, the consequences would be disastrous for herself and her daughter, for they had made many enemies. She may have consulted Queen Supayalat, or perhaps taken her into confidence. (Writer U Than Swe feels 'Supayalat was aware but not instrumental'.[19])

Yanaung and the Taingda Mingyi were both actively involved in planning and carrying out the massacre. It appears the massacre also had the implicit approval of many in the government including the Kinwun Mingyi (he supported it because he believed it would lead to greater stability, as there would be lesser possibilities of uprisings against the king.)[20] King Thibaw later denied he had either ordered or even known of the massacre before it occurred, and this is what many believe.[21]

The British Resident in Mandalay had met many of the murdered princesses: 'the most delightful and feminine women in the world . . . their flattering politeness, their heady hint of submissiveness . . .' Overwhelmed and repelled he informed his head office and sent a letter to the palace denouncing the massacre. He ended by saying that should any more murders take place he would be obliged to shut down the British Residency in protest.[22] The Kinwun Mingyi sent a carefully worded reply politely asking Britain to mind its own business. He indicated that every country had the right to ensure its own stability, and added that the massacre had been carried out as per custom.[23]

The British government now seriously contemplated ousting King Thibaw and replacing him with the Nyaungyan Prince, who had been spirited away and was living in Calcutta, India.[24] The relationship between the Kingdom of Ava and the British had continued to be strained after the two wars that had previously been fought between them. There were three main reasons for this. First, since King Mindon's time, the Kingdom of Ava had been making overtly friendly overtures to a very receptive France. This was a period of blatant British imperialism, and French influence in the kingdom was viewed unfavourably. Second, the British business community in Lower Burma was persistently clamouring for annexation of the kingdom for easier and more profitable trade. As the king of Ava had monopolies over certain goods that the kingdom produced, and control over its exports and imports, the free trade that British merchants wanted was not possible.[25] Additionally, the safety of British subjects travelling to and through the kingdom was always at risk, due to the rapidly deteriorating law and order situation. Third, the relationship between the two countries had been further exacerbated by the fact that the British Resident in Mandalay had not been able to meet the king, making the sorting out of pending issues almost impossible. This lack of access was for an odd reason. All those seeking an audience with the king had to take off their footwear before ascending the palace platform because the platform was thought to represent the mythical Mount Meru, the abode of Lord Indra, the Hindu king of gods, and the king of Ava was considered to be the earthly representative of Indra (many Burmese traditions and beliefs have their roots in India). The British found this shoe removing custom demeaning; the Resident refused to do so, and therefore could not visit the king. This 'Shoe Question', as it was commonly called, became a surprisingly contentious issue between the Burmese and the British.[26]

Preparations were made for the deposition of King Thibaw but were not carried out as the British, at the time, had more urgent problems to deal with in other parts of the world. However, after a few months of posturing on both sides, in October 1879, the British Resident and his staff were suddenly withdrawn from Mandalay.[27] King Thibaw and his ministers were greatly alarmed by this abrupt departure. They felt that this portended British invasion of the kingdom. Acting on the advice of the Kinwun Mingyi, King Thibaw immediately sent a goodwill mission to Rangoon to the government of India (that is, to the British government as Burma came under the jurisdiction of a division of the British administration called 'Government of India'—India was by this time part of the British Empire) to express the palace's dismay at the Resident's withdrawal. The king, in his letter, called the friendship between the kingdom and Britain 'a precious heirloom' of the family since the days of his grandfather, and pleaded that it be resumed. However, the British government did not permit the mission to proceed beyond Thayetmyo (a frontier town in Lower Burma). Over the next several months King Thibaw repeatedly gave increasing negotiating authority to his mission, but not the unlimited scope that the British seemed to want. As a result, after seven months of camping in Thayetmyo, the mission had to return to Mandalay, disappointed at not having been able to achieve anything despite its best efforts.[28]

King Thibaw, angered by the failure of the mission and emboldened by the lack of a forceful reaction by the British to the massacre, had gong-beating criers proclaim throughout his kingdom that he had forced the British out of Mandalay, and would soon clear them from the rest of the country too. He also vowed that he would never again meet a 'white-faced' *kala* (foreigner).[29] On another occasion, Queen Supayalat is supposed to have told a gathering of her maids and attendants, 'The Poon-dawgyi-paya [King Thibaw] has driven the English from the country because he made them fear him. If the spur is long and ready to prick, cut the spur. If the beak is long and ready to fight, cut the beak. If the wing is long and ready to fly, cut the wings.'[30]

One 'white-faced' kala, Kirkman Finlay, who met King Thibaw in the first year of his reign (before the king's vow) recalls his visit in vivid detail in a handwritten journal:

> We were ushered into a side wing of the palace, evidently newly erected. It was devoid of gilding or any ornament whatsoever and presented the appearance of a respectable shed. A raised stage occupied one side. This was enclosed by a thick railing except about 3 feet in the centre which was left open. Here a crimson velvet cloth, bordered with gold; a velvet cushion; a gold spittoon; and a betel box of gold showed that the King would appear at this point. The ministers and officials of all kinds to the number of about one hundred and fifty were squatted on the ground in a circle, leaving a hiatus of about twelve feet at all points from the centre of the dais. The royal guards—in a crouching position, with their arms grounded, presented a most ludicrous appearance having no uniform.

In a few minutes the King appeared from behind the stage and squatted down in a reclining position resting his arm on the cushion. One of the ministers read out of a book in a very loud monotonous voice a full description of our antecedents and our intentions generally in paying our respects to his majesty . . .

A desultory conversation of the most common character, with many painful pauses ensued. One of the ministers then presented each of us in the king's name with a ruby ring; two silver cups; and a fur coat of some value. We thanked the King and another pause ensued during which he seemed uneasy and nervous. This was not surprising considering his age and it was his first reception of Europeans . . .

The King, turning to his ministers, requested them in a firm steady voice and with some 'impressement' to be regular in their attendance at their courts and in the administration of justice. Having said this he retired followed by his body-guard.[31]

Although the king presided over the Hluttaw, although he ceremoniously met visitors and held audiences, by the time King Thibaw's first year of rule was over it became common knowledge that 'Thibaw although King remained an amiable cipher. The old Queen, Supayalat's mother, was safely tucked away where she could do little more than annoy her daughter with her constant advice. Supayalat was in fact the real ruler of Upper Burma.'[32] Her control and authority was described as *dah-htet-te* or 'as sharp as a razor'.[33] On 9 September 1879, at 3.00 a.m., Queen Supayalat greatly cemented her already strong position by giving birth to a son and possible heir.[34]

3

LIFE AT THE PALACE

For fear of being overthrown in their absence, King Thibaw and Queen Supayalat hardly, if ever, left the Golden Palace grounds. They sometimes climbed the seventy-nine-foot-high Watch Tower that King Thibaw had erected on the palace platform[1] to cast a glance over the land they ruled but could not risk visiting. From here they got a panoramic view of Mandalay and the Irrawaddy River glistening in the distance. On a clear day, they could discern the outline of the blue Shan Hills, and the pagoda-dotted Sagaing Hills. Mandalay Hill stood just to the north-east of the palace.

It is believed that Lord Buddha had visited Mandalay Hill and had foretold that in 1857 AD, just south of the hill, a grand city would come up. This city would be an important centre of Buddhism. After consulting astrologers, King Mindon, a staunch Buddhist, decided to shift his capital from Amarapura, which was a few miles down the Irrawaddy, to this auspicious location. In 1857, on a day considered propitious, a carnival-like mass migration of palace occupants and town residents took place. It was hoped that this shift would bring

22

good fortune to the king and his people, and instill new energy into their religion. (Theravada Buddhism—believed to be the oldest existing school of Buddhism—had been the main religion of Burma since 1056 AD.) Mandalay, also called Ratanapoun (pronounced Yadanabon) or the City of Gems, took almost two years to be built. On 23 May 1859, the city was officially deemed completed and founded, and inscriptions to this effect were engraved on the tall red teakwood post outside each of its gates.[2]

Rumour has it that a number of people were buried alive under the gates and at the corners of the new Royal Golden City, as it was believed that people who died a violent death would become *nats* (spirit-beings), and haunt the place where they had died. These nats could sense when people with evil intentions crossed their territory and would attack them, thus safeguarding the city.[3] (Some historians are of the opinion that this barbaric practice, in fact, had been discontinued by this time.[4]) For further safety, the square Royal Golden City was encompassed by a moat and four imposing fortified walls, each over a mile and a quarter long. Twelve gates led into the city; forty-eight exquisitely carved wooden pyatthats topped the bastions of the city wall, including at each of the gates, at regular intervals. The main entrance into the Royal Golden City was through the east gate. The most inauspicious of the gates was the south gate on the western side, also known as the funeral gate, through which condemned and dead people were carried out.[5]

A twelve-feet high stockade of teakwood posts separated the Royal Golden City from the Golden Palace, which lay at its centre. A sixty-foot wide grass lawn separated the stockade from a brick wall that further enclosed and protected the palace. There were four gates that led into the Golden Palace, and the eastern gate, red in colour, was for the king's exclusive use.[6]

The town of Mandalay lay beyond the walls of the Royal Golden City, and was laid out in a neat grid-like pattern with straight, wide, tree-lined avenues.[7] Most of the homes were simple and made mainly of bamboo with thatched roofs. Brightly coloured bullock carts transported people around the town, and the mud roads were quickly deeply rutted by the wooden wheels of the carts.[8] As the town had been built as a religious centre, it had pagodas scattered all over. Although Rudyard Kipling forever romanticized Mandalay with his famous poem 'Mandalay', the actual town was not supposed to have been a pretty one. In fact, George Orwell, who worked as a policeman in Burma in the 1920s, described Mandalay in very unflattering terms, as the town of the five Ps—'pagodas, pariahs, pigs, priests and prostitutes'.[9]

Compared to the rest of Mandalay, the palace was a glittering jewel. Comprising a cluster of about a 120[10] highly stylized, intricately carved one-storeyed wooden structures that were richly gilded, the palace could not fail to impress and dazzle. The main buildings were built on a sizeable roughly rectangular platform, almost seven feet above the ground.[11] High over the palace walls, towards the east end of the platform, was an imposing seven-tiered gilded pyatthat that could be seen for miles around. This pyatthat was topped with a *hti*, a delicate gem-studded gold umbrella-shaped structure edged with small bells that tinkled melodiously in the breeze.

The pyatthat stood directly above the Lion Throne room, the room which housed the most important throne in the palace. The Lion Throne was ornate and rich with symbolic carvings including that of the peacock, the motif of the royal family. The peacock stood for the sun; the sun represented the ancient Indian solar dynasty from which Konbaung kings were believed to have descended. There was also a rabbit carved on this throne that stood for the moon, the moon representing the ancient Indian lunar dynasty from which Konbaung kings were also believed to have descended. The lion symbolized bravery. Thirty-three gods of the Tavatimsa Heaven (one of the heavens in Buddhist cosmology) were carved on the top part of the throne symbolically protecting the king and indicating that he was their agent on earth. Lotus designs indicated purity. No one but the king could sit on the Lion Throne; the chief queen, however, was permitted to sit along with the king on his right-hand side. As the east was considered to be the 'most honourable point of the compass' the Lion Throne faced east.[12] Earth brought specially from holy Buddhist sites in India was buried beneath the Lion Throne.[13]

In front of the Lion Throne room, and perpendicular to it, lay the large rectangular many-columned Great Audience Hall, with an ornamental roof. Important ceremonies and receptions were held here. These ceremonies, according to many who saw them, were astonishingly splendid. Queen Supayalat had her own audience hall, at the west end of the palace platform. It lay before the Lily Throne room. It was here that the queen sat for formal audiences with her female subjects and visitors. The western half of the platform was exclusively the female section with buildings comprising the residences of the senior queens, junior queens and maids of honour.[14]

The eastern portion of the palace, apart from the Great Audience Hall and the Lion Throne room, had six other thrones and throne rooms, and various other rooms including the king's private treasury, the Watch Tower, the Fountain Apartment (one of the few brick buildings, its walls were hand painted with frescoes by an Italian artist and it was used by the king and queen as a summer sitting room; a pretty water fountain was situated right outside the apartment), the king's private apartment and the Perfume Palace (used by the royal couple as a private living area), the Theatre Drawing Room (where they sat to watch pwes), and various structures for armaments, guards, pages, and so on.[15] Most of the apartments were richly laid with carpets and cushions for their occupants to sit on, and large imported mirrors liberally adorned the walls.[16]

While the buildings on the palace platform were all rich and ornate inside and outside, the Glass Palace was the largest and most stunning of them all, its inner surfaces covered with multi-coloured glass mosaics, heavy lacquering, gilt and exquisite carpets.[17] Tall gilded wax candles were used throughout the palace even though parts of it had recently been electrified;[18] in the Glass Palace the millions of minute glass mosaic pieces twinkled resplendently in the soft candlelight, creating a divinely magical atmosphere. It was this building that contained the auspicious Bee Throne. King Thibaw's principal living room was in the Glass Palace, and only he and his senior queens could sleep in the special bedroom located here.[19] A section of the Glass Palace was used to make notes on parabeiks (dried palm-leaf tablets) about significant occurrences in the palace and the kingdom.

The roofs on all the buildings on the palace platform had more than one tier—the number of tiers signifying the importance of the building. Although the roofs, as per tradition, were made of simple painted corrugated iron sheets, they were edged with carved and gilded wooden panels. These carvings were particularly lavish at the four corners of all the roofs, with the angle always representing highly stylized peacocks. On top of all the main buildings was a small wooden construction in which squatted, round the clock, men armed with mud pellets and catapults to scare away birds of prey, as they were considered to be harbingers of misfortune.[20]

To the north and south of the palace platform were many beautiful gardens with attractive plants, fragrant flowers, shady trees and little lakes and streams with small wooden bridges to cross over. Queen Supayalat would sometimes have picnics or play hide-and-seek with the other princesses and her maids of honour in the Southern gardens. A maid of honour recalls one of her first hide-and-seek games with the queen, before the maid quite understood the rules:

> I could see her kneeling down on a little hill behind a clump of bamboos. Everyone who looked could see. I went up and found her . . . She boxed my ears . . . No one could ever find her but the king, if he were playing with us. Then after a time when she was tired of seeing us wander . . . she would come out laughing, and say she was too clever for us . . . [21]

Off the palace platform, just north of the east gate, was the Clock Tower from which a loud gong was sounded every three hours, followed by an announcer shouting in the direction of the city, 'By the favour of the King, it is six (or nine, or twelve) o'clock' and then sheiko-ing three times in the direction of the Lion Throne.[22] Not far from the Clock Tower, to the north of it, stood King Mindon's tomb. The Royal Mint, a building with a tall chimney, that had been producing coins since 1865, lay north of the tomb. The Tooth-Relic Tower (containing a statue of Lord Buddha) stood just south of the east gate. On the south-eastern periphery of the palace grounds was the Royal Golden monastery where King Thibaw had once studied. Also on the eastern end stood the Hluttaw which had a replica of the Lion Throne.[23] When attending the Hluttaw, the king always sat on this throne. Princes and senior palace officials sat near him on special cushions, and touched the Lion Throne whenever they recited any order, thus symbolizing that the order was directly from the king.[24]

It has been said that no other people in the world enjoy theatrical performances more than the Burmese.[25] Since the king and queen never ventured out of the Golden Palace, almost every evening some form of entertainment was brought in to them. Sometimes the king's most accomplished dancer performed alone. She was reputedly very beautiful and was said to have danced as gracefully as 'a grass stem swaying in the wind.'[26] Occasionally a show by the famous puppeteer Maung Tha Byaw would be staged. Some pwes, with elegant dances and elaborate costumes, told religious stories from the Jatakas. At times the pwe was not religious at all and told tales of heroic princes and savage demons. Other pwes dealt with social or political issues in light-hearted, humorous ways. In many pwes, improvisation was common and clowns provided comic relief. Pwes would often go on for hours, sometimes the whole night, and la-hpet (pickled tea-leaf) would be served to keep everyone awake.[27]

During these performances, the king and queen sat on cushions, and behind them sat a sea of maids of honour. A golden gem-encrusted betel-nut box and spittoon would be placed near the king. A maid of honour sitting right behind the queen would roll fresh cheroots for her.[28] (Smoking was very common in Burma and apparently almost everyone smoked—men, women and even young children.[29])

In addition to pwes, storytelling was another very popular activity in the palace. This served the dual purpose of informing and entertaining Queen Supayalat and the ladies of the court. In an attempt to pass on her own views and beliefs the queen often moralized at the end of a story. Surrounded by princesses and maids of honour, she would ask one of them to narrate a tale. She regularly reminded everyone that she did not enjoy stories that were frightening or inappropriate, and that she preferred stories of victory, stories with happy endings.[30] Now and then a mistake would be made and perhaps a tale would be told of a dying hero or a philandering king, and the queen would be very annoyed. The errant maid would be reprimanded with perhaps a harsh word or with an accurate pitch of the queen's crimson velvet slipper.[31]

A European visitor—perhaps the wife of a businessman visiting

Mandalay—would occasionally call on the queen. With almost no opportunities for interaction with the outside world, such visits would evoke much interest and curiosity, and princesses and maids of honour would attend them in droves. One such visitor, a Mrs Rowett, visiting the queen perhaps in late October 1881, wrote an article for *Fraser's Magazine* describing her visit:

> The Queen kept us waiting two hours. At length there arose a slight hubbub, which meant that she was coming, and all the court put itself into the usual attitude for receiving majesty in Burmah, i.e. they prostrated themselves, and folded their hands far in front of them, as if in prayer. The Queen is only 21 years old. She is very nice looking, unusually fair for a Burmese, and her expression is really good . . . I had to sit in front of her Majesty, who herself did not occupy the throne, but sat on a purple carpet with a cushion for her elbow to rest on . . . My presents were then mentioned, and then a maid of honour handed me a beautiful gold cup, and a piece of silk—the Queen's gifts. I made a low bow. The Queen then took a puff at a huge cheroot, and then asked my age, and several other personal questions. She seemed a little shy herself, and when the conversation flagged, she once or twice laughed like a school-girl, and made all the prostrate ones, including the nuns, laugh, too, by some remark of hers . . . The Queen asked how I liked Mandalay, and of course I had nothing but praises of all I saw . . . I then asked if I might see the Princess—the baby. The Queen smiled a gratified maternal smile, but said baby— aged two months and a half—was asleep . . . the interview came to a sudden end through my foot being a little cramped, so that I tried to wriggle into a more comfortable position, seeing which the Queen considerately remarked to Sister Teresa that I must be tired of sitting on the ground, and, rising herself, left the room . . . When the Queen left, the Princesses clustered around me again, and one of them took my hand and said something that seemed very amiable. It turned out to be that she loved me very much. Already! Poor things, they have not much outlet for their affections, for they are more closely immured than the nuns in the convent.[32]

Queen Supayalat had about three hundred maids of honour. Many of them were from known families—daughters of ministers, of Shan chiefs, princesses, etc. They had to be well dressed and well groomed at all times, and always barefoot on the palace platform.[33] A European maid of honour, according to a visitor, was 'rewarded by a salary of Pounds 50 a month, a permanent place, and a profusion of princely gifts ... barefoot of course, but blazing in diamonds. Ear-rings, brooches, and rings adorned her person ...'[34]

The queen, many say, was very generous with those she liked. Stories of her munificence, perhaps embellished over the years, include one told by her granddaughter:

> If she liked a person, she would load them with presents—piles of silk and satins and velvets as high as one's head when sitting. [She would] bring out great bowls of precious stones, gold sovereigns and make them help themselves [to] as much as [their] hand[s] could hold or grasp.[35]

Queen Supayalat took great trouble over her grooming. After she awoke (the king and queen were never woken up for fear that their leip-bya would not be able to return to their bodies in time), which was usually quite early, she would call out for her maids, who would be waiting outside her room. After a cup of tea that would be carried in to her, she would bathe to the sound of Pali chants. Her dressing ritual was elaborate and carried out in precise order: her hair was tied in a *sadan* or top knot and decorated with a diamond pin and flowers; *thana'kha* (a paste made from the bark of a plant and commonly used as a cosmetic) was applied carefully to her face; a rich silk *tamein* was wrapped around her waist; her feet were inserted into crimson velvet slippers (only royalty could have their feet shod on the palace platform); a silk cloth was wound around her chest, over which was placed a pure white muslin jacket adorned with a silk *pawa* or scarf; lastly she was bedecked with multiple diamond necklaces, bracelets, and sizeable diamond earrings. Twice more during the day, her maids would help her freshen up, rearrange her hair, and change her clothes; the queen always wanted to look good, she always wanted to look her best for the king.[36] On state occasions she dressed in special attire and glittered in heavier jewellery. There were strict sumptuary rules that governed what everyone in the kingdom could wear—what you wore defined who you were—and the queen was at her impressive best on these occasions.[37]

The king was not so particular. Some kalas who visited him reported this. One such visitor, Sir George Scott, commented that during one of his visits he found the king dressed carelessly and casually in not very clean looking clothes, and although he wore magnificent jewels, it was obvious he had 'neglected his toilet'. Before she became queen, Supayalat had moved into the king's apartment under the guise of dressing his hair, but she evidently paid little attention to it anymore! According to Scott, the king's *yaung* (long hair tied in a top knot) was nowadays sloppy, which he found odd as the Burmese took great pride in their hair.[38]

Since the kingdom was financially strapped, the king had thought it prudent to retract his oath of never setting eyes on a 'white-faced' kala again. It had therefore been possible for Scott to be admitted into his presence. (Obliging courtiers had found a way for the king to withdraw his oath without compromising his pride. It had apparently been put to him that Buddhism was a religion of charity and acceptance; that it was unfair not to grant foreigners the privilege of coming to pay their respects to him.) Foreigners willing to follow palace protocol could now visit him, and many did—some for business and some out of curiosity. It is said that King Thibaw was never really comfortable with them like his father had been. He never learnt to make small talk with these culturally alien strangers. [39]

There was formal court etiquette in every sphere of life in the palace. A battalion of hundreds of retainers attended on the king day and night, each with clearly defined functions. The king had 'thirty-five pages who carried the royal insignia on state occasions; forty royal tea servers; sixty bearers of the royal betel box; one hundred royal slipper bearers; forty bearers of the royal white umbrella; ten lectors who read aloud from religious books; fifteen messengers; four hundred and fifty gentlemen-at-arms; two hundred and twenty bearers of the royal swords; one hundred and fifty-five lectors whose duties included policing of the palace'. In addition, protocol demanded that a queen be always in attendance on the king for everything he did, from eating to wearing his slippers.[40] But with Queen Supayalat being King Thibaw's only queen, this was a protocol that had to be abandoned.

Speech in the palace was also based on clearly defined rules. To avoid causing offence, words had to be well chosen. For example, 'the ordinary man "ate his food", whilst a Buddhist monk "nourished his body with alms of the pious". His Majesty "ascended to the lordly table"'.[41] For formal audiences with the king the use of appropriate language was vital and this necessitated the use of a royal interpreter, even for people who spoke Burmese but were not well versed in court etiquette. Sir George Scott, conversant with the Burmese language, describes how when he met the king, the interpreter transformed everything that was said into the appropriately sycophantic. For instance, when King Thibaw asked Scott the purpose of his visit, the interpreter replied on his behalf that he had 'come to view the glories of his majesty's mighty kingdom, and to lay [his] head under [the King's] golden feet'.[42]

Apropos their own children, just as their forefathers before them, King Thibaw and Queen Supayalat followed established custom. Their children did not live with their parents, but in a separate section of the palace. They were brought every morning to sheiko to their parents.[43] Although well looked after and pampered by numerous maids of honour, their relationship with their parents was a very formal one: 'they came to the presence of their parents when they were summoned and answered what they were asked.'[44] They called their mother 'Ashin Nanmadaw Phaya' (which is a title for the chief queen) and their father 'Poon Dawgyi Phaya' (Lord of Great Glory).[45]

There was a set code even for the way Burmese royalty moved. Other than short distances on the immediate palace grounds (which queens and princesses were supposed to walk with small, delicate steps), royalty did not walk. (There is an extraordinary story told of a would-be assassin, sent by the Myngun Prince, who was waiting to kill King Mindon at the Royal Golden City gate with a *dah* (dagger) tucked in the folds of his *pasoe* (a piece of cloth worn in place of trousers). An attempt had already been made on King Mindon's life while he was near the foot of Mandalay Hill, and he was rushing back inside the protective walls of the palace when he spotted the man and ordered him to carry him into the palace. The man obligingly bent over and King Mindon climbed on. It was only when King Mindon alighted in the palace, and the dah fell clattering down, that the man's original

purpose was discovered; the unfortunate man was quicky beheaded.[46])
This is why some Burmese historians question—in spite of the
various protocol changes that Queen Supayalat instituted, and the
many norms she defied—whether she ever climbed the tall, many-
stepped Watch Tower, or whether her having done so was just a
figment of someone's vivid imagination.[47]

One of the changes Queen Supayalat made was that she was the first
Konbaung queen ever to sit and eat with her husband.[48] The king and
queen usually breakfasted together at nine in the morning. They also
dined together at around five in the evening. Says a maid of honour,
'Their breakfast and dinner were just rice like those of other Burmans
. . . The king and queen ate rice, and of course, there was curry too. It
was brought in golden bowls by the man who cooked it, and he had to
eat a little of each dish to show there was no poison in it.'[49] The king
and queen also departed from the prescribed etiquette when addressing
each other in private. When feeling affectionate the queen would call
the king 'Maung Maung' ('Maung' literally means younger brother,
but it is also used by a woman to address her husband); otherwise she
called him 'Kodaw' meaning royal body; and sometimes when she lost
her temper she'd pull at his top knot and call him a 'Shan-boke'
meaning 'you rotten Shan' (King Thibaw's mother was a Shan princess).
The king called her 'Su Su' and 'Supaya'.[50]

The royal couple prayed at the royal pagoda morning and evening.[51]
They first recited the precepts; then they asked for blessings and
favours, and lastly they 'sent out the sharing of [their] merits with the
spirits [nats] etc.', says their grandson, Prince Taw Phaya.[52] As
Buddhists they believed that a man's place in the great ladder of
existence, in the constant cycle of death and rebirth, depended upon
the arithmetic of the merits and demerits performed by him. And
therefore to have become the king and queen of Ava was not by
chance—as they had sown, so had they reaped.

Since one of the biggest acts of merit was the erecting of a pagoda
or monastery, Queen Supayalat had built the Mya Taung monastery in
Mandalay. Ironically, it was completed just before she became a British
prisoner and unfortunately she was taken away before she had had a
chance to conduct the all-important *yeizet-cha* ceremony[53] (water pouring

ceremony—performed to share the benefactor's good deeds with all on earth, and to register the good deeds in the benefactor's bank of good deeds.[54])

The king accumulated some merit of his own by performing a variety of good acts. As per custom, twice a year he threw a large sum of money from the palace platform for his subjects to jostle for.[55] He made significant donations for the construction of new monasteries and gave generous offerings to monks.[56] According to a maid of honour, the king was

> very fond of quoting from the sacred book, and he was full of proverbs and wise sayings . . . he would have done very well as a monk, he would have been a very good man, a very good man in a monastery where all temptation was kept from him. But it is very hard to be a king. When you have the power to do things, it is very difficult not to do them.[57]

4

SUPAYALAT, THE QUEEN

Upper Burma was not an easy kingdom to rule. All Konbaung rulers, including King Thibaw, concentrated their attention and energy on governing their capital. People in villages and the countryside were the responsibility primarily of local hereditary chiefs. Various factors, including defeat in two Anglo-Burmese wars (in 1824–26 and 1852–53), had led to erosion in the power of the monarchy. There was mounting turmoil and rebellion. Gangs of bandits had taken over many regions of the kingdom, and there was a general breakdown in law and order leading droves of people to flee the kingdom to British-occupied Lower Burma. Adding to the instability was the increasing number of revolts by Shan chiefs. It had been the custom in the past for the king to take daughters of Shan chiefs as his junior queens, thereby cementing ties with the Shan states. With Queen Supayalat dictating that King Thibaw could not take any more wives, this system had to be abandoned.[1] All of this made the kingdom politically unstable, and many felt that King Thibaw ruled only in name outside Mandalay.[2]

Revenues were also a constant source of concern. Many hereditary chiefs took advantage of the political turmoil during King Thibaw's reign and paid less and less into the royal coffers. Compounding the problem was the fact that the kingdom now had to, on and off, import some staple goods including rice. British-occupied Lower Burma contained the Irrawaddy delta, which was the rice-growing bowl of the region, and Upper Burma had had several years of bad rainfall. Rice prices kept rising due to increased international demand and this had an inflationary effect on the whole economy, as rice was (and still is) the staple diet,[3] or more picturesquely, 'wun-sa, food for the womb'[4] of the Burmese. To increase revenues, various methods were tried. Royal monopolies and concessions were sold, taxes and various duties were restructured, lotteries were experimented with, and loans were resorted to. But corruption and nepotism were rife and none of these efforts worked to provide a stable, prosperous economy.

It is not that King Thibaw and Queen Supayalat were oblivious to the problems facing them. Many attempts were made by the king to improve the situation. According to Dr Thant Myint-U (a Burmese scholar and fellow of Trinity College, Cambridge 1995–98), although the reign of King Thibaw is judged poorly vis-à-vis that of his father, 'his policies were only an intensification, if anything, of the reform process begun under his father'. However, external forces and circumstances were rapidly changing,[5] and neither the king nor the queen had the political dexterity or astuteness of some of their forefathers, including that of their father, King Mindon. This was compounded by their inexperience, insularity and their very limited education. In his youth King Thibaw had excelled in religious studies and, according to Dr Michael Charney (Reader, South East Asian and Imperial History, SOAS, University of London), 'as king, he remained focused on Pali learning' and there is nothing to indicate that he had any desire for Western knowledge.[6]

Life within the palace was complex, and there was much to occupy the king's and queen's attention and time. Custom and superstition dominated their everyday life. There were numerous elaborate religious and family functions that the king had to preside over. Both Buddhist and Hindu festivals were celebrated, some for days on end. (The reason why some Hindu gods were revered, and why some Hindu rituals and festivals were followed, is that since Buddhism essentially shunned rituals of any kind, in order 'to give itself a highly visible aura of mystery and majesty' Burmese courts 'appropriated aspects of Vedic ceremony and Brahmanic ritual'.[7] The most important festivals observed were the *Thingyan* and *Thadingyut* festivals. The Thingyan or 'water festival' was celebrated around April and marked the start of the Burmese new year. The Thadingyut festival, the 'festival of light', marked the end of Buddhist Lent. This took place around October. For both these festivals (and at the beginning of Buddhist Lent in June/July) the magnificent *Kadaw* ceremony (a ceremony for paying respect and renewing an oath of fealty to the king) was held, with the ornately dressed king and queen sitting on the Lion Throne and reverential multitudes crowding the Audience Hall. Ceremonies to propitiate nats (spirit-beings) were also regularly held, for though the royal family was staunchly Buddhist (in fact, King Thibaw, by virtue of being the king, was officially the patron and protector of Buddhism in the Kingdom of Ava), the animistic worship of nats was deeply woven into the fabric of their beliefs, as it was into that of almost all Burmese. Rituals and ceremonies also always accompanied important events in the large extended royal family's life—births, attainment of puberty, marriages and funerals.[8]

Queen Supayalat had the additional burden of bearing babies (more precisely sons), of ensuring that the king's eye did not wander, and that he did not acquire any more queens. Power struggles and politics within the palace were also time consuming and worrisome. In fact, the whole business of life within the palace walls so preoccupied both the king and queen that some felt they had time for little else; that it was the ministers who ruled, or misruled, the kingdom.[9] But this view is neither fair nor accurate.

Though there was a coterie of ministers, most of them were more interested in personal gain than good governance. They were also sycophantic. After all, the king and queen could have sentenced any one of them to death for the slightest offence; additionally, they had limited powers. As mentioned earlier, although the Kinwun Mingyi had tried to wrest some of the king's absolute authority, his wings had been clipped. Therefore, in spite of the time constraints brought on by all the ceremonies, rituals, palace politics and entertainment within the palace, it was the king who continued to have the final say on most matters brought to his attention, political or otherwise. With the king's involvement came the involvement of Queen Supayalat.

In spite of the fact that she had no love for foreigners, Supayalat's window to the outside world was a group of *kalamas* or foreign women—Europeans, Armenians and Eurasians—residing in Mandalay. This group included Mattie, her European maid of honour and close confidante; Hosannah Manook, an Armenian, who was also one of her maids of honour (her father served as King Thibaw's Kalawun or Minister of Foreigners); and some French Catholic nuns including Sister Teresa and Sister Sophia. Most of these women were politically ignorant and, like the ministers, had vested interests, and were therefore not the ideal group to rely on for information and advice. In return for information, Queen Supayalat gave them expensive gifts; in order to remain in favour, they told the queen what she wanted to hear. Foreigners and foreign companies, including British companies, wanting commercial or political favours in Mandalay, realized that often the best approach would be through a kalama. The kalamas' influence in Mandalay was as a result considerable, especially after the British Resident left in 1879.[10]

The queen's much-celebrated son tragically died of smallpox in March 1880, six months after his birth.[11] She was pregnant with her second child at the time of his death, and it was deeply hoped that this child would also be a son. Preparations for the child's birth began three months before the due date. A pure gold dagger embedded with seven rows of rubies was ordered to cut the umbilical cord. Large and small bowls, platters and basins, all made of gold, were readied. The Golden Bed studded with gems was placed in the confinement room. An umbrella was installed for the royal baby.[12]

On the morning of 5 September 1880 (a Sunday) Queen Supayalat gave birth to a daughter,[13] and this significant event was recorded for posterity on a parabeik in the Glass Palace. A series of elaborately ritualistic ceremonies, befitting her regal status, were performed after her birth. The 'showing the face of the baby to elders' ceremony took place after four days. When the baby was seventy-five days old the 'feeding the baby a tiny bit of betel ceremony' was performed. When she was ninety days, her face was shown to the sun and the moon. But the grandest of all was the Dawthakarana (cradling) ceremony for which she was put in an emerald-studded cradle in front of the Bee Throne in the Glass Palace. Hundreds of lavish gifts in the form of precious stones, pearls, jewellery, golden bowls, bolts of expensive cloth, etc., were presented to her. Two princesses, the Thonze Princess and the Taungzin Princess, were selected as her head nurse and her second nurse, and numerous maids were appointed to assist them.[14]

The baby was given the title Ashin Hteik Su Myat Phaya Gyi, meaning the Exalted Senior Mistress of the Head Group of Goddesses[15] (the British re-christened this princess the First Princess during the royal family's exile) and she was entitled to be declared tabindaing—in other words she was eligible to be the next king's chief queen, since she had pure Konbaung blood and was her parent's eldest daughter.

Although the ceremonies were plentiful, extravagant and outwardly celebratory, her daughter's birth heralded neither a joyful nor peaceful time for Queen Supayalat. She was acutely aware that it was a son that she had been expected to produce, and her failure to have done so would have consequences. From the time Thibaw had become king there had been constant pressure on him to take more wives; this, after all, was what *all* the Konbaung kings before him had done. So far she had been able to prevail, but just as she feared, the death of her son followed by the birth of a daughter caused her influence over the king, and therefore in the palace, to falter and diminish.[16]

Yanaung, quickly perceiving the opportunity, pressed the king to take more queens to ensure the all-important male heir. (A well-known womanizer, a much-married man, Yanaung was King Thibaw's closest friend, confidante and advisor; they had been monk-novices at the Royal Golden monastery together and shared a strong bond. The king treated him as a brother and had bestowed the title of 'prince' upon him.) Many in the palace agreed with Yanaung: an heir was vital. Besides, the king's devotion to just one wife was seen as a sign of weakness[17] and the 'lordly demeanour' of Queen Supayalat had resulted in people wanting to see her put in her place. Even the royal astrologers informed Thibaw that 'there was a spell thrown over Soo-Payah-Lat, and that she would never bear him an heir'.[18]

The king wavered under the renewed pressure and Yanaung, seizing the moment, found a charming and beautiful seventeen-year-old girl called Daing Khin Khin (later and more commonly known as Mi Khingyi) from a reputable family, and introduced her to the king. The king, immediately infatuated, declared he wanted to marry her and make her his Northern Golden Chamber Queen (a queen of eighth rank).[19] When Mi Khingyi's father expressed his reluctance for fear of Queen Supayalat's wrath, King Thibaw is purported to have reassured him that he had nothing to worry about. He said that he would inform Queen Supayalat when the time was right, and that he would personally protect Mi Khingyi from any danger. He added that if any harm was to befall her, may he be cursed with the loss of his throne.[20] The father, convinced of the king's sincerity, caved in. Mi Khingyi was snuck into the palace dressed as a page and hidden in the servants' quarters, so that the king could clandestinely meet her.[21]

In 1881 when the queen was heavily pregnant with her third child, King Thibaw suggested that both of them undergo a fast in two separate locations for seven days, as forerunner to getting a *bei thei* (a blessing). Supayalat readily agreed, and while she fasted in isolation, the king closeted himself with Mi Khingyi. It appears that almost the entire palace, with the exception of the queen, was privy to this. No one dared tell her—not even those close and loyal to her—and many enjoyed a private laugh at her expense.[22]

On 11 August 1881, Queen Supayalat gave birth to a second daughter.[23] This daughter, later called the Second Princess by the British, was titled Ashin Hteik Su Myat Phaya Lat. King Thibaw most insensitively told the queen about Mi Khingyi just after the birth of this daughter.[24] The queen, deeply humiliated, hurt and hysterical with anger, pounced on the king, screaming, 'You smell of slaves! . . . you smell of slaves!' (All the king's subjects were considered his slaves.) A spirited fight followed, resulting in two deep scratches springing up across King Thibaw's face.[25] As the bewildered king beat a hasty retreat, Yanaung accosted him and beseeched him to be firm. So, clutching a spear King Thibaw ran back into Queen Supayalat's chamber. A dramatic chase across the palace ensued: king, spear in hand, lumbering after the queen. Queen Supayalat ran swiftly to the safety of her mother's apartments, where she momentarily ensconced herself. And very temporarily she turned to her mother and the person her mother trusted the most, the Kinwun Mingyi, for help and advice.[26]

The queen considered her options. The king had strayed in the past. There had been Pyin Khin Khin—one of Queen Supayalat's maids of honour. King Thibaw had promised to make her a queen, but Pyin Khin Khin's not-so-trusting aunt, terrified of what might happen to her niece when the queen found out about the affair, had whisked her away from the palace. By the time Queen Supayalat heard about the goings-on, Pyin Khin Khin had already left and been married off to a government official.[27] Then there had been a Shan princess, another of her maids of honour. Queen Supayalat had had her beaten up and thrown out of the palace grounds. Although on these occasions, 'her eyes were big with tears for several days',[28] nothing before had been as serious a threat as the one she now faced. She realized that in spite of the betrayal, and the wretched manner in which it had been effected, she loved being queen and she really loved King Thibaw. In fact, according to one of Queen Supayalat's maids, 'of all her passions this was the greatest, her passion for the king'.[29] Getting rid of Mi Khingyi would take some cunning but she recognized this was not an insurmountable task for her. However she knew that there would be many more Mi Khingyis, and therefore decided to eliminate the source of this unhappy problem. She was well aware that Yanaung had cajoled, admonished and swayed her husband to take another wife, and would do so again and again. No other man had as much influence over the king as he did. So she firmly resolved that 'removing' Yanaung was what she had to do.[30] And this, she knew, would be considerably trickier than dealing with Mi Khingyi.

The queen first tackled Mi Khingyi. She summoned her and treated her very kindly, even offering her some of her own jewellery to wear and gifting her many new rich silk clothes. She told Mi Khingyi that she was taking her under her care and instructed everyone to treat her with respect. After all, she said, the king himself had selected this girl.

King Thibaw in court dress with Queen Supayalat. The Graphic, *27 February 1886.*

The dancing peacock, the emblem of the royal family, on a Konbaung-period silver coin.

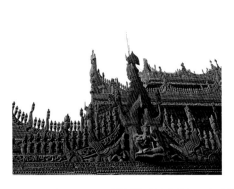

Left: A segment of the Shwenandaw Kyaung (earlier King Mindon's apartment), demonstrating the extraordinary carvings on buildings of the original palace. Photograph by author 2009.

Below: The Golden Palace, Mandalay. Photographer and date unknown; perhaps taken in the late 1800s.

Opposite, above: King Thibaw and Queen Supayalat in state robes, on the Lion Throne.

Opposite, below: An old postcard of the Golden Monastery where the young Thibaw spent three years as a novice monk. Photographer D.A. Ahuja.

King Theebaw's Monastry — Mandalay.

Right: An old postcard depicting a pwe. Photographer D.A. Ahuja.
Below: King Thibaw's barge. The Graphic, 31 January 1880.
Overleaf: King Thibaw with his two wives. The Graphic, 16 January 1886.

Burmese Poay.

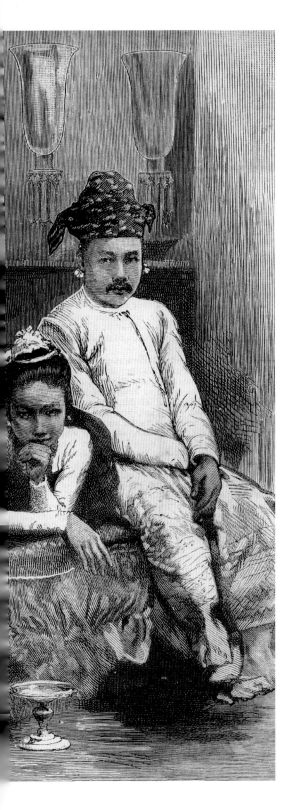

Above, top: The First Princess, with her maid of honour, in Mandalay.

Centre: The Second Princess, with her maid of honour, in Mandalay.

Bottom: King Thibaw and Queen Supayalat in Mandalay.

THE ILLUSTRATED LONDON NEWS.

REGISTERED AT THE GENERAL POST-OFFICE FOR TRANSMISSION ABROAD.

No. 2441.—VOL. LXXXVIII.　　　　SATURDAY, JANUARY 30, 1886.　　　　TWO WHOLE SHEETS } SIXPENCE. BY POST 6½D.

THE BURMAH EXPEDITION: DEPOSITION OF KING THEEBAW—GENERAL PRENDERGAST GIVES HIM TEN MINUTES' GRACE.
FROM A SKETCH SUPPLIED TO OUR SPECIAL ARTIST, MR. MELTON PRIOR.

Deposition of King Thibaw: General Prendergast allows him ten minutes more. Artist Melton Prior.
The Illustrated London News, 30 January 1886.

She now ensured that Mi Khingyi was always near her, giving the king absolutely no opportunity to see Mi Khingyi alone.[31] Why did the king not take a stand? Because, in spite of his brief flashes of defiance, as one of Queen Supayalat's maids of honour eloquently put it:

> No one could stand against [Queen Supayalat] when she was angry. Not the ministers, not the king, nor any one. It [was] better to face a tigress. Everyone bent and shivered before her ... No words can say how angry she was at being disdained and plotted against by little people, at having the king's affection stolen from her. She was fighting for her life, for what was more than life to her.[32]

As far as Mi Khingyi was concerned, the king now had to make do with a few discreet glances and some very public words.

In early 1882, petition boxes were placed all around Mandalay for people to submit complaints and suggestions for the king's consideration.[33] This had been a long-held custom. It is said that Queen Supayalat ensured that numerous petitions against Yanaung were deposited. It is not that all the petitions were fabricated, for Yanaung was a much feared and hated man in Mandalay. Many saw him as Queen Supayalat now did—an arrogant, dishonest, unsavoury and highly immoral character with far too much influence over the king.[34]

At least one unsigned anti-Yanaung petition is supposed to have been very skilfully worded by the Kinwun Mingyi outlining Yanaung's role in the economic ruin and oppression of the people. Another petition, signed by thirty-six people, accused Yanaung of plotting to have King Thibaw removed.[35] The effect of these petitions on the king was profound, and in his distress and fear he turned for help to the one person he truly trusted and knew he could depend on: Queen Supayalat. Yanaung's house was searched, and a stash of weapons, a great deal of cash, and gold and diamonds of such magnitude was found that a very indignant Queen Supayalat is said to have commented, 'Why, he has more than I do!'[36] Perhaps worse, however, was the fact that proof of kingly aspirations was also found: in his home was a bed, big and golden, designed just like the king's, proving beyond doubt that 'he was plotting to be king and was in his heart king already'.[37]

The infuriated king ordered Yanaung's arrest, but thought he'd take his time deliberating the next step. He was very fond of this man, and his execution was not something he could easily authorize. Says Dr Tin Maung Aye (a Burmese doctor cum historian):

> Shwe Lan Bo (Yanaung's archenemy) was sent to arrest Yanaung on Supayalat's instructions. Shwe Lan Bo slapped Yanaung like a woman (men have to box; slapping was an added insult), dragged him to jail, and had him tied up. He then lifted Yanaung's chin with his foot (a terrible insult). As Shwe Lan Bo was triumphantly striding out of jail to report matters to the queen, he met the Taingda Mingyi, who very helpfully pointed out that if the king decided to forgive Yanaung, Shwe Lan Bo would be put to death for his treatment of Yanaung. Highly alarmed at this prospect, Shwe Lan Bo rushed back in and killed Yanaung with a common pair of long scissors (used for cutting cheroots[38]) that he found lying around. He left the scissors in Yanaung's hand to make it appear a suicide. So well known is this story that to this day similar scissors are known as 'Yanaung scissors' in Mandalay.[39]

It was Queen Supayalat who informed King Thibaw of Yanaung's death. The king immediately realized that his friend had been executed, and as his anger against him had considerably ebbed, he deeply grieved the loss.[40] Mi Khingyi's father was also executed, and Mi Khingyi was quietly removed from the palace. But by now the king's infatuation had waned and although he must have noticed her absence, he felt in no position to question it. Shortly after her removal she too was executed on Queen Supayalat's order. Mi Khingyi was pregnant with the king's child at the time she was killed, although it appears the king was unaware of this fact.[41]

The preoccupation of ensuring her own husband's fidelity probably reinforced the queen's very strong and moralistic views on the importance of faithfulness in all marriages, and about socially appropriate behaviour. These views were applied to all in the palace, and to all her subjects. She wanted her reign to be 'a reign of virtue' and she dealt with infringements brought to her attention most harshly. When one of her half-sisters, a beautiful young princess, fell in love and carried on a clandestine affair with someone considered unsuitable, the queen was outraged. An inquiry was held and the lover was put to death in the customary manner: he was put in a sack loaded with heavy stones and chucked into the Irrawaddy River. The distraught princess was imprisoned to live with only memories of her lover, and memories of the tender love-letters they had exchanged (letters written on tiny scraps of paper, rolled thin, and inserted into her faithful nanny's earring hole, to be carried secretly to and fro).[42]

In 1882 Queen Supayalat gave birth to another daughter and in October 1883 to yet another. In March 1884, the queen's two youngest daughters died of small pox. The queen, in the five and a half years since her investiture, had borne five children of whom only one had been a son.[43] She now had two surviving daughters, and by now there was acute concern among the ministers and everyone else in the palace that the king would never have an heir.

In 1884, around the time she was grieving the death of her two small daughters, she suddenly had another predicament to contend with, and perhaps from a totally unexpected quarter—her own mother. Sinbyumashin was sick of being marginalized. Always the master schemer, she realized she had one trump card left: her youngest daughter, Supayagalae. She conspired to marry Supayagalae to the Myngun Prince, one of King Mindon's few surviving sons who at this time was living in India, have King Thibaw overthrown, and have her new son-in-law installed as king.[44] Although the Myngun Prince was no meek prince—he had attempted to seize the Lion Throne in 1866 by having tried, unsuccessfully, to kill his own father and having killed the eingshe-min Prince Kanaung—Sinbyumashin realized she didn't have many choices as most of the eligible princes had been massacred in 1879. She could only hope that the Myngun Prince would be more appreciative and grateful than King Thibaw had been.

It must have reassured the old queen to know that her youngest daughter was nothing at all like Supayalat. She was a sweet and mild-mannered girl, very obedient and pliant. Unluckily for Sinbyumashin, Queen Supayalat got wind of the plot, and planned an equally inspired countermove. The queen realized that if her younger sister was also married to King Thibaw, then all of Sinbyumashin's three daughters would be married to him, so a change in monarch would be to her mother's distinct disadvantage.[45]

When the queen approached her youngest sister with the proposal,

Supayagalae immediately voiced her refusal as politely as she could. Supayagalae knew her sister. She knew of her tremendous possessiveness, of her ruthless vindictiveness. She had seen with her own shocked eyes how her eldest sister, Supayagyi, had been disgraced and removed; how Mi Khingyi had been disposed of. But Queen Supayalat would not— could not—take no for an answer, and furiously ordered Supayagalae to do her bidding. Supayagalae, a timid girl and very fearful of her sister's wrath, felt she had no choice. No ceremony was held; the queen just presented her sister to the king as his junior wife and queen. Regrettably, even after this, Queen Supayalat treated her sister with no generosity or kindness. Rather, it is said that she constantly snubbed and humiliated her in public, to make it abundantly clear where the power still lay.[46]

5

RUMBLINGS OF WAR

There was a distant feeling of superiority vis-à-vis the Burmese in the minds of many British businessmen, missionaries, travellers and government officials who lived in or dealt with Burma during the 1800s and the first half of the1900s. Many felt what Cecil Rhodes—businessman, statesman and a well-known colonizer after whom Rhodesia (now Zimbabwe) was named—so memorably said, 'We happen to be the best people in the world, with the highest ideals of decency and justice and liberty and peace, and the more of the world we inhabit, the better it is for humanity.'[1]

This mindset resulted in many British visitors not even attempting to understand the Burmese in their own context, and there was an ocean of cultural differences that separated the British from the Burmese. As one Burmese minister observed to a British envoy in 1826, 'Your and our customs are so completely opposite in so many points. You write on white, we on black paper. You stand up, we sit down; you cover your head, we our feet in token of respect.'[2] The numerous differences led to unnecessary misunderstandings. For example, the Burmese were very reluctant to wake up a sleeping person for fear that his leip-bya or 'butterfly spirit' may not return in time to his body. As a result, wrote Sir George Scott:

> [I]t is useless to tell a Burman servant to wake you at a certain hour. He will come in at the appointed time and look wistfully at you, and wish something would fall down and make a noise; but he himself would tread as softly as a housebreaker . . . Consequently the master is not wakened and gets up an hour and a half after he wanted to, and storms at the poor Burman for [being] a lazy scoundrel who snores away till the sun is as high in the sky as a pagoda spire . . .'[3]

It was incidents like this, however insignificant, viewed through the filter of their own culture, that led to mistaken opinions being formed by many foreign visitors about the Burmese people. These opinions led to cultural stereotyping, which was inaccurate and often derogatory. Additionally, from the British point of view, the Burmese, as the Indian, 'had to be inferior in order to justify his subjection; generally his inferiority was supposed to lie not so much in his intellectual caliber, as in his lack of those qualities of "character" which made the Englishman by contrast so much his better'.[4]

Dr Marks, the missionary, was warned before he went to Burma that the Burmese were 'treacherous savages, and would murder any European on the slightest provocation'.[5] A British traveller described them as the 'merriest—and perhaps laziest—people in the world . . .', and stated, 'It is to be deplored that this rich country is in the hands of the Burmese, like a rich jewel in a pig's snout.'[6]

A far worse picture was painted of the king and the queen. From the time Thibaw became king, in order to promote their own commercial interests, the British business community in British-occupied Rangoon began a systematic, long-term campaign to discredit and vilify the royal couple, hoping that this would convince the powers that be in Britain to annex the kingdom.[7] Unfortunately this led to many exaggerated, biased and even fabricated accounts and press reports, which resulted in the image of the king and queen snowballing into the very epitome of primitiveness and wickedness. No attempt was ever made, by any representative of the kingdom, to correct these impressions.[8]

King Thibaw was portrayed as a cruel, incompetent drunkard. He was called an 'inconceivable brute'[9], a 'monster in human form'.[10] Unarguably King Thibaw was not a particularly able king, but as a devout Buddhist it is most unlikely he ever drank. In fact, when he was being sent into exile, the officers transporting him on the steamer en route to India offered him a variety of alcohol, which he always declined.[11] Certainly there was not even a hint of him ever having touched an alcoholic drink during his entire thirty-year exile in India, when he and his family were closely monitored by a series of British officers.

Queen Supayalat was portrayed as a darkly malevolent force, a 'savage'.[12] It was reported that taxes in the kingdom had to be increased due to 'her insatiable love for finery'.[13] She was also accused of making 'her position more secure by fostering the King's taste for strong drink'.[14] Increasingly fantastic stories were circulated about her, including one in which she supposedly locked up an erring maid in a wooden chest for several days; the maid is said to have survived by eating the clothes stored in the chest![15] Although Queen Supayalat was ruthless and manipulative, although she was extravagant and enjoyed fine and expensive things, and although she did authorize executions during her reign and may have had a hand in the 1879 massacre, she did no more or less than many Konbaung kings and queens before her. While this undoubtedly does not justify some of her actions, perhaps it explains the context in which they occurred.

Apart from the British business community even some missionaries in Lower Burma had, for evangelical reasons, been maligning the Burmese, including its royalty, and pushing for war. They had been doing this ever since the time of King Tharrawaddy (1837–46) as they believed that war leading to the colonization of all of Burma was 'the best, if not the only means of eventually introducing the humanizing influences of the Christian religion.'[16] The missionaries truly believed that Buddhism was 'an absurd, backward system of belief' that hindered the Burmese from learning and progressing.[17]

It was not only the British who were critical of the royal couple—their own people had grouses which the British were aware of, and which they would later capitalize upon. Every year the king (viewed by his subjects as the earthly image of Lord Indra) was supposed to perform the all-important Ploughing Ceremony by running a plough through a field in an ornately decorated bullock-cart drawn by white bulls, and reciting prayers that were supposed to bring the rains and yield better crops. For fear of leaving his throne unprotected for over three hours, in all the years of his rule, King Thibaw never staged this ceremony. Poor rainfall in the kingdom between 1883 and 1885 resulted in crop failure that King Thibaw was blamed for.[18] The well-known extravagant lifestyle of the royal couple also did nothing to endear them to their increasingly impoverished people. In addition, the Burmese were disillusioned with the poor administration and the growing lawlessness in the country. However, it does not appear that his people ever considered King Thibaw to be the despot the British painted him to be. Rather, they viewed him as someone not as strong or as competent as his father had been.

King Thibaw has been blamed in history for the loss of the Kingdom of Ava. In actuality the process of colonization of Burma, as of India, began seemingly innocuously with Britain's interest in trade with the country. Whenever Britain felt her commercial interests were threatened, she had the strength and influence to resort to military and political intervention, and she often did. Large tracts of Burma had already been lost to the British, including all access to the sea, and the British viewed the rest of the kingdom as not only a potential market for her goods but also as a source for valuable natural resources.[19] Additionally, the kingdom's proximity to a new and very important trading partner, China, and to the jewel in its crown, India, made Britain regard the kingdom as a defence zone that no foreign power should be allowed to infiltrate.[20]

King Mindon had understood well the strength and power of the British, and had concentrated his energies on improving his relationship with them, to the extent that when the Indian Mutiny took place in 1857, and Britain's attention and manpower was diverted, he made no attempt to recapture parts of Burma lost in the two previous wars but is said to have opined, 'We do not strike a friend when he is in distress.' He had sincerely hoped to regain lost territory through diplomacy.[21] What he was able to achieve was the retention of what was left of his kingdom. Although King Thibaw was unable to maintain a healthy relationship with the British, and in fact played into their hands, it was still really just a matter of time before the creeping tide of colonialism would have washed away any king sitting on the Lion Throne.

If Britain had not colonized the kingdom, France with its presence in Indo-China probably would have. In 1882, proposed commercial and friendship treaties between the kingdom and Britain, which, among other things, would have given the kingdom access to arms from British territory and the British a Resident in Mandalay, fell through. It is said that Queen Supayalat had been influenced against the treaties by the kalamas, who did not want the British Resident reinstalled, as that would have meant significant erosion in their power. A treaty with the British also went against the interests of Italian and French arms dealers and manufacturers who were supplying antiquated weapons to the palace, so they too strongly advised against signing the treaties. Now Mandalay turned increasingly towards France for arms and assistance, and in August 1883, King Thibaw sent some of his representatives to France. This mission stayed there for almost two years. During this period, to the increasing suspicion and irritation of the British government, discussions were held both with the French government and private businesses.[22]

The British, meanwhile, were holding talks with the Myngun, Nyaungyan and Nyaungok Princes (all three were living safely in India) as possible replacements for King Thibaw.[23] (The British, throughout King Thibaw's reign, continued discussions with these princes, to the acute discomfort of King Thibaw and Queen Supayalat. In fact, it is rumoured, so fed up was the king with the constant tension that sitting on the Lion Throne involved, that on a few occasions he thought of just giving it up himself in favour of another prince; an appalled Queen Supayalat would hear none of it: 'You are king, I am queen—we will *have* to continue' she is purported to have told him very firmly.[24])

In late September 1884, during the Thadingyut festival, about three hundred prisoners allegedly tried to escape from Mandalay jail and were massacred. The British blamed the king, surmising that he had staged the break out as an excuse to execute political prisoners. A flurry of newspaper articles in Lower Burma deplored the massacre and condemned King Thibaw's 'misrule'. A public meeting was held in Rangoon, and a memorial was submitted to the chief commissioner of British Burma urging the 'absolute necessity of immediate interference.' The memorandum strongly recommended 'the annexation of Upper Burma, or, failing that . . . it should be placed in the position of a protected state within the Empire, with a prince, other than the present ruler, on the throne.' The memorial was signed by a group of Englishmen including Dr Marks, King Thibaw's old teacher.[25] (Dr Marks had, at the meeting, given a rabble rousing speech referring to King Thibaw as 'the vile young ruffian, whom I regret to say was once one of my pupils . . .'). But Thibaw was not even the real perpetuator of the Mandalay jail massacre— some of his ministers had staged it for personal reasons.[26]

　The Kinwun, Taingda and the Taungwin Mingyis had been in touch with the same three princes in India as the British—the Myngun, Nyaungyan and Nyaungok Princes. The ministers knew King Thibaw was unpopular with the British, and each had tried to secure his own position by supporting a different one of these princes in the event a change of monarch became inevitable. Word of this treachery had reached Queen Supayalat's ears, and the messengers used for this purpose had been intercepted and imprisoned in Mandalay jail. The queen had been anxiously awaiting their questioning in the hope of discovering the identities of the betraying ministers. Additionally, some ministers, including the Taingda Mingyi, had been taking large kickbacks to protect dacoit gangs operating in and around Mandalay. Some of these dacoits had recently been captured and interred in the jail, and confessions were not something an involved minister wanted. It was for both these reasons that a group of rival ministers banded together to orchestrate the jailbreak, and the subsequent massacre. King Thibaw's involvement was manipulated and peripheral. When lied to by his ministers that the famous dacoit Yanmin was about to break out of Mandalay jail to start an uprising in support of the Myngun Prince, the king gave orders that Yanmin be executed. The ministers then bribed the head jailer to inform Yanmin of his imminent execution and to allow a jailbreak. The jailbreak was a defining moment in the relationship between the British government and the kingdom. After the massacre, and the resultant public outrage, no further attempts were made by the British to reconcile differences with the kingdom,[27] and its eventual formal colonization was just around the corner.

In February 1885 word reached the British government that the kingdom had signed a treaty with France giving it special privileges. Lord Dufferin, viceroy and governor general of India at that time, under whose jurisdiction Burma came, reacted that if 'the French proceedings should eventuate in any serious attempt to forestall us in Upper Burmah, I should not hesitate to annex the country . . .'[28] Proof of the kingdom's various agreements (with France, and with French companies and individuals), was supposedly provided to the British in June/July 1885 thanks to none other than Queen Supayalat's long-time favourite, her Burmese–Greek maid of honour and close confidante, Mattie Calogreedy.

Mattie had been intimately involved with a Mandalay-based Frenchman, P.H. Bonvillian, who largely due to Mattie's influence with the queen, had been granted a contract for the Royal Ruby Mines. Mattie always thought of herself as Bonvillian's wife and as per Burmese custom her marriage was not an invalid one. But in May 1885, when Bonvillian returned to Mandalay after a long absence in France, he brought back with him a newly acquired young French bride. When a distraught Mattie confronted him with the fact that he was already married to her, he is supposed to have indicated that that was impossible; that he had been engaged to the French lady for a very long time. He went on to say, 'A Frenchman does not marry . . .' Although he stopped himself mid-sentence, no further words were needed. Mattie knew exactly what he meant; to him she was a half-caste, a native, a mistress who had performed her service and was now being discarded. He had never meant to marry her; to him their common-law marriage never held any validity. He did thank her for 'all her sweetness'; he did offer her a consolatory trip, on her own, to Europe. Overwhelmed with despair Mattie took to her bed. Though probably not aware of the reason behind her infirmity Queen Supayalat, caring and concerned, visited her and sent her gifts.[29]

After pulling herself together, Mattie plotted revenge. Having been privy to so many political discussions, she knew of the unease with which Britain viewed the kingdom's growing closeness to France. She hoped that if the British had tangible proof of the agreements between the two countries, they would intervene. And if they intervened she concluded the French, and with them Bonvillian, who had hoped to make his fortune off the ruby mines, would be routed from the kingdom. The possible consequence of her very personal revenge on the kingdom, on Queen Supayalat who had showered nothing but kindness on her, and even on herself whose life now lay solely within the palace walls, did not deter her from the single-mindedness of her purpose. To obtain copies of these critical agreements, Mattie seduced one of the Kinwun Mingyi's secretaries. She then took the documents to Andreino, the Italian consul general.[30] More importantly Andreino was also an agent representing the interests of a couple of British companies in the kingdom. One of these companies was the Bombay-Burma Trading Company.[31]

The Bombay-Burma Trading Company held licenses for logging and exporting timber from specified forests in the kingdom. The company had been accused of underpaying royalty on timber exported from the Ningyan forest, and a large and potentially ruinous settlement had been asked for, and it had appealed to the Hluttaw. Andreino, as its agent, was the man on the spot. He had lived and worked in Mandalay for most of his life, and earned a considerable income from the company. He was therefore desperate for the matter to be resolved in its favour.[32]

Mattie, with the copies of the French agreements, could not have approached Andreino at a more opportune time. When she first approached him, on the mail boat, he was rather condescending. Word had spread about Bonvillian's newly acquired French wife, and perhaps he thought she was casting a net around for a new man. However, when she told him about the papers she held, his attitude changed dramatically. He realized these papers could bring intervention by the British government, and that could be his salvation. After he assured Mattie that he would not disclose how he had got them, she slipped the documents into his eager hands.[33] Andreino passed them on to the

British government in Rangoon. (Some historians believe that the papers the Kinwun Mingyi's secretary gave Mattie were of no particular significance; that Andreino forged more meaningful 'agreements', with the objective of galvanizing the British into action.[34])

In August 1885 the Hluttaw rejected the appeal and indicated that a large payment was due from the Bombay-Burma Trading Company. The British asked that an arbitrator, selected by Lord Dufferin, be appointed to settle the matter fairly. The kingdom refused this request mainly because it felt that formally accepting the arbitration would imply that the Hluttaw's decision had not been a fair one. Besides, how fair would an arbitrator selected by Lord Dufferin be to Burmese interest? However, the kingdom did send many verbal feelers to the Bombay-Burma Trading Company and the British government implying that a mutually acceptable solution *could* be worked out. In fact, a Burmese minister directly approached the Bombay-Burma Trading Company stating that requesting King Thibaw for a royal review would quickly settle the matter for a relatively small amount. But a mutually acceptable solution was *not* what the British government now wanted. The refusal for arbitration had, very providentially, provided them with an excuse to send an ultimatum to Thibaw, an ultimatum that, most importantly, would end French influence in the kingdom once and for all.[35]

In October 1885, while deliberations and correspondence pertaining to the future of the kingdom was going on in British government circles, the Thadingyut festival was celebrated in the palace over several days, with the usual pomp and seemingly without a care in the world. For the Kadaw ceremony, the Great Audience Hall was thronged with ministers, governors, Shan chiefs, various officials, soldiers and others, all in rich ceremonial dresses for the occasion, all bearing gifts. According to a maid of honour, for her reception in the Lily Throne room, the Queen sat 'with princesses and maids of honour about her, a glory of gold and jewels . . .' At night, the palace gardens were lit with thousands of coloured paper lanterns and small lamps, giving it a magical fairy-tale atmosphere. During the festival, races of rowboats with gilded paddles were held on the moat surrounding the Royal Golden City, much to the excitement and pleasure of everyone.[36] In short, the royal couple continued living the way they always had and gave no indication whatsoever of being aware of how perilous their present position was.

The British sent the king an ultimatum dated 22 October 1885.[37] King Thibaw was told that it had been 'decided to place . . . the throne of Burma in the position of a feudatory of British India. He and his successors according to national custom will be allowed to remain on the throne so long as they loyally adhere to the position of, and faithfully discharge the duties and responsibilities of a feudatory of British India.'[38] The five main points contained in the ultimatum were: a special envoy would be sent to settle the Bombay-Burma Trading Company dispute and he should not be submitted to 'any humiliating ceremony' (that is, removing his shoes); no action should be taken against the Bombay-Burma Trading Company until the envoy had decided on the case; a permanent British Resident must be accepted in Mandalay, and he must be permitted proper defence in the form of armed guards and an armed steamer (and he must be received with his shoes on); all future relations between the kingdom and any foreign country had to have the British government's approval; and proper facilities had to be given to permit British trade with China through the kingdom.[39] Thibaw was not given a choice—it was indicated that only under these conditions would the kingdom be allowed to function 'independently'. King Thibaw was also, very pointedly, referred to as His Highness the Prince of Upper Burma, and not as His Majesty the King of Upper Burma, as he had always earlier been referred to. (His Highness was also the British nomenclature for the feudatory Indian princes in British India.)[40]

The British government made it clear that if it did not receive a written acceptance of the ultimatum by 10 November, it would feel free to exercise whatever option it wished.[41] To impress upon Mandalay the option it had in mind, and the seriousness of its intention, ten thousand British troops were positioned ready for action in Thayetmyo, a small town 400 miles away from Mandalay,[42] on the Irrawaddy, near the border that divided Upper and Lower Burma.

The ultimatum arrived in Mandalay on 30 October and was presented by the Kinwun Mingyi to the Hluttaw on 31 October 1885. When

King Thibaw first heard its contents he was shocked into silence. The Kinwun Mingyi expressed surprise at the ultimatum; the Taingda Mingyi immediately advocated rejection. The king left the Hluttaw and consulted the kingdom's head priest who advised acceptance.[43]

The next day, the Hluttaw met again to consider the ultimatum. This time Queen Supayalat was also present at the meeting (as was her mother, Sinbyumashin). Mattie with some other maids of honour sat behind the queen. Perhaps Mattie now regretted what she had done.[44] The bazaar gossip was that the British government was not going to allow one of its companies to be punished and fined and as a result they had begun preparations for war. And war was what all the maids in the palace whispered about when the queen was out of earshot.[45] At this meeting the Kinwun Mingyi and the Taingda Mingyi took diametrically opposite stands, creating a gaping schism in the Hluttaw, as they so often had in the past. Unfortunately, each of them had vested interest in the advice he gave. Each of them had his own supporters.[46]

The Taingda Mingyi advised war. He argued that the ultimatum would in effect make the new British Resident the real king of Upper Burma. As commander of some of the royal armed forces he assured the Hluttaw that Burmese soldiers and their weapons were as good as anybody else's.[47] He dramatically beseeched the king to 'drive the heretic kalas into the sea whence they came'[48] and declared, 'In this war the King shall be victorious'. Queen Supayalat smiled her approval; King Thibaw said nothing, but turned to the Kinwun Mingyi for his advice.[49]

The Kinwun Mingyi said that although the ultimatum was very demeaning, it was better to accept it, in toto, in order to avoid a conflict. He reminded the Hluttaw that compared to the Taingda Mingyi who had never left the shores of Burma, he was a much travelled man. He had actually *seen* the British army and weaponry. From his position as the commander of some of the royal armed forces, he knew that they were totally outclassed and had no chance of winning a war against the British. He tried to soften his stance by saying that they could buy time by accepting the ultimatum, and some years later, when their soldiers were better trained, and the kingdom had closer alliances with other powerful countries, resistance against the British could be contemplated.[50] He advised the king to 'bide his time, and strike when the blow will tell.'[51] Throughout his speech Sinbyumashin nodded her approval.[52]

Then various other ministers and officials offered their points of view. Some agreed with the Kinwun Mingyi. Some, influenced by the indignation and anger they felt at the tone of the ultimatum, pushed for war. Queen Supayalat smiled encouragingly at anyone who spoke of war and winning. But Thibaw didn't smile, didn't say anything. The Kinwun Mingyi, very anxious by now to convince the king of his point of view, reminded him of the two earlier wars lost to the British and the large parts of the kingdom lost as a result.[53] He then ominously added, 'Would His Majesty [like to] go down in history as the King who lost the *rest* of Burma?'[54]

The very thought of being so ignominiously labelled had a profound effect on King Thibaw.[55] Perhaps at this moment he also recalled that his royal astrologers had warned him, as early as 1879, that he would be the last king of Burma.[56] Sensing that the alarmed king was on the verge of accepting the Kinwun Mingyi's advice, Queen Supayalat acted swiftly. She was five months pregnant with what she desperately hoped and prayed was a son, a future heir. She certainly didn't want to give up the Lion Throne without a fight.[57] So leaning forward, she furiously said that even if the Kinwun Mingyi was right and the kingdom was lost in the war, 'better it were to lose the Golden Kingdom than to listen to orders like slaves . . . But all this talk of defeat is the talk of old men and cowards. There is no fear . . . The Taingda Mingyi shall command, and all shall go well.' Then pointing a trembling finger at the Kinwun Mingyi she shouted, 'As to the Kinwun Mingyi, he is old and afraid. He is not a man, a minister, but a woman, an old, old, woman . . .'[58] Paying no heed to the shocked silence, she turned to her maids of honour and ordered them to bring 'a *tamein* and a fan, and the Kinwoon Mingyi shall go and live amongst the women!'[59] Although ignored before, the Kinwun Mingyi had never been so openly and devastatingly belittled. According to a long missive written many years later by the Fourth Princess, it was because of this very public humiliation by her mother, who at that time was 'young and child-like in temper', that the Kinwun Mingyi 'made a plan for the dethronement of my parents'.[60]

Queen Supayalat's opposition to accepting the ultimatum could not have been made clearer. As no one dared contradict her, only those who supported its rejection now spoke up. The only exception was the Kinwun Mingyi who, in spite of everything, valiantly tried again to justify his point of view. But the king suddenly saw him as a spent old force. Confused, unsure of whom to trust, hearing the general call in the room for war, being ignorant both about the true state of his army and about the modernized British armed forces, perhaps sensing that both options were dismal ones, and hoping against hope the French would come to his defence, King Thibaw swayed towards Queen Supayalat's point of view as he had for so many years, and declared that rejecting the ultimatum, even if it meant war, was his only honourable option.[61] So saying he 'put out his hand and held Supayalat's . . . warm strong and comforting, in his'.[62]

In all probability the king realized that war meant defeat, although of course he hoped this would not be the case. If he had *not* opted for rejecting the ultimatum he risked losing the respect of his subjects or even of being assassinated.[63] When his half-brother, the Nyaungok Prince, was interviewed by *The Times of India* in early November 1885, he said that he felt the king had no choice and was sure that the king would fight rather than accept the ultimatum because 'The King of Burmah is regarded by the nation with great veneration, and according to the Buddhist religion is the representative of the deity, and for the King to humble himself before his subjects would be to strike a blow to their faith.'[64]

The Hluttaw met again immediately, in another room and without the king and queen, to vote on a decision. The custom was that the ministers would come to whatever decision the king wanted, because the king in turn would have ensured that his view was not contradictory to that of the majority of his ministers. Whatever the Hluttaw voted at this follow-up meeting, the king generally accepted although he had the power not to do so. Due to the very intimidating presence of Queen Supayalat at the earlier meeting, only the pro-war faction of the Hluttaw had felt free to speak, leading the king to believe that most of the Hluttaw favoured war. But this was not the case. Now, in the queen's absence, and bowing to the deep gravity of the situation, the Hluttaw did the unthinkable—they voted *not* to reject the ultimatum but to send an ambiguously acquiescing reply as they were not in favour of risking war.[65]

News of the Hluttaw's vote reached the king, queen and Sinbyumashin in the Summer Pavilion in the palace gardens, where they were sitting together on that very still, hot afternoon. Shocked and infuriated by this unprecedented defiance, Queen Supayalat urged the king to consider 'what sort of ministers yours are. You give them orders to declare war and they send you a message that they think peace would be better. Your father the great king would have executed or dismissed them.' Sinbyumashin asked Supayalat to bear in mind why the ministers had so voted: only in an attempt to save the throne, the throne that *she* had manipulated and obtained for King Thibaw. She also reminded the queen that she was young and inexperienced compared to the Kinwun Mingyi, who had so forcefully spoken in support of accepting the ultimatum. At the very mention of the Kinwun Mingyi, the man Queen Supayalat knew had influenced the Hluttaw to vote against the king's decision,[66] she screamed bitterly at her mother, 'You two should marry . . . You are well suited . . . You are both cowards . . .'[67] King Thibaw, though horrified that a daughter should speak so disrespectfully to her mother, said nothing. A tearful Sinbyumashin, realizing there was nothing more she could say or do, walked quietly back to her own apartments.[68]

King Thibaw made the very difficult choice of not accepting the Hluttaw's decision. He seems to have been greatly influenced by his pride, his not wanting to lose face,[69] for if a Burmese king lost his honour, 'he [was] left with nothing but his umbrella.'[70] So he indicated that while the other not-so-important points could be conditionally accepted, the all-important clause in which the kingdom had been asked to put all its foreign affairs under British supervision was not to be. The Kinwun Mingyi was asked to prepare a reply. Although the reply was carefully and cleverly drafted, and left room for further negotiations, the British were in no mood to parley. When Bernard (the chief commissioner of Lower Burma) received the reply on

8 November, he considered it a rejection of the ultimatum.[71] On 11 November, Lord Dufferin issued the order for war.[72] Now there was no turning back.

(It is interesting to note that when *The Times of India* interviewer, who had interviewed the Nyaungok Prince in early November, had asked him what he would have done had he been in King Thibaw's shoes, he had replied:

> I know how loth the [British] Government is to extend the responsibilities of the Empire by fresh annexations. It would be a comparatively easy matter for the King of Burmah to make such an arrangement as would fully satisfy the Indian Government [as the British government in India were called], and yet sacrifice nothing that the Burmese regard as precious. But to do this knowledge of the English which Theebaw does not possess and confidence in your intentions, which if you will excuse me for saying so, Theebaw does not feel.[73]

With war looming on the horizon the Irrawaddy Flotilla Company, the British company that operated steamers up and down the Irrawaddy, stopped sending boats into the kingdom's waters. Many foreigners fled in alarm, as did many Burmese. King Thibaw reacted by issuing a proclamation to all his subjects, dated 7 November 1885, informing them about the possible war, asking them to remain calm and to continue with their usual business. He also requested voluntary enlistment in the Royal Armed Services, and indicated that he would lead his forces not only to wipe out the English kalas but also to seize their country![74] This proclamation poignantly demonstrated either the unrealistic view the king had of his own ability to win this war (unlikely) or his desire to save face and to inspire confidence in his subjects.

The Taingda Mingyi, who, just a few days earlier, had been made the minister for war responsible for defence of the kingdom, believed that the British would not actually attack the kingdom. After all nothing had come of their posturing following the massacre of royals in 1879. He believed, incredibly, that the 10,000 men gathered at Thayetmyo was just an 'armed demonstration'. So he made half-hearted preparations for the war. On 14 November 1885 General Prendergast and his men, the British Burma Expeditionary Force, comprising a flotilla that extended almost five miles, left Thayetmyo and began travelling up the Irrawaddy with the clear objective of capturing Mandalay and deposing King Thibaw. Only then did the Taingda Mingyi wake up and realize that they really meant business.[75]

6
THE WAR AND THE LIES

In spite of the Taingda Mingyi's grandiose assertions at the Hluttaw meeting, the king's army did not stand the slightest chance against the British Burma Expeditionary Force; the Burmese army was poorly trained and badly equipped with antiquated and ill-functioning weapons. An oft-repeated story of a memorable drill, held during King Mindon's reign, gives an indication of the kind of instruction the soldiers received. Once a Frenchman, hired by King Mindon to train his soldiers, enthusiastically took his charges just outside Mandalay to practise the various arms that they had been outfitted with. The firing of these arms was heard all over Mandalay, including in the palace, and led to pandemonium. An exercise of this kind—the actual firing of arms *for practice*—had never happened before, leading to wild speculation and total panic. When the cause for the commotion was discovered, the king was furious. The Frenchman was told that he was *never* to hold such a drill again. The Burmese officer assisting the Frenchman suffered a worse fate for his role—he was publicly whipped. The guns were taken away from the soldiers and stacked safely in the palace, and subsequent sessions were ceremonial and spectacular, with dragon-tattooed soldiers marching in brilliant uniforms accompanied by bands of musicians and assistants carrying betel boxes, spittoons and cheroots.[1] Although King Thibaw did make some attempts to improve both the arms and the training of his army during his reign,[2] he had neither the financial resources nor the access to know-how to make a real difference.

The British army in contrast was extremely well trained and had the latest equipment at its disposal. Compared to the sixty-four-pound guns used by the British forces in this war, the Burmese army was equipped with swords and spears and with guns ranging from three to eight pounds. Additionally the British had decided to press into use machine guns.[3] General Prendergast's well thought-out strategy, contrasted with the Taingda Mingyi's barely existent one, also played a significant role. Once war had been decided upon, the general's advance upriver was so rapid that it gave the Burmese almost no time to cobble together a coherent defence plan. Not even the full army was available; not expecting the war, the Taingda Mingyi had given no orders to recall the many Burmese soldiers scattered in various parts of the kingdom (to quell the numerous rebellions and gangs of dacoits that had overrun the countryside), and now it was too late to do so.[4]

The swift advance of the British Burma Expeditionary Force also greatly startled the Italians Comotto and Molinari—the two engineers in the employment of King Thibaw—who had assisted in defence plans including in the fortification of the river forts along the Irrawaddy.[5] On 14 November 1885, the two Italians were engaged in the process of barricading the river between Thayetmyo and Minhla with submerged sharply pointed teak logs that they hoped would lacerate and sink any steamer going over them. When the first shot was fired at them, the terrified Italians jumped overboard and in their hurry left behind detailed maps of the various river forts. These maps were under General Prendergast's careful scrutiny before the end of the very first day of the war![6]

The British also exploited King Thibaw's lack of popular support. In an inspired last-minute strategy, they pretended they were coming with a Konbaung prince on board. Although the so-called prince was no prince at all but a Burmese clerk who worked for Bernard, for the moment no one was to know any better. Many on shore caught a glimpse of someone in princely attire, surrounded by attendants, and this sighting made many Burmese soldiers reluctant to risk their lives in a pointless war.[7] So long as there was a Konbaung king to sit on the Lion Throne, to many it mattered little who he was. For them it was an internal palace matter, as they had no particular loyalty to King Thibaw.

A proclamation signed by General Prendergast was widely distributed as the flotilla progressed upriver. The proclamation declared that the British government had decided that 'His Majesty (King Thibaw) shall cease to reign'; it explained Britain's reasons for declaring war, and informed the Burmese population that the British sincerely wished

> that bloodshed should be avoided, and that the peaceable inhabitants of all classes should be encouraged to pursue their usual callings without fear of molestation. None will have anything to apprehend so long as you do not oppose the passage of the troops under my command. Your private rights, your religions, and the national customs will be scrupulously respected . . .[8]

This reassuring proclamation, coupled with the fact that the British were not total strangers to the Burmese (they had ruled their countrymen in Lower Burma for decades) must have further weakened the will to resist in some Burmese soldiers and other people encountered along the way.

Ironically the kingdom's two most powerful ministers—the Kinwun Mingyi and the Taingda Mingyi—unwittingly assisted the British by sending conflicting and therefore confusing orders to the various units of the Burmese army. The Kinwun Mingyi ordered submission as he seemed to believe that this, with acceptance of the ultimatum, might persuade the British to let King Thibaw or another Konbaung prince remain on the throne. The Taingda Mingyi, on the other hand, ordered opposition. He could not do otherwise—it was he who had pushed so hard for war, it was he who had spoken so convincingly about the strength of the king's army, and it was he who had assured victory.[9]

Prendergast and his men advanced upriver virtually unopposed. At Minhla there was strong resistance, but it fell on 17 November. On the 19th Magwe was taken.[10] At Magwe the king's two Italian engineers (highly alarmed by the facility with which the frontier forts had been captured) surrendered to the British forces, thinking this was their safer option.[11] On 20 November, Yaynankhyown was occupied. By 21 November, the British flotilla was 145 miles south of Mandalay, and on that day they occupied Tsillemyo. On 22 November, the convoy reached Pagan (Bagan) and occupied it the next day without much difficulty. The expedition continued to Myingyan and after heavy firing on 24 November, it was captured on the 25th.[12]

Although Myingyan was eighty-five miles by river to Mandalay, it was only thirty-five miles as the crow flies. In Mandalay Queen Supayalat heard the echoing boom of the sixty-four-pound guns and it terrified her. She wondered whether all the information she had been receiving about the progress of the war was accurate. She had not questioned it before; she had great faith in her tattooed 'army of immortals'.[13] Just a couple of weeks earlier she had personally seen off many of the army officers with pep talks, gifts and promises, and they had been most confident and reassuring.[14] And she and the king had been *guaranteed* that Mandalay was impregnable. Comotto and Molinari had strengthened the river forts at a considerable cost, and had reassured everyone that an enemy could not possibly sail up the river undefeated.[15]

Right after the 14 November tragicomic confrontation involving the Italian engineers, the royal couple had been told that there had been fierce fighting downstream at Minhla, and although many had died, the king's force had ultimately won and two British ships had been captured. In celebration of this early first victory a particularly magnificent pwe was organized in the palace. All through the night many references were made in song and speech to the greatness of the king and queen, to the strength and bravery of the Burmese army,[16] and clowns made the Kinwun Mingyi the butt of many derogatory jokes.[17] When a particularly talented actress sang a deeply flattering song, a visibly moved queen removed a richly bejewelled bracelet from her wrist, gifted it to the actress, and said—and her words were

repeated loudly by a maid of honour for the entire audience to hear—
'soon there would be more to sing of than the capture of little
ships. . .'[18]

News conveyed to the royal couple after the so-called victory,
although sometimes contradictory, was generally upbeat. Not being
privy to the bazaar gossip of the rapidly approaching British expedition,
or to the fact that all business in Mandalay had been paralysed with
fear, the king and queen were ignorant about the true state of the
war.[19] However, the king was informed when the British flotilla passed
Pagan (23 November) and, deeply worried, he seriously considered
escaping to the Shan Hills with a cavalcade of fifty elephants and two
hundred ponies.[20] The next day, a flurry of telegrams was sent from
Mandalay to Commander Hlay Thin (at Myingyan). One tellingly
desperate telegram is reproduced below:

> How could heretics get through your troops of Pagan Nyaung U and
> reach Kun Ywa? STOP His Majesty expects you to do your best
> STOP Fight with courage and determination STOP His Majesty said
> he would lead the forces STOP So exalted a person need not do it
> STOP You do it as you had promised STOP Chase all heretics right
> back to their own land STOP Report success by telegram STOP[21]

As asked to, Commander Hlay Thin obligingly reported success by
telegram. The vanquished commander decided to report the 24
November shelling of Myingyan, the sound of which was heard by
Queen Supayalat, as having ended in Burmese victory. Totally in the
dark regarding the true position of the battle, the delighted king
instructed the Hluttaw to send a telegram to Hlay Thin saying:

> Nga Khine, Nga Tha Aung and Nga Aung . . . are going posthaste on
> horseback to deliver to you 100 viss of gold and 240 gold cups STOP
> Give them as rewards of bravery STOP Give most liberally STOP
> More is coming STOP[22]

The king also decided that his people had to be told the good news, so
a gong-beating crier was sent all across the town with the message that
three English warships had been destroyed and four had been captured,
and the captured four were being brought to Mandalay.[23]

Queen Supayalat, however, was by now deeply suspicious. How

could the stories of victory be true when the British had advanced so far? Explanations such as 'they were only being allowed to ascend the river so as to be more severely defeated' did not satisfy her. She guessed she was being lied to; she realized she needed to learn the truth.[24]

It was probably in the early morning hours of 25 November that Queen Supayalat walked with one of her maids of honour to a pagoda just at the edge of the palace gardens. On a clearing in front of the pagoda many young children were playing. The queen knew these to be the children of palace employees. Standing in the shade of a large tamarind tree, she told her maid to summon one of the children to her. When an eight-year-old girl was brought, the queen instructed her to repeat what her parents said to each other about the ongoing war. After some coaxing the frightened little girl replied that her parents talked about fighting, about Burmese soldiers being defeated and about foreigners rapidly advancing towards Mandalay. The queen said nothing, but rewarded the girl with a gold bangle. Then the queen repeated this exercise with four more young children and they all had more or less the same thing to say. By now visibly pale, the queen sadly commented that it was through these children, who were too young to tell a lie, that she had finally learnt the truth.[25]

A meeting with the ministers was hastily summoned and a chastened king and queen turned to the wise old Kinwun Mingyi to save the situation, and the throne. The Kinwun Mingyi and the Taingda Mingyi had been aware of the exact nature of the progression of the war but both, for their own reasons, had chosen to keep quiet. An increasingly worried Taingda Mingyi had recently been trying to win over the Kinwun Mingyi. The Taingda Mingyi had much to be fearful of: he knew he would be blamed for the defeat and perhaps even be executed. Also he knew he was unpopular with the British for advocating and supporting a pro-France stand, for the fight against the Bombay-Burma Trading Company and for this war for which he had pushed. He needed the Kinwun Mingyi's support. The Kinwun Mingyi, for his own selfish reasons, backed the Taingda Mingyi. Both the Mingyis had a common goal now, which was to try for armistice, failing which to ensure that King Thibaw was delivered safely into the hands of the victorious British, who in their gratitude might reward the Mingyis with important positions in the new government.[26]

The Kinwun and Taingda Mingyis combined forces to convince the king and queen that no attempt at escape should be made. They indicated that the British were really coming to ensure compliance with the ultimatum and if they agreed to all the conditions laid out in it, all would be well.[27] The king turned to the Kinwun Mingyi and requested him to think of something a little less mortifying than agreeing to *all* the conditions in the ultimatum. The Kinwun Mingyi gently reminded him that the British army was almost at his doorstep, that he no longer had any bargaining power whatsoever, and that he better agree to everything they asked for. The king looked hopefully at Queen Supayalat, and when she said nothing to contradict the Kinwun Mingyi, he gave the Kinwun Mingyi full authority to draft a letter agreeing to all conditions of the ultimatum and asking for armistice.[28]

Late at night on 25 November the Kinwun Mingyi, the Taingda Mingyi and a few others sat down to write the letter.[29] Carefully worded, it began by saying that the Burmese government was taken aback by the war. The time given to reply to the ultimatum had been so short and the matter so serious, that the ultimatum could not be adequately considered which was why everything asked for by the British had not been fully agreed to. But the *tone* of its reply to the ultimatum should have made it amply clear to the British that the Burmese had no desire to breach its 'loyal friendship'. The letter clarified that armed opposition by Burmese soldiers in the war was only 'to maintain the reputation and honour of the kingdom and people of Burmah'. The British were known to be fair and in this case also it was hoped that the right thing would be done.[30] The letter appealed that the kingdom not be occupied, and reminded 'the Commander-in-Chief of the English War Boats'[31] that 'the most powerful and gracious English Queen-Empress was pleased to declare publicly that the English Government had no wish to take possession of Burmah except [if] great necessity existed for doing so'. To clearly demonstrate the lack of necessity, the letter went on to concede unqualifiedly to every single condition of the ultimatum, and to request that the fighting be immediately stopped and a friendly relationship be quickly resumed.[32]

On 25 November the British flotilla anchored for the night off the village of Yandabo.[33] On the 26th, as the flotilla proceeded upriver towards the forts of Ava and Sagaing (which lie on opposite banks of the Irrawaddy), officers spotted through binoculars that both forts were teeming with soldiers. A few flashing golden umbrellas indicated the presence of senior Burmese officials. The British assumed that the Burmese were readying to attack the flotilla.[34]

What the British did not expect was the sighting, at around 4 p.m., of one of the king's magnificent gilded war-barges being paddled furiously towards them by forty-four oarsmen. In the boat were two of King Thibaw's high-ranking officials who sat under colossal golden umbrellas. The envoys, in an unusual show of respect, removed their shoes before being ushered onto General Prendergast's steamer,[35] and presented to him the letter requesting armistice. The letter was read and translated, and then it was discovered that it had not been signed! It would have been considered unauthorized and invalid had General Prendergast not had with him Colonel Edward Sladen, who during King Mindon's reign had been the British Resident in Mandalay. Sladen was considered an authority on palace matters, and he clarified that 'no Burmese king ever signed an official document. No minister ever presumed to sign a document made out in the King's name, but instead stamped the document with the Royal Peacock Seal . . . if the armistice letter had been signed it would have been unofficial and worthless.'[36]

General Prendergast informed the king's envoys that he had no authority to grant armistice, or to halt the advance of the army. He recommended that the king agree to unconditionally surrender, and that he order the Burmese army to immediately lay down their arms. He promised that if this was done, and if the Europeans in Mandalay were found unharmed, King Thibaw's life would not be taken and Mandalay would not be attacked but just occupied. The envoys were told that if the king did not accept these conditions by 4 a.m. of 27 November, the forts of Ava and Sagaing would be shelled. By 6 p.m. the envoys had left the general's steamer with the burden of conveying this unexpectedly bad news to their king. The British were now less than thirty miles away from Mandalay.[37]

Once the armistice-request letter was on its way, the tension in the palace must have visibly diffused. Parts of Burma had been lost to the British in the two previous Anglo-Burmese wars, but agreements had always been reached, that allowed a Konbaung king to continue sitting on the Lion Throne. The king and queen saw no reason why things should be different this time. They did not know that the unambiguous brief given to General Prendergast by his government had left no room for any type of compromise; that his instructions were: 'You will understand that after you cross the frontier no offer of submission can be accepted or can affect the movement of troops; Mandalay must be occupied and Thibaw dethroned . . .'[38]

The reply denying the armistice appeal must have come as a profound shock. Perhaps the royal couple again considered the option of escaping before the British flotilla arrived. They could try and make their way to Shwebo, the town where the first Konbaung king had come from. Here they could hope to rally support, mount a resistance and at some stage try to win the kingdom back. But Queen Supayalat was over five months pregnant, and in no state to travel long distances by elephant or pony. As Thibaw refused to go anywhere without her,[39] they could do nothing but await Prendergast's arrival with mounting dread.

On the morning of 27 November the British flotilla advanced towards Ava and Sagaing, with the full intention of attacking and capturing these forts. However, before they could do so, at around 10 a.m., the king's barge with the same two envoys appeared and indicated that the king had agreed to accept all the general's conditions.[40] The forts of Ava and Sagaing were peacefully subjugated, and about 200 members of the Burmese force surrendered and laid down their arms. (A vast majority of the Burmese troops, however, absconded with their arms and many later went on to form dacoit gangs. General Prendergast was afterwards blamed for not having launched an attack and confiscated their weapons.[41])

Mandalay now lay just a few miles ahead, awaiting occupation. The Third Anglo-Burmese war leading to the deposition of King Thibaw, and to the end of the Konbaung dynasty's 133-year rule over the Kingdom of Ava, ended almost before it had begun. General Prendergast's force had taken only two weeks to win the war. *The Times*

(London) irreverentially wondered whether history would even accord this war the title of a war! But Prendergast was kinder in his reaction. He was later to say that it was unfair to criticize the way the Burmese soldiers had fought because 'how would it be if the weapons (and positions) were changed? Till fighting under such conditions has been tried, are we entitled to consider Burmans cowards? They certainly face death with the greatest composure.'[42]

On the night of 27 November 1885, the penultimate day of Konbaung rule, a rare astral phenomenon—an immense and spectacular Andromedids storm—occurred. All night long, thousands of shooting stars filled the clear sky. In the Kingdom of Ava, people stared nervously at the heavens above, pondering on the ill fortune this dramatic celestial display portended.[43]

7

THE DEFEAT AND EXILE

On 28 November 1885, people gathered from dawn on the banks of the Irrawaddy to witness the arrival of the British flotilla in Mandalay. All kinds of rumours had been swirling around in the preceding days, one of these being that the expected flotilla was actually the four captured British ships (the news of which had been declared by gong-beating criers only a few days earlier).[1] Before long there was a sizeable crowd, and vendors were doing brisk business selling not only food and cheroots, but also toys for the numerous children who had accompanied their parents. The festival-like atmosphere was so devoid of any palpable apprehension that it seemed as if people had come to attend a pwe and not to watch the arrival of the enemy.[2]

Instructions had been received from the palace that there was to be no opposition, and when the British flotilla finally arrived at 9 a.m. the Burmese displayed no hostility.[3] Upon mooring, Colonel Sladen sent a letter to the Kinwun Mingyi that he should come to General Prendergast's steamer by one in the afternoon, and that 'it would be convenient if he brought the King with him'.[4] At best this request was insensitive. Well aware of the godlike esteem the Burmese kings had for themselves, and which their people had for them, the British must have realized that it would have been a further humiliation for King Thibaw to have to come to the steamer to surrender.[5]

A quiet dread had hung palpably over the palace on the night of 27 November, and had prevented almost everyone from sleeping. Queen Supayalat was out of bed well before dawn the next morning. In the very early hours, in one of the palace rooms overlooking the garden, some of her maids saw her and her mother weeping in each other's arms. The queen bathed and got ready as usual, and after a few tense hours, a messenger came to her with the report that the British had arrived at the shores of Mandalay.[6]

Wanting to confirm this for herself, the queen walked over to the Watch Tower, which she and her husband had, in happier days, sometimes climbed up together. A guard was always posted on top of the tower and when the queen arrived, she noticed he was facing west, the direction of the river. Looking through binoculars, he informed her that he could see the British fleet on the river, right off the banks of Mandalay. A few hours later, he shouted out that countless soldiers were disembarking, lining up, and advancing towards the palace.[7]

On hearing this, in spite of her pregnancy, the queen slowly climbed up the long, arduous spiral stairs of the tower to witness this spectacle for herself. The sight of thousands of British troops marching towards the palace seems to have been her moment of truth—the moment that finally drove home the inevitability of what was to come, and which destroyed in her any hope of a miraculous salvation. She carefully descended the stairs, and then collapsed in the courtyard. An embarrassed crowd watched as she sobbed[8] and 'rose upon her knees and beat her breast with her hands and cried out loud . . . "It is I—I alone—I the queen that have brought destruction to the king my husband and my people. It is I—I alone".' Then quickly composing herself, she disappeared into an inner room of the palace.[9]

Meanwhile, by the one o'clock deadline neither the king nor the Kinwun Mingyi had made an appearance before General Prendergast, nor had there been any reply to Colonel Sladen's letter. The British troops were now assembled in order to advance towards the palace. Sladen, accompanied by a couple of people, left for the palace just ahead of the troops. Almost as soon as they entered the gates of the Royal Golden City, Sladen saw the Kinwun Mingyi hurriedly approaching him on an elephant. The minister apologized for having just missed the colonel at the river (where he said he had gone to meet him). He requested that the British troops not enter the Golden Palace as yet, and that Sladen accompany him to meet the king.[10]

By 2 p.m. the British troops began their three-mile march towards the Royal Golden City. They marched in three separate columns, each column taking a different route down three of Mandalay's broad tree-lined avenues (on what are today the 22nd, 26th and 35th Streets). People lined the streets to watch the extraordinary display of British troops marching in unison to the beat of accompanying bands. After about an hour of marching, the vast reddish-pink crenellated walls of the Royal Golden City came into view.[11] Major Browne, a member of the British Burma Expeditionary Force, later commented in his memoirs how much the 'extent and grandeur' of the Royal Golden City had impressed him. Upon arrival the gates were found wide open. The guards did not oppose or question the entry of the troops, and quickly gave up their arms when asked. The streets inside were deserted, except for some curious onlookers. The troops surrounded the city and secured all the palace gates.[12]

The king, the queen (who, according to one of her maids of honour, had had 'her tears washed away and jewels put about her neck and arms, that she might appear before her conquerors the queen she was'[13]) and Sinbyumashin were in the Great Audience Hall when the Kinwun Mingyi brought in Colonel Sladen.[14] Sladen, defying palace protocol, walked in with his shoes on. The king, sitting on the Lion Throne for the last time, looked nervous and his hands shook as he tried to smoke a cheroot. The queen was composed, but she did lean over and whisper something to the king in what appeared to be an attempt to calm him. After entering the hall, Sladen, defying protocol again, did not sit down, but stood upright in front of the royal family.[15]

Colonel Sladen noticed that the king was 'in a very prostrate condition'.[16] King Thibaw's first words to him were, 'Are you well? Do you remember me? So glad you have come.'[17] Sladen reassured him that he did remember him from the time he had been the British Resident in Mandalay (1865–69), when the king had been just a young boy.[18] The king, calmer now, went on to explain that he had not come to General Prendergast's steamer to surrender, as Colonel Sladen had requested him to do, because he was afraid of being assassinated if he left the palace grounds. He then proceeded, in his own fashion, to surrender himself and his country to Colonel Sladen by saying, 'All is finished; I have been badly advised by my ministers; I leave all to you, Sladen; I will allow you to govern my country. If I cannot live in the palace give me a little house in Mandalay.' Colonel Sladen told the king that it would not be possible for him to stay in Mandalay. When the king asked Colonel Sladen what his advice was, it appears that Sladen attempted to soften the news of the proposed exile to India by saying that as the king's 'future rested with the Viceroy . . . the best course for the King to take was to go to India, where he might see the Viceroy'.[19]

The king now shifted his attention to something else that had been weighing heavily on his mind—Queen Supayalat's pregnancy. He requested that they be allowed to remain on the palace grounds for the next few months, until after the baby was born. The colonel politely informed him that this was impossible and that although he would ask General Prendergast's permission for time until the next day, the king had better 'prepare for an immediate departure from his capital and country'. Colonel Sladen, who had heard rumours about a possible attempt at escape by the king, cautioned him that the palace had been well secured by British troops and no escape should be endeavoured, to which the king replied, 'Where can I go? I have no wish to go anywhere.'[20]

After an audience of about half an hour, a visibly moved Colonel Sladen emerged from the Great Audience Hall and convinced General Prendergast that the king needed some time to prepare for his departure. Prendergast agreed to give the king until noon the next day, at which time the king was expected to formally surrender to the general.[21] Shortly after his audience with the king, Colonel Sladen was approached by the kingdom's ministers, who questioned him as to what lay in store for the country, and wasted no time at all in switching allegiance and suggesting an alternative for King Thibaw. The Myngun Prince, and not the Nyaungok Prince, was the one they wanted as the puppet king on the Lion throne. (The Nyaungyan Prince, who at one time had been considered the most likely to succeed his father, had recently died.[22]) Colonel Sladen indicated that he was not in a position to answer any of their questions, or give any pointers on what might be decided.[23]

Plans were made for Colonel Sladen, along with some troops, to spend the night in the Hluttaw. British troops now marched into the palace grounds, with a band robustly playing, took possession of all arms, and secured all exits. The Taingda Mingyi was put in charge of the king, and was to spend the night in the palace along with some guards to ensure that the king made no attempt at escape. (Ironically, it was not the king but the Taingda Mingyi who tried to escape, disguised as a coolie, that night. He was recognized, stopped and promptly sent back.[24]) King Thibaw's ministers assured Sladen that if they were unable to hand over the king to him in the morning they were ready to be penalized by death.[25]

Some of the ministers requested the colonel that the queen's maids of honour be permitted to leave and enter the palace grounds unimpeded. Perhaps the request was to enable some of the maids to meet their families who were, in the present circumstance, naturally very concerned about them. Perhaps it was to enable them to collect their dinners, which used to be cooked outside the palace grounds and delivered to them. Colonel Sladen put the matter up to General Prendergast who objected on the grounds that the king might try to escape in disguise. However, Prendergast ultimately relented and an order was passed permitting their easy passage.[26]

This order was to have disastrous consequences. Knowing that a foreign force had defeated their king and queen, most of the queen's maids of honour, perhaps worried about their own safety, decided to leave. Taking advantage of the situation some carried away rich spoils from the palace. Word quickly spread in Mandalay that there was much in the palace to be had for the picking—from jewels, to imported silk bolts, to gold utensils. In place of the maids of honour, hordes of common women from town entered the palace to capitalize on this rare opportunity. The British soldiers, in the dark and in the confusion, were unable to distinguish between them and the well-dressed maids of honour. All night long, the king and queen and a handful of faithful maids could do nothing but cower in their apartments, silently and helplessly watching the silhouettes of lantern-bearing women looting at will amid muted shouts and much jostling. By the morning of 29 November, many of the palace rooms had been overturned and plundered, and the king had finally been able to persuade the Taingda Mingyi to appeal to Colonel Sladen for help.[27]

The king conveyed to the colonel his deep apprehension that if so many unauthorized people had been able to enter so freely, then an assassin would be able to slip in with equal ease. Colonel Sladen, shocked to see scores of women running all over the palace, immediately summoned some British troops to guard the family and the gold, jewels and other valuable items that the king and queen had gathered and that were in their immediate possession.[28] The shaken king was comforted by the presence of the British troops, but when a very dark-skinned man—an assistant to one of the British soldiers—appeared the frightened king asked 'if he was the executioner'.[29] Colonel Sladen decided to shift the king and his family to the small Summer Pavilion on the grounds of the Southern gardens. British soldiers surrounded the pavilion to ensure the royal family's safety.[30]

Perhaps even more tragic than the looting of the palace rooms was that the Shwe-Taik, the king's private treasury, was also ransacked that night. Apart from holding many jewels, precious stones, crowns and other valuables (some of which had been part of the royal family for generations) the treasury also held the archives and records of the kingdom.[31] Much of this very valuable collection of records was destroyed for reasons unknown (some say out of 'pure wantonness') by the British army after it occupied Mandalay.[32] An ex-minister (U Tin) witnessed with horror this looting and burning, and salvaged 'thirty-five cartloads of palm leaf and bark manuscripts', which he later deposited in the British chief secretary's office in Rangoon.[33]

Many conflicting stories are told about the disappearance of the priceless eighty-carat Nga Mauk ruby belonging to the royal family. This 'ruby among rubies', apparently the size of a betel nut, was said to be 'worth a kingdom'.[34] According to a letter written by the Second Princess in 1948, 'the late U Po Kya, the Burmese historian, valued it at ten thousand crores of rupees at the lowest. The value of the said Nga-mauk Ruby depends not only on its weight, colour and flawlessness, but also depends on its spiritual or magnetic qualities.'[35] According to some of King Thibaw's ministers, on the morning of 29 November, the king handed over many valuables including the Nga Mauk ruby ring to Colonel Sladen for safekeeping.[36]

When Sladen was later questioned by letter about the ruby, he wrote that he had no recollection of the ring. There was just too much confusion, he wrote: 'the Palace was being overrun by crowds of common women who were looting in all directions and carrying away boxes and bundles . . .' The king and queen were in a state of 'great grief and trepidation', and had to be quickly moved to the Summer Pavilion. Sladen said that after the couple were in the pavilion,

> [their] attendants were busy removing Royal baggage, consisting of numerous boxes and bundles, from the Palace—it is impossible to say whether any or what portion of the Regalia may have been taken away at this time, or during the previous night when most of the minor Queens and Princesses and some 300 maids of honour are known to have made good their departure![37]

A correspondent of *The Times* (London) who interviewed King Thibaw on the morning of his exile, *after* he was in the Summer Pavilion, noticed the king had on 'a magnificent ruby ring'.[38] Was this the Nga Mauk? The king's daughter, the Fourth Princess, states in a missive that when her parents were leaving Mandalay 'the priceless Crown Ruby' was 'in their betel-box. Sladen asked my parents to let him have a look at it and they gave it to him. My parents said that after looking at it for a while, Sladen put it into his pocket, and pretending to be absentminded, did not return it.'[39] One of the Fourth Princess's sons believes that Colonel Sladen carried the Nga Mauk ruby back to England, and it is perhaps now part of the British Crown Jewels. Perhaps it has been re-cut and re-set. Many valuables forming part of the regalia were sent to Britain—a piece or two to Queen Victoria, and the vast majority to the South Kensington Museum (now the Victoria and Albert Museum).[40]

U Than Swe has a different take on the disappearance of the Nga Mauk ruby. He believes that King Thibaw probably *gifted* it to Colonel Sladen 'to ensure their future'. He argues that when a man as desperate and frightened as King Thibaw was at the time is pushed into such a tight corner and is bargaining for his life and that of his family, wouldn't he give up his most precious possession to someone whom he believes has a great say on what is to become of him? So when Colonel Sladen asked to have a look at the Nga Mauk ruby, and hesitated to return it, the king told him to keep it.[41] Sladen's 1885 handwritten diary today lies in the British Library in London. A significant portion of a 29 November 1885 entry has been thoroughly blackened out, making one wonder what it was that he recorded that day that he wanted so completely and totally obliterated (other entries in this diary needing deletion have been crossed out with just a simple line).[42]

At about 10 a.m. on 29 November, the British troops again began their band-accompanied march towards the palace from the flotilla where the majority of them had spent the night. Upon reaching the eastern gate, General Prendergast and his men waited outside for word from Colonel Sladen that the king was ready to formally surrender and leave the palace grounds.[43]

King Thibaw, Queen Supayalat, Sinbyumashin and her two other daughters were sitting on the verandah of the Summer Pavilion with some maids of honour behind them, when Colonel Sladen—along with a reporter from *The Times* (London) and an interpreter—arrived. The king permitted the reporter to interview him and this resulted in a detailed and fascinating article in the 5 December 1885 issue of the newspaper, much of which has been reproduced below:

Colonel Sladen and I remained standing during the interview, the Royal party being seated in the gallery of the garden pavillion, raised about four feet from the ground. Soopyalat sat next to the King, and closely followed the conversation at the interview, in which she occasionally took part.

Thebaw is a stout, young, good-looking man of about thirty . . .

Since he found that he had no violence to fear, King Thebaw has recovered his nerve, and he displayed a good deal of quiet dignity . . . He [said] that he was anxious the English people should hear his words, and he requested me to write down what he said. At the close of the interview I read over my notes, through the interpreter, to Thebaw, who said they were correct.

Thebaw said: 'I wish to be kept quiet. I have given over everything to the English. I want Sladen to govern the country now and in the future. If Sladen had remained as Resident and not left, this war would never have occurred. I have been badly advised.'

I then said that I thought Tinedah Mengyee [the Taingda Mingyi] had been a bad advisor.

Thebaw: 'Yes; I was seized when young, and made a mere puppet. I have now to suffer for what Tinedah and others forced me to do. I know now that I was altogether wrong. Tinedah, the Athlaym Woon, and the Kyoung Moung Woon urged me on to war, and when the fighting commenced they were the first to abandon me. I did not hear of the English taking Minhla; but when I heard of your arrival in Pagan, I said, No more fighting must occur, as the Burmese could not resist.'

'My Ministers told me that only five vessels with 2,000 soldiers were coming to make a treaty. My mother-in-law was always very anxious to prevent war. My ministers are very ungrateful. Not one of them has waited on me since the English arrived in Mandalay.'

Colonel Sladen here said, 'It will not raise your Ministers in English public opinion that they should thus desert you.'

Soopyalat, turning to the interpreter, said, 'Tell him that the day before yesterday I had 300 maids of honour. Yesterday evening only 16 remained with me. We have two children alive, and three are buried in the northern garden.'

Thebaw, resuming, said, 'Let Sladen govern the country for five years.' The King added: 'When he has got affairs in good order then I will come back and be guided by him. I have known Sladen since I was a boy, and have most confidence in him, or in any Englishman.'

'You English think that I killed all my relatives, but it is not so. I was under a guard myself, and they were murdered. The reason that I was not murdered myself was that before the King died he told the Queen I was the quiet son. A horoscope was also drawn by the priests, and my name came out first. For the first seven months after I became King I was not allowed to interfere. I was not even crowned . . .'

'After eight months the Yenout Mengyee [Yanaung], who killed the Princes, tried to murder me. The English people knew much that I did, but not of what was going on behind me. I never left the palace.'

'I wish the English to know that I am not a drunkard. I am a religious Buddhist. I have given up all my Crown jewels, and I am sure the English, who are great people, will not object to me, as a King, keeping my ring' (showing me a magnificent ruby ring he was wearing), 'or to my wife keeping her jewels' (pointing to a diamond necklace on the Queen).

Colonel Sladen answered: 'I am certain that the English people would not wish you to be deprived of those jewels.'[44]

Never once during the interview did King Thibaw take any responsibility for the disastrous war that had cost him his kingdom. Neither did he blame Queen Supayalat. He did, however, give his mother-in-law credit for opposing it. Blame for everything, from the 1879 massacre to the war, was heaped on his ministers. While no attempt had been made earlier to improve his image in the Western world, at this very vulnerable point King Thibaw was understandably very anxious to clarify matters. There is much pathos in the naiveté and the lack of perception he demonstrated during this interview. It is apparent that, at this point in time, the king had no idea that he was being permanently exiled to India.

The sky was unusually cloudy, and it had been raining lightly on and off[45] as General Prendergast waited patiently for Colonel Sladen to finish his audience with the king. When the king was finally convinced that he could no longer delay his departure, a large column of troops marched in through the eastern gate, towards the palace platform, and formed two lines extending all the way from the gate to the steps leading up to the Great Audience Hall. The soldiers in both lines faced each other and it was to be through the passage created between the bayonet-holding soldiers that King Thibaw and his entourage would have to leave the palace. They stayed in position while General Prendergast went on ahead to meet King Thibaw for his formal surrender.[46]

A sizeable crowd comprising, among others, officers and Burmese ministers, accompanied the general as he walked through the palace and the Southern gardens to where the king and his family were awaiting them. Major Browne, who had accompanied Prendergast, later wrote that as they approached King Thibaw, his face 'bore unmistakable evidence of the dread which had taken possession of his soul'. The general stood in front of the king and politely bowed to him.[47] A reporter from the *Illustrated London News*, present at this time, wrote that the king 'had no particular richness to his dress . . . The only royal appendage that I noticed was a huge gold spittoon, so heavy that it is said to take two men to carry it . . . The Queen crouched behind the King in the orthodox Court position of respect. She was eagerly whispering to the King nearly all the time . . .'[48] *The Times of India* reported:

> the King at once began an animated conversation in Burmese with Colonel Sladen, to whom he seemed to cling in his fallen state with touching confidence. He made enquires about the steamer which was to take him down, asking that no troops might be allowed on board the vessel itself. To this he was answered that his privacy would be respected, and that although it was necessary to place troops on board the steamer, they would occupy another deck to that reserved for him.[49]

Colonel Sladen now reminded the king of his promise to surrender himself. Before doing so the king wanted reassurance from the general that he would spare his life and that of his family, and would protect him from any assault or assassination attempts. The king was assured of this. He was also told that he could take whatever and whomever he wanted with him when he left. As the king wished for some of his ministers to accompany him, he said to them, 'When I go into captivity those who love me will follow me, but those who like themselves best will stay, and look after their own property.' It must have come as a shock to him when only one old minister responded to his invitation while all the others stared resolutely at the ground before them. He now 'regarded them with a somewhat scornful, incredulous look . . . He then shook his hand angrily, intimating that he would have nothing to say to any of them.' The king then asked Colonel Sladen whether he would accompany him 'as you are an old friend'. Sladen politely declined.[50]

The king was told that the time for departure could no longer be delayed, prompting him to ask General Prendergast how much longer he could have. The general glanced at his pocket watch and said ten minutes. The general and his men then withdrew, giving the king and his entourage a few final private moments.[51]

An hour and a half later the king asked for more time to be able to organize some money to take along with him. He was told that he would not require any, and needed to leave at once.[52] When the king still showed no signs of being ready, Sladen climbed up onto the verandah of the Summer Pavilion. The king, never having had anyone tower over him like this before, was startled into getting up himself. He was now encouraged by the colonel to climb down the steps of the pavilion. As the king walked towards the palace platform followed by his entourage, General Prendergast approached him for a formal handshake. Extending his hand towards that of the surprised king, he unwittingly became the first person in history to ever shake hands with a Burmese monarch![53]

King Thibaw held Queen Supayalat and Sinbyumashin's hands as he led the way.[54] A brigadier who witnessed their departure commented on the 'dignity and tenderness' the king showed towards the queens, which he thought was 'chivalrous at such a time'.[55] Colonel Sladen, a couple of ministers, and about fifteen to twenty women and girls, some holding babies, all holding an assortment of packages and bundles, followed them. The procession walked through the palace, past the Lion Throne, through the imposing columns in the Great Audience Hall. From here, the sight of two endless parallel lines of soldiers, their bayonets glistening in the sun, caused the royal couple to pause. Perhaps they also paused to look back at the Lion Throne, on which they had sat so many times in the past. Then the king's entourage moved down the steps of the platform and walked slowly forward.[56] According to an Englishman, Mr Noyce, who witnessed the surrender, the band accompanying the soldiers played "Tis but a little faded flower' as soon as the royal family exited through the auspicious inner eastern gate. He noted that King Thibaw and the queens now stopped and sheiko-ed in the direction of King Mindon's tomb.[57]

Two covered bullock carts, the kind that was commonly used in Mandalay, were waiting to transport the family to the Irrawaddy, where a steamer had been readied for boarding.[58] King Thibaw, who had earlier requested General Prendergast to be allowed to leave Mandalay 'in state, riding on an elephant or in a palanquin',[59] turned up his nose at these rickety carts and, in protest, started walking with his queens. However, they were soon convinced to use them. King Thibaw, Queen Supayalat and Queen Supayagalae got into one of the carts; Sinbyumashin, Queen Supayagyi and the two little princesses (the First and Second) got into the other. The maids of honour walked. A couple of Burmese officials hurriedly produced two white umbrellas, and not even having the time to get their footwear on, they 'follow[ed] the king, holding the umbrella over him. They [went] all the way barefoot.'[60]

The band, followed by an officer holding up the British flag, led the procession. Then marched General Prendergast and a column of soldiers. The bullock carts carrying the royal family trailed by the maids of honour came next. Another column of soldiers and Colonel Sladen brought up the rear.[61] A line of troops marched on either side of the procession.[62] One hundred coolies had been engaged to carry the various boxes, bundles and packages of the royal family, and they followed. The procession exited the walled city through the southern gate a little after 4 p.m. The streets of Mandalay were thronged with people, many of whom sank to the ground in the traditional sheiko, and 'uttered loud cries of lamentation' as the carts passed. The band stepped up its volume in an attempt to drown out these cries.[63]

Major Browne rode beside the king's bullock cart. He noticed that along the way Queen Supayalat stuck her head out of the cart and asked for something. Realizing she had not been understood, 'she held up her cigar to express her desires, and quite a rush [of British soldiers] took place to supply the required light. She honored someone, smiled, and began puffing away.'[64] Rumour has it that the queen stuck her head out one more time: when her cart went past the Mya Taung monastery.[65] Its monks had lined the street to catch a glimpse of their fallen benefactor. This was the monastery she had recently had constructed, and she anxiously looked out to try and discern—in the rapidly fading light—the magnificent form of her biggest act of merit. Perhaps she drew some much-needed strength from this fortuitous sighting, one of her last in Mandalay.

It was after 6 p.m. and dark by the time the procession arrived[66] at the Gaw Wein jetty. A huge crowd had gathered and soldiers had to clear the way for the carts. However the crowd displayed no sign of aggression, except for an occasional hurled stone.[67] Most people had come simply for a glimpse of their departing king and queen whom many had never seen.[68] Alighting from the cart, the king walked tentatively down the uneven and rather steep slope of the embankment leading to the river. He was supported by a Major Symons on one side, and his mother-in-law and Queen Supayalat on the other.[69] When they reached the lantern-lit narrow wooden gangplank to board the *Thooreah*, the triple-decked steamer that was to carry them down the Irrawaddy to Rangoon, the king hesitated.

A rush of emotions and apprehensions must have overwhelmed him. He was leaving his kingdom, where he had been an absolute monarch. He, who had never ventured out of Mandalay in his entire life, was leaving behind all he knew for the totally unfamiliar, as prisoner of a foreign force. In the words of one of Queen Supayalat's maids of honour:

[I]t was hard for him to take his foot from off his kingdom, from off the land that was his. And so he hesitated. Then the officer grew impatient and signed again, and the queen went forward and put her hand in that of the king and led him up the way to the steamer as a mother leads her child when it is lost and afraid. They went on board the steamer, and my queen was lost to me forever. In a few moments the steamer let go her moorings and stood out in the great river . . . you may say she was not a good queen, he was not a good king, but they were our own. Do you think we can love a foreign master as we loved our king, who was, as it were, part of ourselves?[70]

PART II

DURING THE EXILE

8

THE ROYAL FAMILY IN MADRAS

Aboard the *Thooreah*, King Thibaw and his family were escorted to the saloon. The king did not linger here; he immediately asked to be taken to his cabin.[1] Events of the last few days had taken its toll on him and he wished to retire. The steamer anchored mid-river for the night, and according to an Englishman who witnessed the event,

> All that night patrol launches with naval officers and blue jackets on board kept sentry duty and saw that no one got on the ship and no one left it. It was a tremendous responsibility. What if Thibaw left the boat in disguise and escaped? Nothing untoward happened, however, and at daybreak the *Thooreah* was steaming full speed ahead for Rangoon . . .[2]

Not much is known about the five-day journey down the Irrawaddy, but we do know that the officers on board the steamer were very courteous with the king and his family. Lord Dufferin, the viceroy and governor general of India, had requested this in an internal memo, expressly stating that they be 'treated with all possible consideration and spared any unnecessary inconvenience or humiliation of any kind'.[3] The king was repeatedly offered alcoholic beverages during the trip, which he invariably turned down;[4] perhaps now the officers accompanying him questioned the validity of the endless press reports that had painted him a drunkard.

It is difficult to guess what the king and queen thought and felt as they were being carried away from their kingdom. Perhaps the sound of the lamentation uttered by the crowds on the streets of Mandalay ricocheted in their minds. The loud army band had been unable to drown out the peoples' oft-repeated pithy chant of 'Taing-kat-lo, kin-tok-ta hpaya', the literal translation of which is 'when you leaned on the post, the scorpion stung you'. What it implied was that the king had leaned on or trusted the Taingda Mingyi's bad advice for war ('taing' means post) and was stung by the scorpion, the Kinwin Mingyi ('kin' means scorpion), who handed him over to the British.[5] Did they dwell on their disastrous decision for war, on their betrayal by the Kinwun Mingyi (for they certainly believed, until their dying day, that he had been in cahoots with the British[6])? Did they, as staunch Buddhists and believers in karma, dredge through sins of the past to try and determine which ones had landed them in this miserable predicament? Or did fear of what was to come paralyse every other thought? King Thibaw did, more than once, betray dread that execution was what awaited him and his family.

As the king and his entourage travelled towards Rangoon, letters and telegrams flew back and forth between India and Burma discussing the burning issue of where in India the king and his family were to be resettled.[7] The British government certainly did not want the king lingering anywhere in Burma.[7] And Lord Dufferin had made it amply[8] clear that he did not want him to be sent to a town of any importance in India.[9] Various locations were suggested and dismissed—Bangalore (an important centre), Ranipett (too close to Pondicherry,[10] the town occupied by the king's old ally, France). Ratnagiri (on the western coast of India about 217 miles south of Bombay) was put forward as it was well off the beaten track. It lacked any railway connection and this, it was felt, would discourage all but the most intrepid of visitors. The climate was considered healthy, and the local government

administrator, the collector of Ratnagiri (to whom the police officer
in charge of the king would have to report[11]) was not overburdened
with work and would therefore have time to devote to the deposed
king.[12]

When the family arrived in Rangoon on 5 December 1885, they
were not permitted to disembark but were immediately transferred to
the *Clive*, a government steamer.[13] Here, after assuring King Thibaw
that he would not be deprived of any of the property he was carrying
with him, the government arranged for its inventory and evaluation.
The king's valuables were estimated at Rs 4 lacs and Sinbyumashin's
Rs 1.7 lacs. To the government's surprise, no large precious rubies
were found. It suspected that the royal family, wary of the government's
intentions, had concealed some of their treasures, but so as not to
humiliate them any further, it was decided not to conduct personal
searches.[14]

While an entourage of eighty people had loyally travelled with the
king to Rangoon, when realization dawned that he was being sent away
to India, the majority of them balked at the idea of sharing his exile.
Only about seventeen female attendants (mostly young girls), two
court officials and an interpreter agreed to accompany the family any
further. Sinbyumashin also requested that she not be sent away from
Burma, saying that she 'greatly dreads going to India'.[15] The government
refused to let her return to Mandalay—she was too influential a
person—but instead sent her and Supayagyi (her eldest daughter and
King Thibaw's discarded queen), with twelve female followers, to
Tavoy in southern Burma.[16]

On the evening of 10 December, as the *Canning*,[17] the ship carrying
the royal family to India, sailed downriver in the descending darkness
and entered the Gulf of Martaban, the king and queen got their very
first glimpse of the sea. It had been decided to temporarily send the
family to Madras in south India, and they arrived there on the
afternoon of 14 December. Their landing the next morning was a
muted but ceremonious affair, with various officials accompanying
them off the ship onto the pier, escorting them (with mounted
police) to their new residence, and with the chief secretary personally
greeting them there on their arrival. The nervous king was deeply

relieved by all this pomp and fuss, and enthusiastically 'expressed himself greatly pleased with his treatment on the ship and the arrangements made for his landing'.[18]

A day after their arrival, Colonel Cox, assistant inspector-general of police, was appointed as the police officer in charge of ex-king Thibaw (as King Thibaw was called in all official correspondence from 11 December 1885, one day after his departure from Burma.[19] A few months later, the style of address accorded him by the viceroy of India was 'His Highness the ex-King Thibaw',[20] and the king was forbidden to write letters using his earlier titles.) Now orders that would dictate almost all aspects of his and his family's life began to be spelt out in Orwellian form and detail: 'the conditions on which the ex-King and members of his party should be allowed to take exercise, see traders, and be supplied with local newspapers' were specified, and it was indicated that 'subject to [Colonel Cox's] inspection, the ex-King and his party might dispatch telegrams and letters ... and he and they might receive communications addressed to him or them, after they had been opened by, and passed through the hands of the (Police) Officer'.[21] A warrant for King Thibaw's custody as state prisoner was also drawn up, but so as not to unnecessarily further distress the family, its existence was kept confidential.[22] (This warrant was renewed on 1 January every year—coincidentally King Thibaw's birthday—for the rest of his life.) To thwart any escape attempts, the family was to be guarded round the clock by an officer, six policemen and two mounted orderlies.[23]

The precedent of Indian princes and kings—whose kingdoms had also been seized by the British—was available to the government in arriving at the monthly allowance to be given to King Thibaw. Colonel Sladen recommended Rs 5,000 per month. The chief commissioner of British Burma (it seems quite unsympathetically and arbitrarily) suggested Rs 3,000 per month,[24] and this was the amount that was settled upon, because it was felt this amount would enable him and his family to live with 'reasonable luxuries, but ... not in any kingly state'.[25]

Colonel Cox visited the king twice daily (except on his weekly day off), and submitted amazingly comprehensive written reports. In these he commented on mundane aspects of the king's daily life: that the king hardly left the house, in fact after a drive around Madras, he had not left the upper rooms of his house for a week; that the king overindulged in ham and other tinned goods leading to repeated attacks of dyspepsia; that both the queens sheiko-ed to the king every morning and offered him flowers; that the king was fascinated by the variety of capsicums available in Madras![26] He dutifully reported whatever the king and he discussed: the king's explanations regarding the war; his curiosity about the administration of British India, about English social custom; his desire for the daily paper; his complaint that time passed slowly as he had nothing to occupy himself with; and his plea for Burmese books. Cox also wrote down his impressions of the king: 'he is certainly not the simpleminded, unsophisticated youth of whom his countenance speaks. I do not think he is a *strong* man, but he is not without a certain force of character. He is intelligent and shrewd. . .'[27]

Colonel Cox additionally submitted accounts of the goings-on in the king's entourage. He wrote about a not-so-young maid who one Tuesday morning scooted up a tree and refused all entreaties to come down; that it was finally the threat of bringing the king himself to the tree that made her scamper down 'like a squirrel'.[28] He described how troublesome a patient the junior queen was: she refused to stick out her tongue for the doctor; she got a maid to taste the quinine mixture the doctor had prescribed, and based on the maid's grimace refused to have any of it herself![29]

Colonel Cox's 'juicy' reports, sometimes very judgemental and biased, led to reams and reams of information of questionable use to the government. This pattern would be followed by many of the numerous police officers in charge of the family throughout their long exile. The royal family, desperate to hold on to vestiges of their privacy and dignity, often resorted to concealing whatever information it could, significant or insignificant, and got increasingly adept at doing so.

Details of the king's expenses were also meticulously recorded. It was observed that, as per custom, members of the king's entourage were not paid a regular salary but were periodically gifted money or jewels. A monthly statement of household expenses (paid by the government) was prepared in minutiae. It was noted that the king's private expense (paid by the king) was about Rs 4,000 a month. Colonel Cox commented on the king's extravagance, and listed some of his purchases: a gold calendar repeating watch, two sewing machines, two opera glasses, hand mirrors and numerous items of clothing. These purchases were brought to Lord Dufferin's attention, and his office immediately telegrammed that the personal expenditure needed to be controlled; there were many personal claims against the king in Burma, and part of the property in his possession might have to be used in the future to settle some of these claims.[30] (In the end the government took care of both the public and private claims against King Thibaw for debts incurred during his reign without any recourse to him. While the majority of these claims were rejected, those that the government deemed genuine were paid, though often for a fraction of what had been asked for.[31])

Apart from closely monitoring the king and his family in India, the government also attempted to weaken their link with Burma. This was done systematically over the years; an early example occurred not long after their arrival in Madras. Queen Supayalat had been en route to Madras on her twenty-sixth birthday (13 December). Shortly after reaching Madras, King Thibaw requested the government to convey his donation of Rs 1,000 to the Shwedagon Pagoda in Rangoon to commemorate both their birthdays (he was turning twenty-seven on 1 January).[32] The government refused to officially permit or transmit any gifts to Burma on his behalf on the grounds that it 'did not want to keep alive his connection with Burma', but it added that if the king wanted to give the donation privately through friends, it would not prevent him from doing so.[33]

The government also tried to ensure that the king got minimal publicity, in the hope that he would gradually fade from public memory. Autograph hunters who arrived at The Mansion (as the king's three-storeyed[34] home in Madras was called) were turned away, as were any visitors from Burma or elsewhere. When Lord Dufferin arrived in Madras in March 1886, he did not meet the king,[35] perhaps to avoid the attendant spotlight such a visit would have thrown. This had to have been deeply bewildering and alarming for the king, who still desperately clung to the hope that the *raison d'etre* for his journey to India, as explained by Colonel Sladen, *was to meet the viceroy.*

In an attempt to recreate a semblance of the past, of the comfortingly familiar, the king poignantly 'beg[ged] that every inducement may be offered' to three of his ministers to come and stay with him in India,[36] but the government was not in favour of this (it spelt out that it had no desire for him to set up a 'sham' court in India).[37] The king submitted a list of people whose services the royal couple desired for more menial matters: Queen Supayalat's hair dresser, her cheroot maker and betel-box keeper, maids to look after the princesses and the royal infant, etc.[38]

Queen Supayalat yearned for companionship in Madras—in Mandalay not only had countless maids of honour constantly surrounded her, hanging onto her every word, but European nuns and others would also visit to pay their respects. She requested that 'ladies' in Madras be permitted to call on her. This request was granted.[39] The king, however, was strictly not allowed any visitors. On one occasion when some of the queen's visitors asked to see the king, he obligingly (and perhaps unwittingly) came into the drawing room and met them. Colonel Cox apologized for this breach in his weekly report and provided assurances that he would ensure this did not recur. So threatened was the government by this seemingly insignificant infraction, that Lord Dufferin himself immediately responded with an order that henceforth no European was to be permitted to visit King Thibaw or his wife.[40] (He later retracted this order. Just that week in February, the heavily pregnant Queen Supayalat had had five lady visitors. Aware that the sudden stoppage of visitors might increase her sense of despondency at this vulnerable time, he later clarified that the ladies were not to be prevented but discouraged from calling on the ex-queen, and that their visits were to be gradually petered out.[41] The king, of course, like before, was not to be permitted any visitors.)

Shortly after reaching Madras, King Thibaw sent a telegram to his mother-in-law stating: 'Arrived Madras safely. Well treated and comfortably housed by English Government. Letter will follow.' He sent a similar telegram to his ex-ministers.[42] King Thibaw evidently missed his mother-in-law, for he exchanged frequent letters with her, made frantic enquires about her, requested permission to send her gifts, and in February 1886, begged that she be permitted to join him. Although Sinbyumashin declined the king's invitation (and informed the government that she had no wish to go as she and her eldest daughter did not get along with him),[43] she wrote frequently to him. In one letter she stated that she 'longed to see you all' and requested that her daughters and granddaughters apply for permission to visit her in Tavoy. She sent gifts whenever she could—one parcel contained jasmine oil and toys; another contained a hundred dolls and some toy torpedoes. (The dolls were delivered, but the toy torpedoes were not!)[44]

Apart from people left behind, the family also missed their possessions, and comforts—big and small—not available in India. King Thibaw requested for his betel box and spittoon (encrusted with diamonds and other precious stones),[45] a black panther skin, herbal medicines and snuff for Queen Supayalat, Burmese calendars, and books on casting a horoscope.[46] He also asked for commonly used Burmese food items, like *ngapi* (fermented fish paste) and la-hpet (pickled tea), and clothing.[47] The government responded that the valuable gold betel box and spittoon could no longer be considered the king's; the rest of the items would be shipped over.[48] For all the years of their exile, the king paid for regular shipments from Burma of clothing, food, condiments and other things that the family needed and wanted.

Superstition and custom had dominated the royal family's life in Mandalay, and those who had lived around them had fomented and reinforced these beliefs. It must have therefore been deeply disturbing for the king to now have to offer explanations to the culturally alien Colonel Cox on matters of great importance to him, only to have these tersely dismissed. The king was very keen that his and the queen's horoscopes be sent for from Mandalay where they were stored in a special room. He painstakingly explained that the value of these horoscopes would be compromised if they were not carried observing certain ceremonies. He indicated that he would instruct three of his retainers (currently with him in Madras) on these ceremonies and requested that they be permitted to go to Mandalay to bring the horoscopes. The government responded, very curtly, that if found the horoscopes would be shipped to the king, but without the benefit of any special ceremonies or escorting retainers.[49]

It is not that the government was always inconsiderate towards the family; during the many years of exile there were officers in charge of the king who were compassionate and sympathetic, who made many representations on behalf of the family to their seniors, but almost invariably this was only done when the frame of reference coincided with their own. Sensitivity could not be counted upon consistently even from the same officer, and the proud bruised family—who never before in their lives had had to ask permission for *anything*—took offence quickly. Soon after his arrival in Madras, the king indicated that he would like to visit the museum—a harmless request made by a man who badly needed some distraction. Cox's knee-jerk reaction was to refuse permission. Although authorization for this visit was later granted, it appears the insulted king never raised the subject again. Paradoxically, on another occasion, knowing of the king's fascination for fruits and flowers, Cox thoughtfully bought from an exhibition (at his own expense) unusual varieties for the delighted king to examine.[50]

Unfortunately, but not unexpectedly, King Thibaw from time to time was gripped by 'fears and anxieties'. He was 'uneasy and anxious' when newspapers were withheld; he was distrustful when a professional photographer made a formal request to take a photograph of him and his queens. He voiced his suspicion that interpreters were acting as spies for the government, and that the government had 'designs upon his life'.[51] Perhaps in order to understand his adversary better, he asked for an English tutor.[52] While his request was agreed to, the government could not find someone sufficiently fluent in both English and Burmese.[53]

As Colonel Cox and subsequent police officers dealt almost exclusively with the king, archival material unfortunately does not contain much about Queen Supayalat's views and emotions during the exile. However, at this point in time, it is known that the matter foremost on both their minds was the impending birth of their child.

The king expressed to Cox their desire to have brought over from Mandalay the queen's masseur (officially titled the 'Royal Shampooer') and two Brahmin astrologers to cast the newborn's horoscope. The British government acceded to the request for the shampooer (and he soon arrived), but refused to send for the Brahmins from Mandalay as it felt that Madras was flooded with them, and that the king's 'eagerness for them [was] probably connected more with a desire to learn the events that [had] transpired since his deportation and to relieve his ennui, than with astrological aspirations.'[54] Dr Branfoot was selected as the queen's doctor, and a certified midwife was installed in The Mansion after the queen had a false labour alarm.[55]

It did not take long for the maids of honour and other retainers to sense the royal couple's anxiety about the queen's anticipated confinement, and to take advantage of the situation. They also clearly comprehended the dramatic change in their *own* positions: they were no longer slaves but employees of the family. Much to the chagrin of the king and queen, the very same maids who had been so humble and reverential in Mandalay were now suddenly lacking in even basic courtesies. The king complained bitterly that they made 'a noise and [used] improper and immodest expressions in his hearing'. He grumbled to Colonel Cox (the *only* outlet for his grievances) that while this kind of behaviour may not seem particularly objectionable to an ordinary onlooker, he and the queen found it absolutely 'intolerable'.[56]

The king indicated that he wished to dismiss seven of the impudent maids.[57] A couple of maids left when their families summoned them, and the air was awash with constant tension of the others leaving. Although it was possible to replace Burmese maids with Indian ayahs—and this was resorted to fairly quickly—the royal family was picky (one candidate was rejected as she was found to be 'too ugly'). Additionally, the family required the ayahs to pay their respects in the Burmese style (to remain in the sheiko position in the family's presence), which the new arrivals took a while to learn. (The government informed the English midwife, a Mrs Wright, that while she was expected to be respectful to the queen, 'on no account' was she to get down on all fours.) The new maids were also unfamiliar with rolling cheroots, and the king piteously narrated to Colonel Cox 'the [many] hardships he and the ex-Queens [had] to endure for want of efficient attendants'.[58]

Other members of the entourage also gave trouble—Colonel Cox wrote that the interpreter Maung Gyi was unhappy and constantly complained, and anticipated that it would not be long before the king wanted to get rid of him.[59] Sure enough, very soon the king dismissed him. The government now decided to take a firm stand; the king was informed that henceforth whosoever he dismissed would not be allowed to return, and that others would not be brought in their place. (The poor king was constantly submitting lists of people he wanted sent over to be part of his entourage. In a very moving letter asking for yet more people, he implored the British government to 'graciously grant this request, taking into merciful consideration his fallen state and his comparatively friendless and isolated condition in a foreign land . . .'[60])

In February 1886 the king was informed that the royal family was being sent to Ratnagiri after the queen's confinement. If everything went smoothly, the shift was to take place in April.[61] King Thibaw naturally asked Cox numerous questions about the move including the proposed tenure of his stay in Ratnagiri. Upon his persistent questioning, he was told that it was forever—that he was *never* going to be permitted to return to Burma. This was the first time that the king was categorically informed of his fate-to-be, and this bit of information clearly had a devastating impact on him. He was well aware, however, that Colonel Cox was only the messenger; that officers much higher up in the government ladder made the decisions. He begged the colonel that his queens not be told, that he would break the news to them himself at a later date.[62] Although Queen Supayalat had been such a pillar of strength to him in the past, in deference to her advanced pregnancy, it appears he gallantly shouldered this distressing burden alone for the time being.

Ashin Hteik Su Myat Phaya (later rechristened the Third Princess by the British) was born on a Sunday, 7 March 1886. High drama followed her birth. Colonel Cox reported that Queen Supayalat had thrown a terrible tantrum, and King Thibaw 'completely cowed, fled as if for his life. After a while he made several ineffectual attempts to conciliate her with peace-offerings of sorts, but whenever he approached, the storm began to rage more violently than ever. At last in despair the ex-King entreated the shampooer to intercede on his behalf and peace was restored.'[63]

Dr Branfoot certified the queen medically fit to travel anytime after 29 March, and the family realized that their departure for Ratnagiri was now very imminent. To show their appreciation, the queen offered the doctor a ruby ring, and the king offered precious stones to a sergeant stationed in his home and cash to some ayahs who had been temporarily retained. When Colonel Cox heard about this, he harshly admonished a doubtlessly bemused king and indicated that if anything similar happened again, the government would probably take over all his property. While it is true that the king had earlier been informed that he and the queens could not offer gifts to any government servant, Cox could not have understood how foreign and incomprehensible a concept this was to the royal family. However, the king, it seems, took the rebuke and the departure for Ratnagiri in his stride, for Colonel Cox reported that just before leaving Madras the king 'was quiet and dignified, and appeared to be cheerful'. He asked for (and was granted) permission to give a piece of cloth to each of his servants before departure, but his request to throw Rs 150 in coins for people waiting at the gate of The Mansion to scramble for was denied.[64]

On 10 April 1886, King Thibaw, accompanied by his family, attendants (a nurse, two assistant nurses, six maids, two male attendants, a page, an interpreter, the shampooer, a butler, and five Indian ayahs), the new police officer (Fanshawe), an inspector of police and a sergeant of police,[65] boarded the *Clive* a little after 5 p.m. A portion of the deck had been screened off, and a carpet and easy chairs installed. Colonel Cox went aboard to see the family comfortably settled, and to bid them farewell.[66] If the royal family viewed the partial similarity in the names of Ratanapoun (as Mandalay was also called) and Ratnagiri as an encouraging omen, they were to be deeply disappointed. Any resemblance between the two began and ended right there.

9

BURMA WITHOUT A KING

T he royal white elephant died in the Golden Palace the very day
King Thibaw left the shores of Burma.[1] The king learnt of his
death in Madras, and is said to have remarked to Colonel Cox that the
elephant must have starved to death as his keepers must have abandoned
him.[2] During his reign, King Thibaw had accorded this elephant
appropriately honorific treatment. A hundred soldiers had guarded his
enclosure. Everything he ate and drank from was made of solid gold;
he was bathed with sandalwood scented water; palace dancers performed
every day to entertain him; and every night lullabies were sung to put
him to sleep. The reason for all these privileges was that it was
believed that in his last birth on earth, the Lord Buddha had entered
his mother's womb in the form of a white elephant. Therefore the
white elephant was one of the 'seven precious things' the ownership of
which marked great kings.[3] King Thibaw must have consequently seen
the death of his elephant as a great tragedy and as a sinister omen of
things to come.

As it turned out, the royal white elephant's death heralded bad times

not just for the royal family but also for the people of Burma. Less
than a month after his death, Burma ceased to be an independent
nation. On 1 January 1886 Lord Dufferin issued a proclamation
making Burma a part of the British Empire.[4]

Many in the British government had expected the Burmese people
to welcome them with open arms[5] for having freed their country from
a despotic ruler. They were disappointed. The Burmese saw the British
as colonizers rather than liberators, in Burma for the pursuit of their
own interests. Additionally, the fact that a non-Buddhist power had
occupied all of their country (including Mandalay—the centre of
Buddhism in Burma), and that with King Thibaw's departure their
religion had no patron was disturbing to many Burmese. Moreover, as
a proud race who valued their heritage, culture and identity, they
deeply resented the presence of an omnipotent foreign ruler.

Almost immediately after King Thibaw's deposition, spontaneous
uprisings were witnessed all over Upper Burma. Gangs of dacoits who
had plundered and looted during the king's days and bands of ex-army
men still equipped with palace-provided rifles and ammunition appeared
to have found a common cause.[6] Both presented a surprisingly vicious
and sustained guerrilla-style resistance. All trade came to a standstill
with the collapse of any semblance of law and order. This led to
shortages of food and other essentials, which in turn led to further
attacks and robberies for the acquisition of these necessities.[7] The
British government tried to use the Hluttaw to restore law and order
and to govern the newly acquired kingdom while it deliberated its next
step—whether to make Burma a protectorate and place a titular prince
on the Lion Throne, or dispense completely with any form of monarchy
and annex the country.

Since the Kinwun Mingyi had sailed off to Rangoon with King
Thibaw (some believe in an attempt to assuage his guilty conscience[8]),
the Taingda Mingyi was put in charge of the Hluttaw. But as the
uprisings continued unabated and rumours reached the government
that the Taingda Mingyi was actually fostering dacoits, he was arrested.[9]
The Kinwun Mingyi was called back from Rangoon and re-inducted as
head of the Hluttaw, but the disorder continued.[10] He pressed for the
quick investiture of a Konbaung prince as king, who could rule under

directions from the British government. He argued that as the monarchy was such a hallowed institution in Burma, rebellions could be more effectively quelled after someone—however nominal his authority— was sitting on the Lion Throne.[11] However, this was not to be. In February 1886, the British government decided to dissolve the Hluttaw, annex Burma, and make it a part of its Indian empire. This momentous decision was reached during Lord Dufferin's visit to Burma and appears to have been precipitated by, of all things, an insult.

In February 1886, while the royal family was adjusting to life in exile, Lord and Lady Dufferin set off for Burma on the *Clive*—the same ship that had housed the royal family in Rangoon, and that would carry them to Ratnagiri. The Dufferins sailed in style carrying on board their 'own servants, cooks, horses, cows, calves, chicken, sheep and quails . . .' They were graciously received and duly entertained everywhere in Burma, and everything was going better than planned until they reached Mandalay. In Mandalay, although they were received ceremoniously, were seated on ornate throne-like chairs decorated with embroidered peacocks and imitation stones, were shaded by a white umbrella, and were accorded a thirty-one gun salute,[12] members of the Hluttaw publicly showed their resentment—none of them made a speech, none of them extended any welcome.[13] The reason for this 'insult' was twofold. First the Hluttaw was highly frustrated because it was being blamed for its ineffectiveness in restoring law and order, when in reality it had been given no authority. Additionally, members of the Hluttaw (and countless other Burmese) were offended by the splendidly elaborate arrangements made for the arrival of the viceroy, which contrasted very sharply with 'the shame and tragedy of the King's final departure from his city' just a couple of months earlier.[14]

On 13 February 1886—a day after his ignominious reception by the Hluttaw—Lord Dufferin telegraphed London recommending full annexation of Burma.[15] Of course there were many reasons for this decision (the spiralling unrest, the inability of the Hluttaw to perform effectively for whatever reason, the lack of a suitable prince, pressure from various sources including the British press and the British business community in Lower Burma, opinion in government circles in favour of annexation, etc.) but the insult is what seems to have triggered it. Not only was the decision taken to annex Burma, says the Burmese historian Maung Htin Aung, but so annoyed was the viceroy that he followed the recommendation of the British business community that the Burmese must be forced to accept that

> they were now a conquered people. As a result, on February 26, the whole of Burma was proclaimed a mere province of the Indian empire, which made the administration of Burma easier for the British, and which at the same time struck a grievous blow to Burmese pride. The Hluttaw was abolished and its buildings pulled down ... the whole area within the palace moat and walls was renamed *Fort Dufferin*.'[16]

(The Kinwun Mingyi was later made Chief Burmese Counsellor of Government, and was honoured in 1887 with the 'Companion Star of India'.[17] The Taingda Mingyi, on the other hand, was exiled to Hazaribagh, India, from where he wrote piteous memorials begging to be permitted to return, even as a state prisoner, to Burma, to live among 'his fellow-countrymen and co-religionists'.[18])

Lord Dufferin's rebuff in Mandalay seems not to have tarnished the visit for Lady Dufferin. 'Mandalay is a lovely place, and we, at any rate, have had a delightful visit there', she wrote in her journal towards the end of her stay. She was dazzled by the palace and commented: 'A marvellous place it is. What is not gold is a sort of glass mosaic which is very bright and effective . . .' Her journal, later published as a book, provides an interesting palace-centric glimpse of Mandalay soon after the deposition. It also demonstrates that the British government knew by now that the press had maliciously maligned King Thibaw—'he did not drink as he was said to do', Lady Dufferin jotted in her journal.[19]

While in Mandalay, Lady Dufferin gossiped with French nuns, who had spent a lot of time with Queen Supayalat during her reign. They told her that the queen used to send for them regularly, sometimes to translate French novels, and sometimes to show them her jewellery: '[S]uch diamonds and rubies! . . . dazzling heaps of them covering the floor'. They indicated that the queen loved music, and enjoyed listening to the piano. They described how once, on a whim, the queen had them stitch trousers for all the ladies of the court, although everyone, including her, wore only the traditional Burmese tamein. They described her generosity and said that she gave 'quantities of presents' to those she liked. They remembered that on important occasions the queen liked to sit behind an enormous pile of coins, and people who streamed past to pay their respects could carry away as much money as they could hold. Lady Dufferin evidently greatly enjoyed these stories and surmised that Queen Supayalat reminded her of a queen of 'ancient history'.[20]

Officers of the British Burma Expeditionary Force who had come to Mandalay to depose King Thibaw were also curious about the royal couple and life at the palace, and mined for information and material. Many carried away mementos from the Golden Palace—a certain Colonel Pollard, for example, took home one of Queen Supayalat's *yinzis* (breast cloths) from her apartment, which his wife later donated to the South Kensington Museum.[21] The dying confession, many years later, of a private who had been part of the expedition raised public suspicion that British soldiers had not only carried away memorabilia but had also stolen 'a large portion of the royal treasure'.[22] Certainly the size and value of the property found in the palace after King Thibaw's deposition was not commensurate with what the British government had expected.

U Than Swe, the well-known Burmese writer on the Konbaung dynasty, says the following on what he thinks happened to much of the palace valuables:

> On the night of occupation there was wholesale looting. The maids and other women would steal from the palace and come out, and there many of them would be looted from by the British soldiers and the dacoits. They were waiting for the maids to come out. No Burmese soldiers at all—they are all gone. When the *pardawmu* procession (the procession when King Thibaw and family left the palace to go into exile) comes there are so many maids all carrying jewelry. Slowly slowly they break off with the jewelry ... *Everybody* plundered, the maids, the British soldiers, the dacoits, *everybody*.[23]

The British government claimed as 'prize of war' everything left behind, including the property entrusted by King Thibaw and Sinbyumashin to Colonel Sladen. King Thibaw's crown, some emeralds and a diamond necklace were sent to Queen Victoria, and a pair of carved ivory tusks and a gold Buddha figure were sent to the prince and princess of Wales respectively.[24] Other 'treasures, looted [by the government] from the palace of Mandalay', (in the words of *The Telegraph*, London) were sent to Britain, and exhibited at the South Kensington Museum. The article went on to narrate the bejewelled magnificence of this collection (the Mandalay Regalia, as it came to be called, comprising 168 pieces). The collection included the betel box that King Thibaw had repeatedly asked for in Madras, which was described as having on its lid 'a remarkably costly specimen of the mystic group of nine stones (*nauratna*). The middle gem is a ruby of 39 ¼ carats, with only one fault. . .'[25]

The Times of India commented that there was 'something undignified' in the manner in which 'the best part of the furniture of King Theebaw's Palace . . . [including] chairs, tables, sofas, mirrors, etc.' was removed and sent to Simla, India, for the viceroy's use.[26] Unfortunately, even a rare collection of eleven gold statues of past Konbaung kings and queens, of great historic value, were taken to Calcutta, melted down, and sold for the price of the gold.[27]

Not only was the palace stripped of everything valuable for the purposes of gifting, exhibiting, using or selling, but the palace itself was now turned into the headquarters of the occupying force leaving only 'traces of its gorgeous past in the chandeliers, golden pillars, carved images etc'.[28] Many of the old wooden structures in the walled city were pulled down to make space for parade grounds and a prison. Palace buildings were modified for use as offices, residences, a club and a church. Queen Supayalat's Lily Throne room was converted into the Upper Burma Club, and fitted with a bar and a billiards table. The Great Audience Hall was transformed into the army church,[29] with an altar set up in front of the Lion Throne, and presided over by the same Reverend Dr John Marks whose missionary school King Thibaw had once attended.[30] Now people strutted all over the palace platform with their shoes on. Needless to say, it offended the sensibilities of the Burmese to see the palace grounds being thus defiled. It was only in 1901 that Viceroy Curzon had it vacated, restored to the extent possible, and preserved.[31]

The British did make desultory attempts to be sensitive to the

Burmese viewpoint, but this did not mitigate the resistance to British occupation. It would take the British army four years and much violence to 'pacify' Burma as guerilla warfare continued unabated. All rebels (including members of the Burmese army) were labelled dacoits, and were summarily executed. Those sheltering these so-called dacoits were also dealt with ruthlessly—at times entire villages were burnt down, and its inhabitants massacred. The British mercantile community—which had earlier so vociferously condemned King Thibaw for the massacres in Mandalay during his reign—applauded the government's firm effort to quell the disorder.[32]

So keen was the new government to erase memories of the royal family and ensure that there was no attempt to revive the monarchy with another Konbaung prince, that Mandalay was drained of major Konbaung descendants—male and female, old and young. Most were sent off to Rangoon (many of the old queens were settled in its Sanchaung area) and other towns in Lower Burma, but the potentially more troublesome ones were sent to different locations in India. Local newspapers were banned from printing articles about the royal family,[33] but reports did occasionally appear. News of the Third Princess's birth in Madras filtered through, and a moving song was composed in her honour by one of the king's ex-subjects. The birth of a royal child in an alien country was 'a never before heard of event in our history', it said, and one that led people to feel great compassion for the exiled royal family.[34]

Missionary effort was intensified in Burma after the annexation, but did not have much of an impact. That the Burmese were very 'satisfied with Buddha and their pagodas' and showed no interest at all in the Gospel, was the complaint of many a missionary, including a Charles Lambert who went on to comment (in January 1891) that 'a lot of Burmese are waiting for their King to come back'.[35] And according to the historian Thant Myint-U, a sense of dislocation and aimlessness permeated Burmese society for several decades after King Thibaw's deposition, because a British-occupied Burma with no king was an incomprehensible break from the past, from all 'the ideas and institutions that had underpinned society in the Irrawaddy Valley since before medieval times'.[36]

10

THE KING IN RATNAGIRI

Two of the finest bungalows in Ratnagiri, west-facing and at the edge of a plateau with a breathtaking view of the Arabian Sea, were rented to accommodate the royal family and its entourage. The bungalows, about four hundred yards from each other, were set in a large compound. Though somewhat isolated, they were not far from the European section of the town, which lay to the south. The native or old town of Ratnagiri was to the west, at the foot of the plateau on which the bungalows stood, and well hidden by an abundance of coconut palms.[1] Three police *chowkies* (stalls) were erected in the compound to house the policemen who were to guard the family, and who were to monitor the king's movements at all times. Word had been spread that nobody would be allowed to meet the king, and that all communication with the family had to be routed through the police officer, Mr Fanshawe.[2] Fanshawe and all succeeding officers in charge of the king were to have an enormous influence on the day-to-day life of the family.

The bungalows had been completely overhauled and refitted before

the family's arrival. As one entered the compound, the first bungalow
(Outram Hall) was for the staff. The other bungalow (Baker's
Bungalow) was to be occupied by the royal family, *and* Fanshawe.
Baker's Bungalow, reported a special correspondent sent by *The Times of
India* to cover the king's arrival, was 'furnished in excellent style'. The
floor of the not-too-large drawing room was covered with matting
overlaid with rich Persian carpets. Handsome furniture, tastefully
upholstered, filled this and other rooms. Elegant hanging and pedestal
kerosene oil lamps were to provide the lighting. To the left of the
drawing room were two well-appointed bedrooms for use by the
family, and behind them another similar bedroom for Fanshawe's use
(this arrangement fortunately was a temporary one; Outram Hall was
where he later stayed[3]). On the right hand side of the drawing room
was the dining room, and a study for King Thibaw that was equipped
with a desk, chairs and a bookshelf. A large verandah ran across the rear
of the bungalow, and was dotted with easy chairs and—in deference to
the family's seating preference—cushioned wooden platforms. Two
carriages and two pairs of horses were to be stationed in the compound.
Apart from the staff already employed by the family, the government
retained an additional twenty-five male servants and six female ones.
'In fact,' commented the reporter, 'nothing has been left undone by
those entrusted by the Government to arrange for the housing of the
ex-King and his party.'[4]

   The *Clive* sailed into Ratnagiri on the afternoon of 16 April 1886. A
bevy of government officials—including the collector of Ratnagiri
and the inspector general of police—were present to assist in the
landing the next morning.[5] *The Times of India* correspondent described
King Thibaw as 'a strong built middle sized man, with a round fair
Chinese complexion, [wearing] a slight moustache. He has a
prepossessing appearance, and the gait and behavior of a refined
person.' The king wore a long white silk coat that reached up to his
knees, a silk multi-coloured pasoe (a piece of cloth worn in the place
of trousers), a white silk *gaung baung* (Burmese turban), silk stockings
and kid leather shoes. On both sides of his coat, at breast level, were
attached 'two rows of diamonds and rubies of the size of small
chestnuts in gold setting, which shone brightly in the morning rays of

the sun'. Queen Supayalat was also reported to be well dressed, in a small white jacket, a pink and blue silk breast cloth, a silk tamein (worn in place of a skirt), stockings and English-style shoes. Around her neck glittered 'a huge diamond necklace some three or four rows deep', on her sadan or hair top knot was a jewelled ornament set with rubies, emeralds and diamonds, and her ears shone with earrings set with a very large diamond and emerald.[6]

Once the entire family was safely on shore, they were signalled to move towards the two carriages. As officials led the way Queen Supayalat 'immediately turn[ed] towards her royal consort, cast a wistful glance at him and offer[ed] him her left hand'. The king and queen went hand in hand, with Queen Supayagalae trailing behind them. The maids, it was noticed, were also very smartly dressed; each one had 'a mine of wealth [on] her'. After the Burmese interpreter clambered into the second carriage, and two colossal conspicuously flashing pure gold bowls were lifted into it, the carriages immediately departed for their hill top destination. The press waiting by the beach was not permitted to interview the king, and curious Ratnagiri residents had been kept at a distance.[7]

Ratnagiri had a population of around eleven thousand when King Thibaw first arrived there. As the chief town of a district (the district was also called Ratnagiri, and was located in the Bombay Presidency), it housed a handful of government officials and had the trappings of any small district headquarter in British-administered India. It contained a revenue survey office, a custom house, a jail, a post office, schools and chapels. Ratnagiri had no manufacturing base, and was mainly an agricultural and fishing economy. To help the European officers and missionaries survive in this sleepy outpost, a club had been built for their use, with a library, reading room, covered racket court, swimming pool, garden and recreational grounds.[8]

From day one King Thibaw and his queens did not like Ratnagiri, and deeply resented having been transplanted here. As soon as he was permitted to by the police officer (in June 1886), the king dashed off a heart-rending memorial to the viceroy. He complained bitterly about Ratnagiri, calling it 'a very unpleasant place to live in', comparable 'to the wild villages of the Kachins and Karens' in Burma, abounding with 'snakes and scorpions'. He objected to his 'small brick house' and to the fact that policemen guarded him; he also indicated that he found the climate unsuitable. He pleaded for an interview with the government, 'a fair trial'. He and his family were very homesick for Burma, and he expressed his desire 'to be allowed to return to his own country on any conditions that the British Government may make, and that if he misbehaves himself in any way, he will be quite willing to be sent back and placed in confinement'.[9]

He said that Colonel Sladen had assured him that he was being sent to India for three months only, to discuss matters with the viceroy, and that after this period 'he would be replaced on the Throne of Burma'. He pointed out that so many months had passed, and no interview with the government had been granted to him, although he had been most cooperative. He said that he was in 'very low spirits', and could not recall 'any breach of faith or intentional fault that could have brought all these troubles upon him'.[10]

He ended his memorial by submitting a detailed long list of the very valuable articles (many diamond-, ruby- and emerald-encrusted gold spittoons, betel boxes and other containers; a gold hand-wash basin and a gold stand also similarly encrusted; a large gold sofa; necklaces, rings—including the ring holding the priceless Nga Mauk ruby and seven other rings set with large notable rubies, earrings, combs, official caps, court dresses all set with diamonds, emeralds and rubies; loose precious stones; silver ornaments, cups, ingots; gem-encrusted ornaments for elephants and horses, etc.) entrusted by him to Colonel Sladen, which he said he had handed over as he was afraid that they might get lost during his journey, and which he stated Colonel Sladen 'promised . . . would be returned to him when he wanted it back'. King Thibaw went on to say that he had recently been informed that all this property could not be located. He requested the viceroy to 'issue an order' for their return.[11]

Response to the memorial was quick. He was firmly told that under no circumstances could he be restored to the throne or allowed to return to Burma. Regarding the property he had left behind, the government reminded him that he had 'been liberally treated in being allowed to take away with him so much property as he now possesses', and that he had many debts outstanding in Burma. All the property left behind, therefore, was to be considered confiscated as 'prize of war'.[12] This reply, and the finality of its tone, must have squashed the family's hopes on many fronts, and had to have plunged the king and his queens, already in very low spirits, into deeper despondency.

The deeply religious king now turned to Buddhist high priests in Mandalay for comfort. He wrote them letters seeking their blessings. In one letter, he desperately beseeched them to 'pity me and absolve me from my sins both great and small'.[13] He wrote in the only style he knew—reverential, rambling and highly stylized. In a letter written to them in late 1886, the king implied that he was still the head of the Buddhist faith (which he justifiably believed he was). This letter was brought to the attention of the commissioner of Mandalay (all the family's letters, it will be recalled, were scrutinized by the government), who felt it was designed to 'stir the recollection of [the King] and his pious qualities, excite pity and compassion, and call up the memory of past favours', and this irked the commissioner. The king's overarching objective was quite clearly to solicit a favour on a subject that continued to trouble him—his staffing. He asked that the priests 'instruct and persuade men and women and suitable ministers to join him and relieve his distress'. But the suspicious commissioner, his attitude hardened by a rumour that a recent charitable distribution of rice by the British government had in fact really been funded by King Thibaw, strongly advocated that 'measures be taken to cut off *all* communication between King Thibaw and the country he once ruled'.[14]

Although this recommendation was not implemented, the government became much more vigilant. In December 1886, the chief commissioner of Burma blocked permission for King Thibaw to contribute towards the funeral expenses of his and his father King Mindon's revered spiritual advisor.[15] And while the government had had no objection to King Thibaw being photographed in Madras, in Ratnagiri (in April 1887) it turned down permission sought by a professional photographer to take the king's picture. It opined that recent photographs of the king and the queens 'would again invite public attention to the ex-King and his wives, whereas the Government of India ... wish[es] that His Highness Thebaw should be kept in perfect retirement'.[16]

The government did, however, make an effort to make the family comfortable—secluded, forgotten, but comfortable. The shrill whistle of the steamer from Bombay announced the arrival of supplies like ice and fruit, which was unfailingly sent down bi-weekly for the family (eventually an ice machine was installed in the king's compound).[17] Tins of biscuits and crystallized fruit were procured;[18] since the family was very fond of pork, two piggeries were erected in the compound; to supplement the milk bought, a shed was built to house cows.[19] To stir the still and humid air during the warmer months, men and women were employed to pull *punkha*s (fans) in Baker's Bungalow day and night.[20] The civil surgeon visited the compound daily to ensure sanitary conditions, but so as not to impose on the royal family he only met them when asked for.[21] When King Thibaw asked again for an English tutor, the government readily sanctioned his request,[22] but a tutor fluent in English and Burmese was never found.

In mid 1887 the king again pursued the matter that was foremost on the family's mind. He represented to a senior government official that he found Ratnagiri intolerable. The reason he gave this time was the very heavy monsoon rainfall there (Mandalay, in the central dry zone of Burma, experienced considerably less rain). The officer was unsympathetic—the government had incurred considerable expense to settle the family in Ratnagiri and would definitely not agree to a shift, he indicated.[23] But the king decided to anyway submit another written petition on the subject. So despondent was he in Ratnagiri, that this time he asked for nothing except that he and his family be permitted to live *anywhere* else, his only specification being that the new location be a major centre. He ended his petition by trying to appeal to the government's sense of fairness, saying that he hoped his request would be favourably considered 'as the Government is generous and the protector of the poor and helpless'.[24]

As in all his requests to the British government, here too the king adopted a self-effacing humble tone, in deference to where the power now clearly lay. Once, not so long ago, a royal interpreter had been used to transform everything any visitor said in the king's presence into the appropriately sycophantic; now the king's interpreter helped him write appropriately sycophantic petitions to the British—the autocrat now the supplicant, zenith to nadir. Although individual government officers were sometimes truly sympathetic to the family's fallen position, in this case too the king's request was quickly turned down.[25]

Early on in the exile the British had noted that the king and his queens were very careless with their valuables. They gifted gems at the drop of a hat. They were unaware of the value of their possessions, and sold to people who unscrupulously cheated them. They made no attempt to conceal their valuables, so theft by staff was a constant threat. All this alarmed the government and it tightened its control in this area of the king's life as well. The reason for this was not only to help the unworldly king best preserve his assets, but also to forestall him selling valuables to finance a conspiracy or an attempt at escape: 'he might at any moment get a ship hired, bribe the Police guard and be off'.[26]

In late 1886, the government made another inventory of the king's jewels,[27] and by March 1887 insisted that any payment the king wished to make *had* to be routed through the police officer. By the following month the collector and police officer were instructed to take steps to strictly monitor *all* the king's transactions.[28] This was easier said than done.

For the seven years of their reign, the king and queen had spent as they chose, and had lived as they wanted. In exile, they found it impossible to come to terms with their drastically changed situation, and were unable to do without certain goods, services and celebrations they regarded as basic. The government's monthly allowance of Rs 3,000 was insufficient for their needs, and the king spent on average an additional Rs 1,500–2,000 per month.[29] He sold his valuables in bits and pieces to buy new jewellery, clothes, trinkets and other things the family needed or wanted;[30] to pay for priests, and for religious and birthday ceremonies; and to compensate the bandsmen he had hired both to entertain the family[31] and to scare away wild animals that the family occasionally spotted lurking around in their compound.[32]

In order to better manage his expenses, the government set up a bank account in the king's name. His monthly allowance was credited into this account. Cash realized from the sale of the king's valuables (that was now to be sold *only* through the police officer) was also credited to his account. All bills to suppliers were paid off by cheque. The only cash the king was supposed to lay his hands on was the Rs 100 pocket money sanctioned to him every month. But even in this he was tightly corralled by the police officer: 'With part of [his pocket money], he gets the Police Officer to buy him miscellaneous things he may want from the bazaar; and with part of it, he keeps five or six [additional] servants—a *malli* [gardener], an assistant cook, 3 tailors, and a dog-boy ...'[33] (Servants hired by the government were paid salaries by the police officer from the king's monthly allowance—there were about forty of them at this stage;[34] maids from Burma were not paid regularly, but were compensated with occasional bejewelled gifts from the king or queen.[35]) Sadly, so strapped for petty cash was the king and the rest of the royal family, that, as revealed by the Third Princess in an interview many years later, 'the British gave us five cans of biscuits daily. We did not eat them but sold them.'[36]

Although kept under strict surveillance,[37] the king also used his increasing army of servants to raise money and to buy the things the family wanted. The policemen on duty were richly tipped by the king and saw no more than they could help. Servants found guilty of helping the king were sacked, but proof of guilt was difficult, and new servants were soon tempted to fall into the same pattern of behaviour as the old ones.[38] The police officer or collector periodically attempted to examine the king's valuables and compare it to the list made in late 1886, but as one collector commented, he and his colleagues were no jewel experts. It was therefore impractical for them to be asked to judge whether what was shown to them was the same as before or inferior stones/metals substituted for the original.[39]

In addition to administering the king's financial transactions, the government also felt it could not give the king a free hand in appointments as this would lead 'to the indefinite increase of Burmese followers'.[40] Permission was required to both hire and fire staff.[41] Countless letters therefore went back and forth between King Thibaw and the government regarding his staffing requirements. Also not in the king's hand was the authority to even reprimand his own servants;

the police officer was responsible for this.[42] King Thibaw found it
truly annoying, demeaning and uncalled for to be mired in such
endless red tape for all aspects of his staffing.

By late 1888/early 1889 the government felt that it could quite
safely permit King Thibaw greater liberty in Ratnagiri—it had realized
that the possibility of him engaging in an intrigue of any consequence
was minimal, and the last three years had demonstrated that he was
unlikely to make an attempt at escape. He was therefore now allowed
to meet 'any respectable native gentleman' of Ratnagiri if he chose to,
with the police officer responsible for preventing him becoming close
to people of doubtful character. The king and his family were also
permitted to visit European officers, and were encouraged to use the
horse carriages provided by the government. But the king and his
queens seldom did. The princesses, on the other hand, made good use
of the transport provided. On a few rare occasions in 1888—two or
three at the most—the royal family did emerge as a family and visit
the collector's house and the club.[43]

Like in Madras, the police officer in whose charge the family had
been put called on the king almost daily. Through the years of exile
there were some officers that the king tolerated, some he liked, and
others he could barely stand. In the first decade of his exile, the king
particularly disliked Mr Allbon who was with him from 1888 to 1894
(following Cox and Fanshawe, both of whom the king had gotten
along with). It appears that King Thibaw did not take to Mr Allbon
right from the start, his prejudice probably triggered by the fact that
Allbon was junior in rank to the two preceding officers. The king
viewed this as a slight, for the collector noticed that he behaved
somewhat arrogantly with the new officer and asked numerous questions
about his authority. The relationship between the two steadily
deteriorated, and Mr Allbon was a source of escalating irritation for
the king (the historian W.S. Desai opines that Allbon, unlike his
predecessors, was unimaginative and therefore unable to keep the king
happy).[44]

By 1892, the king had had enough of Allbon. The despondency
arising from almost seven years of exile, coupled with Allbon's irksome
and constant presence, seems to have led to a crescendo of frustration.

The king hired a solicitor—Frederick Edgelow—to help him get Allbon removed (and to represent some of his other grievances), and informed him (on some points with a certain degree of inspired creativity!) of all of Allbon's misdeeds. Based on this information, Edgelow wrote to the government accusing Allbon of, among other things, 'practicing unjustifiable zoolum [oppression]', and 'practically blackmailing' the king. He requested that Allbon be immediately replaced by 'a gentleman of higher position, and if there be any objection to this on the score of expense, [the king] offers to defray a portion of such expense'.[45]

Apart from the removal of Allbon, the main thrust of Edgelow's representation was that King Thibaw wished to manage, even with a smaller allowance, his own affairs. He wanted control over his own jewellery—no more inspections—and the freedom to sell items whenever he chose to, with Edgelow's help when necessary. He wanted to be able to hire and fire his own staff. He wanted control over his own banking account—open always, however, to government inspection.[46]

The king's aggravation was not always one-sided. As is evident in some of the communication generated over the years, many of these foot soldiers of the British Empire felt equally frustrated by the petty nature of their responsibilities, and by the pot shots the family occasionally took at them. The government took no accusation made by the king lightly—each had to be vigorously defended by the man charged. Edgelow's missive of June 1892 was investigated. The collector of Ratnagiri's seventy-one-page handwritten letter passionately defending his subordinate (after numerous interviews with him) supplemented Allbon's own relatively brief and indignant explanation.[47]

The government informed King Thibaw that it found his complaints embellished and unsubstantiated, and saw no justification to remove Allbon. He was also informed that, should he need to in the future, his complaints could be addressed directly to the collector. Since this would enable him to bypass Allbon, it would eliminate his need for any future interaction with his solicitor Edgelow. The king, more troubled by Allbon's presence than Edgelow's absence, did not immediately press to see the latter again. Edgelow, however, was extremely keen to continue his alliance with the king. During their first meeting (which had taken place with government consent) the king had paid him Rs 17,000 in jewels, with promises of much more to come. [48] The lawyer now wrote numerous letters to the government pleading that he be permitted to visit the king again, and it was only in February 1894 that his request was finally granted. He rushed immediately to Ratnagiri. The king warmly welcomed him and confided that his 'troubles had become so unbearable that he saw no way out of them but to commit suicide'. Edgelow attempted to reassure the king,[49] and the king generously promised him Rs 100,000 if he succeeded in getting Allbon transferred and the management of his household put under his (the king's) control.[50] Edgelow hurriedly prepared another memorial, travelled to Calcutta to push the matter with the foreign office, and in May 1894, thanks mainly to his efforts, Allbon was finally removed.[51]

Although King Thibaw got along well with Police Officer Barber who succeeded Allbon, he was still desperate to have the freedom to manage his own home. He, who had once ruled a country, wanted to have the authority to run *at least* his own home. Edgelow petitioned the government again in August 1895.[52] Although the collector did not recommend it, the government decided it was no longer justified in withholding the permission that the king so badly wanted. As a prelude to the permission, in cognizance of his both his extravagance and lack of financial acumen, and in order to protect both the government and the king from any lawsuits, an act (called Ex-King Thebaw's Act 1895) was passed in October 1895 disabling King Thibaw from entering into any contract that resulted in a financial obligation. All existing debt was to be estimated and repaid by recourse to the valuables owned by the king.[53]

Finally, from January 1896, the king was allowed to manage his own household with an allowance of Rs 3,000 per month.[54] Visitors and employees still had to be screened by the government, but the king no longer had to justify each request. Promptly—in February 1896— King Thibaw added nine people from Mandalay to his establishment.[55] A monthly expenditure statement of the king in 1896 interestingly reflects the family's priorities—nearly 20 per cent of their allowance was spent on priests and religious ceremonies:

Clerical establishment	Rs 184
Household establishment	Rs 606
Food and other household expenses	Rs 1,120
Clothing	Rs 750
Bandsmen	Rs 295
Priests	Rs 120
Religious ceremonies	Rs 766
Miscellaneous	Rs 100
Repayment of debt	Rs 500
Total	Rs 4,441[56]

The king had by now been in exile for just over ten years and had run through almost all the valuables he had brought along with him. Although Edgelow had persevered and had got the king what he had asked for, in April 1896 the king wrote and very regretfully informed him of his inability to pay the promised amount—all he owned, he explained, had been either sold or mortgaged. Edgelow, aware of the new law recently passed, presented his claim to the government.[57] A committee considered it, and decided to award him a further Rs 55,000 (on top of the Rs 17,000 that had already been paid to him by the king). This payment was made by the government in March 1898, and while it was entitled to sell some of the king's assets to offset the amount it decided not to do so.[58]

This was not an act of generosity. The collector, a few weeks earlier, had attempted to value King Thibaw's possessions. The king submitted a list of his valuables, but claimed that as everything on the list had been pawned, he was unable to actually show any of it. Due to the difficulty of tracing and assessing each piece, the collector submitted to the government the value the king had assigned to his residual assets—Rs 10,005 [59] (later re-estimated by a local jeweller at no more than Rs 3,704[60]). As everything had been mortgaged, little could have been gained by attempting to dispose off the king's belongings. However, under the Ex-King Thebaw's Act 1895 and on paper at least, since the government had settled his debt to Edgelow, all the

king's assets now belonged to the government, and in late May/early
June 1898 public notices were released cautioning people of the king's
revised position:

> It is hereby publicly notified that His Highness the *Ex*-King Thebaw
> is by Section 2 of Act XX of 1895 incapable of entering into any
> contract so as to give rise to any pecuniary obligation on his part.
>
> Under Section 10 (1) of the same Act the moveable property of the
> *Ex*-King was valued under the orders of the Governor-General in
> Council, and, thereupon, under the said Section the whole of the said
> property has now vested in the Secretary of State for India on behalf
> of Her Majesty, Her heirs and successors.
>
> All people are, therefore, warned not to deal in any moveable
> property hitherto belonging to His Highness the *Ex*-King.[61]

Highly alarmed by the fact that he now legally owned *nothing* (rumour
had it that the family still had some undeclared assets), and by the
humiliation and inconvenience of the public notice (which had resulted
in him, as he wrote, being 'unable to get credit for the smallest amount
... unless I produce the actual cash before delivery, tradesmen refuse
to supply me with even the necessaries of life'), the mortified king
immediately appealed to the government. Although the two requests
in his letter were reasonable (an increase in his monthly allowance, and
a financial provision for his family in the event of his death), the
argument he used to justify his request demonstrated that, in spite of
all that had happened in the intervening years, his distantly regal past
still sharply informed his radically altered present, and probably
always would. He wrote:

> This amount [of Rs 3,000] is not sufficient even to clothe myself
> and the Ex-Royal family. My own clothing must consist of silk, velvet,
> and satin, and there is not sufficient balance left out of the Rs 3000
> to properly clothe the Ex-Queens and Royal family. I therefore
> beg that His Excellency the Viceroy be pleased to increase my
> allowance ...'[62]

In late 1898 the government assured the king that a provision would
be made for his family on his death,[63] and from December 1899 it
increased his allowance to Rs 4,150 a month. [64] In spite of the

increase, the king was never able to live within a budget. He did not stop borrowing, and continued doing so until his dying day. Promissory notes signed by him still exist in Ratnagiri—he borrowed liberally from just about everybody, including his grocer.[65] (Also still existent, in a tiny back room in a home in Ratnagiri, is a cupboard especially built with secret compartments to conceal the valuable jewellery pledged by the king to a moneylender in the earlier years of his exile.[66])

The government by now no longer perceived King Thibaw as a threat. As a result, it loosened its grip, softened its stand and showed more compassion in its dealings with the moping ex-monarch. It noted, rather sympathetically, that he had not gone out of his compound for years, and that he seemed 'thoroughly resigned to the circumstances in which he [found] himself'.[67] The role of the officer in charge of the king could now be changed, successive collectors of Ratnagiri opined, and one of them recommended that the person selected need not be from the police department, but 'should be an officer of experience and courteous manners, well acquainted with the Burmese language and one who understands the customs, manners and sentiments of His Highness and be able to act as a friendly advisor to him and a useful assistant to the Collector.'[68] More than someone controlling him and trying to prevent his escape, felt another collector, the king needed a friend, philosopher and guide—'Thebaw is without energy and has few resources within himself and requires a man who will read with him, teach him English and give him interest in life. Time must hang very heavily on his hands and he wants some one to show him out. . .'[69]

11

THE ROYAL FAMILY IN RATNAGIRI

Queen Supayalat came from a line of strong determined women. Although her mother Sinbyumashin had not been King Mindon's chief queen, she had ably elbowed herself to the forefront after the chief queen's death. Sinbyumashin's mother, Mae Nu, was also highly manipulative and her story—partly accurate and partly embellished over the years—is a truly fascinating one: Mae Nu was the daughter of a military officer. One day, during a raging storm, her tamein blew away and got caught very high up on the palace hti (the palace in those days stood in Ava, or Inwa as it is today called). The palace astrologer saw this as an omen that could not be ignored. The owner of the tamein must be found and installed in the palace, he declared, as her presence would be very auspicious. Mae Nu, then fourteen, was accordingly inducted as a maid of honour to the chief queen. At the palace she met the future King Bagyidaw, enthralled him, and later became his queen. After the Burmese lost the First Anglo-Burmese war in 1826, King Bagyidaw grew increasingly mentally unstable, giving Queen Mae Nu and her brother Maung O (who was supposedly also her lover) the opportunity to grasp the reins of the kingdom. When Tharrawaddy (King Bagyidaw's brother) revolted and seized the throne (1837), Queen Mae Nu schemed to have him killed, and Maung O crowned king.[1]

Queen Mae Nu had had constructed many years earlier, as a work of merit, a stone monastery on the banks of the Irrawaddy, and she now ordered a secret tunnel to be built from the monastery to the river. She conspired to have King Tharrawaddy thrown in a sack, carried through this tunnel, and drowned in the Irrawaddy. King Tharrawaddy got wind of this unsavoury plot, and ordered Queen Mae Nu's death—by drowning in the Irrawaddy. While being taken through the grounds of her monastery to her watery grave, she is believed to have desperately shouted to her old abbott for help, but all he was able to offer her were words of very questionable comfort: 'You go to your death first, we will all follow you someday!' Sinbyumashin was nineteen at the time,[2] and the pain of her mother's sudden and brutal end must have made her realize how ephemeral power and life was, and must have taught her the vital importance of meticulously planned intrigues. Both she and her daughter, Queen Supayalat, were well versed in this art, and both were very intelligent and ambitious. Queen Supayalat, in early 1887, was poised to finally pass on this legacy.

Ashin Hteik Su Myat Phaya Galae—the Fourth Princess—was born in Ratnagiri on the evening of 25 April 1887.[3] Birth of yet another daughter had to have been deeply disappointing to the royal couple who had hoped so long and so hard for a son and heir. Queen Supayalat had borne King Thibaw a total of seven children, of which four daughters now survived (and would into adulthood). Although they were not to know it at the time, this daughter, more than any of the others, was of the same mould as her mother, grandmother and great grandmother, and would grow up to display the same intelligence and mettle that they all had.

Around the time of the Fourth Princess's birth, the government briefly thought of relocating Queen Supayagalae, the junior queen, as her health had considerably deteriorated. The reason for this was a series of back-to-back miscarriages, and the civil surgeon of Ratnagiri felt it imperative that she be separated from the king, at least for a few months, for he warned she no longer had the strength to get over yet another pregnancy. Her health was not all that was troubling Queen Supayagalae. The police officer in charge of the king indicated that she had approached him on a few occasions in the past with the plea that she be allowed to go to her mother in Tavoy. She had complained that both the king and the queen bullied her, and following one disagreement she had cut off her hair to demonstrate her anguish. In early 1888, Sinbyumashin wrote to the government complaining of her youngest daughter's unhappiness and requesting that she be permitted to come and stay with her in Tavoy. [4]

Queen Supayagalae was not sent to Tavoy, but a few months later, as a result of a rather unexpected turn of events, her mother was brought to Ratnagiri. Sinbyumashin was exiled to Ratnagiri as there had been trouble in Tavoy, and the government suspected a connection between Sinbyumashin and a Shan sawbwa who had been accused of dacoity. [5] When she arrived at her first port of call in India—Calcutta—Sinbyumashin indicated that she was keen to remain there. She 'disliked' King Thibaw, she said, and did not wish to live in the same town as him [6] (she must have also shrewdly assessed that Calcutta was a far larger and more cosmopolitan location than Ratnagiri, and that it had a fair number of Burmese). But the government insisted otherwise, and Sinbyumashin, her eldest daughter Supayagyi, and their female attendants reached Ratnagiri in June 1888. [7] The king, when he had earlier been asked by the government, had declined to accommodate Sinbyumashin, [8] but he was so delighted to actually see her that he insisted that she and her entourage stay with him. His joyous welcome, however, was short-lived—about five weeks after her arrival, she and the king had a serious misunderstanding. There was such acrimony in the air that the government (on the advice of the king's interpreter) had to have all the *datura* plants (a highly toxic commonly found wild herb) in the compound meticulously weeded for fear of an attempt at poisoning. This, however, could not be a long-term solution, and it was decided that the wisest course of action would be to physically separate the warring factions. Rooms in a mission house in Ratnagiri

(close to the king's compound) were rented to accommodate
Sinbyumashin and her entourage.[9] Queen Supayagalae did not move
in with her mother but continued to stay in her marital home.

Although it is not known what the massive fallout was about, one
can attempt a reasonable guess. Before her arrival King Thibaw and
Sinbyumashin had exchanged frequent warm letters, gifts and
photographs. But underneath the affection there had been undercurrents
of discord. In one letter King Thibaw had written 'we cannot help
thinking with grief and sorrow that although Your Majesty's children
and grandchildren are in Ratnagiri, Your Majesty has been pleased to
stay apart with one daughter alone in Tavoy having been led away by
the persuasions of a certain individual. We have daily been longing for
a meeting . . .'[10] Supayagyi—the discarded queen—evidently continued
to be the bone of contention. Additionally, and very importantly, in all
probability Sinbyumashin laid the blame for the loss of the kingdom
squarely on King Thibaw and Queen Supayalat's shoulders. And it is
extremely unlikely that, when in such close and daily proximity, she
kept this opinion to herself.

There had earlier been no audible murmur of discontent between
Supayagyi and her mother, but now Supayagyi complained to the
government that her mother ill-treated her, and indicated that she no
longer wished to stay with her. In early 1890 Supayagyi was permitted
to return to Rangoon.[11] In March 1890 Sinbyumashin also requested
to be sent back to Burma, saying that while she had been 'delighted to
find my daughters enjoying good health . . . unfortunately the climate
[in Ratnagiri] does not agree with me . . .' She begged that she be
allowed to rejoin her eldest daughter, as she couldn't bear to be parted
from her.[12] Supayagyi wrote as well to the government pleading that
her 'innocent' seventy-one-year-old mother be allowed to return to
Burma to stay with her.[13] The government was understandably
suspicious by the inconsistency between Supayagyi's earlier statements
and her present request, and still believing that Sinbyumashin had
been responsible for the disturbance in Tavoy, refused to let her
return.[14] However, in early 1891 she was allowed to.[15] She would never
again see her two younger daughters, her granddaughters, or the king.

Sinbyumashin moved to Rangoon, bought a home on Boundary

Road,[16] and stayed there with Supayagyi. But peace did not reign in this home for long. After another fallout with her mother, Supayagyi departed forever for Mingun, a town a few miles upriver from Mandalay, and lived as a Buddhist nun until her death a few years later (she predeceased her mother).[17] Sinbyumashin now lived alone with her staff until she passed away on 27 February 1900.[18]

King Thibaw laid claim on Sinbyumashin's property (after setting off all her liabilities, her residual assets were not worth much) and generously offered to pay 'any amount' for her funeral expenses.[19] The government permitted Sinbyumashin's coffin to be taken upriver to Mandalay with stops in towns and villages along the way to enable people to pay their last respects. Her mortal remains were laid to rest in the Golden Palace in a specially built mausoleum next to that of King Mindon's.[20] The funeral was elaborate and was carried out according to prescribed royal protocol of the past. The Sawbwa of Nyaungshwe (a Shan chief very close to the royal family—as a young boy he had been 'adopted' by King Mindon and had been brought up in the Golden Palace[21]) personally paid more than half the expenses.[22]

Their own lineage, heritage and customs were of paramount importance to the royal family. Therefore, in spite of their differences, the king and queen must have looked back at Sinbyumashin's extended stay in Ratnagiri with some gratitude, for this had enabled their daughters to interact with their royal grandmother. The princesses ranged in age from three to ten at the time of Sinbyumashin's departure, and it was Queen Supayalat who home schooled them. In fact, unlike King Thibaw and Queen Supayalat, none of the four princesses ever went to school. The Third Princess said in an interview many years later:

> We had to study [to read and write[23]] under the chief queen. She was very strict and well disciplined. She used to beat us with rulers [wrapped with silk ribbons[24]]. We were not afraid of the king, but we were very afraid of the chief queen. We dared not even cough in her presence . . . We had to sleep at the foot of the chief queen's bed . . . She also taught us how to cook food . . . We also had to study Buddhist scriptures . . . The chief queen often said that we had become village girls in India as we had lost the royal manners. My father also said we were speaking just like Indians . . .

From the Indian servants the princesses learnt various languages including Hindustani, Marathi and Konkani ('Goan' is what the royal family called Konkani).[25] (Not too many years into the exile the king and queens could also communicate well with their servants in these languages.[26])

Although the family spoke to each other in Burmese, the sisters' accent was greatly influenced by their Indian surroundings, and it is said that they developed a distinct dialect of their own comprising a mix of Burmese and Hindustani.[27] They called each other Suphayagyi (First Princess), Suphayalat (Second Princess), Suphaya (Third Princess) and Suphayagalae (Fourth Princess).[28] That the four princesses had each other to lean on, conspire and play with was the saving grace of their childhood, for their existence was a lonely one, and they knew no local children. They found numerous small ways to entertain themselves, says the Third Princess's daughter, and provides an example: 'My mother and her sisters were adept at giving names and mischievously dubbed [one of the king's secretaries] "Mr Warty Toad" since he was rather stout and when he prostrated before the King must have looked like an old squatting toad!'[29]

The king, who could recite traditional Burmese poems and play the piano, harp and concertina, occasionally entertained the princesses. Classical Burmese music was his forte, and he even composed songs. While the princesses 'were not allowed to sing or to whistle ...' because Queen Supayalat did not permit it, they were all taught to play a musical instrument.[30]

By 1892 the government decided that the two older princesses' education needed some attention (the First Princess was around twelve and the Second Princess eleven). In spite of King Thibaw's great dislike of Mr Allbon, he did not object to Allbon's daughter's engagement as governess for the two princesses. A report indicates that in the first half of 1892 the princesses 'made steady progress, and [had] gone through Longman's three primers, [had] learnt to write easy sentences of words of one syllable, and work out easy sums in simple addition'.[31] But the teaching was erratic and in May 1993 the government gave permission for Miss Allbon to be employed for an uninterrupted period of one year.[32] This arrangement, which was to be renewed each year, ended with Allbon's removal from Ratnagiri in May 1994, and there are no records to show that another governess was ever hired in her place.

The royal family had carried some images of Lord Buddha with them, and these were used for worship. The king and queen taught their daughters the various traditions and rituals that they themselves had been brought up with.[33] The Burmese festivals of Thingyan (the Burmese new year), Thadingyut (the end of lent), and Tazaungdaing (the end of the rainy season observed on full moon day in November) were celebrated each year in their compound. The king was rather adept at carpentry, and according to the Third Princess, himself designed the *mandup* (pavilion) for these festivals.[34] Since the Hindu festivals of Diwali and Holi fell approximately at the same time as Thadingyut and Thingyan respectively, the family celebrated the Buddhist and Hindu festivals together,[35] and invitation cards with a gold peacock crest embossed on top (the symbol of the royal family) were liberally sent out inviting townsfolk for the celebrations.[36] These festivals generated tremendous excitement in the quiet town.[37]

During the festivals a feeble semblance of the Kadaw or the paying respect ceremony that had always been held with great splendour in Mandalay, was replayed in Ratnagiri. Locals came to bow deeply before the royal couple and were served refreshments and given small gifts in return.[38] The family's residence was beautifully illuminated with kerosene lamps and oil diyas, and at Diwali children would shriek with delight at the sight of a specially constructed enormous coloured-paper serpent, lit from within, and made to slither sinuously all over the compound.[39] People in Ratnagiri remember stories told by their forefathers of the king's majestic bearing and lavish expenditure during these festivals.[40]

As had been the case from the beginning of the exile, the government allowance was woefully mismatched with the king's spending. In addition to the festivals, birthdays of all the family members were also celebrated—especially King Thibaw's and Queen Supayalat's (this was not vanity but tradition). One of King Thibaw's police officers reported that the king and queen were both always 'very generous and charitable to the poor', who were frequently fed. The couple was also obliged to send charitable donations to priests and pagodas, and gifts to close relatives in Burma.[41] Queen Supayalat voiced many years later that 'giving money and things after counting and measuring was actually the practice of commoners', and not something that either the king or she found possible to do.[42]

A compassionate collector tried to explain to his senior why the king spent the way he did, especially for festivals:

> He has always been accustomed to hold these festivals on this scale, and he considers them indispensable to the due observation of his religion and the proper maintenance of his dignity. They are the chief consolations of his exile, and the preparations for them form his principal occupation during the greater part of the year. They are thus really necessities of his existence. It was largely his determination to keep them up in befitting style that made him part with his private property, bit by bit, and then incur debt when that was exhausted. He cannot pay for them out of his ordinary allowance, but it would make him so desperately unhappy not to be able to celebrate them as heretofore ... [43]

The king and the queen often brooded on their terrible misfortune. Religion provided the king with some comfort. It was his very unfortunate destiny, he reasoned, that had led to the loss of the kingdom, and he once wrote to Buddhist priests in Mandalay that 'he exonerates his ministers and servants from all blame, and attributes the sole fault of what has happened to his own destiny'.[44] Religion did not provide Queen Supayalat with the same answer. She continued to blame the Kinwun Mingyi, and when informed that he had been honoured with the 'Companion Star of India' by the British, she regarded this as ample proof of his betrayal.[45]

It was a matter of great regret to King Thibaw that he lived in a land where the teachings of the Buddha were no longer practised. Every day he paid homage to the three gems—Buddha, Dhamma (Buddha's teachings), Sangha (order of Buddhist monks).[46] He said his prayers twice a day, in the morning and in the evening. One of King Thibaw's grandsons repeats a telling story his mother, the Fourth Princess, told him: King Thibaw, at the conclusion of his morning prayers, always asked for peace and good health for all beings. Queen Supayalat watched him silently (and apparently disapprovingly) for days on end, until finally she could contain herself no more. In the words of their grandson:

> 'What did you say after the prayers?' asked my grandmother.
> 'I said let everyone be peaceful and healthy,' replied my grandfather.
> 'When you say "all" don't include the British!'
> 'Well, my dear, the British are also people!'
> '*People*—they are our enemies! See what they have done to us, we are suffering because of the British, so don't you give them any blessings!'[47]

The king repeatedly demonstrated that he bore no malice towards the government that had toppled him. All other things being equal, he made an effort to be congenial. Even when half frightened to death by an outbreak of plague in his compound, the police officer reported that the king continued to be cooperative. The ten-year-old daughter of one of the king's Burmese attendants died of plague in July 1899, and then it was discovered that two of the king's other servants had died of the same disease. Dead rats were also found in the outhouses of the compound, and the very alarmed king, queens and princesses desperately pleaded with the collector to relocate them as quickly as possible. The government acted swiftly, and in a matter of days shifted the family to another bungalow in Ratnagiri.[48] Plague haunted Ratnagiri for several years, and the family had to be evacuated twice.[49]

Unlike her more forgiving husband, Queen Supayalat could never let go of the anger and bitterness she felt towards the British. Contoured by the beliefs and superstitions of her past, she read messages in everything that happened around her including in the multiplication of the huts near their compound (was this a form of mental torture deliberately inflicted by the British?), and the outbreak of plague in Ratnagiri (a stratagem of the British?), and these views were later articulated by one of her grandsons.[50]

According to the Third Princess, as her mother did not approve of any 'English habits', to the extent they could the family clung to Burmese practices (Indian ones were also eschewed). Coconut oil was never used for the hair (as is done in India), but sesame and jasmine flowers were pounded together to prepare a special oil. In place of scents bought from the store, *tharaphe* flowers were dried, shaped into small cakes, broken as and when needed, and ground with rose water to create a strong fragrance. All of them used only thana'kha and were not permitted to use face powder. The clothes worn by the royal family were always of Burmese style—the queens and princesses never wore the Indian sari but tameins and simple blouses. The blouses had to be hip length to conceal the shape of the hips as Queen Supayalat disapproved of anything revealing. When they could still afford it, Ko Ba Shin (an honorary magistrate in Rangoon who took over the job of supplying whatever the royal family needed from Burma[51]) arranged for their clothes to be tailored for them in Rangoon.[52] However, later into the exile when money was so scant, 'the four girls [were] practically kept without any of the little luxuries of life and their clothing consist[ed] of the ordinary common cotton material purchased in the Native bazaar'.[53] Queen Supayalat always wore a *yinzi* (breast cloth—a piece of cloth wrapped tightly over the breasts) day and night.[54] The First and Third Princesses found sleeping with a yinzi impossible because, as the Third Princess later commented, it caused such 'difficulty in breathing!'[55]

In spite of all the Burmese cooks that went back and forth, and all the Indian cooks that were hired, so nervous was the queen of British intentions that she took to cooking most of the family's meals herself, with the assistance of these cooks. The Third Princess mentioned in an interview years later that Queen Supayalat believed that the British had planted many of the Indian servants as spies, and worse, that an attempt could be made to poison the royal family. But it was on these Indian servants that the queen eventually had to rely. Very hurt by the behaviour of the Burmese that came to serve the family in India, and totally put off by the insolence shown by the daughters of the Hanlingyi Myosar (who arrived in Ratnagiri in 1896[56]), the queen decided that she no longer wanted any staff from Burma. Most of their maids thereafter were Indians—'We had to look in the mirror to see ourselves if we wished to see a Burmese!' says the Third Princess.[57] As 'it was the court habit that the children were looked after by nannies, ayahs, and not parents', the Indian ayahs were the ones who took care of the everyday needs of the four princesses.[58] (Konbaung queens always handed over their babies to wet nurses and maids. They could neither afford to lose their figures nor spend too much time with their offspring, as competition was fierce and their positions always precarious.[59])

It was Queen Supayagalae who helped bring up the girls, and the princesses 'were more close to their aunt than to their mother. Because it was under the aunt's control that the daughters grew up. Poor thing, she had no children, only had these four little nieces to look after.'[60] Queen Supayagalae at some stage 'adopted' Mary Dinshaw or D'Anjou, a Eurasian girl whose father was a Frenchman and mother a Burmese; this girl though close to the family was never considered a member. She went on to become the family's housekeeper.[61]

Old palace customs were observed to the extent possible. Servants not wearing shoes in their home continued to be important to the queen.[62] One of her grandchildren says that as per tradition the queen continued to treat the king very deferentially: 'My grandmother held King Thibaw in very high esteem. She was very respectful. We have heard she has a strong character, and King Thibaw was very pious, naturally she can control Thibaw, but she was so careful.' Queen Supalayat, however, confided in her daughters that her husband 'didn't have a strong character. He was too pious . . . he shouldn't have been king, but should have continued as a monk.'[63] The king, who his daughters saw as 'a shy quiet person',[64] rather ingenuously indicated to a collector, with whom he had established a rather cordial relationship, that 'worries of a kingdom were not to his taste'. On another occasion, perhaps recalling the threat of violence so omnipresent in the lives of Konbaung kings, he is purported to have blurted out that in some ways he should consider it a 'blessing' that he was removed from Burma, otherwise he may not have been still alive![65]

A formal relationship existed between the royal couple and the rest of the household including their daughters: 'Being king and queen their word was law; they order, finish, then others have to do the job . . .' The princesses therefore could not argue, contradict, or even freely discuss any issue with their parents. The king, however, occasionally relaxed his guard. On the princesses' birthdays, he and his four daughters would gather around a table and play. Not surprisingly, one of these games centred on money, on coins. This game would also make use of the numerous flies flitting around ('in those days there were so many flies. Because their residence was very close to a plague area'): each person sat behind a small pile of coins, and whoever's pile a fly visited was the winner and could claim everybody else's piles! The Third Princess used to cheat, she later confessed. She would sweeten her coins with a touch of jaggery. Queen Supayalat never joined them in any such frivolous activity, says one of the Fourth Princess's sons, adding—'they were very afraid of the queen, she wouldn't stand any nonsense from them. And if they had to go and see her they had to sheiko and, in this position, approach her.'[66]

Years later when talking about herself and her sisters, the Third Princess described the Fourth Princess as a quiet and well-behaved child, and the most intelligent and motivated of the four, and someone her father leaned on. The First Princess was a 'perfect little lady, gentle and kind and generous'. The Second Princess was portrayed as rather heavily built, and someone who loved children. She was also the queen's least favourite child, and was sadly often the target of her anger. The queen believed that since she had been carrying the Second Princess when the king had had his affair with Mi Khingyi, this child brought her ill luck. The Third Princess herself was a mischievous tomboy and the queen's favourite child. [67]

Being her favourite however did not save the Third Princess from being punished by her very strict mother. The queen had forbidden the princesses to wander around alone on the grounds as she considered such behaviour 'vulgar'. Servants were instructed to report, for a princely reward of a sovereign, any princess found flouting this rule. The Third Princess remembers how much she loved chasing butterflies in the garden (when she was around twelve), and how she was often caught. Sometimes a kind-hearted servant would let her go, but more often than not the servant would drag her to the queen for the reward. The Third Princess would apologize profusely and beg her mother for mercy. The queen, smiling dourly at her cowering daughter, would say, 'Ah! My daughter is a good girl, but it is these adventurous feet that took her', and proceed to mercilessly whip the soles of her offending feet. The princess's screams would bring the king rushing in and he would exclaim, 'Supaya, you will tire yourself—let me punish [her] for you!' He would then render a soft thump between his daughter's shoulder blades with his elbow. The Third Princess remembers her father tenderly nursing her and her sisters' wounds with ointment after particularly severe beatings.[68]

Time hung heavily on everyone's heads. One of King Thibaw's secretaries provides an interesting albeit cursory account of the king's daily schedule: he rose every morning at 8 o'clock, and on seeing him his bandsmen would strike up their morning performance. He breakfasted at 9 a.m. and lunched at 12 noon. Again the band played when the king had his tea at 5 p.m. He ate dinner at 9 p.m. and went to bed at midnight. It was in the afternoons that he met his visitors. Visitors were permitted to retain their footwear when calling on the king, and to sit on chairs, but the king always sat at a higher level than them.[69]

The family rarely went out. The planning for the numerous festivals that the family celebrated, the making of endless representations to the government for things big and small, the constant worry over his finances, and the overseeing of his home and family took up much of the king's time. What was left of it was spent on hobbies, says a granddaughter. She elaborates:

> He was a gold and silver smith, for he made silver filigree pagodas and ornaments. He carved figurines out of wood and was quite a good carpenter and handyman. Perhaps because of these hobbies he was kept busy and sane! Though he was called lazy and good for nothing by some Burmese writers for not having done any scholarly work for the benefit of Burma since he was a learned scholar who had passed the Tripitakas Exam (with honours), the highest in religious literature. But the poor man had no time to call his soul his own, and being a peaceful person had a hard time trying to keep his wives and family happy and harmonious.[70]

Some years into the exile, a collector of Ratnagiri opined:

> I think the ex-King is of a very kindly disposition, free from vice and very well behaved. He takes pleasure in little things and is quite happy. He has however one fault. He is absolutely incapable financially to make both ends meet. Money passes through his fingers like water,

and it is impossible for him to restrict his expenditure. His one hobby
is the spending of money.[71]

Queen Supayalat also tried to find ways to fill her day. Apart from all
the time she spent cooking, she prayed daily, and crocheted handmade
tablecloths and doilies too (unfortunately none of these remain with
the family today).[72] For news of Burma, she read the *Hanthawady Daily*
and *Myanma Alin*.[73] And, says one of her granddaughters, 'she would
often look over the sea . . . she misses her home . . . her power . . . her
rule . . . the voice she had over the whole Palace . . . and now to be a
captive. She was very very sad. My mother [the Fourth Princess] told
me that.'[74]

By the early 1900s Queen Supayalat's deep despondency overwhelmed
her. She fell ill, and medical treatment did nothing to improve her
health. After a point she refused to see the doctor anymore. She never
left the compound; in fact she stayed in bed most of the time, and
declined to meet anyone other than family. Unlike in the past, she now
took no interest at all in household affairs.[75] She also neglected her
personal grooming, paying no attention to 'even her ordinary toilet'.[76]
The dire lack of money, the total absence of power, the forced
alienation from her beloved homeland to a country that she could
never call her own, and the absence of any hope of reclamation of any
part of her past, was, it appears, just too much for her to bear. And the
once 'strong' queen visibly and completely crumbled, while the once
'weak' king valiantly attempted to hold it all together.

Then a truly heartbreaking misfortune took place that profoundly
impacted the already battered royal family. In the words of a Burmese
superintendent of police from Upper Burma (who got the information
many years later from a couple of Burmese returning from Ratnagiri):

An Indian Fakir with extremely cringing manners appeared before the
ex-King and performed or exhibited miracles transforming brass or
copper into gold, etc., presumably by hand changing tricks. The ex-
King readily believed him and started practicing Alchemy with this
Fakir. The ex-Queen Supayalat rightly suspecting the Fakir to be a
swindler ejected him against the wish of Thebaw. Thebaw trusted the
Fakir so much that he took no heed to Supayalat but retained the
services of the Fakir in spite of repeated protestations. The ex-Queen

began to despair and refused to take her meals. According to information the Fakir, under the pretext of giving her medicine, gave her a dose of Datura which made her speechless for a time and subsequently drove her to semi-insanity.[77]

Queen Supayalat's illness and depression lingered on for many, many years. In a letter written some years later the Fourth Princess indicated that the medicine 'so affected her brain that she used to try and kill herself. My father spent a great amount of money over her illness. For some years she never spoke to anyone . . . She cannot bear noise, the slamming of any door seems to upset her at once; all she asks for is quiet; just to live a quiet life . . .'[78]

By 1909 the king was at his wits' end, and accused Maung Po Gaung, his private secretary, of 'bewitching' Queen Supayalat. He told the police officer that he and the rest of his family were frightened of Maung Po Gaung because of his 'magical powers', and were keen that he be made to leave not just Ratnagiri, but the shores of India forever. At first the government was reluctant to permit his dismissal as he provided them with insider information on the royal family. However when the collector discovered that Maung Po Gaung was in cahoots with the servants and traders cheating the king, he immediately pressed for his quick deportation. In his place, King Thibaw asked for the husband of the Pinya Princess, Maung San Shwe, as he felt the couple would be suitable companions for himself and his family.[79] Perhaps the king thought that their familiar presence would help soothe Queen Supayalat. The queen had been very fond of the Pinya Princess whom she considered a close relative, and who had served her faithfully in the Golden Palace.[80] Maung San Shwe and his wife were sent for, and in 1910 Maung San Shwe reported to a relative in Mandalay:

> His Majesty is in robust health, but some blackish spots have appeared on the face. As regards Her Majesty, she is, as before, not in good health, but on account of medical treatment Her Majesty is now able to speak slowly and gently. Her Majesty's features are changed, because she has lost her teeth and her hair has become grey . . .[81]

As they were growing up, the princesses had silently and helplessly watched their tough mother sink into protracted ill health, depression and premature old age, and their good-natured father get increasingly embroiled in a mire of never-ending financial debt and anxiety. They had watched their family being systematically looted and taken advantage of—'There were all sorts of crooks and swindlers, faith-healers and magicians coming to the royal house . . . they came to cheat the family of the dethroned King as they had no knowledge of the outside world', said the Third Princess in an interview many years later.[82] While Queen Supayagalae lovingly looked after the princesses to the extent she could, she was not a strong, forceful or influential presence. The lack of guidance or discipline after Queen Supayalat's 'unavailability' from the early 1900s, combined with the princesses' increasing sense of boredom and pent-up frustration as they got older, led to events that would deeply affect the family, and would forever alter the dynamics within it.

12

THE PRINCESSES GROW UP

Two Celebrations, a Birth and
a Death

It was in December 1905 that King Thibaw officially broached the subject of his desire for a new home, his overwhelming need for one well reflected in the greater than usual supplicant tone of his letter to the governor of Bombay: 'I beg to offer my best respects to Your Excellency and I pray for your health and happiness. May every day, every month, every year, be more prosperous than the last. I am deeply gratified and delighted at the prospect of greeting Your Excellency at Ratnagiri and I offer you a most cordial welcome.' He went on to say that while he had had no complaints earlier, now that his daughters had grown up (they ranged in age from nineteen to twenty-six), he needed more space. He also indicated that as plague had been rampant for the past five years in the huts that had sprung up near his home, he had been very anxious and greatly inconvenienced. He asked for a

Above: Deposed King Thibaw arriving in Prome. Artist Melton Prior.
The Illustrated London News, 9 January 1886.
Below: A pwe being held at the Golden Palace, Mandalay, for Lady Dufferin. Artist Melton Prior.
The Illustrated London News, 17 April 1886.

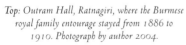

*Top: Outram Hall, Ratnagiri, where the Burmese
royal family entourage stayed from 1886 to
1910. Photograph by author 2004.*

*Right: The Royal Residence, Ratnagiri.
Photograph by author 2004.*

*Middle: The Darbar Hall in the Royal Residence.
Photograph by author 2004.*

*Bottom: The courtyard in the Royal Residence.
Photograph by author 2004.*

Below, left: The peacock emblem, that the queen insisted upon, on a pediment at the Royal Residence.
Right: The idol in King Thibaw's pagoda at Outram House; fresh flowers show that it is still worshipped.
Both photographs by author, left 2007 and right 2004.

The Third Princess in Ratnagiri in 1902.

Left: The Third Princess in Ratnagiri in 1893.

Below: A photograph of the Third and Fourth Princesses taken after their earboring ceremony in 1914 in Ratnagiri.

Top: The four daughters of King Thibaw, left to right: the Fourth, First, Third and Second Princesses.
Photograph taken after their earboring ceremony in 1914.

Opposite: King Thibaw's funeral in February 1917. Photographer M.V. Apte.

The Second Princess, perhaps at the time of her wedding in 1917.

larger home further away from town. He also asked for an increase in his monthly allowance.[1]

All those in frequent contact with the king—the police officer (Comber, with whom the king shared a friendly relationship), the collector, the civil surgeon—were very sympathetic to his request, and wrote detailed memos strongly recommending it, with the collector going to the extent of saying that 'the bare requirements of comfort, convenience and decency call for a larger and more suitable accommodation'. The present accommodation had been chosen twenty years earlier, when the princesses were very young, he argued, and now that they were young women, a reassessment was required. The civil surgeon added that apart from the living/dining rooms, the study, and the storeroom, the family basically had just two bedrooms and two bathrooms. The king and queen used one of these bedrooms as a day room; the junior queen and the four princesses used the other. At night one of these bedrooms served as the sleeping chamber of the entire family of seven members—only sixty square feet per person— leading to grossly inadequate fresh air.[2]

As no home suitable for the family was readily available in Ratnagiri, Mr Comber suggested that one be specially built on an isolated plateau. The king had requested for a many-roomed double storeyed house, and this is what Comber recommended. He also recommended that this building be set in a big compound with sufficient outhouses to accommodate the retinue of servants the king had accumulated over the years—130 to be precise, including his bandsmen and female attendants. Comber compassionately represented that since the king had always had a large retinue of people around him, this was what he was used to, and it would now be impossible to pare down the numbers. It was imperative to house as many of the servants as possible in the king's compound, the civil surgeon indicated, to prevent them ferrying plague and other diseases from town.[3]

The king's annual allowance also needed revision, felt the collector and police officer, as it had been fixed when the princesses were younger and their wants fewer. Comber described the princesses' present condition as appalling, indicating that 'they have nothing but a bare room to live in and they are unable to buy anything for want of funds'. Perhaps because they no longer had any decent clothes to wear, the princesses had stopped taking even an occasional ride in the horse carriages. (The king and the queens too could now only afford to dress very simply, he said.[4])

That the all-important earboring ceremony had not been performed for any of the princesses clearly demonstrated the family's financial difficulties and the inadequacy of their annual allowance, opined the collector. The king and queens constantly fretted about the ceremony, he indicated, which was usually held when a Burmese Buddhist girl was about thirteen years old (around puberty). All Burmese parents considered it their duty to have it for their daughters, and it was a significant source of shame if they did not.[5]

In view of the king's character and behavior over twenty years of exile, and the family's impecunious condition, the collector felt that there was strong justification for the government to substantially increase his annual allowance.[6] Based on these recommendations, in August 1906, the king's allowance was increased to Rs 100,000 a year broken up as follows:

Pension of Rs 5,000 a month	Rs 60,000
'Dress' allowance of Rs 125 a month to each princess	Rs 6,000
Festival allowance	Rs 15,500
To be credited to Reserve Fund	Rs 18,500
Total per annum	Rs 100,000

The festival allowance was to be disbursed in instalments, as required. The Reserve Fund was to be used for various one-off expenses of the family, and would have to be approved in each instance by the government.[7]

The government also agreed to the king's request of a new, much more commodious home, and eventually sanctioned Rs 125,711 for this purpose. (This amount, contrary to the opinion held by some royal descendants, was at no stage debited to the Reserve Fund.[8]) The government also gave the king a special grant of Rs 10,000 to enable him to clear a portion of his debt, and made him undertake that he would not take any further loans but would apply to the government for any additional funding required (which, if sanctioned, would be debited to the Reserve Fund).[9] From this point in time, the king and his family were able to live much better, with some of the comforts previously denied. For this the king felt deeply grateful, and repeatedly expressed his appreciation to the collector. The collector felt that the king was 'content for the first time in twenty years'.[10] But sadly this contentment would not last long. The king, incapable of any financial prudence, increased his expenses disproportionately, and soon began to borrow again in the market behind the government's back.

Although the king had never personally brought up with the government the question of the marriage of his daughters, in 1906 the government raised the matter.[11] Numerous interdepartmental letters were exchanged between the governments in India and Burma, and most regrettably political considerations totally eclipsed humanitarian ones. In early 1907, the government in Burma callously opined that the best course of action would be to keep the princesses unmarried. Their rationale for this recommendation was that the princesses' 'proximity to the throne of the late dynasty and their father's misfortunes would render them of more than ordinary interest'. It therefore felt that it would be inadvisable

> to allow them to marry and live in Burma. Even if they married commoners, their husbands might be unduly elevated by so high an alliance and be led into disloyal acts ... Politically, there can be no doubt that the course least likely to be productive of embarrassment would be to allow them to remain unmarried. It is not only the ladies themselves and their husbands but their prospective descendants also that have to be considered ...[12]

The government in Burma went on to say that *if* the government in India saw it *obligatory* to get the princesses married, then marriage with a Burmese prince would require the princess and her husband to reside outside Burma; marriage with a Burmese commoner would need prior approval of the prospective bridegroom by the lieutenant governor of Burma, and then residence in Burma may be permitted; marriage into the religiously similar royal families of Siam or Ceylon would be the least complicated option for the government.[13] But, best of all, it said, would be not to bring up the question of the princesses' marriage at all.[14] The government in Burma hoped that the king would continue to consider the matter too personal and delicate to raise himself.

But Comber, being the man on the spot, and being very sympathetic to the plight of the young ladies, *did* bring up the subject with the king. Both he and the collector were taken aback by the king's response. The king indicated that the earboring ceremony was a necessary forerunner to the princesses' marriage; that he would not even consider marrying his daughters to anyone outside the Burmese royal family; that even within the Burmese royal family most princes were not good enough for his daughters because Queen Supayalat and he were both of pure royal descent, whereas most of the surviving princes' mothers were of very humble birth (most of the pure blooded ones had been killed, it will be recalled, in the 1879 palace massacre); and that if suitable husbands could not be found, he would prefer his daughters to remain unmarried. On this subject, he was uncompromising. And he was in no hurry to look for potential husbands. He indicated that only once his new house was ready, would he have the earboring ceremony (together with a housewarming 'festival'). As his house would not be ready for another 2–3 years, he indicated that there was no choice but for his daughters to wait to see if matrimony was what the future held for them—the king himself being of the opinion that the possibility of any of them marrying being, unfortunately, very unlikely.[15]

None of the princesses had ever left Ratnagiri, and yet Ratnagiri was not a town any of them either understood or knew. Their ancestry, the importance of which was often and emphatically stressed by their parents, had entitled them to no benefits or privileges but had rather deprived them of all freedom and even basic comforts. As girls they had had each other to play with, but now as young women, there was nothing other than the celebration of festivals to take away from the monotony and frustration of their day-to-day existence. The older princesses did ask their father (due to the strict protocol followed in the family, probably only when the subject could be politely raised) when he planned on getting them married or were they to live like this forever?[16] They were acutely aware of their father's stringent requirements for suitable bridegrooms, and if they despaired at the impossibility of his conditions being met, their upbringing prevented them from openly discussing it.

By now the older princesses desired male companionship, and, needless to say, they were not spoilt for choice. Perhaps when younger, they had regarded their staff as nothing more than people there to do their bidding, and of a standing much lower than their own. They had certainly watched and noticed the servility with which all employees behaved in their parent's presence. But by now this had changed. Comber had earlier intercepted a letter from the First Princess making plans to meet a young Burmese man under a tree in the compound at midnight. His peon, employed as well by the family, had also been found trying to get the attention of the princesses. The collector wrote to the government that there had been similar incidents in the past, that

> cooped up as they are with nothing to do, it is only natural they should intrigue. Theebaw himself lives in mortal dread of a scandal. I believe the Government of India undertook to dower and marry them off suitably when the time should come, and it has certainly come now. The suggestion of the Burma Government that the question should not be touched means ruining the girls' lives.[17]

Sadly, Comber's warning was not only a bit late, but was also lost both on his superiors and on the obdurate king.

What Comber, and for that matter the king and the queens, had been unaware of was that by early 1906 the First Princess had fallen in love with Gopal Bhaurao Sawant, a strapping, young, good-looking Maratha, who worked as a gatekeeper at the family's residence. The First Princess had been put in charge of doling out the daily cash for the purchase of food for the family's dogs, and Gopal's duties included buying their food. Every morning he visited her to collect money for this purpose. It is said that the physical attraction was strong, meaningful glances were exchanged, and although the sequence of events can at best be conjectured, the First Princess began to steal away at night to meet Gopal in his quarters, located near the entrance of the compound. While she took no family member into confidence, it is believed her sisters were aware of the affair, but felt completely unable to share this dark secret with their parents or aunt.[18]

The First Princess's stolen trysts with Gopal resulted in the birth of a baby girl (later named Tu Tu) on 26 November 1906. Descendants of the family assert that the king and the queen were unaware of her pregnancy until she went into labor. And U Than Swe tries to explain this assertion: 'the parents do not know about it . . . their dress—their skirt is tightly bound and on top a loose jacket. And in (Burma) a young girl, the first pregnancy is not so visible. So it *is* possible.'[19] It is not known when and how the First Princess confessed to her shocked and horrified parents that the father of the baby was Gopal, or whether one of her sisters or someone else informed them. Not only was Gopal a foreigner (or as foreigners were derogatorily called, a kala), and a man of a different religion, but he was also a lowly employee. On making inquiries the family must have been additionally dismayed to discover that he was also a newly married man. Certainly he did not even remotely meet any of the king's stringent requirements.

Queen Supayalat, still unwell and depressed, was almost destroyed by the birth of a half-caste granddaughter. The government noted in a memo (in December 1906) that Queen Supayalat 'seems to be moping to death; she is not seen, never leaves her room . . .'[20] The family now tried its best to close ranks and conceal this mother of all scandals from the government that so closely scrutinized its every move. Amazingly, in spite of informers planted in the compound, it took some time for the incident to surface and to come to the government's attention.[21]

It was their deep faith, their religion, which enabled the king and queen to cope (the king much quicker than the queen). Says someone married into the extended Burmese royal family (based on what some family members who visited Ratnagiri in 1914 told their descendants): the king and queen were overwhelmed with 'intense grief that the bright future of their eldest daughter had been shattered to pieces by this servant . . .' While neither the king nor the queen ever forgave or accepted Gopal, and while the tragedy continued to 'wring their hearts', they 'forbore it in accordance with the [Buddhist] Mangala Sutta'.[22]

Past reactions and actions of the king and queen make some of what is said to have followed seem totally incomprehensible and out of character. But as the exile did distort and change their personalities, their initial reaction to this calamity was perhaps informed by the change. Perhaps it was also a result of the prevailing Burmese custom that, whether they liked it or not, the First Princess and Gopal were deemed married. Whatever the reason(s), Gopal was *not* sacked on the spot. Certainly (since January 1896) the king had the authority to fire whomsoever he wanted, and could have done so without involving the government. In fact, according to Maung San Shwe's (the king's secretary for about three years up to late 1912) version of events (retold by U Than Swe) 'after their affair, after their marriage', the First Princess would sometimes go spend the night at the gatehouse with Gopal. Gopal, however, was never permitted to come into the family's home.[23] During the day, the little girl offered Queen Supayalat some distraction and entertainment. Tu Tu, says one of the queen's grandsons, would spend her days 'sitting on her grandmother's chest and pulling her grandmother's hair'. Queen Supayalat would tell Tu Tu stories, and was 'a very good grandmother to Tu Tu'.[24] But all this, unfortunately, was to change very dramatically in a few years.

The king, soon after Tu Tu's birth, immersed himself in the planning of the family's proposed new home, and took deep interest and considerable pleasure in its construction. He drove out, in early December 1906, to see the selected site, which was located on a breezy plateau above Ratnagiri. The plot commanded a magnificent view of the sea (to the west) and the Ratnagiri creek (to the south), and was at a distance of about a mile and a half from the centre of town. The king expressed his satisfaction and work commenced after government sanction in June 1907.[25]

Although the family's proposed residence in Ratnagiri was of course not comparable to the Golden Palace in Mandalay, there is no doubt that the government was generous. The new two-storeyed home was to be in a twenty-seven-acre compound. The main building was to comprise sixteen spacious rooms, covering 25,000 square feet in carpet area. Sixty servants' quarters; stables and garages to accommodate six horses, three carriages, and one car (for a car to be soon bought); two kitchens and two storerooms connected to the main building by a covered path; a police guardroom; and two wells for water were all to be constructed on the property, which was to be surrounded by a stone compound wall. Various building materials were considered, and in the end the local laterite stone and lime mortar was settled on for the main building. The design (with considerable inputs from the king) was to be an amalgamation of styles, both western and eastern. Quantities of Burmese teakwood were to be used for beams, ceilings, staircases, shutters, railings, etc. The roof was to be constructed of Mangalore tiles, and the flooring was to be of marble and minton tiles in the main halls, and of concrete in the rest of the house.[26] The building was to face the sea in the west. This is perfectly logical until one recalls that the Golden Palace had faced the opposite direction, east, as the east was supposedly the 'most honorable point of the compass'.[27] Details such as this were important to the king, and this deviation must have given him much pause for thought.

The king had specified the number of rooms he wanted and the dimensions of each room. Although everything was eventually not exactly as the king had asked for, it appears that he was involved in every step of the revision. The ground floor was to comprise a drawing room; two dining rooms—one for the king and queen, the other for the junior queen and the princesses; an office room for the king; a spare room; and at the rear of the building separated by a courtyard, three sitting rooms, one for the junior queen, one for the older two princesses, and one for the younger two princesses. (These rooms were very large and were later partitioned so each of the princesses could have her own 'apartment'.) The front portion of the first floor was to contain a large, double-storeyed imposing reception room called the Darbar Hall, and to have the living quarters of the king and queen. Each of them was to have their own bedroom and sitting room with an attached bathroom and dressing room. At the rear of the building, and connected by two passages were to be three bedrooms, the central largest one for the junior queen, and two of equal size to be shared by the princesses (these again appear to have been partitioned to create separate spaces for each of the princesses). The house was to have eight bathrooms in all, four on each floor. There was to be a porch at the front of the house, with a terrace above the porch. A verandah was to encircle the house on both floors.[28] (See Appendix III for the floor plans.)

In 1908, on the occasion of the governor of Bombay's visit to Ratnagiri, Rs 10,000 was granted to King Thibaw from the Reserve Fund for the purchase of a two-cylinder 10/12 H.P. De Dion car.[29] Mr Parulekar (a Ratnagiri resident, whose grandfather was an advocate that King Thibaw sometimes consulted) tells a story that demonstrates how cocooned Ratnagiri was from changes taking place in other parts of the world: 'King Thibaw's car was the first in the district. People used to prostrate themselves before it and put grass in front of it, because they thought it had to eat, that it had to be some kind of a newfangled bullock cart or horse carriage!' It appears that the increased allowance and the new car encouraged the king and the queens to finally venture out again, at least very occasionally—including the not-so-well Queen Supayalat—for Parulekar mentions that the royal couple attended his grandparent's housewarming ceremony in 1908 and gifted them an emerald ring, a gold, jewel-encrusted pillbox and two small silver peacocks, items his family still has and cherishes.[30] The princesses also took fairly frequent evening drives in the car.[31]

In 1909 the king requested the government to sanction him Rs 5,000 from his Reserve Fund to enable him to build a summer house for the queens and the princesses in the compound of his new house (modelled perhaps after the Summer Pavilion in the Southern gardens of the Golden Palace, where he had surrendered to General Prendergast).[32] This request was granted; the king proceeded to have built a four-room, four-bathroom structure, with a large verandah, for the pleasure of the ladies.[33]

The main house, the Royal Residence (the name by which the royal descendants in Burma call it), was completed in 1910, and new furniture, carpets, lamps, etc. were ordered for a cost of approximately Rs 19,000, which was debited to the Reserve Fund.[34] Many years later the queen said in an interview that their new home was a 'grand mansion' and the furniture and carpets in it were 'excellent'.[35] The princesses also found the house to their liking, with the Third Princess years later remembering the furniture and fittings in glowing terms: the 'heavy brocaded chairs and sofas . . . great shining brass four-poster beds with springs, and fat flowered china basins and jugs and chamber pots . . . long velvet and damask curtains and great crystal chandeliers . . .'[36] Certainly they all now had a lot more space, and much more privacy.

When the family went to see the property just before moving in, Queen Supayalat noticed that an emblem on the terrace pediment was of British design, and strongly objected to this. The king brushed the matter aside, saying that it was unimportant, but the queen insisted that it be changed. It was a dancing peacock—the insignia of the Burmese royal family—that she wanted.[37] After this was done, the family occupied the Royal Residence on 13 November 1910.[38] A housewarming ceremony was held around the same time.[39] Preparations for the housewarming ceremony had been elaborate—the king had ordered from Mandalay, among other things, royal court dresses, three kinds of court cushions, and military short and long coats.[40] The whole family was caught up in the excitement and the princesses, too, were given specially prepared silk clothing from Mandalay to wear. The king had been permitted to invite Burmese priests and musicians (including the well-known musician, Ywasargyi Sein Beida, who had put together a troupe of twenty comprising some of the best dancers, comedians, singers, and a harpist[41]). The government of Burma approved each person individually before permitting him/her to go.[42] Not only was the ceremony lavish, but the family also marked the occasion with handouts to the poor in Ratnagiri.[43]

Early in the exile the king had written to Buddhist high priests (sayadaw) in Mandalay lamenting: '[A]mongst all my trials the sorrow of not being able to behold you my teachers is the greatest.'[44] Now, after a hiatus of almost twenty-five years, as he finally beheld the five permitted sayadaws at his housewarming ceremony, the king bowed low before them, and was so overwhelmed that tears rolled down his cheeks. The monks also choked with emotion and nobody could utter a word for a while. Finally the most senior monk, Bemei Sayadawgyi, 'retold the story of King Vissandara so as to encourage the King and to dissipate his sorrow and despair. The Sayadawgyi then urged King Thibaw to take refuge in Dhamma, the teachings of Lord Buddha, to nurture a spirit of goodwill and to lead a peaceful and tranquill life.'[45] The princesses too had the opportunity to make their obeisance to the visiting monks, and were apparently taken aback by the obvious depth of feeling shown by the monks and by other Burmese visitors for their parents.[46]

All through the happiness of the move and the housewarming ceremony, there was an undercurrent of tension from a front that had been calm for many years. After the departure of police officer Albon in May 1894, King Thibaw got along fairly well with almost all the officers who followed. Over the years the work of the officer in charge got lighter and lighter, as most officers stuck to the government's unofficial directive of being a friend, philosopher and guide to the king. In fact, King Thibaw is said to have indicated to the collector that Comber, his officer for almost seven years until mid-1910, was 'the greatest friend [he] had'.[47] Then along came Mr Inmam. A blustering man with no tact at all, he took his job title literally and treated the king as a prisoner who needed constant watching.[48] He told the king that he was required to take permission every time he wished to venture out (the king, by now, was required to *inform* the officer, not get his permission). The king, very sensitive to anything he perceived as a slight, was highly offended. 'Am I a criminal prisoner?' he indignantly asked of the collector. Inmam also began doing something that had not been done for many, many years. He regularly and overtly inspected the police guard to check that rifles were clean and bullets were readily on hand. This highly alarmed the king. He immediately enquired of the collector *whom* the police planned to fire upon. Tension between the king and Inmam escalated. The collector realized that Inmam was unfit for the job, pulled him up, and in late 1910, after having been in Ratnagiri for only a few months, Inmam submitted his resignation.[49]

As the collector (by now a Mr Ghosal, with whom the king had a strong rapport) was also to leave Ratnagiri at the end of 1910, he advised the government that the objective of all future supervision of the king should be with the view of controlling his debt. He had been horrified to discover that the king was heavily in debt once again—to the tune of Rs 60,700—and that he was paying interest alone of Rs 3,260 a month. Since the king's monthly allowance was at present Rs 5,500 a month, this did not leave much margin for other expenses. He was therefore compelled to borrow even more to settle his monthly bills.[50]

When Ghosal pointed out to the king that he could take shelter behind the Ex-King Thebaw's Act, 1895 (which made him legally incapable of incurring debt, and therefore not legally obligated to repay any loans), the king denied having any debt, and then went on to provide a quixotic explanation of why he felt obliged not to renege on commitments made to even those who cheated him with an unfairly high interest rate. He explained 'that *supposing* he had borrowed money and agreed to pay a certain interest it will be against his *kingly dignity* to refuse to pay that interest or capital, taking shelter behind the Act'. The collector realized that he would not be able to influence the king in this matter, and that the king would probably always struggle with debt. Obligated to show the government's displeasure, and to stem the king's borrowing, he forbade entry into the compound to all of Ratnagiri's larger moneylenders. He, however, was fully aware that the king would soon devise ways to bypass this obstacle. [51]

The government had advanced Rs 7,000 from the Reserve Fund to the king for the housewarming ceremony, but, as usual, the actual expenses exceeded the amount sanctioned. As a result, the king applied for an urgent additional sanction, which was granted.[52] Then again a few months later the king asked for Rs 5,000. His sister had passed away in Mandalay, and he wanted to contribute to her funeral expenses. He pleaded, 'She is my only full sister . . . I cannot see and I cannot go. I am much grieved . . .'[53] (See Appendix II.) By now the Reserve Fund had dipped rather low, and the government, foreseeing other expenses, was reluctant to sanction this amount.[54] In the end it was the viceroy who personally intervened to allow it.[55] Then, in September 1911, the king wanted twenty people (priests and musicians) brought over for the consecration of a shrine he had had built in the compound.[56] He also wanted money to complete the shrine, and to illuminate and decorate his compound during the ceremony. The new officer in charge (Mr Roussac) was most sympathetic. He had watched the building of the shrine with some fascination (detailing in a memo 'the small gilted dome . . . a brass umbrella known as "Hti" . . . a large and small bell with clappers . . .') and seemed to have shared some of the king's enthusiasm for it. He recommended sanction of Rs 3,000 from the Reserve Fund.[57] As can be seen, the king's demands on the Reserve

Fund were fast and furious, and he deeply resented the difficulty in drawing money—which he saw as his right—from it.

In January 1911 the governor of Bombay visited King Thibaw[58] in his new residence. The king graciously entertained him—Ywasargyi Sein Beida and his troupe were still in Ratnagiri, and the governor and his wife are said to have greatly enjoyed the show put on by them.[59] The king handed over to the governor a memorial for the consideration of the viceroy. While the king voiced his displeasure in this memorial at the government's control over his Reserve Fund and the inadequacy of his allowance, perhaps as significantly he requested that both he and the police officer be addressed differently. Of all the memorials submitted by King Thibaw over the years, in some ways this was the most heart-wrenching. Perhaps the housewarming ceremony had served to vividly refresh dormant memories, and he ached again for tributes of the past. He wrote:

> Once I had the same footing as the King of Siam, the Emperor of China, the Emperor of Japan and other Kings. It seems to me rather inconsistent to address such a King as His Highness even if he be an ex-King. I shall be very glad if I am allowed to keep my titles and honours, namely, His Majesty, and to change the address of 'Officer in charge of His Highness the ex-King Thibaw' to 'Political Officer to His Majesty'. I am not saying these with a view to glorify myself, for I am beyond these. Personally any form of address will be acceptable to me, I do not seek for shadow when I know I have lost the substance. But I feel it very much when they address me as His Highness, as it reminds me of my fall . . .[60]

Certainly the king now felt, with renewed vigour, as he himself later put it, 'the pang of being precipitated into extreme littleness from the most exalted and commanding' position that he once held. Some months after he had penned his memorial to the viceroy, he heard that King George V was to visit India for his coronation as Emperor of India. King Thibaw was very keen to meet King George V personally. Perhaps he hoped that a reigning king would empathize with a former king, and would intervene to substantially improve his position. Realizing the unlikelihood of being permitted to leave Ratnagiri, King Thibaw eventually made his appeal (asking for exactly the same things as he had just asked the viceroy) through a memorial.[61]

King George V was not shown King Thibaw's memorial until he was back in England. His office replied on his behalf that His Majesty concurred with the viceroy of India's decision: a higher allowance was not warranted, but some concession could be permitted regarding King Thibaw's request for form of address. In official correspondence the present title was to be retained, but in the more frequent local correspondence between the collector or police officer and the king, he could be called 'His Majesty the ex-King'. The officer in charge of the king could henceforth be styled 'Political Officer to the ex-King'.[62]

Right after the housewarming ceremony, the government periodically brought up the question of the princesses' marriages. But as the lieutenant governor of Burma was still reluctant (in 1911) to let the princesses return to Burma[63] as there were changes in both the collector and political officer in charge of the king and as, most importantly, the king was himself silent on the subject,[64] the matter was not pursued. The subject of the earboring ceremony, the necessary precursor to their weddings, was only occasionally and desultorily raised. Then a tragedy occurred that spurred the government into action.

On 28 June 1912 the junior queen, Queen Supayagalae, suddenly died of gastric tetany after just twelve hours of illness. The shocked and bereaved king requested that her mortal remains be sent back to Mandalay for internment. But the lieutenant governor of Burma turned down this request on the grounds that although Queen Supayagalae was of no political importance, it would set a precedent. He definitely did not want King Thibaw or Queen Supayalat's mortal remains sent to Burma after their deaths, for he felt that this would cause 'great excitement' in the country, and could lead to trouble.[65] She would have to be entombed in Ratnagiri, it was spelt out. Having no choice in the matter, the king arranged to have Queen Supayagalae's embalmed body[66] placed in a coffin and entombed within the compound.[67]

The Second Princess said, many years later, that the entire family was in shock and distress, not only at Queen Supayagalae's sudden death, but also at the manner in which it had happened. She indicated that she herself had always loved her 'small mother' more; that King

Thibaw (who over the years had gotten increasing dependent on Queen Supayagalae) was devastated, distracted, and for a long while unable to focus on anything; that even Queen Supayalat (who had never shown her younger sister any affection) was so disturbed that for months she endlessly and restlessly paced up and down on the front verandah.[68] The Third Princess's daughter says that 'a medicine man' gave Queen Supayagalae (who was menopausing) 'some medicine supposed to be iron tonic which poisoned the poor lady and I believe she died a horrible death by having terrible convulsions . . .'[69]

The government was also perturbed by Queen Supayagalae's death, and felt that the princesses' marriages now had to be urgently pushed. The collector explained: 'The late queen seems to have been the one capable and responsible person in Theebaw's household. The elder queen is apparently verging on imbecility; the King himself is an amiable old spendthrift, who does nothing but potter about his palace . . . Then there are the princesses. What is to become of them, living on here in Ratnagiri?'[70]

The government in India wrote off to the government in Burma mentioning the altered state of affairs and urgently requesting their help in locating appropriate husbands for the princesses. It also asked that objection to the princesses returning to Burma to settle down be relaxed. By December 1912, the government in Burma wrote back with a list of fourteen male members of the Burmese royal family who were unmarried and over twenty years of age, but it did caution that none of the listed people were of pure royal descent. It said that as far as it knew all princes of pure royal blood were already married. It also conceded that if suitable husbands were found for the princesses in Burma, they were free to return.[71]

By February 1913 this list had been forwarded to Ratnagiri, and by March 1913 King Thibaw, who pondered long and hard over it, replied that only no. 12, a Maung Pe Gyi, was eligible for one of his daughters' hands. (Maung Pe Gyi was a grandson of Prince Kanaung, and both his parents were of royal descent.[72]). The king also reiterated that his daughters could not marry until the earboring ceremony had taken place.[73] As the king's crippling debt had rendered him completely at the government's mercy to finance every aspect of this ceremony, for over a year after his housewarming ceremony he seems to have awaited replies to his two memorials (to the viceroy and to King George V), perhaps hoping a favourable reply would enable him to hold a more befitting ceremony for his daughters. A more practical father would certainly have been more influenced by his daughters' ages, than by the type of ceremony appropriate for them, but King Thibaw, completely frozen in a now irrelevant time-frame, was unyielding.

Estimates of the cost for the princesses' earboring ceremony varied between Rs 15,000 and Rs 455,488. Hluttaw records showed that just before the annexation Rs 100,000 was usually spent on the earboring ceremony of a princess. The king and the government now haggled over how much should be sanctioned, their views vastly divided on the matter. After many months of discussion, in August 1913 the government was able to pressurize the king (who was by now himself getting increasingly anxious on the subject) into agreeing to go ahead with the ceremony based on the promise that it would give him as generous an allowance as possible (a figure of Rs 30,000 for a common ceremony for all four princesses had been decided upon, but this was not revealed to the king).[74]

Preparations for the ceremony, which was to be held on the auspicious date of 5 March 1914, now began in earnest. The king made detailed enquiries in Mandalay on palace customs in respect of the ceremony. He made arrangements for elaborate pwes to be staged, and for appropriate gifts to be distributed to the poor in Ratnagiri. He planned for the erection of temporary buildings and pathways, the lighting arrangements, the printing of cards, etc. In planning of festivals the king truly excelled, in budgeting and economizing he did not. A couple of months before the ceremony, money fell short and a further Rs 10,000 was sanctioned (the entire cost of the ceremony was to be debited to the Reserve Fund). What the king borrowed privately to tweak the ceremony into the appropriately lavish is unknown. Eighty-two people including priests, guests (including the Chun Taung Princess and a junior ex-minister, the Wet-masoot Wundauk, both of whom had been acting on behalf of the king in Mandalay), musicians and actors, left Burma for Ratnagiri in the third week of February 1914.[75]

On the first and third day of this important ceremony (called the *natwin mingala*), the princesses' hair was ceremonially washed in a structure specially erected in the compound for the purpose. The main ceremony was held in the impressive Darbar Hall of the Royal Residence. Chairs had been set up on one side for European guests, whereas Burmese guests sat, as per custom, on little mats on the carpet. Royal golden umbrellas had been strategically positioned and a stage had been erected where the actual ceremony would take place. Everyone was dressed in elaborate formal attire, the Burmese observing the etiquette of the past in the clothes and jewellery that they wore for the occasion.[76] The four princesses wore special headdresses (*sipon*) and ceremonial robes—adorned with gold, rubies and emeralds—that the Wet-masoot Wundauk had had made for them in Mandalay. Both *ponnas* (Indian Brahmin priests) and *pongyis* (Burmese Buddhist priests) were present to officiate at the ceremony and to bless the princesses.[77] At a time deemed auspicious, the princesses' ears were pierced with a pure gold needle.[78]

Once the ceremony was over, a photograph of the princesses was taken (the only photograph in existence today of the four sisters together), and the princesses were taken for a formal ride around Ratnagiri in horse carriages, royal umbrellas held high over their heads, to enable the townspeople to offer them their good wishes, garlands and gifts.[79]

Visitors from Burma had also come with generous gifts, and the felicitation, revelry, and feasting continued over many days. Burmese musicians and actors performed for the guests, as did bandsmen from Goa. Just like the housewarming ceremony had opened a floodgate of memories for the king and queen, so must have this ceremony, but this perhaps more so because present now were royal relatives. For the princesses the experience must have been a spectacular and moving one. The Third Princess many years later told her daughter that it had been 'thrilling' to see Burmese ladies of the court 'so dainty and charming and soft-spoken—relics of the old days'.[80] The ceremony must have also served to sharply highlight a life that the princesses had repeatedly been told was their birthright, but which they must have realized could never be theirs.

13

THE FRUSTRATIONS AND
THE SQUABBLES

Even after almost thirty years of exile, life in the Royal Residence continued to have trappings of the family's royal past. The band played in the morning when the king got up, and whenever the king and queen sat down to eat. A butler supervised an army of servants during each meal. The king and the queen ate together seated on a raised dais on which velvet mats were placed around a circular table about five feet in diameter and about one foot high. The princesses dined alone in their own rooms. They sat Western-style on a chair at a table, with their ayahs waiting on them. The kitchens were staffed with three cooks—English, Goan and Burmese—and although each of the princesses cooked herself whatever special dish she wished to eat, at meal times trays of food were sent up to their rooms from the kitchens.[1]

While all the princesses (in the words of the Third Princess's daughter) 'excelled in all womanly arts—cooking, sewing and in handicrafts like paper flower making ... knitting, crocheting etc.',[2] the only princess to continue her education and to learn English was the Fourth Princess. An intelligent and driven young lady, it was solely on her own initiative that she did so. Perhaps the value many attached to the language was first brought forcefully to her attention when the Maharaj Kumar of Sikkim had refused, in early 1911, to consider any of King Thibaw's daughters in matrimony because they did not know English.[3] Sometime in 1913, the Fourth Princess acquired an English lady companion, a Mrs Vickery, who not only helped her learn the language, but also became her faithful ally.[4] By 1915, the Fourth Princess was able to speak, read and write English, and was independently penning letters to the government.[5] In 1915, with Mrs Vickery's help, the princess hired a second junior companion, a Miss McDiarmid. But this new employee lasted only a few weeks because, among her other failings, she also had had the temerity to sit on the same bench as the Fourth Princess.[6] All the princesses were conscious of their ancestry, the Fourth Princess much more so than her sisters.

King Thibaw represented to the government, in June 1916, that he wished to pay an additional Rs 75 per month from his Reserve Fund to the Fourth Princess (she, like the other princesses, received a dress allowance of Rs 125 per month). She was the only daughter for whom he made this request and he justified it by saying that it was she who ran his house, met with the wives of visiting officials, best looked after the comfort of her parents, and that she, unlike the others, had educated herself. The collector endorsed the king's request and it was immediately sanctioned.[7] With this sanction came official recognition of what had unofficially been the Fourth Princess's elevated status in the house for some time now.

The Fourth Princess's strong sense of filial responsibility had made her shoulder household responsibilities from the age of seven, say her children.[8] While according to archival material it was supposedly Queen Supayagalae who had run the family home until her death in 1912, the government was never fully informed as to what exactly went on within the four walls of the Royal Residence. The Fourth Princess probably helped her aunt out from a fairly young age, played an ever-increasing role over the years, and completely took over after her death. The king was completely dependent on her to run his large, unwieldy home (with a staff strength that ranged at various times between 150 and 200[9]). Therefore it was not at all surprising that the Fourth Princess exercised great influence over him,[10] or that the authority she had been granted made her somewhat peremptory in her dealings with those around her, including with her sisters.

In 1912 the Fourth Princess had helped unearth an affair between the Second Princess and a nephew of the king's private secretary Maung San Shwe, and the nephew had been immediately packed off to Burma.[11] It had been around this time that ill will between these two sisters had germinated, and had soon become deep-rooted. Before long, the king's attitude towards the Second Princess echoed those of the Fourth Princess (the Second Princess already was, it may be recalled, Queen Supayalat's least favourite child). Things weren't easy for the First Princess either,[12] although it is impossible to pinpoint at what stage prejudices resurfaced and attitudes changed. Tu Tu's birth in 1906 had to have altered the First Princess's standing in this deeply traditional, status-conscious family. It appears for some years the shame was buried and both she and her daughter were more than tolerated. Perhaps it was when visitors from Burma stayed with the family during the housewarming and the earboring ceremonies that latent biases were awoken and reinforced. While this will never be known for sure, it is known that in the years following the ceremonies, tension ran high in the Royal Residence. Alliances were formed. The two older princesses sympathized with each other; the Fourth Princess took the fragile Third Princess (who was of a very nervous disposition and prone to fits[13]) under her wing, and ruled the roost.[14]

Although authoritarian, the Fourth Princess was not without charm. It appears that she, like her mother, was blessed with grace and a certain magnetism. She was able to forge friendships with some of the visitors who came to call on the king. She corresponded with, among others, the Ferreres (Mr Ferrer had spent some time in Ratnagiri as the district judge), the Palmers, and the Smarts after they left Ratnagiri, and these couples warmly invited her to vacation with them (subject of course to government permission, which was never granted).[15] And then there was a Mark Tennant of the Indian Custom

Service who fell in love with the 'pretty', 'dainty', 'engaging', 'disarmingly outspoken' Fourth Princess. He felt she would be 'a warm-hearted companion', and he dreamt of whisking her away from her claustrophobic surroundings to 'make an Englishman's wife of her', until she rebuffed, in no uncertain terms, his gentlemanly overtures.[16] Like her father, the Fourth Princess firmly believed that she and her sisters should marry only those of an equivalent status or remain unsullied,[17] and an employee of the government did not meet her exacting standards.[18] She was happy to wait.

The Second Princess was sure, in 1916, that *she* had found the right man. Says U Than Swe,

> Kin Maung Lat—the king's young secretary—used to offer flowers to all the princesses every day. All the princesses liked him, as he was handsome. Although the Second Princess was the least attractive of the princesses, Kin Maung Lat fell in love with her, and gave her an additional big jasmine flower every day. In Burma, jasmine means love, so she understood and gave him chances.

(Kin Maung Lat and his family had come to Ratnagiri in 1914 at the time of the earboring ceremony at the invitation of the king. His mother, Hmanthagyi Ywasar, had been one of Queen Supayalat's most trusted maids of honour. After the earboring ceremony the king had asked the family to stay back in Ratnagiri to work for the royal family.) [19]

On 14 September 1916, the Second Princess wrote a long petition to the governor of Bombay begging for her freedom. The family had strongly opposed her relationship with Kin Maung Lat, she had made up her mind that she wanted to marry him, and she wanted the government's support and help. This petition (together with the letters and interviews that followed) forever shred the veil of secrecy that had shrouded the politics rife in the Royal Residence over the last few years. Given that her upbringing had taught her not even to *privately* voice a dissenting viewpoint, she had to have been driven by overwhelming desperation to *write in such detail* to the government about matters so deeply personal. While she had voiced some discontent to the government before, it had never been done so plainly and specifically.[20] Her detailed letter (partly reproduced below) demonstrates how the long years of isolation had taken a tragic and severe toll on the family, and how the Royal Residence had by now become a veritable cauldron of pent-up emotions.

The Second Princess wrote:

> As for years I am in a very unhappy state and have no others to ask for help and depend upon than your Gracious Excellency, I venture to write ... I hope to bring to your notice that I have reached the full grown age and have not done the least wrong to the British Government. I therefore am afraid that I have the right to claim my independence under the kind control of the British Government and to go on in my own way, and in my own personal affairs without any unjust and unlawful interference by others ...

She went on to detail some of the reasons for her unhappiness:

> In the first place, I beg to observe that the authorities at Ratnagiri, more or less, might be aware of how my position has grown wretched in contrast with that of my younger sisters ... although I am the 2nd daughter of the King, yet my position is not only unlike that of the youngest sister, but is made like that of an outcast or a menial of the lowest type of existence. I am almost everyday unjustly found fault with, given severe reproaches, upbraidings, and taunts and accused in many a different way for nothing ... Of all the four daughters of my parents, the youngest or Sopaya Galay is the dearest of my beloved father. She alone is freely allowed to do and say anything she pleases ... My father agrees with and approves of whatever she does and says ... She superintends all the affairs of the palace and manages them as if she were an eldest daughter with the assistance of her two favourites namely Mrs Vickery [the Fourth Princess's present companion] and Mary [Miss Mary Dinshaw, the Eurasian housekeeper]. My father lets her alone do all the works except the menial ones ... What our grievances is that he always speaks well of her but never a word of good of the others especially of me ... The eldest Princess and I besides have by turns sit watching half night each while my parents are sleeping. The other two Princesses have no such duty. It is not as if my parents are naturally unkind and I, in fact, do not mind such troubles only if I were to be happy otherwise ...'[21]

She indicated that she had expressed her unhappiness to the government a few years earlier (although she doesn't specify when, perhaps it was at the time when Maung San Shwe's nephew had been sent away). At that time the government asked the king when he planned on getting his daughters married, and her father replied that

> his daughters are not to be married unless the lovers are Kings [she means pure blooded princes]. It is for your Excellency to consider whether that is proper under the circumstances. The Princesses are to await until certain kings ask their hands and remain in the wretched state they are in. It is not possible that kings will ask their hands . . .[22]

She went on to say, 'I have now found a Burman of a very high family on whom I can rely in all respects.' She then detailed how she and Kin Maung Lat wrote frequent love letters to each other, and how one day (in July 1916[23]) the Fourth Princess, who disapproved of the relationship, 'all of a sudden, came up to me and robbed me of my letters'. The Second Princess dramatically added, 'I may very well prefer being put into a prison and undergoing any other suffering to being put under the tyranny and persecution of my youngest sister.'[24]

The Second Princess described how the housekeeper, Mary, seeing the tug of war over the letters between her and the Fourth Princess, screamed at the top of her voice, setting the dogs off barking. As a result of all this commotion

> my father being naturally nervous and of weak constitution was laid up with sickness . . . They say that my father fell sick because he heard of my having been in love with [Kin Maung Lat] and got ashamed. On the contrary, the real reason of his being laid up with sickness is the horrible noises perpetrated by the Princess and her favourites. Neither Kin Maung Lat nor myself are wrong in loving each other . . .

According to the Second Princess her father sided as usual with the Fourth Princess, and the next day 'accused me of having practiced black magic on him and caused his serious sickness the previous night'.[25] (From this point in time—July 1916—the king's health fluctuated and was generally poor. In July he suffered from temporary partial facial paralysis; and in August he complained of chest pains.[26])

She begged for *urgent* intervention saying that the Fourth Princess was in the process of making arrangements to send Kin Maung Lat and his family back to Burma, and she proclaimed, 'I cannot live without him as I love him most dearly. If he is to go without me I may be desperate.' She evidently felt some remorse and embarrassment at publicly exposing her family for towards the end of her letter she added, 'of course I love my parents but I have to pity them. It is not that I do not love them but circumstances compel me.'[27]

As Kin Maung Lat and his family were to leave in October the Second Princess quickly shot off yet another letter (handwritten in Marathi), and a telegram to the government begging for immediate intervention. Kin Maung Lat also personally went to see the collector (Brander) to inform him that the Second Princess needed to see him right away. Brander responded by calling on the king on 22 September. He asked the king why he objected to the Second Princess's marriage with Kin Maung Lat, requested him to think of the Second Princess's future before making a decision, and asked for an interview with the Second Princess. The king refused permission for the interview,[28] and the next day expostulated in an indignant letter to the governor of Bombay, 'We are all of the Royal family while (Kin Maung Lat) is of a much lower caste, so how can he marry my daughter ...' He very firmly asked that the government not interfere in his 'private family affairs', and reiterated his demand that immediate arrangements be made for the deportation of Kin Maung Lat and his family ('servants' as he called them) to Burma.[29]

The Second Princess is said to have anxiously pleaded with her mother. She argued that although Kin Maung Lat may not have been a prince, his family had numerous royal connections through marriage. The queen, it is said, was deeply hurt at the source of the betrayal—the son of one of her oldest and most trusted maids of honour. The maid of honour and her family understood very well the unalterable order of things that separated Burmese royalty from its subjects, so the transgression was unpardonable. Kin Maung Lat's tenuous connections with the royal family carried absolutely no weight with the infuriated queen, and she bitterly pointed out to the daughter, who she felt had brought her nothing but trouble from the very beginning, 'Kin Maung Lat is the son of our maid of honour and officer, they are all our slaves ... And he himself is our secretary. So you are wanting to marry a slave!'[30]

On the evening of 12 October 1916 the Second Princess secretly ran away from the family compound. Her version of events is that she left her room, went to the summer house where she met Kin Maung Lat, and stole away with him to the Ratnagiri Club (a path ran downhill from the Royal Residence to the club; the compounds abutted each other[31]). According to the king, Kin Maung Lat came up to the Second Princess's bedroom and 'took her away. My wife and eldest daughter saw him. He was also armed with a knife and threatened any one that came to interfere with him.' The Second Princess arrived at the club at 8 p.m., and met with the political officer, Mr Head, and the collector, both of whom, luckily for her, still happened to be there. The officers asked Kin Maung Lat to stand apart, while the Second Princess, jittery and voluble, explained why she was there. In a report written a few days later the collector pointed out that both he and Head had 'tried in vain to persuade her to return. She clung on to us greatly agitated . . . the Heads, at my request, kindly put her up that night. . .'[32]

Head went later that night to the Royal Residence to meet the king in order to apprise him of the situation. He afterwards stated that the king and the rest of the family had shown great anger and resentment that the officers had entertained the Second Princess's complaints, and had not forced her to return at once to her own home. They accused Head of having plotted and planned the entire affair along with Brander.[33]

The very next morning Brander called on the king and interrogated him, rather severely, on the subject of *all* the princesses' marriages. He felt both the king and the government had neglected this subject for far too long, and this is what had led to this untoward occurrence. The king, unwell, and still reeling under the shock of all that had so recently happened, could not have been in any frame of mind for this kind of a discussion. His private affairs had already been so publicly aired; he had just been so humiliatingly defied. He stated in no uncertain terms that he would not give his permission for the Second Princess's marriage to Kin Maung Lat, and in view of her insolent disobedience he stated he did not want her back (by 17 October he had calmed down and offered to send transportation to bring her home[34]). He also declared to Brander that 'none of the other Princesses want to marry, none but a royal husband would do'.[35] A very unconvinced and annoyed Brander walked out of the king's residence that morning.

Brander then interviewed the Second Princess who said she was willing to marry none other than Kin Maung Lat. Suggestions of marriage to Maung Pe Gyi (the only bachelor approved by the king of the list of fourteen sent by the government in Burma in 1913), or a son of the Meik Hti Lar Princess (King Thibaw's sister), or her own previous paramour Maung San Shwe's nephew (whom the king now said he would no longer object to, as he at least had *some* royal blood) were immediately rejected by her. She threatened suicide if forced to return to the Royal Residence.[36]

For now onwards there was a radical shift in the way those in charge of the king viewed him, their stance towards him considerably stiffened, and they judged him harshly. Almost every interaction between the king and the government (represented by Brander or Head) was henceforth filled with rancour and misunderstandings. Mr Brander wrote to his superiors squarely blaming the king for the Second Princess's affair saying it was nothing but foolishness on his part to keep his daughters unmarried, and then, in spite of the Second Princess's earlier affair, to again bring home for an extended stay another virile young Burmese bachelor. In the circumstances, he opined, an intrigue was inevitable. He went on to stress that three of the princesses were already in their thirties, and that he believed that the king, for the following reasons, *never* had any intentions of getting any of his daughters married:

> The first is his inflated pride . . . hence only royal persons are good enough husbands, and one or two at most of them. The second is his selfishness . . . He is of an amiable but weak and self-indulgent nature, and would miss the Princesses if they left, so he has sacrificed their future to his convenience. Of course his position commands one's sympathy, he and the ex-Queen are exiles in a strange land and growing old, and would be lonely if their daughters left them . . .[37]

He pointed out that the position of all the princesses was extremely unfortunate, and suggested that in future the government act only on what it thought was in the girls' best interest, and ignore the king's

opposition, if any. Brander strongly recommended that the Second
Princess's marriage with Kin Maung Lat be permitted, and that the
wishes of the other princesses regarding marriage be ascertained
through individual interviews at a location other than at the Royal
Residence. (All conversations in the Royal Residence, he said, were
subject to eavesdropping.)[38]

The Second Princess continued to reside with the Heads while the
government contemplated how and where to effect her marriage with
Kin Maung Lat. Mrs Head and the Second Princess shared a room, as
the Second Princess was too nervous to sleep alone. Perhaps to avoid
any possible accusation, Mr Head moved out of his house into a tent
in the compound. Kin Maung Lat was told to wait for the government's
decision, and was prohibited from visiting the Heads' residence in the
meanwhile.[39] The king, increasingly desperate with each passing day, is
said to have sent his horse carriage (probably with one of the princesses
in it) to try and persuade his daughter to come home. Both he and
Queen Supayalat are said to have waited very anxiously on their front
terrace for its return, and as they heard the approaching clattering
hooves, they strained to see if she was in it. When the king saw she was
not, he fainted,[40] because, says one of his granddaughters, 'the hurt
and the insult' were just too much for him to bear.[41]

In November 1916, the king wrote to the viceroy of India, elaborating
his troubles, citing his bad health, and throwing himself at the
government's mercy as he said there was no one else for him to turn
to.[42] And he wrote again, and yet again, to the governor of Bombay
requesting him to order the political officer to send off Kin Maung
Lat and his family. But the viceroy of India and governor of Bombay
were greatly influenced by the views of their men on the spot, and
turned a deaf ear to all the king's frantic pleas.[43]

Cultural, social and language differences made it difficult for the
government to understand the situation from the king's point of view,
and for the king to understand where the government was coming
from. The king's pride, the need to save face, was a deep-rooted and
intrinsic part of him. It may be recalled that one of the main reasons
he rejected the ultimatum, fought the war, and lost his kingdom, was
not to lose face. More recently, he honoured his word and continued to

repay loans he knew were highly exploitive, in order to preserve his 'kingly dignity'. And amazingly, when World War I commenced shortly after the earboring ceremony in 1914, the king, debt-ridden though he was, with 'kingly' pride and magnanimity had wanted to donate Rs 20,000 to the War Fund! (The government thanked him for this very generous offer and accepted Rs 2,500.)[44] Although it is unmistakable that the king had set an impossibly high bar for any prospective bridegroom for his daughters, he did it in the context of his own beliefs and experiences. Certainly he was very impractical and unreasonable, but it is very unlikely that he, as accused by Brander, *deliberately* withheld his daughters' happiness to cater to his own.

When the Second Princess ran away the king suffered a major blow; a mortal blow was dealt by the government's subsequent handing of the situation. Though the support it gave the Second Princess was fully justified, though the Heads' help and sacrifice was commendable, surely it could have been done with a display of more tact and diplomacy towards the king? The role of the officers in charge of the king had been redefined years ago as that of a friend, philosopher and guide—this unfortunately was now completely ignored. Tragically, the collector and political officer were needlessly graceless, insensitive, and harsh with an ageing, ailing, power-stripped king with nothing but an ego left to call his own.

14

DEATH OF THE KING AND THE ENSUING UNREST

A t the time of the Second Princess–Fourth Princess brawl in July
1916, the king had fallen seriously ill and had since preferred to
rely on doctors of his own choice. In particular, a Goan doctor (with
questionable qualifications[1]) had been brought in, and was staying
with the family.[2] The king's health had thereafter fluctuated; there had
been good days and bad days, but unfortunately every day had been a
stressful one. By December 1916, he had had a couple of attacks of
angina pectoris[3] and having also suffered from diabetes for many
years, his kidneys by now had considerably weakened.[4] On 15 December
his health suddenly took a turn for the worse and the civil surgeon was
urgently sent for. Sadly nothing more could be done for him.[5] As his
distressed family huddled anxiously around him, the pious king
indicated with his fingers that he wanted his rosary. Queen Supayalat,
sharply attentive to his every need, immediately 'put his rosary in
his hand so he started counting it ... when his heart stopped, he

stopped . . .' King Thibaw passed away that night a little after midnight, on the sixth waning day of Nataw 1278 (16 December 1916).[6] (See Appendix II.) At the time of his death he was just a couple of weeks short of his fifty-eighth birthday, and had endured exile for thirty-one years (the ancient Greeks had thought exile a fate worse than death!). The cause of his death was stated in government records to be 'heart and kidney trouble'.[7]

The lights within the Royal Residence were immediately dimmed. By morning, a notice, handwritten by the Fourth Princess, was hung at the compound entrance. Under the Burmese script was the English translation: 'The Great King of Righteousness has wearied of the world of men, and ascended to rule among the Gods.'[8] Queen Supayalat, who had fiercely loved King Thibaw since her teenage days, was drained and shattered, but managed to keep her composure. It is said she did not weep, but 'looked at the face of King Thibaw for a long time and went into her bedroom without speaking a word'.[9] She draped herself fully in white,[10] and would soon turn to religion with an unprecedented vigour, which would remain undiminished for the rest of her life. The town of Ratnagiri plunged into mourning along with the bereaved family. With the passing away of their most famous and generous resident, an era in their lives had also ended.

Brander and Head went to condole with the family soon after the king's death. Their empathy for the family had significantly waned since their recent arguments with the king; sadly even at this most vulnerable of times, they were reserved and somewhat hostile in their dealings with the family. Language, as before, led to misunderstandings. Although the Fourth Princess had learnt English, her knowledge was still shallow and ungrammatical. She asked the officers' permission for her father's coffin to 'be kept always in the Palace' and went on to clarify 'till to mount gold leaf to whole of the coffin box'. However, the collector and the political officer took this to mean that the family hoped to *always* keep the coffin in the Royal Residence. The officers brusquely replied that they doubted such permission could be granted (and went on to telegram the government that they found the idea totally 'revolting'[11]). The Fourth Princess, genuinely perplexed as to why such a simple request had not immediately been granted, wrote a long letter to the private secretary of the governor of Bombay clarifying her position and begging for the permission. Also, she pleaded for intervention in another matter. She mentioned that when the queen had said to the officers that she needed Rs 15,000 for the king's funeral, the officers had commented (with amazing insensitivity) that they first wanted to ensure there was enough money in the Reserve Fund for the Second Princess's marriage (the balance in the Reserve Fund at the time of the king's death was later determined to be Rs 43,874[12]). The livid queen pointed out to them that it was not Burmese custom to marry so soon after a death in the family. Besides, she also pointed out, she *disapproved* of the marriage.[13]

Things rapidly got increasingly bitter between the Fourth Princess and the collector and political officer, and on 20 December—just four days after the king's death—Brander wrote to the government indicating that the Fourth Princess had seized the reins of the Royal Residence. He said that as the Fourth Princess's companion, Mrs Vickery, encouraged her in everything she did, including in her hostility towards Head and Brander, it would be better if she was dismissed. He wanted to send Miss Mary Dinshaw, the housekeeper, away too for he said she also was in cahoots with the Fourth Princess.[14] While the government did discontinue Mrs Vickery's service, Miss Mary Dinshaw was not removed.

Many decisions had to be taken by the government immediately after the king's death, the most pressing ones being the management of the Royal Residence; the revision, if any, in the family pension; the amount to be sanctioned for, and the date of, the king's funeral; and the mechanics of the where and when of the Second Princess's marriage. And it appeared to Brander and Head that the Fourth Princess resisted, intrigued and attempted to foil them at every turn.

The queen left everything in the Fourth Princess's hands, and did 'nothing herself' (in the words of the collector). The Third Princess supported the Fourth Princess, and the First Princess did not oppose her. Therefore, with the whole family so to say behind her, the Fourth Princess resisted any interference from the government. She went to the extent of threatening to dismiss any servant who accepted his or her wage from Head! At first the government tussled to take over, but it soon realized that the family owed its servants a large sum in arrears (Rs 29,122[15]), and that if the government was to handle the payment of wages, it might be seen to have a responsibility to clear this amount. So it decided to leave matters status quo; it would hand over the wages to the queen, who would promptly hand them over to the Fourth Princess.[16] The king's outstanding total debt at the time of his death was estimated (unreliably) to be just under Rs 55,000. What Brander recommended was that in order to avoid any possible future law suits or embarrassment to the family and the government, the queen and the princesses be brought, as quickly as possible, under the Ex-King Thebaw's Act, 1895, so they too would not be legally liable for any debt.[17] (This could not be done as the Act became invalid with the king's death. A new Act would have to be passed, and the government opined that this was unnecessary; it would just have to try and informally supervise the family's financial transactions.[18])

The king's funeral was originally supposed to take place on 29 December,[19] but it had to be postponed due to the slow and gradual sanction of funds by the government.[20] After many representations, in January 1917, a total of Rs 15,000 was finally sanctioned (the amount was to be debited to the Reserve Fund).[21] In spite of approval of the full amount requested by the queen, there was no concerted move by the family to quickly organize the king's funeral. This worried both Brander and Head. The family had understandably been keen that the king's mortal remains be sent to the Golden Palace, Mandalay, for entombment. The Fourth Princess had raised the subject with Brander soon after the king's death, and Brander had responded that this definitely would not be permitted.[22] The officers wondered whether the funeral was being delayed in the hope of somehow getting this permission. Or was it being stalled in an attempt to hinder the Second Princess's wedding, which could not be held until after the funeral took place?[23] It appears the officers were right on both counts.

Not satisfied with the answer Brander had given her, the Fourth Princess had tried to obtain, without his knowledge, authorization from other sources for her father's body to be entombed in Mandalay. She had written to the family's representatives in Mandalay (the

Chun Taung Princess and the Wet-masoot Wundauk) to ask them to apply for permission in Burma for the construction of a brick mausoleum next to that of King Mindon's. She had also written to Ko Ba Shin (the honorary magistrate in Rangoon, who supplied the royal family with whatever they needed from Burma), requesting him to get permission to have the king's body properly conveyed to Mandalay.[24] Ko Ba Shin had responded warmly:

> [I]n connection with the burial of the dead body at Mandalay I myself with my son and relations will carry out everything. We ourselves will lift the dead body until it reaches Mandalay. His Majesty getting tired of the human world went to the world of the Nats. As I would like to serve faithfully under Her Majesty and your Highness, kindly let me know.[25]

These letters were uncovered by the government and, in spite of the Fourth Princess's best efforts, in spite of a spirited movement in Mandalay to bring the king's mortal remains back to his former capital, much to the royal family's disappointment, the government indicated in no uncertain terms that it would not permit its entombment anywhere in Burma.[26]

The queen and the Fourth Princess realized that, in spite of the king's very recent death, the government was rapidly moving ahead with plans to get the Second Princess married. This prompted the queen, in December 1916 itself, to send a telegram to the governor of Bombay saying that she did not wish to give her daughter in marriage to Kin Maung Lat.[27] Over the next few days the Fourth Princess also shot off numerous letters in a desperate attempt to stop her sister's wedding. She wrote to the private secretary to the governor of Bombay; she wrote to the king's representatives in Mandalay; and she wrote to Ko Ba Shin. In her letter to Ko Ba Shin, which she got the First and Third Princesses to also sign, she accused Kin Maung Lat's family of not only influencing the Second Princess to elope with Kin Maung Lat, but much more insidiously, of 'bewitching' the king and *causing* his death. In order to create an outcry in Burma against the Second Princess-Kin Maung Lat marriage, she asked Ko Ba Shin to get the letter published in the *Hanthawaddy Weekly Review*.[28] Ko Ba Shin balked at her request, but it was through him, the Chun Taung

Princess and the Wet-masoot Wundauk that the Fourth Princess succeeded in generating considerable disapproval in Burma for the marriage.[29]

A couple of days after the king's death, the government in Burma had telegrammed the government in India asking whether, in view of the changed circumstances, the Second Princess's marriage could be held in Ratnagiri. It indicated, however, that it had no objection to her and her husband settling in Burma after their marriage.[30] The Second Princess and Kin Maung Lat, impatient to wed, readily agreed to this request, and asked that the wedding be arranged on any auspicious day in early February[31] (as 20 February was the last day of the Burmese marriage season[32]). Brander pressed for Rs 5,000 to be sanctioned for the marriage expenses.[33] Aware that opposition to her marriage in Burma was strong, the Second Princess appealed to the government that after her wedding she and her husband be permitted to stay in Calcutta for six months. She hoped that after this period the indignation and excitement would die down.[34]

The government now put considerable pressure on the family to carry out the funeral, and on 5 February 1917, the entombment finally took place[35] with as much solemn pomp and ceremony as was possible. The king's body had been placed in a zinc coffin filled with charcoal and camphor.[36] Three more coffins had been used to encase this innermost coffin—a wooden one, which had been placed in another zinc one, which had finally been put in another wooden coffin. The external wooden coffin had been covered with a purple velvet cloth, and onto this cloth had been nailed sheets of gold and silver.[37]

The coffin was brought down from the first floor of the Royal Residence via a wooden platform and staircase temporarily erected in front of the porch. The coffin was shaded by eight royal white umbrellas, and was carried in a procession comprising an army of white-clad, turbaned male servants. The coffin was first taken to circumambulate the pagoda in the compound,[38] and was then placed in a chamber-like mausoleum also in the compound. The mausoleum, to the great suspicion of the government, was not cemented up and the coffin could easily be accessed through a gate.[39] (It is not known exactly when, but at some stage Queen Supayagalae's coffin was brought into the king's mausoleum, and both coffins were housed here together.[40]) Religious ceremonies with pongyis had been planned,[41] but surprisingly the details of what actually took place appear not to have been recorded, or have been misplaced, and are therefore today unknown. An official photographer was called; government officials must have been invited. Also present must have been hordes of sombre townspeople—people who year after year had flocked to the king's compound to celebrate festivals with the royal family.

On 20 February 1917, two weeks after the funeral, and on the very last day of the auspicious Burmese marriage period, the Second Princess and Kin Maung Lat married.[42] No one from the royal family attended the wedding, and the queen and the Fourth Princess never forgave the Second Princess for it (or for that matter for the king's death for which they both held her responsible). The wedding was held at Brander's bungalow. The Second Princess looked attractive in a white satin jacket and a pale pink tamein richly embroidered with gold. Kin Maung Lat's mother accompanied her; a band played; the police fired a salute at the appropriate time; and Monginis, from Bombay, served refreshments to the numerous guests.[43]

Not long after the king's death, the government raised the subject of sending the family back to Burma, and Brander was asked to submit his recommendation. Although for years Queen Supayalat had been ill and depressed, and not the strong driving force that she once had been, Brander's portrayal of her is still poignant:

> The ex-queen is aged fifty-seven. She is resigned enough to life here, and for her to end her days here would be no great hardship, as she has a comfortable palace, a good climate, a large pension, and her three daughters. She is a quiet, dull, respectable old lady, though obstinate and not amenable to advice. She is entirely under the sway of the fourth princess. It is hard to get her to attend to any business. She would not be capable of active intrigue but might be made a catspaw of by others. This would be the only danger from her if she went to Burma.[44]

Of the First Princess he said: she is 'a harmless and amiable woman with no force of character'; of the Second Princess he had nothing much to say other than she was 'an amiable girl' now married to a commoner and would settle in Mandalay; of the Third Princess he was dismissive saying that she was 'weak and often ailing. A mere cipher, under the thumb of the fourth princess, with whom she sides'. While the others in the family would not be of any threat in Burma, the Fourth Princess could be, he indicated. His diatribe on the Fourth Princess was long and detailed. He said that she had 'brains and force of character . . . unfortunately however she has been the spoilt child of the family. She thrusts her sisters into the background and behaved to them with the utmost selfishness . . . she has a great idea of the dignity and rank of the family . . .' He concluded that she was 'an intractable and intriguing character. Personally I consider that in Burma she would be likely to prove a firebrand and dangerous politically, at any rate while she remained unmarried, owing to her royal notions, ability, venom and unscrupulousness.' He recommended that the government in Burma should be forewarned about her, and if the family were permitted to return, they should be located as far away from Mandalay as possible.[45]

Mr Brander also indicated that the queen, the Third Princess and the Fourth Princess were all eager to return to their homeland, but that the First Princess was not. She had told him that she wished to stay on in Ratnagiri and marry Gopal (by now the family's car driver). Gopal already had a wife and child, and in Brander's opinion, was not at all keen on marrying her. He wrote that 'morality apart' Gopal appeared to be 'respectable and well behaved', but doubted that there was any chance of a happy marriage for the First Princess with him.[46]

The situation, he thought, put the government in a difficult position, for if the First Princess was to stay on in Ratnagiri unmarried, the queen would also have to remain in the interest of maintaining at least an outward appearance of decorum. If the government tried to influence Gopal to marry her, he felt people in Burma might conclude that the government had forced her marriage with a married man of a different nationality and a much lower status with the objective of besmirching the royal family's reputation. It is evident that Brander felt compassion for the First Princess, for he repeatedly turned the issue over in his mind (and on paper) and went on to say that perhaps if she was forced to go to Burma, she might forget Gopal. He indicated that although she was no longer young (she was thirty-seven), and had an eleven-year-old daughter, her chances of marriage in Burma were perhaps good because of the lure of her government pension.[47]

The First Princess, it seems, was highly alarmed at this discussion about a possible return to Burma. She and Gopal now clung to each other with increased intensity, leading a very disapproving Fourth Princess to shoot off a letter in February 1917 to Lady Willingdon (wife of the governor of Bombay). She raised two issues in her letter. The first was a complaint that although she had appealed to Brander to forbid Gopal's visits to the First Princess, he had responded that the First Princess could do whatever she wished. The second was:

> [T]he Collector & Political [officer] gave orders to our servants which[ever] princess they like they can have for wife and bring to their house . . . [S]ome servants run into our rooms pulling [the] poor third princess. [She was] shouting & screaming calling for help, now she is so afraid [for] her life & she is staying with me . . .[48]

The Third Princess, in an interview many, many years later, repeated a similar account of this event.[49] This incident is oft repeated in the royal family's descendants' circle in Burma, and it still rankles.

Mr Head claims that there had earlier been a physical fight between the Third Princess and Gregorto (a Goan clerk employed in the Royal Residence), after which she took shelter with the Fourth Princess, and that it was this incident that had been distorted and blown up. A government inquiry followed the Fourth Princess's letter, and Brander and Head strenuously denied ever having made such a statement.[50] However, it is true that after the king's death, harsh words and false accusations were freely exchanged between the Fourth Princess and the collector and the political officer. It will never be known whether the unsavoury incident described by the princesses was triggered by a demeaning remark made by the collector or political officer in the presence of staff or whether two separate unrelated events (a very offensive remark; misbehaviour by staff) were conflated and reported as one by the princesses.

When the government in India wrote to the government in Burma (with Brander's detailed family report enclosed) suggesting it was time to send the family back, the government in Burma quickly responded that their return was sure to cause a flutter, and was better avoided until the end of World War I. It was also internally decided that at no time would the queen be permitted back to Mandalay; the princesses, however, would not be so restricted.[51] Now that the family was to continue in Ratnagiri for an unspecified period, the government once again brought up the subject of the marriage of the princesses, and the government in Burma was once again asked to suggest names.[52] This time around, unfortunately, it was unable to come up with any names,[53] and so, for the umpteenth time, this pressing matter was depressingly put on the backburner and indefinitely postponed.

What the government did not postpone was the deliberation of how to cut down the cost of keeping the family in Ratnagiri. In June 1917 a decision was reached to considerably reduce (by over 60 per cent!) the family's pension to the following revised scale (implementation would be after some months—from February 1918):

Pension to the queen of Rs 2,000 a month	Rs 24,000
Allowance of Rs 150 a month to each princess in Ratnagiri	Rs 5,400
Festival allowance	Rs 4,000
To be credited to Reserve Fund	Rs 4,000
Total per annum	Rs 37,400[54]

The post of the political officer was also to be dispensed with by 30 November 1917; the huzur deputy collector, who had other responsibilities as well, would deal with matters pertaining to the family. The police guard was to be reduced from sixteen to eight.[55] It was Brander who had recommended all these changes. Regarding the reduction in pension, he opined it would cause no great hardship, but would encourage better economy and management. And he pointed out that money was needed for intrigues—something the king had not indulged in, but which the Fourth Princess was proving to be proficient at—so it was wise to curtail the amount available to her via the queen.[56]

In August 1917, Mr Head reported that he had heard from various sources that the Fourth Princess was spending on festivals only a very small percentage of the allowance given for the purpose; that she was converting the bulk of it into gold sovereigns. It appears that in preparation for their long awaited return to their homeland, the family was at last not only economizing (as repeatedly prescribed by the government) but was actually saving for the future! Although admittedly money was not being used for the purpose allocated, perhaps another collector and political officer would have viewed the aberration with a little more understanding. A very disapproving Head, however, recommended extreme caution in disbursing any future large amounts to the family, and a very distrustful Brander again warned the government that the Fourth Princess was 'a dangerous woman' and was certain to use her savings for intrigues in Burma.[57]

The family had been told that its departure for Burma had been postponed until the end of the war. While the First Princess must have been relieved by this decision, other family members were not. Their disappointment served to intensify the already highly charged atmosphere in the Royal Residence. The Third Princess took ill and the civil surgeon recommended (in April 1917) a change. He indicated that she was 'of delicate constitution and of neurotic temperament . . . subject to hysterical fits, which, of late, have become very frequent.'[58] In June 1917, the Fourth Princess complained of being 'very miserable' in Ratnagiri and requested that she also be permitted a change for a few months.[59] While the Third Princess was permitted, in November 1917, to go to Matheran for a few months,[60] the Fourth Princess's request was turned down as the government was concerned about the trouble she may stir up if allowed to venture out from its watchful presence.[61]

In July 1917, the First Princess confided in Brander that she was unhappy in the Royal Residence, and that her family was 'unfriendly' with her. She repeatedly requested him to persuade the government to arrange her marriage with Gopal (perhaps encouraged by the role the government had played in bringing about the Second Princess's marriage a few months earlier). He reported that the family strongly opposed the First Princess's liaison and marriage with Gopal. Of Gopal he said,

He is a Hindu of no special rank or position. He has accumulated considerable landed property, estimated at Rs 10,000. He resorts to the palace at nights, but during the day goes to his house for meals. He has not left his wife and child, but supports them, as also his own relations. He is respectable looking. He now expresses his wish to marry the Princess. When I reported last February, he was reluctant. But the news that the second Princess gets since her marriage Rs 1,000 a month has, it seems, changed his mind. I consider he wants the First Princess mainly for pecuniary advantage.[62]

Although she had earlier told Mr Brander that she would hate to stay behind in Ratnagiri not married to Gopal because of the shame that would involve, she would rather put up with that, she now said, than return to Burma. Apart from her despair at the thought of being torn apart from Gopal, the First Princess explained that there was also another reason why she did not wish to return: the Burmese would 'jeer at her' seeing her half-caste child.[63]

Brander did not recommend sanctioning her marriage to Gopal, but he put the matter up for the government's consideration. The government's reaction was swift and unequivocal: Brander was informed in July 1917 to tell the First Princess that her marriage to Gopal was impossible, and moreover that she should immediately stop seeing him as doing so demeaned her. Brander was also told to issue an order forbidding Gopal (who had by now been dismissed from service by the Fourth Princess[64]) from visiting the Royal Residence.[65]

Then there was the discovery that the First Princess was pregnant again with Gopal's child. With their return to Burma just around the corner, the family felt deeply betrayed and completely disgraced and began treating her like 'an outcaste'. The queen refused to speak to her any more and objected to even meeting her.[66] The government was informed of her pregnancy in December 1917. Aghast, it resolved that once she delivered it would be best to pack her off to her sister in Calcutta, until the whole family was sent to Burma.[67] The First Princess, terribly miserable by now in the Royal Residence, said she wanted to go to Calcutta right away 'and have her confinement there, and (was) willing to go to Burma if the Second Princess goes there'. She did, however, once again stress that she greatly 'felt the shame of going to Burma with [half-caste] children' and would prefer to live anywhere in India other than in Ratnagiri.[68] The government immediately wrote to the Second Princess requesting her to accommodate her sister.[69]

The Second Princess and Kin Maung Lat had left Ratnagiri shortly after their marriage and had arrived in Calcutta on 7 March 1917 after stopping en route for a couple of days in the sacred Buddhist town of Bodhgaya. In Calcutta, they stayed at the Grand Hotel for four days and then were invited to move into the home of a Burmese merchant. Not long after arriving in Calcutta the Second Princess wrote a number of letters to the government complaining that Calcutta was a very expensive city to live in, especially since she had 'to keep up [her] position' (Calcutta was after all full of Indian royalty, she explained); that she needed an allowance of at least Rs 2,000 a month to live in 'an economical and unostentatious style'; and that she needed an additional special allowance of Rs 3,000 right away to furnish her new home 'decently and fittingly'. She also said that while her husband very much wanted to join the Burmese Battalion, as she had no one else to live with, she could not permit him to, and was he not entitled to a government pension since he was a grandson of the Taingda Mingyi who had been exiled about the same time as her father? She also indicated that she had recently been to a Red Cross sale, and had purchased some oil paintings. And she requested for an introduction to His Excellency Lord Carmichael, the governor of Bengal.[70]

These letters were so out of character, that Mr Brander (to whom the letters were ultimately sent) immediately realized it was not the Second Princess but Kin Maung Lat who had penned them. Another volley of letters signed by Kin Maung Lat himself followed these. This prompted Brander to write a very firm letter to Kin Maung Lat indicating that the sanctioned monthly allowance of Rs 1,000 to the Second Princess was a temporary figure, and that when the family pension was reduced, so would be the Second Princess's, therefore they had better get used to restricting their expenses to their likely allowance of Rs 300 per month. He pointed out that no one had compelled the couple to live in Calcutta, advised him that they leave immediately for Burma, and suggested that he take up some gainful business or employment there. In an internal memo to his seniors he wrote that Kin Maung Lat 'has little sense, but boundless assertiveness', and wanted to live life 'as a gentleman at ease'.[71] But by April 1917 the couple seemed to be settling down—they had moved into their own rented home at 22 McLeod Street, and Kin Maung Lat had begun a course in pottery with the aim of starting his own factory in Burma.[72]

Then, out of the blue, the Second Princess wrote a letter to the Heads (in May 1917) saying that she wished to return to Ratnagiri and settle in a 'little house' there![73] In a letter that palpably radiated high alarm, Brander told the government that their return to Ratnagiri had to be avoided 'at all costs, otherwise my life and that of the political officer will not be worth living, we, judging from past experience, will be expected by them to attend to them hand and foot. We have enough trouble now with the three princesses at the palace who are quarrelling vigorously.'[74] He recommended that the couple be ordered to leave for Burma *right away*.[75]

Orders were hastily issued in June 1917 informing the Second Princess and her husband that they were to return to Burma as soon as possible and that upon reaching there their allowance would be reduced to Rs 300 a month.[76] The Second Princess protested by letter to the viceroy of India, requesting him to overrule this order and permit her and her husband to stay in Calcutta for two years, to fix her allowance permanently at least at Rs 1,000 a month, and to sanction enough money to enable her to buy land and build a house in Burma.[77] The Second Princess was permitted to stay in Calcutta for a further two years,[78] and she was told that her monthly allowance would remain status quo until March 1918 when it would be reduced to Rs 300.[79]

In December 1917, when the government asked the Second Princess to accommodate the First Princess, she, very unfortunately, perhaps at her husband's instigation, seized the opportunity to make her own demands. She said she would be happy to have her sister if the government met certain conditions—a larger house, a more generous pension, etc. Discussions with the government went back and forth but no agreement was reached,[80] and on 24 February 1918, the First Princess gave birth to a daughter.[81]

While the government was debating how to reach a fair compromise with the Second Princess, the civil surgeon reported (in April 1918) that the Third Princess was unhappy and unwell. He indicated that she would 'lose her reason' if immediate action was not taken, said that she was anxious to go stay with the Second Princess for some time, and recommended that this be permitted.[82] Brander endorsed this recommendation, adding that 'an undesirable young man is trying to approach her, and it is most necessary to get her away, in view of what happened to her sister'.[83]

With *two* of her sisters now wanting to come stay with her, and with the government strongly supporting the idea, both Kin Maung Lat and the Second Princess again tried to turn the situation in their favour. Kin Maung Lat wrote that he was looking for a suitably large house to accommodate the First and Third Princesses, as well as his wife and himself.[84] The Second Princess complained about the woefully inadequate pension: '[R]e. my sisters and my monthly allowance of three hundred each it is better for the Government to put us in confinement in the jail instead of sending out into the world with a small and insufficient allowance'.[85] (By this time the Second Princess's allowance had been cut to Rs 300, which the couple had refused to accept.[86] Petition after petition after petition followed, each more indignant than the previous one; none garnered any result.[87] Then the Second Princess tried to stake a claim on her inheritance, citing the balance in the Reserve Fund; the government replied that the fund had been set up to defray the cost of one-off occurrences, and that the family had no legal right to it.[88] Fed up with her constant demands, and the tone of her letters, someone in the government advised the couple to be more 'submissive'. The Second Princess's response to this was to petulantly proclaim that her present position was 'too lowly as it is to be bent down any more'.[89])

Another development also took place while the government was negotiating with the Second Princess. In late March 1918 the First Princess lost her newborn baby. This naturally made her very distraught. Additionally, she developed a fever and breast abscesses. Out of kindness, and at the civil surgeon's recommendation, in April 1918 Mr Brander permitted Gopal to resume his visits to the First Princess.

(This, as was to be soon evident, was a really tragic and irreversible mistake.) Of course the Fourth Princess vigorously and indignantly protested; of course Brander ignored these protests.[90] Then the Fourth Princess did something unconscionable—she spread rumours in Ratnagiri that it was Brander who had fathered the First Princess's newborn. The Fourth Princess's basis for this allegation was the fact that Brander used to visit the First Princess often, and during these visits the two were often closeted together alone. By July 1918, a new collector, a Mr Brendon, had taken over, and it was he who investigated the matter. He immediately realized that there had been considerable friction between his predecessor and the Fourth Princess. He also understood that the two had frequently exchanged allegations. The government dismissed the Fourth Princess's accusation as malicious and unfounded, and threatened to substantially cut the family allowance 'if [the Fourth Princess] does not mend her ways'.[91]

It is evident that the Fourth Princess, and the job that lay ahead of him, intimidated the new collector. In July 1918 he nervously opined of the Fourth Princess: 'it is quite impossible for any man to control her'. He worried about the Third Princess who had run away from the Royal Residence a few days earlier. He urged, with a tinge of panic, that the government act quickly, for he said, 'If she [the Third Princess] doesn't marry she may go off her head at any time or cause another scandal. Miss Trewby, who is a lady doctor (and the Fourth Princess's latest companion), supports this view.' He didn't know quite how to handle the First Princess who just wanted 'to be left in the company of her servant–lover'. He seemed downright relieved that the Second Princess was married and living far away in Calcutta, and that the queen was not causing much trouble as she seemed to have 'no interest in life except to be left in peace'.[92]

Unfortunately the peace the queen had so wanted for so many years was never to be hers—not when she so desperately needed it right after her dearly loved husband had died, and not anytime thereafter. In February 1918, she had been greatly irked by the substantial cut in her pension, and this spurred her into writing a long memorial to the governor of Bombay complaining about it. (While she said in this memorial that her pension had been reduced from Rs 5,500 to 1,625, it had actually been revised to Rs 2,000,[93] but deductions were made each month to recover advances.) The queen condemned the reduction saying the family was trying very hard to pay off its debts; she pointed out that prices had risen considerably. She piteously pleaded:

> Our lot is already too hard. The tale of our domestic woes and sufferings is too long to narrate here . . . We have no patrimony, no other source of income. It is not given to us to earn our own living. We, therefore, absolutely depend upon the charity of our benign Government . . . It is certainly the worst irony of fate, that the widow of the mighty king of a large territory like Burma, should be reduced to such straits.[94]

Of the revised pension of Rs 2,000 the queen appropriated Rs 600 each month as her pocket money—something she had been doing for many years—for remittances, probably of a charitable nature, to Burma.[95] Both she and her daughter wrote increasingly frantic letters to the government, and in October 1918 the Fourth Princess begged to be granted permission to go and call on Lady Willingdon to personally explain why, 'Rs 1400 is not enough to manage. I pay our monthly stores bills what is there left [for] daily expenses[?] . . . we are starving here and no one to help me in my troubles. The merchant man said he will not give us any more without money . . . I feel very miserable . . .' Brendon reported that the Fourth Princess *was* trying hard to curtail expenses, and, much to the irritation of the queen, had dismissed many servants.[96] (The staff strength by August 1918 was reported to be seventy-four—less than half of the number employed during the last years of the king's life.[97]) But their entreaties were all ignored.

While the government paid no heed to their pleas, there was someone else who greatly sympathized with the family's plight, and around this time offered his assistance (though not of a financial nature). According to U Than Swe and the descendants of the Fourth Princess, there was a pongyi or Buddhist monk by the name of Ko Ko Naing who happened to be in Madras around the time King Thibaw died. Ko Ko Naing heard about the trouble the family was undergoing after the king's death, and wrote a letter to the Fourth Princess to the effect: 'Don't worry the whole of Burma is on your side, and I'm in

Madras and I'm available for all the help you need'. This letter was the
first of many letters between Ko Ko Naing and the Fourth Princess,
and one day he arrived in Ratnagiri quite suddenly and presented
himself at the Royal Residence. The queen immediately invited him to
live in the pagoda in the compound.[98]

Ko Ko Naing had his breakfast and lunch in the Royal Residence
every day. As per custom, after he finished eating the family carried
out the water pouring ceremony. In U Than Swe's words,

> After a donation or a good deed is done—in this case the good deed is
> feeding the pongyi—water is poured to inform others of the good
> deed. This is our culture . . . One day while this ceremony is being
> performed, Ko Ko Naing was on a raised platform as always, raised 12
> inches off the ground. As the golden bowl overflows with water that
> the Fourth Princess is pouring the water goes straight to Ko Ko
> Naing . . . like a miracle. The water doesn't of course climb the
> platform but just goes towards him. That's one instance. Another
> time the Fourth Princess's scarf is blown off by the wind and wraps
> itself around the pongyi's stand. The queen notices these and sees
> them as omens, as does the Fourth Princess. Probably their [the
> Fourth Princess and Ko Ko Naing's] romance starts around now,
> although he is still a pongyi.[99]

There is no evidence to suggest that anyone apart from the family was
ever aware of the Fourth Princess's burgeoning romance, and so it was
never an area of concern to the government. It was the future of the
First and the Third Princesses that continued to worry the government,
and in July 1918 (while the government and the Second Princess were
still haggling) both the First and Third Princesses, for reasons unstated,
changed their minds and firmly declined to go to stay with their
sister.[100]

In September 1918 the government pushed for the entire family to
be sent back to Burma. An internal memo stated that 'the situation in
the palace has by now become a little short of scandalous', and went on
to say:

> The Governor in Council recognizes that the enforced residence in
> Ratnagiri of these young ladies during the lifetime of their father was
> probably unavoidable. The reasons for detaining them there since his

death are less cogent, and it is evident that the conditions of their detention, the lack of suitable society and opportunities for healthy recreation are having a demoralizing effect on them. Moreover he considers that it is not entirely creditable to our administration that they should be condemned indefinitely to an existence which offers small prospects of their ever being able to lead a reasonably happy and useful life. He would urge most strongly that a further effort should be made to induce the Government of Burma to receive the whole family back into that province. There, the daughters could presumably find husbands of a rank suitable to their changed position in life, and could settle down to a domesticity which they cannot find in the artificial and irksome conditions of their present environment.[101]

Other letters followed this one detailing the situation. The government in Burma was approached, and it replied by telegram (it appears in late October 1918) agreeing to the immediate return of only the First and Third Princesses.[102]

Brander's permission in April 1918 to allow Gopal to visit the First Princess[103] had made it possible for Gopal to visit her openly and frequently and had enabled him to reignite in the First Princess her infatuation for him, which had ebbed after his visits had been stopped (in December 1917 she had readily agreed to be sent to her sister in Calcutta, and had also agreed, though reluctantly, to go on to settle in Burma with her[104]). When Brendon told the First and Third Princesses (in mid-November 1918) of plans to send them to Burma, the First Princess protested excitedly and vociferously and said that she 'would rather kill herself than go'. The Third Princess also expressed her great unwillingness to go, not only because she didn't wish to, she said, but also because of the effect her absence would have on her mother, who was 'very attached to her and dependent on her'. The queen indicated her disinclination to *ever* be separated for any length of time from the Third Princess. She told the collector that if the Third Princess should marry, she wanted her and her husband to continue living with her. The Fourth Princess put forth yet another argument saying that it would be very unfair on the part of the government to send the Third Princess to Burma with the First Princess 'who [had] lost her reputation'.[105]

By this time, World War I had recently concluded, and before ignoring the family's protests and sending the First and Third Princesses off, the government in India thought it wise to once again appeal to the government in Burma to take back the entire family.[106] A memo reading 'It is the intention of government to get rid of this whole troublesome family . . .' and other similar statements in other memos demonstrated how much governmental frustration had also peaked by now.[107] When, in late November 1918, the government in Burma *finally* gave the green light for the entire royal family to be sent home[108] (to Rangoon and not to Mandalay), preparations for their return were effected with tremendous caution, resulting in considerable further friction between the government and the careworn but still feisty family.

15

PRELUDE TO THE END
OF THE EXILE

When informed of the decision to send the family back to Burma, the queen requested that they be allowed to leave after January 1919—until then they would be observing a period of mourning for the king's death anniversary. She also asked for permission to take back with her the coffins of King Thibaw and Queen Supayagalae, and that she be permitted to take her nurse Miss Hill, her housekeeper Miss Mary Dinshaw, the old Burman Tandawzin whose job it was to look after the coffins and to write her letters,[1] and some servants. The Fourth Princess, who was present during this interview, requested that her companion Miss Trewby also be permitted to accompany them, and that they be allowed to take some furniture, two cars and a piano. And then, on a much more personal note, she stressed that the First Princess and her daughter be sent back and housed separately in Rangoon. This last request was made in the queen's presence, and the queen did not oppose it.[2] It is apparent that the Fourth Princess did not want the First Princess's reputation to tarnish that of the rest of the family. The family was returning after thirty-three years and wanted to do all it could to ensure its welcome by the people of Burma. This was important to Queen Supayalat who had been the all-powerful queen of the Kingdom of Ava in the past, and to the Fourth Princess who was returning full of hope for the future.

The family now began preparing for their departure. Silk cloth for the queen and the princesses (including the First) was ordered at the then considerable sum of Rs 2,000, and tailors were given an additional allowance to stitch appropriate garments so that the family could be well attired for their arrival.[3] On 25 January, the traders and storekeepers of Ratnagiri held a *pan-supari* (a good luck ceremony) for the Third and Fourth Princesses. Around three hundred people attended the event at the Shri Vithal temple. Mr Sakhalkar, the huzur deputy collector, was present, as was the editor of the local newspaper. Sakhalkar gave a speech in which he 'thanked the Princess for the benefits accruing to Ratnagiri as a consequence of Thebaw's residence there'.[4] At a later unknown date the First Princess sold some of her furniture and presented the proceeds as donations to some Hindu temples,[5] but it does not appear that any farewell ceremony was held for her—her standing in Ratnagiri was very different from that of the powerful Fourth Princess's who managed the large household and dealt regularly with tradesmen.

The First Princess's donation did not signal that she was willing to leave. She continued to plead to be allowed to stay back, but Brendon repeatedly and firmly informed her that she had to go.[6] Strongly suspecting that money played an important role in Gopal's attraction to her, he had, from September 1918, withheld two-thirds of her monthly allowance, and had invested it for her in post office cash certificates.[7] But this measure evidently did not have the desired effect: in late January 1919 the Fourth Princess wrote a letter to Brendon's wife announcing that the First Princess was pregnant once again, and that the baby was due in June.[8]

In spite of this development, the government insisted that the First Princess would still have to leave Ratnagiri. It also insisted that she would have to travel back with the rest of the family, but in view of their strong sentiment on the subject, a concession was made: a separate compartment would be arranged for her and her daughter for the train journey up to Calcutta.[9] It would be up to the government in Burma to decide whether she stayed with the rest of the family or not in Burma.[10]

While the details of their return were being ironed out, word arrived (around the third week of January) from the government in Burma that it would not under any circumstance permit the mortal remains of the late king and junior queen to be brought to the country.[11] The explanation provided to the government in India was that the 'possibility of using them symbolically, to stimulate, among a credulous race like the Burmese, political aspirations of an exceedingly dangerous character would be ever present, and they would be a never ending source of extreme anxiety'.[12] On receiving this devastating bit of news, the family immediately stopped all preparations for their departure. The queen stated that she was not leaving without the coffins. Then, out of the blue, around 28 January, the queen indicated that she was willing to have the coffins entombed above ground (Burmese royalty were never buried underground) in a mausoleum in Ratnagiri. Her sudden change of mind, combined with the Fourth Princess's request to remove the gold and silver sheets attached to the king's coffin (said to be worth Rs 10,000), and the information that the junior queen's remains was in mummified condition (and therefore perhaps so was the king's) made the collector suspicious. Was the family planning to take the bodies back *without* the coffins?[13]

Other factors served to compound Brendon's suspicion on the subject. On 15 January 1919, the queen had petitioned the viceroy of India that he allow it to be publicly announced in India and Burma that the late king had indicated that the Fourth Princess should be considered head of the family after his death.[14] (The queen's request was turned down on the grounds that this was a purely domestic matter and needed no public announcement.[15]) Brendon also recalled that Miss Trewby had recently questioned him 'as to the possibility of the fourth Princess marrying an English prince or an Englishman and regaining her father's throne'. Adding these to 'the extraordinary importance' given by the queen to taking the king's remains to Burma made him conclude that the family wanted to use it 'for the furtherance of the fourth Princess' political ambitions'.[16]

On 30 January the family changed its mind yet again. The queen indicated that she would not leave Ratnagiri without the coffins. The reason she gave was that if the government considered it dangerous to send the coffins back, then it was dangerous for *her* to go back to Burma. Brendon saw no logic in her argument and, very frustrated, threatened the family that if they didn't cooperate they 'would be removed without preparation and the coffins would be entombed by strangers'. And he wrote off to his immediate senior that he be given permission to use force, if necessary, to ensure the family's departure. This permission was granted,[17] and Mr Brendon promptly (and perhaps gleefully) informed the Fourth Princess of it.[18]

The queen now turned to the governor of Bombay for help. She pleaded in a long letter dated 11 February 1919 for permission for

> taking with us the two coffins, one of our beloved Lord and the other of our sister . . . the final obsequial rites have not been gone through with respect to the dead . . . the local officers seem determined to coerce us to leave them here behind us in some nasty unconsecrated place. While as a matter of fact, a suitable and decent ground has been specifically prepared long ago for the location of these two coffins and our own in Burma . . . We therefore earnestly request your Excellency to take this question of having the last rites rendered to the dead and allow the two coffins to be conveyed with us to Burma.[19]

While taking the coffins back with her was the primary reason for her letter, she also made some other representations. She explained that the allowance given to them had never been sufficient to meet their expenses as they were, after all, accustomed 'to Royal and high ways of living'. They therefore had to sell jewellery to meet expenses, and after that was no longer an option they had to incur debt. She indicated that she was very keen to clear all debts as the family was leaving Ratnagiri for good, and did not wish 'to be termed cheats in a place where we passed almost the whole of our life'. She requested that their debts be scrutinized by the government and repaid from the Reserve Fund.[20]

She went on to say that she had attached to the letter a list of

servants, the bare minimum, who she wished to take back with her, and
begged that this not be curtailed. [Her list totalled thirty-seven of
which eighteen were for her, five for the First Princess; and seven each
for the Third and Fourth Princesses. Each of them was to have
separate cooks, butlers (except for the First Princess), *hamals* (bearers)
and ayahs. She pleaded for special arrangements to take the family to
Burma—a chartered ship to take them all the way, so that they didn't
have to change 'conveyance after conveyance' as she did not think she
could stand the strain. And, besides, she pointed out this would make
it easy to convey the coffins and the furniture too. Her last request
was that an officer and a lady doctor be deputed to accompany them
on this long journey.[21]

The queen's letter crossed one written by the government in Burma
to the government in Bombay. Enquires had been made in Mandalay as
to the correct procedure to entomb the remains of the late king and
the junior queen, so as to avoid, to the extent possible, offending the
family and the Burmese people. The government in Burma now spelt
out in considerable detail the arrangements for the 'honourable disposal
of the remains' in Ratnagiri and requested that they be carried out
before the family left town:

1. A temporary erection called an *Alaungdike* should be constructed
    for the deposit of the body during the funeral ceremony. In
    Burma the *Alaungdike* would be made of bamboo . . .
2. Eight white umbrellas should be carried at the ceremony and
    subsequently placed at the *Alaungdike* . . .
3. Eight drum (*si-daw*) players will be required . . .
4. A minimum of eight or ten pongyis (according [to whether]
    eight or ten percepts are to be recited at the ceremony) will have
    to be invited and a small pandal will have to be erected for them
    at the head of the *Alaungdike*.
5. A permanent masonary edifice called *Oknan Pyatthat* will have to
    be constructed, [with] a cavity in which the bodies . . . will have
    to be placed and bricked in, immediately after the funeral . . .
6. All those who take part in the ceremony including the drum
    bearers and the umbrella bearers should wear the customary
    white dress . . .
7. Arrangements should be made for the distribution of alms or
    food to the poor at Ratnagiri . . .

8. Arrangements should also be made for giving light refreshments
to all who are invited to the ceremony . . .

It suggested that Taik-Ok of the Mya Taung monastery (the monastery
built by the queen in Mandalay as a work of merit just before her
exile) should be one of the pongyis invited.[22]

In the meanwhile, Brendon, blinkered by suspicion, focused on
ensuring that the royal remains were not surreptitiously removed from
the coffins. After government sanction, he purchased a plot of land on
which he was quickly having the tomb constructed. The site he
selected was located about one kilometre from the Royal Residence.[23]
He also ordered the deputy superintendent of police and the huzur
deputy collector to open the coffins and examine the remains, in the
presence of the Fourth Princess, 'if this could be done without doing
violence to the feelings of the family'. However, the horrified family
refused to allow this. The officers, not authorized to press matters
beyond a point, had to satisfy themselves with placing a lock and a
police guard at the temporary tomb, in the compound of the Royal
Residence, after which they retreated (the door to this tomb was now
secured with the queen's lock and the collector's lock).[24]

A volley of indignant telegrams and letters immediately shot forth
from the Royal Residence. The queen telegrammed the viceroy of
India and the lieutenant governor of Burma: 'Please stop order to open
my husband's coffin.'[25] She telegrammed Brendon (who was away on
tour) and followed up by writing a letter brusquely stating: 'I, the Ex-
Queen of Burma refuse to allow you to open the Tomb of my husband,
Ex-King of Burma. It is sealed with the Royal Seal of Burma, and it
will be illegal for you to act against my order in this matter.'[26] The
lieutenant governor, very wary of a public outcry in Burma, immediately
cautioned the government in Bombay that any action, which may
'seriously offend susceptibilities of ex-Royal family', should be
postponed until he had been consulted.[27]

Although Brendon informed the family on 15 February that the
opening of the coffins had been postponed, this just bought them
some time but the threat continued to loom ominously. Maybe it was
the trauma and anxiety of the situation that made the queen fall
ill (details of her illness are unknown),[28] and a few days later, on

17 February, she wrote her will. (The family did not own much by way of assets but it always believed it had a claim on the Reserve Fund that could someday be realized.[29]) The queen explicitly excluded the Second Princess from any share in the family property. For the First Princess, she apparently still felt some affection and/or responsibility— she put in a clause that an allowance should be paid regularly to her. It was to the Third and Fourth Princesses that she bequeathed everything.[30] (Copies of *another* will signed by Queen Supayalat *dated the same day* exists today in Burma with some of the royal descendants. In this will, the queen left everything to the Fourth Princess.[31])

A few days after the officers' attempt to open the coffins, the Fourth Princess wrote a detailed and an obviously anguished letter to the government in Bombay. She lamented 'there seems to be suspicion that our family are going to try and convey my Father's body to Burma' without its coffin and explained 'we don't know where this idea originated but I may state that if the King's body does go it will be as it should be conveyed and not as a package case.'[32] (About this last statement of hers there can be no room for doubt. It may be remembered that when the king had wanted his and the queen's horoscopes sent from Mandalay, he was adamant that it be done in a special ceremonial manner. Certainly the family would have wanted *the king's mortal remains* carried back observing every custom and ritual in the book.)

Apart from the battle over the coffins, there were other fronts on which Brendon and the queen/Fourth Princess combatted. The family wanted to take thirty-seven of their old retainers back with them to Burma (out of a staff of forty-seven currently employed in the Royal Residence[33]); Brendon had been told to inform them that this was excessive.[34] The family wanted to travel the entire way by ship; they were informed this wasn't possible due to a shortage of ships.[35] The family requested for Ko Ba Shin to come from Rangoon to escort them back; Brendon did not consider him suitable for the purpose, and Holland, the district superintendent of police, was to be their only escort.[36]

Even the amount of luggage and furniture to be taken became a bone of contention. The government did not want the family to take back any furniture as a fully furnished house had already been rented for them in Rangoon with hardly any space for anything more.[37] The cars and the piano must be sold, the family was informed, and the amount realized must be credited to the Reserve Fund. The Fourth Princess strongly resisted this and, without Brendon's knowledge, sent the De Dion car and the piano off to Bombay for repairs, with orders for their onward transmission to Rangoon. (By the time the decrepit De Dion reached Bombay it had to be towed about by a bullock cart! The government intervened and both car and piano were sold in Bombay.) The Ford car she sold herself and refused to hand over to Brendon the Rs 2,000 she got for it.[38] Next she sold items of furniture (financed from the Reserve Fund), and again refused to hand over the considerable sale proceeds she got for it.[39] Brendon reported to his seniors that when he had asked the Fourth Princess why the family was so defiant, she had replied, 'We are royalty.'[40] Exhausted and exasperated, he complained that the preparations for sending the family home were causing him 'very heavy work most of which is due to the difficulties created by the family at every turn'.[41]

By the third week of February, a worried Brendon anxiously reminded the government that there might be problems if the family's departure was delayed too much because of the First Princess's pregnancy and pointed out that the new tomb was completely ready now.[42] (Constructed at a cost of Rs 515, it was of 'Burmese design', had a stepped roof, was made of red laterite stone with walls two feet thick, and was plastered and whitewashed.[43]) But the government decided that the family's transfer would have to be postponed because arrangements for the late king's entombment, as suggested in such detail by the government in Burma, had to be faithfully followed, and would take time to implement[44]—especially since pongyis had to be sent for from Burma.

Brendon immediately went over and explained to the queen all the entombment arrangements proposed. He added that he would only send for the pongyis from Burma if she agreed to hand over to him the key to her lock on the temporary tomb once the pongyis arrived. The queen promptly replied that she would *not* give up the key, would *not* instruct the pongyis to carry out the ceremony, and that the pongyis would most certainly *not* carry out the ceremony against her wishes.[45]

Brendon cautioned the queen that this probably was the last opportunity that would be given to her to entomb the coffins herself; that the family was to be soon sent back to Burma. He asked her to think the matter over carefully and send to him, as soon as possible, a decision in writing, co-signed by the Fourth Princess. During this visit he also explained to her why he had wanted to open the coffins and asked her to suggest a less objectionable method for confirming that the coffins had not been tampered with. The queen readily agreed to give a signed declaration that the remains were in the coffins, and unhesitatingly suggested that the family's luggage be searched before their departure.[46]

The very next day the following letter, in the Fourth Princess's handwriting, and signed by the queen and her, was sent to Brendon (see Appendix II):

1. I understand all that was said by Mr Brendon yesterday about bringing Poongyis, band, and umbrellas from Burma. I refuse the Poongyis, on arrival, to entomb the coffins, if that is still the determination. I refuse to give up the key of my husband's tomb.

2. I solemnly affirm that the body of my husband and my sister are in the coffins which are in the tomb in the Palace compound in Ratnagiri.[47]

Enclosing this letter, Brendon wrote to the government in Bombay saying that there was no point in sending for the Burmese priests in view of what had been said and given to him in writing by the queen, and requested for orders for the removal of the family without delay. He added, 'The ex-Queen and her family seem now to be reconciled to the idea of going to Burma without the remains and they informed me that they would go peaceably.' He also informed the government that he had promised the queen that he would not remove the coffins from the tomb in the compound until they received instructions from the government, and suggested that the queen be given the opportunity to make a representation to the lieutenant governor of Burma on the subject before any decision was reached.[48]

The government in Burma, on being told of the latest twist in the coffin saga, immediately and unequivocally responded that the queen could only be sent back when she had understood and accepted that the coffins had to remain in Ratnagiri, that no further discussion on the subject would be entertained, and that the matter was *forever closed*. In fact, the coffins *had* to be entombed *before* the queen left Ratnagiri. It added that the coffins should not be opened prior to entombment; that the lieutenant governor was prepared to accept the queen's written assurance coupled with inspection of her baggage prior to her departure.[49]

From the tone of the correspondence of all parties involved, it is evident that by now everybody had had enough—the family, Mr Brendon, the government in Bombay, and the government in Burma. The family and Brendon were particularly anxious to resolve the deadlock and move ahead. The Fourth Princess had repeatedly asked Brendon when the family was to be sent back, and when he informed her (on 14 March) of the conditions specified by the government in Burma, she immediately wrote agreeing to the entombment of both coffins in the newly constructed tomb.[50]

On 19 March 1919 the mortal remains of late King Thibaw and late Queen Supayagalae were laid to rest in the newly constructed tomb. Neither the queen nor the First Princess attended the ceremony—the former perhaps in symbolic protest; the latter, sadly, probably because her family did not permit her to. Brendon reported in considerable and fascinating detail the entombment (by now he had discovered that the late king's body had not been embalmed and so was much less suspicious of it having been surreptitiously removed from the coffin):

> On the 19th instant at 3.30 p.m. Kabraji (the Deputy Superintendent of Police), after inspecting the seal on his lock on the door of the palace tomb and finding it intact, removed his lock in the presence of the Third and Fourth Princesses. The Fourth Princess also removed her lock. The coffins were then removed in Kabraji's presence. The Huzur Deputy Collector was also present with the men whom he had engaged to carry the coffins. In accordance with the wish of the ex-Queen and the Fourth Princess, whom I had consulted on the 16th instant, these men were dressed in their ordinary clothes. The funeral procession started from the palace at 4 p.m. and reached the new tomb about 4.30 p.m. The following persons accompanied the coffins from the palace to the new tomb:

The Third Princess; The Fourth Princess (both dressed in white); Miss Mary Dinshaw; Tandawzin U. Yaw, the old Burman Secretary; a number of palace servants; Mr Zal K.N. Kabraji, the Deputy Superintendent of Police (with a police escort); Mr V.B. Sakhalkar, Huzur Deputy Collector. The palace servants carried eight white umbrellas supplied by the ex-Queen.

I arrived at the new tomb at the same moment as the funeral procession. The ex-King's coffin was immediately placed on a bier in the tomb under the personal directions of the Fourth Princess and the [eight] white umbrellas were also placed upright in the tomb about the ex-King's coffin. The Fourth Princess then sprinkled two basketfuls of white flowers on the floor of the tomb, chiefly under the ex-King's coffin. The coffin containing the junior ex-Queen's remains was then placed in the tomb, on a wooden bench, alongside the ex-King's coffin. The Third and Fourth Princesses then knelt on the ground in front of the open tomb (all the palace servants were also kneeling) and offered prayers. As soon as the Princesses rose, I ascertained from the Fourth Princess that the ceremony was over and I immediately gave orders for the walling up of the opening. The Princesses and the servants then departed . . .[51]

The extremely cautious government in Burma wired its permission for the family's return only on 1 April 1919,[52] after it had received intimation that the entombment had been carried out, and that the government in Bombay had in its possession three vital documents signed by the queen and the Fourth Princess specifying that they had willingly agreed to permanently entomb the mortal remains of King Thibaw and Queen Supayagalae in Ratnagiri and that they would never ask for their removal; that the government had offered to carry out all ceremonies as suggested by the government in Burma but they had refused this offer and that they confirm the ceremonies carried out instead were to their satisfaction; and lastly, that the remains of the king and junior queen were in their coffins at the time of the entombment.[53]

Within a week of the entombment the family had packed and was anxious to leave.[54] Now everyone (with the exception of the First Princess) cooperated to hastily tie up all loose ends. Just prior to their departure, Holland carefully searched their luggage and found nothing suspicious.[55] The family was finally ready to begin their long-awaited journey home.

Not long after the family's departure, after consultation with the government in Burma, an inscription was placed on the late king's tomb, on its northern wall, facing the Kolhapur–Ratnagiri Road. It reads as follows:[56]

IN THIS TOMB
ON THE 19TH MARCH 1919,
WERE DEPOSITED THE MORTAL REMAINS OF THEBAW
THE LAST KING OF UPPER BURMA,
WHO WAS DEPOSED ON THE 1ST DECEMBER 1885
AND REMOVED TO RATNAGIRI, WHERE HE DIED ON THE
15TH DECEMBER 1916
AT THE AGE OF 58.
ALSO THE REMAINS OF TEIK SUPAYAGALE
THEBAW'S MINOR QUEEN
WHO DIED AT RATNAGIRI ON THE 25TH JUNE 1912, AGED 50.

PART III

AFTER THE EXILE

16

The Homecoming

On the afternoon of 10 April 1919, a rather frail-looking Queen Supayalat, with three daughters and a granddaughter, boarded the *Fairy Queen* to begin the journey that would finally take her back to her homeland. The collector, Mr Brendon, the civil surgeon, and their wives came to see the family off.[1] Also present were crowds of Ratnagiri residents who were sorry to see the family leave.[2] The king's establishment had been more like a corporation (in fact, the largest one in Ratnagiri!) than a family and had, over the years, provided employment to countless locals. Moneylenders and traders had taken full advantage of the loosely run establishment. Many in town had benefited considerably from the family's presence, and everyone warmly remembered the generosity with which the late king, the public face of the family, had celebrated festivals and fed the poor. People had also been touched by the recent gifts given by the princesses to local Hindu temples. Besides, the family, always rather mysterious and alluring, had become an institution in the town, and would be missed.

On that hot and humid afternoon, as the ferry steamer pulled out, it probably was not a sense of liberation that overwhelmed Queen Supayalat. It's not that she had formed any attachment to Ratnagiri; she hated the climate and always deeply resented having to live in, as she put it, 'a strange country with no people of our race and religion'. But she was clearly distraught at having to leave behind the coffins of her 'beloved Lord' and of her sister. Also, she was now nearly sixty years of age, and considered herself 'old and naturally infirm'.[3] All she wanted was peace and quiet to live out the rest of her days. Would this be possible in a land which though very much her own, was nonetheless one from which she had been alienated for so long, and where she was unsure of her reception? She was well aware that she had made many enemies during her reign. And perhaps she worried that she had been blamed over the years for the loss of the kingdom.

An additional anxiety, a source of shame, was that she, who during her husband's rule had preached and moralized to all and sundry, had had no influence over her two elder daughters. She was, after all, going back with a half-caste granddaughter, irrefutable proof of her eldest daughter's unsuitable liaison—an alliance she was sure would be viewed with derision not only by members of the extended royal family but also by every other Burmese. Then there was the other scandal of the Second Princess having run away to marry a man of lower birth. Perhaps the queen drew some comfort from the reassuring presence of the Fourth Princess, her morally upright daughter who had been her crutch for so many years. And, of course, the company of the Third Princess, her favourite daughter[4] and one of her few sources of joy, must have lifted her spirits.

The entire first-class section of the *Fairy Queen* had been booked for the family to ensure their privacy and comfort.[5] All travel arrangements had been made as if for two groups, with the First Princess and her daughter separated from the rest.[6] Apart from the family, the entourage comprised eleven people—Miss Mary Dinshaw, Tandauzin, the butler, the cook and his assistant, two men for odd jobs, and four maids. Three dogs accompanied them, as did eleven cartloads of possessions.[7] Holland, the district superintendent of police, Ratnagiri, along with five orderlies, was to escort the family all the way to Rangoon.[8]

The *Fairy Queen* docked in Bombay harbour on the morning of

11 April. A police officer was waiting on shore, and the family was whisked off in two cars to the plush Taj Mahal Hotel[9] that stood on the city's waterfront. Not much is known about how the family spent their only day in the city, but from Holland's report indicating that they had not been 'in a condition to travel at once' and from their listed expenses one can surmise that they rested in their rooms. The next afternoon the family was taken to the Victoria Terminus Station from where they caught the Nagpur Mail for Calcutta.[10] On 13 April, as their train chugged through the heartland of India, a terrible act of barbarity was being perpetuated in another part of the country. This was the day of the infamous Jallianwala Bagh massacre, where a large gathering of unarmed Indians, including women and children, were repeatedly fired upon in a walled enclosure. The distress and outrage in India at this British brutality sparked off acts of violence in various parts of the country. As the press had been muzzled, and telegraph and telephone lines cut, word of the tragedy took a few days to be known,[11] so the queen's journey was unaffected by its aftermath.

The train reached Calcutta late on the morning of 14 April. Regarding the long train journey that Queen Supayalat had been so apprehensive about, Holland wrote, 'All arrangements worked without a hitch. The heat was trying but unavoidable. The ladies were extremely satisfied with the arrangements for their food and convenience.' At the Howrah railway station in Calcutta they were met by the assistant commissioner of police and sent in two cars to the Grand Hotel.[12]

The next day the Second Princess, with her husband Kin Maung Lat in tow, arrived at the hotel to meet the family. The queen flatly refused to see her. Kin Maung Lat brashly stepped into Queen Supayalat's room, but withdrew immediately when she angrily screamed at him to leave.[13] Unfortunately there is no record of the meeting between the First and Second Princesses; certainly the First would have been happy to see the Second, the only sister sympathetic to her plight. A small bit of billing information highlights the extent of the First Princess's isolation: while in Calcutta the royal family had their clothes washed. Even for this mundane task there was a division, and the First Princess and Tu Tu's clothes were washed and accounted for separately.[14]

On 16 April, at 7 a.m., the family boarded the *S.S. Arankola* sailing for Rangoon. Special food had been pre-ordered for the journey,[15] and cigarettes had been obtained at the Fourth Princess's request.[16] The family travelled first class, as did Miss Dinshaw. The old Burmese secretary was in the second class, and the servants and dogs travelled on deck.[17] The journey to Rangoon seems to have been rather uneventful, with Holland later stating:

> The passage to Rangoon was calm and speedy and made in comfort. None of the party were ill . . . We arrived at Rangoon on the afternoon of Good Friday the 18th April. The Commissioner of Police, Rangoon, and the Collector of Rangoon came on board to receive the ex-Queen and daughters. A special launch came alongside and took the party ashore where motors were in readiness. We all proceeded to the bungalow (23 Churchill Road, Rangoon) prepared for the ex-Queen and family. Here I handed over the whole party safely to the care of the Commissioner of Police, Rangoon.[18]

There were no crowds, big or small, to greet the ex-queen of Burma and her family on their arrival, as the significant news of their return had been withheld from the people of Burma.[19] Although Queen Supayalat was no longer in power, although she had been in exile for over thirty-three years, and although she had been subjected to sustained character assassination in those intervening years (leading 'most Burmese youths who could read English to believe what the British Imperialists wrote'),[20] the government felt they couldn't risk her becoming a rallying point for an anti-British nationalistic movement. Nor did they want her or the Fourth Princess to instigate a movement to restore the monarchy. As a result, the government effected her return as discreetly as possible.

Compared to the relative grandeur of the Royal Residence in Ratnagiri, Queen Supayalat's new home was a 'modest-sized',[21] two-storeyed bungalow with five main rooms. It was located in a large compound on a slight hill, and faced south. From the upper floor the queen had a spectacular view of the Shwedagon Pagoda, and she greatly appreciated this.[22] However, Mandalay was where her heart belonged, not to this very anglicized city of Rangoon, which was nothing like the Burma she remembered.[23] But she accepted that it was here that she would have to live out the rest of her days.

Queen Supayalat ensconced herself on the upper floor of her new home and never went out, never even came downstairs.[24] Although technically not a state prisoner,[25] she and her family were nonetheless guarded night and day, including by a policeman stationed *in* her home at the top of the staircase.[26] (Also, says one of her grandsons, 'anybody going out of that compound had to report to the Commissioner of Police to go out even for their shopping'.[27])

In spite of this very obvious and intimidating police presence, as word of the queen's return spread, people came by, some all the way from Mandalay, to pay their respects to her. Many members of the extended royal family, ex-maids of honour, Burmese nationalists, journalists and common citizens visited her. She received them all in her upstairs living room, dressed in the customary white she now always wore. It is said that as she swept into her living room, often with the Third and Fourth Princesses, everyone would immediately fall down in a sheiko. The queen would settle down on the floor, on a small red velvet mat laid out for her at a short distance from her visitors, then she would ask everyone to sit at ease, and the audience would begin.[28] Monks (including from the Mya Taung monastery in Mandalay, which the queen had had built as a work of merit during King Thibaw's reign) also visited her. At long last, she was able to personally make donations to monks, and hear them preach the teachings of the Buddha. At long last she was back in her homeland, among her own people, who, to her great relief, accorded her a very warm welcome. At long last she was receiving the attention and being given the respect that she felt she deserved. And, over a period of time, although she continued looking older than her years for the long exile had taken its toll, the daily stream of visitors helped revive her. Now no longer withdrawn, disinterested and quiet, she freely expressed her opinions to the audience that sat reverentially before her[29] and soon it was obvious that 'age and long years of her captivity had not broken her spirit'.[30]

While returning to Burma impacted the queen so positively, it had quite the opposite effect on the First Princess. Shortly after reaching Burma, the First Princess gave birth to a stillborn child.[31] It is unlikely that anyone shared her grief or helped to ease her pain. While there had, again, been a shift in the family's attitude towards her, and they no longer isolated her,[32] it is hard to imagine that her severely moralistic family showed much sympathy at the death of an unwanted child born of an unacceptable alliance. In their new home the First Princess closeted herself in her room with her daughter. She did her best to avoid her sisters, although apparently they did make some effort to reconcile with her. The First Princess did, however, occasionally visit her mother who, according to an observer, 'receive[d] her in a perfectly friendly spirit'.[33] On hearing her daughter's incessant pleas to be allowed to go back to Ratnagiri, and on seeing her increasing despair and loneliness, the queen tried to help her settle down by insisting that she accompany her sisters on their rather infrequent outings. The First Princess did go with her sisters at least once to the Shwedagon Pagoda, but details of this excursion are unknown.[34]

In September 1919, the First Princess sent off the first of a series of letters to the lieutenant governor of Burma, Sir Reginald Craddock, pleading to be allowed to return to Ratnagiri. She and Gopal had been writing to each other, and he constantly asked her to return. It was suspected that it was Gopal who penned the First Princess's letter, which is partially reproduced below:

> Ever since I was brought over to Burma from Ratnagiri with my mother, Her Majesty the Queen, and my sister Princesses, I have not been feeling well and comfortable as I was in the climate of Ratnagiri to which I had become acclimatized by a continual stay there from my early childhood. I have been feeling unhappy, gloomy and sickly here, and very much long to be restored to the place of my adoption whose air became as the very breath of my nostrils, and the sudden separation from the associations of which has been my sorrow . . .[35]

Sir Reginald immediately asked his office to interview the First Princess and to write to the collector of Ratnagiri for further information. As interviews were conducted in Ratnagiri and in Rangoon, as letters went back and forth between various government departments in India and Burma, and as the details of the First Princess's circumstance became better known, the lieutenant governor and his office realized that this was not a decision to be made lightly. In the past, Gopal had see-sawed over the question of marriage; he now indicated that 'marriage is impossible' as it would lead to him being 'outcasted', not a small matter in early twentieth-century India. Gopal, a Maratha, could only marry someone of his own caste, and definitely not a non-Hindu. For this reason he could not take the First Princess even as his second or lesser wife (which, in the government's opinion, 'could not be more humiliating than that of being the mother of his illegitimate child'[36]). The British consulted various eminent Marathas to check the veracity of his statements and they confirmed that what Gopal said was indeed true.[37]

There was also no question of the First Princess going to live in Gopal's family home, because even this would lead to Gopal's outcasting and, besides, this would cause Gopal's wife to leave—again something Gopal did not want. The government discovered that what Gopal wanted was for 'the Princess to come and live in a separate house of her own where he could be at liberty to visit her. He says his wife would not object to that . . . in such a case the caste also would have nothing to say.' The lieutenant governor of Burma discovered something else too: Gopal seemed to be more interested in the First Princess's pension than in the princess herself.[38]

During the many months that the matter was being considered, the opinion of leading Burmese, including the Sawbwa of Nyaungshwe (the Shan chief very close to Queen Supayalat), were taken. They were all unanimous in their view that the First Princess should *not* be allowed to return to Ratnagiri; allowing her return, even if she were to marry Gopal, 'would be regarded as a disgrace to the *ex*-Royal family and to the Burmese people as a whole'.[39] The queen and the Fourth Princess refused to publicly voice any view on the matter. All they would say was that it was entirely up to the government to decide what should be done.[40] (According to Prince Taw Phaya Galae—the Fourth Princess's son—his mother told him many years later that the family had strongly opposed the First Princess's return to Ratnagiri, and had privately expressed this to her.[41])

By now, there was a volley of increasingly desperate letters from the First Princess, and she threatened to commit suicide if not permitted to return. Although Burmese public opinion indicated that it preferred 'a tragedy to disgrace', the lieutenant governor's office searched for

solutions. Could a marriage be arranged with a family member of one
of the Shan Sawbwas, or some other respectable Burman, they wondered.
But they realized that the First Princess was in no frame of mind to be
receptive to such a proposition[42] and, besides, they knew that arranging
such a marriage would not be easy because of her age and history.[43]
They offered her various options including a separate house anywhere
she wished in Burma, just for her and her daughter, but she expressed
her unwillingness to stay on in the country. The government by now
realized that it was her royal status that was preventing her from doing
what she desired. As women from European royal families were
permitted to marry commoners if they relinquished their royal status
and privileges, the government asked her whether she was willing to
renounce her royal status. She said yes.[44] All she wanted was permission
to return to Ratnagiri, to Gopal.

The First Princess had to have known that her pension was important
to Gopal. After all, over the years he had constantly taken money and
anything else he could from her. But she still clung to him; she still
drew some solace from their relationship. Perhaps like her late father
who had rejected the British ultimatum, acceptance of which would
have allowed him to continue sitting on the Lion Throne (albeit
without much authority), because he felt he had no other *real* choice,
she too felt returning to Gopal was her only tolerable option.

By this time the lieutenant governor of Burma thought he was no
longer justified in refusing the First Princess's request.[45] After all she
was not a giddy-headed teenager but a mature woman nearing forty. His
office also speculated that because of the long years of exile perhaps

> her return to Burma, instead of being a return to her homeland, is an
> exile from the only country she knows. Her letters and her replies to
> interrogatories present a true picture of a lonely stranger in a strange
> land, cut off by her royal status from the only direction from which
> she can ever hope to receive any alleviation of her pitiable loneliness.[46]

But, like her family, the government also judged her harshly ('one of
the ladies beyond reform'[47] was one of the written comments made
about her) and treated her severely. It was decided that her monthly
allowance would be only a fraction of what her sisters were to be given
once they were respectably married. She was informed that she would

get Rs 200—the personal allowance now given to unmarried daughters of King Thibaw—if she returned to Ratnagiri. This bit of information did nothing to change her mind.[48]

Only after the First Princess had signed a declaration renouncing her 'rank and title and status as a Princess of the Burmese Royal House', giving up on behalf of her children any claim for a government allowance, and indicating she understood that she was returning as a 'private person' for whom the government had absolutely no responsibility, was she given permission to return to Ratnagiri. While there is no doubt that this declaration was carefully explained to her, and she agreed to all the conditions,[49] it is doubtful if she comprehended the ramifications. This was a person who had had almost no exposure to the outside world and almost no education, a person with no ability to react intellectually rather than viscerally. This was also a person who, by this stage, was so anxious to leave that she would have signed *any* declaration.

On 29 June 1920, escorted by Mrs Simpson, a 'respectable Anglo-Indian lady', the First Princess and her daughter left Burma for Ratnagiri via Calcutta,[50] never again to return to the country of her birth or see her mother and sisters. Queen Supayalat, 'very strong-minded and very angry with the First Princess for going back', never spoke, or even mentioned the name of, this daughter again.[51]

17

QUEEN SUPAYALAT

The Fourth Princess and Ko Ko Naing were married on 1 July 1920, just two days after the First Princess departed for Ratnagiri. There had been a slight hiccup in their romance a few months before the wedding: a group of Siamese had called on the queen with a proposal that the Fourth Princess be given in marriage to one of their princes. Queen Supayalat, very pleased, had asked for a photograph of the prince.[1] It wasn't that the queen didn't approve of Ko Ko Naing; she did. She was aware that after the annexation of Burma, many Burmese princesses married monks because monks formed the educated class[2] and were revered by the people. Additionally a monk was considered 'a free man, not a slave'.[3] Besides, Ko Ko Naing had proved his worth by having been a pillar of strength during the family's final days in Ratnagiri, by having loyally followed them back to Rangoon, and by having 'de-robed' to declare his affection for the Fourth Princess. But the queen was not averse to considering all options, especially good royal ones.

It appears that the Fourth Princess was also pleased, or at least flattered, by the proposal. She prominently displayed the handsome prince's photograph on her bedside table as soon as it arrived. Ko Ko Naing, needless to say, was upset by this turn of events. He is said to have put pressure on the Fourth Princess to commit herself to him, which she did. The queen gave her permission for the marriage after Ko Ko Naing agreed to a few conditions she laid down, including that he would 'marry [the princess] till death'.[4]

The marriage was held at the queen's residence with her blessing.[5] Various newspapers printed brief articles about it including *The Times of India,* which reported that the bride 'was simply dressed and wore no jewellery', and that the wedding 'was performed with traditional Brahministic rites by U Than Da, who was chief astrologer at Thebaw's court.' It also mentioned that although the queen did not attend the ceremony herself, she had given instructions for the poor to be fed.[6]

For about a year after their wedding the Fourth Princess and Ko Ko Naing lived with the queen. It was sometime in 1921 that they moved into a rented home of their own, not too far from the queen's house.[7] Even when not living with her mother, the Fourth Princess visited her daily and, just as she had in Ratnagiri, the queen continued to rely on her for advice and help.[8]

The Third Princess got married in 1921, but without the queen's approval. The queen had requested one of her favourite cousins to move in with her, and this cousin had brought along her very personable son, Prince Hteik Tin Kodaw Gyi.[9] The Third Princess was about thirty-six at this time, and was a 'simple, trusting person'. Prince Hteik Tin Kodaw Gyi 'was a 17 year old, fair, handsome and affable young man, an errand and odd job man for the queen . . . the two became very close . . .'[10] Prince Hteik Tin Kodaw Gyi's mother was one of Prince Kanaung's daughters, but his father was a commoner and that made him a prince of no significance. The couple, aware that the queen would disapprove of their relationship (the difference in age seems not to have been as relevant as his lack of standing), hid it from her, and ran away together to Mandalay.[11] Queen Supayalat was devastated; this, after all, was the daughter she was closest to,[12] the daughter without whom she had said she could not live.[13] Besides, she was acutely aware that now three of her daughters had blatantly defied her.

In Mandalay, Prince Kanaung's daughters huddled together to decide on what to do next. One of them had a long-standing grouse against Queen Supayalat: the king and queen's extreme reaction to the Second Princess's marriage to Kin Maung Lat had deeply offended her as Kin Maung Lat was her nephew. She urged her sister to 'have a grand wedding ceremony in Mandalay for her son and the Third Princess . . . not to care about the Queen's reaction'. Influenced by her, and by the awkward presence of the courting couple, Prince Hteik Tin Kodaw Gyi's mother hurriedly arranged a well-attended wedding ceremony in her home. Not only did no one ask the queen for her permission, but she was also given no intimation, and certainly no invitation.[14]

After the Third Princess's elopement, Queen Supayalat lived with just her staff. The Fourth Princess was not in a position to move back in with her mother because it is believed that Ko Ko Naing had taken to the bottle, something the queen would not have tolerated in her home. Troubled at the prospect of her elderly mother living alone with just her staff, the Fourth Princess lobbied very hard to try and get the queen to forgive the Third Princess. The Wet-masoot Wundauk and the Sawbwa of Nyaungshwe (two people the queen trusted) also worked on a resolution, and about a year and a half after the Third Princess's marriage, she was forgiven and she and her husband were invited back by the queen.[15] It seems to have been an extremely well effected reconciliation, for no ill-will ever showed between mother and this daughter,[16] and the Third Princess and her husband lived with the queen until her death. The Third Princess often attended her mother's audiences, sometimes answering questions for her, and Prince Hteik Tin Kodaw Gyi supervised the running of her house and welcomed her visitors.[17]

Her religion, and the audiences she gave to an endless stream of visitors, dominated Queen Supalayat's life after her return to Burma. Around fifteen pongyis or monks visited her daily to collect their morning alms. The queen rose early every day to supervise the making of rice and curry dishes for these revered men.[18] She told a rare British visitor, whom she had permitted into her presence, that she fed pongyis and provided them with the eight necessities (three pieces of cloth for robes, a mat, a bowl, a water strainer, a needle and a razor[19]) because 'now is the time to do good deeds as I am aging so [I need] to wash out all the misdoings of the past'.[20]

There was another reason the queen donated so generously to pongyis, a reason she did not share with her foreign visitor. She regarded herself as the patron of her religion. According to U Than Swe, 'in our divine faith of the kingship, the king and the queen are the supporter for religion, so whether they want or not, they *have* to donate to the pagodas, to the monks.'[21] As to why she always wore white, she said, 'not because of my husband's death. I wear white only for remorse.'[22] And, some years later, she declared that she was still wearing white because she 'had cleaned out all her sin. White is very pure and clean, isn't it? That is why she was wearing white, because she [had] purified herself.'[23] The queen's immersion in her religion was not just ritualistic—it helped her understand and cope. To one visitor she commented, 'I have been well aware of the ups and downs of life for 37 years [since the time of her exile]. I well understand the law of impermanence. I have experienced personally this Dhamma [Buddha's teaching] . . .' and she recalled her journey from a beautiful palace to an ordinary home, from freedom to subjugation.[24]

Queen Supayalat often discussed with her visitors her sorrow at having had to leave her husband's remains behind in Ratnagiri. She stressed that the appropriate last rites had not been conducted for him or her sister.[25] But she never explained that it was she and the Fourth Princess who had turned down repeated offers made by the government to conduct the king's last rites according to Burmese royal custom, including offers to send for pongyis from Mandalay. It is apparent that she and her daughter had fervently hoped that if these rites were not performed, heightened public sympathy might sway the government to change its mind about allowing the entombment of the coffins in Burma.

Most of the queen's visitors found that she did not hesitate to speak her mind, and was straightforward and honest about answering the questions put to her, including about the massacre of the royals in 1879 (she vehemently denied any role in it).[26] The queen's audiences frequently consisted of her royal relatives, and much to her relief they came with no grievances and seemed to harbour no ill-will for events of the past, not for the loss of the kingdom, not for the massacre.[27] Many years later, in the 1960s, one of King Mindon's granddaughters would say in a newspaper interview that it was Sinbyumashin who was responsible for the massacre:

> I bring this up not with any rancour or hatred. It is to clear Supayalat's name. She has been much maligned over this mass killing. It had nothing to do with her ... It had little to do with Thibaw also. Thibaw's fault was his weakness ... We have even forgiven Sinbyumashin but whether history could gloss over her part in this massacre is another thing.[28]

One of the queen's earliest visitors after her return was her old European maid of honour, Hosannah Manook. Mattie Calogreedy (who had supposedly betrayed her in 1885 by passing on confidential French agreements to the British) also visited her.[29] It appears the queen was unaware of Mattie's involvement in the fall of the kingdom. She held a certain U Mye (a Hluttaw clerk) responsible for having leaked the agreements.[30] However in certain circles Mattie's role was known: when W. Somerset Maugham chronicled his visit to Mandalay in his travelogue *The Gentleman in the Parlour,* he wrote that he was taken to meet 'an old lady who in her day had made history'. He described how stoutly Mattie defended Queen Supayalat as 'a very nice woman, and people had been so unkind about her; all those stories of the massacres she had instigated, stuff and nonsense! ... I know for a fact that she did not murder more than two or three people at the outside.'[31]

Many noticed that the queen lived firmly in the past, both in terms of what she dwelt on, and the customs she followed. This anachronistic existence of the last queen of Burma drew curious visitors who came to witness living history.[32] Her daughters, when present, sat next to her, but faced her and not the visitors. Holding audience was a formal occasion and the princesses were not permitted to smile at people, including those they knew.[33] During one long session, it was noticed that the queen and the Third Princess did not even slightly shift their positions. The queen's staff (by one count thirty-eight, most of them Indians[34]) was well trained, very clean and neat, and had been taught 'the good and gentle manners' of her palace days.[35] A young monk served as the queen's reader; he came in daily, at one in the afternoon, to read Burmese literature and poetry. The queen, of course, could read herself, but it had been customary for royalty to have their own personal readers.[36] The queen was also fond of classical Burmese music, and the gifted musician Ywasargyi Sein Beida (who had travelled to Ratnagiri to play at the housewarming ceremony) frequently visited and played for her.[37]

Giving a generous reward to those who came to pay homage, or to those who pleased her, was something the queen had done in her palace days, and to the extent she could, in Ratnagiri. Now back in the land where she had once been queen, it was a constant source of embarrassment and regret for her that she could no longer give gifts liberally to deserving visitors.[38] Trying to hold on to even a feeble semblance of the past caused her pension to often run out. (The queen's pension had been increased to Rs 4,000 per month when she first returned to Burma. However, it had been since reduced to Rs 2,500—after deducting the Third and Fourth Princesses' separate allowances. Apart from her pension, the government paid for the rent of her furnished house.[39]) On one occasion, when a princess read out a poem she had composed in the queen's honour, the deeply moved queen immediately wanted to give her a gift, but was unable to do so. She remarked, rather apologetically, 'I wish to give some money as a reward to the Pinle Princess but I might be able to do so only at the beginning of next month when I get my pension.' The Sawbwa of Nyaungshwe was present in the audience that day and he immediately asked the queen how much she would like to give. When told a hundred rupees, he gave her this amount in a small velvet bag for her to hand over to the Pinle Princess.[40] On another occasion, perhaps not having anything else to hand out, the queen warmly offered a gift-bearing ex-maid of honour *pwedawkya* (the leftovers of a meal eaten by the chief queen).[41]

With many of her visitors she indulged in reminiscing about bygone palace days. On one occasion she and a half-sister, Princess Mintat Hteik Kaung Tin, recalled the first Thingyan (water) festival after her ascension to the throne. Her half-sister had been thirteen at the time, and had had the audacity to pour water on the queen as she walked past. Everyone present had quaked with fear, wondering how the imperious queen would react to such impertinence. But the queen, only twenty, had welcomed this breach of protocol, this spontaneous inclusion in the revelry her exalted position now excluded her from. She had immediately rewarded her sister with two small delicately crafted fishes, made of gold; her sister now told the queen that she had greatly treasured this gift, and had it in her possession to this day.[42]

It appears that not only the queen's spirit but also her sharp wit revived not long after her return. Although protocol prevented people from actually laughing out aloud in her presence, it was evident they appreciated her humour. When told by Princess Mintat Hteik Kaung Tin that her husband was now a town commissioner, Queen Supayalat quipped (not unkindly), 'Oh! A town commissioner! Does he have the *real* authority?'[43] Everyone present knew he didn't; Burma was after all still under British rule. When told that the British had sent this half-sister and her mother off to settle in Rangoon—after Mandalay was captured—on a steamer called *Alaungpaya* the queen is said to have commented, 'How very indecent on the part of the British to give the name of our great ancestor to a steamboat. These British are only white on the skin. [Inside] they have such dark and clever ideas!'[44] (At the time she made this remark, many in her audience would have understood its significance. It was known that the colonizing British made ceaseless attempts to 'wash black people white' by converting them to Christianity. The native who converted to Christianity was viewed as 'black' on the outside, but Christian and therefore good and 'white' on the inside.[45])

A nationalist, Maung Lun, as anti-British as the queen, had been one of her first visitors when she had returned. This man went on to become a towering and revered figure in Burma, well known both for his contributions to Burmese literature and to his country's struggle for independence. A poet, journalist, historian, nationalist and peace activist, Maung Lun is more commonly known as Thakin Kodaw Hmaing (the name he assumed from 1935). Thakin Kodaw Hmaing had been a boarder in the Mya Taung monastery in Mandalay in 1885. Then around ten years old, he had stood and watched his king and queen being ignominiously carted away by British forces. This incident and its implications—the fall of the Konbaung dynasty and with it the occupation of Upper Burma by foreign forces—were seminal ones in Thakin Kodaw Hmaing's life and awakened in him an intense sense of patriotism that would dictate the direction of his life.[46] In a poem he wrote some years later, he described what he had seen and how he had felt:

> From the Mya Taung Monastery, a sacred Buddhist precinct
> I witnessed the taking of the sun and the moon [king and chief queen]
> I was so filled with anguish and disappointment
> That my patriotic spirit was aroused . . . [47]

Queen Supayalat and Thakin Kodaw Hmaing held each other in high esteem.[48] A frequent and welcome visitor to her home, Thakin Kodaw Hmaing became her confidante and ardent supporter. Other nationalists—lawyers, writers, and political and social activists—also often visited the queen.[49] The queen had returned to Burma shortly after latent Burmese nationalism had been awakened by the Montagu–Chelmsford report (which, in 1918, suggested the gradual introduction of limited self-governance in India, but not in Burma, for it was felt that Burma was not as yet ready for it)[50] and, not long after her return, the queen became for some, just as the British had feared, an emblem for the country's independence.[51] While most nationalists did not attempt to romanticize the queen,[52] many empathized with her, and increasingly resented the treatment meted out to her by the British.

Although the queen's home had been refurbished before she had occupied it in 1919, it appears that no repairs were carried out after that. Since it was a wooden structure subjected yearly to Rangoon's heavy monsoon rains, it needed regular maintenance. Visitors to the queen's residence noticed that her home progressively got more decrepit.[53] Written and verbal reports created growing public awareness of the queen's living conditions. Many applauded her for her generosity to men in robes, for whom she had so visibly sacrificed her own creature comforts. Many admired her dignity and composure in the face of sustained adversity. Many respected her for her unyielding anti-colonial stand. Many begrudged the fact that the government not only paid her an inadequate pension, but had also not returned to her the landed property she had held in her own name, or the many valuables (including the priceless Nga Mauk ruby) entrusted by King Thibaw to Colonel Sladen. And many took exception to the fact that permission had been denied for the entombment of the remains of King Thibaw and Queen Supayagalae in Mandalay. The General Council of Burmese Associations set up a committee to study the problems faced by Queen Supayalat, and in early 1925 it came out with a report that listed various grievances and urged the Nationalist Party to take up her case with the government.[54] Nothing came of this except heightened public awareness, and Queen Supayalat's life continued much as before.

The queen lived to see the birth of two granddaughters and three grandsons after her return to Burma. A few years after her return, in answer to reporters' questions about her health, the queen no longer talked of being 'old and naturally infirm' as she had when leaving Ratnagiri, but responded that her health was good.[55] For her birthday on 13 December 1925 the queen had planned special offerings for pongyis; however, just weeks before it she suddenly fell ill. The government-selected Indian doctor, who had been assigned to look after her, had always resented that he had to remove his shoes before entering her room, and on this occasion, perhaps thinking she was too sick to pay attention, came in fully shod. But the queen immediately noticed and sharply ordered him out. The doctor replied that he would leave as soon as he finished examining her. This enraged the queen. Lifting a silver spittoon lying by her side, she hurled it, with surprising strength, at him. The greatly startled and highly indignant doctor beat such a hasty retreat that as he galloped down the steps, he stumbled, fell and broke his little finger. After this he flatly refused to visit her, and the proud, dying old queen did not receive the medical attention she so desperately needed. Her fever continued, and she became increasingly weaker. The doctor was persuaded to return a few days later, but by then it was too late. But even if he had visited earlier (he returned the day before her death) perhaps it would have made little difference because she had always distrusted this British-selected doctor, was afraid of being poisoned, and had specified that none of the medicines suggested by him be given to her. She preferred to rely on plant-based, natural Burmese remedies.[56]

On the morning of 24 November 1925 (less than three weeks shy of her sixty-sixth birthday), Queen Supayalat died of a heart attack.[57] A writer for the *Dagon* magazine came to pay his last respects at about 6 p.m. on the same day, and he recorded his visit as follows:

> There was nobody upstairs. It was very still and quiet under the electric lights. My eyes wandered and I saw the body of the Chief Queen lying on a bed in a small room. There was nobody except the senior maid sitting by the bedside and fanning the body. All was very still and quiet . . .
>
> Suddenly I wanted to take a close look at the Chief Queen, so I got up and moved closer to the bed. The senior maid did not even glance at me. I took a closer look at the Queen and saw that she was an old woman . . . the face seemed to be alive, it looked serene and tranquill; there were no wrinkles. A (crown) was worn on this head once upon a time. Orders which could change the lives of citizens came out from these lips . . . These eyes had witnessed the downfall of the Kingdom . . . And once upon a time she had been the most powerful [person] in the country.[58]

The government paid over 80 per cent of the cost of Queen Supayalat's funeral[59] from the Reserve Fund that had been set up during the exile.[60] The Sawbwa of Nyaungshwe was asked to oversee the arrangements, a funeral committee was set up, and in consultation with the government, it was decided that she be entombed in Queen's Park (now called Kandawmin Gardens), a stone's throw from the Shwedagon Pagoda, the pagoda which had meant so much to her. Queen Supayalat's body was placed in a coffin on 4 December,[61] and the day of her entombment, 17 December 1925, was declared a national holiday.[62] Thousands attended the funeral ceremony, which was grandly conducted with eight ceremonial white umbrellas shading her coffin. A large entourage of monks, followed by a sizeable number of bullock carts loaded with charitable gifts, formed part of the procession.[63] The governor of Burma, Sir Harcourt Butler, joined the cortege on horseback.[64] But in spite of the pomp and pageantry, the disappointment was palpable. It had been the wish of the Burmese people that their queen's remains be entombed in Mandalay next to that of her father's, and that the remains of King Thibaw and Queen Supayagalae also be brought home at this time. But the British government refused both requests.[65] Echoing the sentiment of the people, the funeral committee refused to recognize the queen's entombment in Rangoon as final, but viewed it as a temporary arrangement.[66]

Afraid of the emotions Thakin Kodaw Hmaing might stoke up, the British government did not permit him to attend the funeral of the queen he revered.[67] However, in spite of this precaution, according to U Than Swe, 'the funeral of the Chief Queen played a very important role in nurturing the national spirit among the Burmese people of all classes'.[68] Many were moved to tears on the occasion. Also moved seems to have been the reporter who wrote the following article for *The Rangoon Times* (possibly for the first and last time a British-controlled paper printed an article that did not further vilify the already much maligned last queen of Burma):

> There passed away on 24th November in Churchill Road, Rangoon, a striking figure in the history of Burma—ex-Queen Supayalat . . .
>
> On her return to Burma, one noticed that there had been a complete metamorphosis in her life. The turbulent spirit of the past was quelled and she became a peaceloving lady. She spent the last years of her life in more or less complete seclusion, and in many acts of piety and charity she sought to wipe away the dark stains of her life. She was charitable to a fault and spent a great portion of her allowance in assisting the poor.
>
> The funeral ceremonies were such as befitted her position. Over a lakh people thronged the streets to watch it. H.E. the Governor, Sir Harcourt Butler, was present in the Cantonment Gardens, where, after the usual ritual, the body was laid to rest in a specially constructed mausoleum.
>
> Burma mourned the death of her ex-Queen, not because of her past greatness, for it was blurred; not because of her royalty, which had faded; not even because of the impulse of sentiment; but because of her piety and charity after dethronement. She was a tragic figure in the history of Burma, but she will go down to posterity as one that in her late life had learnt the lesson of true queenliness.[69]

18

THE FOURTH PRINCESS

The first seven years of the Fourth Princess's married life were, in one respect, strikingly like the first seven years of her mother's married life: she was in an almost perpetual state of pregnancy. Over this period, she had four sons and two daughters. Until her mother's death, the Fourth Princess stayed in Rangoon looking after her rapidly increasing brood, attending many of her mother's audiences, and advising her on all matters big and small. Not only was she a dominant force in the queen's home, but she also made an impact on the extended royal family and on various Burmese nationalists who interacted with her,[1] and many regarded her as 'influential and arrogant'.[2]

Adding to the Fourth Princess's authority was the fact that, unlike her mother and sisters, she could communicate in English with ease. (According to her niece, the Fourth Princess spoke with a British accent, acquired, of course, from the English companions she had had in Ratnagiri![3]) Like before, she did not hesitate to express her opinions or demands. Shortly after the royal family's return to Rangoon, the Fourth Princess approached Lady Craddock, wife of the

lieutenant governor of Burma, to complain that the home selected by
the government for the queen was unbefitting, and that the family
'wished to stay in Mandalay Palace, if it was put to repairs'.[4] Although
nothing came of it, this request perhaps served to warn the government
of the Fourth Princess's aspirations. It certainly should have!

After her marriage, the Fourth Princess was given a pension of
Rs 750 and a house rent allowance of Rs 250 a month. (A festival
allowance of Rs 500 per annum was also given, and she was eligible for
grants for ceremonies like marriage, cradling, earboring, and for
medical expenses and school fees.[5]) Although this should have enabled
her and her family to live fairly comfortably, by normal standards, the
Fourth Princess found the amount inadequate. Her son, Prince Taw
Phaya, recalls staying on Wisara Road as a young child and 'in 4 or 5
big houses in Yangon [Rangoon]. The last one on Dama-sedi road was
on a hillock—now a high-rise building is there. The reason for us
shifting houses in Yangon was that there was a tussle between our
mother and the Government over house rent.'[6] The Fourth Princess
staffed these sizeable homes well, borrowed to meet the perpetual
shortfall created by a lifestyle she felt was her right, and wrote
numerous petulant letters to the government complaining about the
inadequacy of her pension.

Every month, after paying salaries to her staff, the Fourth Princess
threw coins as gratuity, for which they all had to scramble. When
paying vendors she magnanimously waived the change. As far as she
was concerned she was just following old royal customs, but to her
husband all this was unnecessary and, in their present circumstances, a
ridiculous waste of money. Ko Ko Naing's disapproval, combined with
the fact that he was now drinking, led to friction between the couple.[7]

Tension was also brewing between the Third and Fourth Princesses.[8]
Of her three sisters, it was with the Third Princess that the Fourth
shared the strongest bond, and the exact reason for their rift is not
known. While the Fourth Princess had herself coaxed the queen to
invite the Third Princess back, perhaps she resented her mother's
continued and obvious attachment to the Third Princess. The queen
leaned heavily on her youngest daughter for advice and support, but
her heart, like before, blatantly belonged to the Third Princess. The

Third Princess perhaps begrudged her mother's continued reliance on the Fourth Princess in spite of her husband, Prince Hteik Tin Kodaw Gyi, now constantly being at the queen's beck and call, ready, available and eager to advise and support. The two brothers-in-law, Prince Hteik Tin Kodaw Gyi and Ko Ko Naing, had nothing in common and felt no particular affinity for each other.[9]

Shortly after the queen's death, both the Third and Fourth Princesses applied (separately) for permission to move to Mandalay. As Mandalay had been their father's capital, the government was apprehensive that his daughters would be able to exert undue influence there. Additionally, it was felt that if they combined forces they would present a greater threat. So, although both sisters were allowed to shift, they were informed that hereafter they could meet each other only with the government's prior permission.[10] The Fourth Princess shifted to Mandalay in late 1927 or early 1928, sometime after the birth of her youngest child.[11] Every summer, she and her family would relocate to Maymyo, a small cool hill town not far from Mandalay. Maymyo was where the Third Princess had settled (after living for a while in Mandalay), but in spite of the proximity of their homes the sisters could rarely meet,[12] making the healing of differences very difficult.

For the Fourth Princess's children, Mandalay has happy memories. Her eldest daughter, Princess Hteik Su Phaya Gyi, says that as children they would often go to the Golden Palace to play. Although it was in poor condition, with many of its original buildings demolished and, in the words of the Fourth Princess, 'full of bats and filthy and dirty with their dung', the children enjoyed their visits. On one occasion, Prince Taw Phaya Gyi, the Fourth Princess's eldest son, climbed up and sat on the Lion Throne. A caretaker materialized instantly, roughly grabbed the young boy by his shirt, and tried to yank him off. According to Princess Hteik Su Phaya Gyi, their old governess—who had come from India with her mother (perhaps Mary Dinshaw)—sternly admonished the caretaker saying, 'don't touch these children, they are the owners of this palace. This palace is their grandparent's. So the caretaker joined his hands, and bowed . . .'[13] (Prince Taw Phaya Gyi was probably the last member of the royal family ever to sit on the Lion Throne. The throne, with the rest of the palace, was destroyed in a fire caused by an Allied attack towards the end of World War II. The Lion Throne now seen in the National Museum in Rangoon was the one that used to be housed in the Hluttaw.[14] It was taken to Calcutta in 1886 as a prize of war— therefore surviving the bombing—and was gifted back in March 1948, a couple of months after Burma's independence.[15])

Prince Taw Phaya recalls that his mother's birthday celebrations were 'tame affairs': five to ten pongyis were given their mid-day meal and gifts of the eight necessities; the pongyis chanted *parittas* (religious passages chanted for protection) and shared merit; the family ate a special meal. The big affairs, he says, were on the queen and king's death anniversaries, especially the king's.

> What I remember was on the Queen's death day my father used to go down from Mandalay to Rangoon and have the same ceremony like the Princess's birthday but on a bigger scale like having 25 or 30 monks. The King's death day was observed in Mandalay . . . After feeding the monks and sharing of merits, the monks would line up to return to their monasteries, and relatives of princes, princesses and the offspring of Palace officials, maids, pageboys and others connected with the monarchy could offer what they could to the monks while the Palace drummers played on their big drums.[16]

For the Fourth Princess, life was neither carefree nor easy in Mandalay. Being in her father's capital meant receiving an endless stream of visitors who came to pay homage to his daughter. Although she appreciated this attention and show of respect, she had to entertain these visitors in a manner she felt befitted her position, and this added considerably to her expenses. Additionally, the power and financial freedom she had enjoyed in her parents' home had evaporated in her marital home. She had neither Ko Ko Naing's unconditional love, nor his blanket approval. Instead, he had become disapproving, dominating and difficult. Not long after their marriage, Ko Ko Naing began asserting his position as the man of the house, and therefore its head.[17] And, over a period of time, his authority pervaded spheres that had always been hers in the past.

For centuries Burmese women had been known to be remarkably equal to men in terms of the law of the land, in the independence and freedom they enjoyed (surprising many Western travellers in the 1800s and early 1900s), and in many of their customs (there was no concept of a surname and Burmese women never changed their names after marriage; nor was any prefix like 'Miss' or 'Mrs' used before their names to spell out their marital status).[18] The vast majority of them, nonetheless, deferred to their men, as they still do. This deference is for various reasons born of their culture and religion. In Buddhism, a man is regarded to be higher on the spiritual ladder of existence than a woman. The relationship between a husband and a wife bears this in mind: the man is *ain oo nat* or the 'spirit head of the house'.[19] And as Aung San Suu Kyi so charmingly puts it, 'Secure in the knowledge of her own worth, the Burmese woman does not mind giving men the kind of respectful treatment that makes them so happy.'[20]

The Fourth Princess had grown up watching her mother treat her father in accordance with Burmese custom. Although very clearly the stronger and the more dominant one in the relationship, she attempted not to dishonour him: 'She was very humble or kind to the king,' says one of their grandsons.[21] Perhaps accepting that this was the way things had to be, the Fourth Princess yielded to Ko Ko Naing, maybe hoping that he would soon appreciate her worth and give her the same free rein her father had. But Ko Ko Naing was no King Thibaw.

Ko Ko Naing not only had a very strong personality, but like the Fourth Princess, was reputed to be sharp and intelligent. Having lived as an austere monk for over ten years, he had been transformed into a highly disciplined and thrifty young man.[22] As the Fourth Princess's consort, Ko Ko Naing did not need to earn a living. He, on the contrary, felt entitled to pocket her monthly pension and to dole out to her whatever he thought fit for her to run the house on. He used the amount he saved to buy houses and land. Not too many years earlier a collector in Ratnagiri had opined, '[I]t is quite impossible for any man to control her';[23] in Ko Ko Naing, the Fourth Princess had more than met her match.

The government, who had always found the Fourth Princess intractable, also tried to contain her in various ways. According to her youngest son, Prince Taw Phaya Galae, '[Our] guardian at the time were not our parents but the British Commissioner . . .'[24] In a long

letter in which she listed a litany of her complaints the Fourth
Princess said, 'Not only have the Government refused us permission
to put our children in the school we want, they have also interfered in
their education. In thus acting, perhaps the Government have not
considered whether they can have more sympathy for the welfare and
progress of the children than their parents.'[25] Her children were
enrolled in missionary schools and, as was then the custom, were given
Christian names. Her children were now known as Prince George,
Princess Tessie, Prince Edward, Prince Terence, Prince Frederick and
Princess Margaret. Staunchly Buddhist and deeply nationalistic, the
Fourth Princess must have hated this, but surprisingly she did not
complain about the renaming—at least not in writing. Perhaps she
realized there was nothing she could do about it,[26] and wanted to
conserve her energy for other battles.

Although called Su Phaya Galae by her family, the Fourth Princess's
title was Ashin Hteik Su Myat Phaya Galae. Her title was, in effect,
the name by which she was known in public. Just as the government
had prevented her parents from using their titles after the king's
deposition, they now prevented the Fourth Princess from using hers.[27]
Highly indignant, she wrote, 'Although the people of the world can use
freely their names, which were given to them by their parents, we, who
are powerless, have not been permitted to use our worthless names.'[28]

The Fourth Princess also resented other restrictions placed on her,
and wrote 'although we have been living lawfully for many years, the
Government have forbidden us from associating with Burmese
nationalists legally; from residing in places which we like, and in
particular they have refused us permission to go to England'. (She had
wished to travel to England to present all her grievances and make all
her claims directly to someone who could address them, instead of
routing her pleas through the quagmire of the British bureaucratic
hierarchy.) Deeply frustrated, she commented bitterly, 'Although we
are still alive, there is no difference between us and dead persons.'[29]

By 1930, the Fourth Princess busied herself with efforts to make
her most dramatic claim: a written claim to her father's kingdom. She
began by putting down on paper details of her ancestors' origins, and
events leading up to the annexation; she listed properties belonging to

her family that had been handed over to Colonel Sladen at the time of
her father's deposition, and listed other properties that had once
belonged to her family and had been appropriated by the government.
She prepared a long and detailed missive, which she ended with a list
of her 'grievances and sufferings' and of her 'legitimate claims'. She
addressed this letter to the Governments of England, India and Burma
and sent it on 27 October 1930, and then sent a more elaborate
version of the same letter on 15 December 1931 (the second letter
was later published as a thirty-four-page booklet entitled 'Private
Affairs'). Not satisfied that her second submission would get the
attention it deserved (her first had been ignored), she defiantly sent
off copies to the League of Nations and to various heads of state.[30]

Her claims included the restoration of 'the paddy lands, garden
lands and other cultivated lands ... which were confiscated by the
Government and which were given to the children of my grandparents
and my parents as gifts during their earboring ceremony, cradling and
other auspicious ceremonies'. She also asked for the restoration of
confiscated 'invaluable properties and jewelleries belonging to my
parents and grandmother' and indicated that if these could not be
returned, the family be monetarily compensated to the value of 'not
less than 5000 crores of rupees.' She demanded the return of the 164
oil wells which according to her were 'the private and personal properties
of my parents' and a compensation of Rs 4 crore for their use by the
government over the previous forty-five years. She ended her letter by
saying: 'While Burma affairs are being considered, that a crore of
rupees be reserved for expenditure connected with the affairs of my
parents and all of us, and that from the 1st April 1886, the Government
pay me Rs 10,000 at least monthly, as previously promised by them,
after deducting the amounts already paid to me.'[31]

Although her inventory of claims was all-encompassing, the most
momentous one was the return of her father's kingdom. Very
interestingly, perhaps in an attempt to make her request more palatable
to the British authorities, she did not press for independence, but for
the return of the kingdom as part of the British Empire. In her words,
'the territories of Upper and Lower Burma be formed into a Burmese
Kingdom within the British Empire, within a prescribed time, and be
handed over to us'.[32]

Compared to what the government felt it owed King Thibaw's family—which was precious little—the Fourth Princess's claims were spectacular, to say the least. Not only that, but she had made her claim public. Not surprisingly, the British government 'almost jumped out of their skins',[33] and immediately came down like a sledgehammer on the Fourth Princess, who was now labelled 'the Rebel Princess'. They accused her of fostering 'a monarchy movement',[34] and decided to muzzle her by removing her from Mandalay, and exiling her and her family to Moulmein, in Lower Burma, far away from her royal relatives, to live 'amongst the Mons' (a Burmese ethnic group).[35] Here they hoped, distant from the influences and energy of her father's capital, she would have no option but to quietly settle down.

The Fourth Princess indignantly refused to be relocated. She complained bitterly that every time the government disapproved of anything she did or said, they threatened her with removal.[36] In January 1932, she was informed that she was being given no choice; that if she did not shift right away, her pension—her only source of income—would be stopped. Sick and tired of being constantly subjugated, the Fourth Princess refused to yield. The government stopped her pension, and in order to make ends meet she took to making paper flowers to sell in the market. (She had learnt this art as a child from her mother and aunt.[37]) Also, very dramatically, she put up notifications in newspapers proclaiming that as she could no longer afford to look after her six children, she was putting them up for adoption.[38]

The Second Princess saw this notice in India. Putting aside the bitter differences she had had with this sister in the past, she immediately offered to take charge of the children.[39] The children were not sent to her, but, says Prince Taw Phaya (who vividly recalls what followed):

> Margaret and Fredrick, the two youngest children, were sent to a royal relative's home, and Tessie was sent to the owner of the house we rented—in the next compound. We three boys stayed behind. Our father tried to put us in the monastery that the queen had built ... But the head monk was the queen's abbot, so he said "No, no". We returned home never to leave again. Only Tessie and the younger two

stayed away for about a month. And everyone started telling our parents that it is no use banging your head against a wall. Just accept [the relocation] and go.[40]

Not having had the education, experience, skills or ability to earn her own living—and being married to a man who, in all fairness, probably could not have earned an amount comparable to her pension even if he had made every attempt to—the Fourth Princess reluctantly agreed to shift to Moulmein. She was informed that within Moulmein she and her family could travel freely, but permission would be required to leave Moulmein.[41] The family departed on 19 May 1932[42] and was seen off at the railway station by friends and well-wishers. A commodious, pillared, 'very grand' two storeyed house with 'four bedrooms . . . 2½ acres . . . the fruits you want . . . the flowers you want . . . a laaaaarge dining room', was selected to accommodate her and her family in Moulmein,[43] and her pension was restarted immediately on her arrival there.[44]

In Rangoon and Mandalay the Fourth Princess had been able to meet members of the extended royal family, nationalists, ex-subjects and people who had served in the Golden Palace, but in Moulmein such interaction was next to impossible. Lower Burma had been under British reign for over eighty years, so Moulmein's population had never been ruled by King Thibaw or his father, and had no recallable personal history with the Fourth Princess's family. A few descendants of Shan chieftains did make some attempts to visit the Fourth Princess but the British, much more vigilant now, discouraged them. Once in a while the Fourth Princess would call on the governor or other visiting dignitaries, but otherwise she was pretty much on her own.[45]

The government did not permit the children to stay at home in Moulmein, but insisted that they be boarded in missionary schools, and permitted them to visit their parents only on their weekly day off.[46] This enforced separation from all her children, compounded by her marital woes, must have been very hard on the Fourth Princess. According to one of her children, their mother 'had to suffer both physically and mentally during her stay in Moulmein . . .'[47] When the children came home, they noticed 'she has a very solemn face . . . she

always has a sad look on her'.[48] While the Fourth Princess had, from a
young age, been rather serious and sombre,[49] these days there was not
much to bring her joy, or for that matter, hope.

With helpless frustration, she watched the steady and systematic
anglicization of all her children. In school, they were known by their
Christian names (given to them at St Joseph's Convent in Mandalay),
and it is by these names that they had to address each other. Since they
were all so young, and in school far more than at home, it is these
names that became second nature to them, and by which they began to
even *think* of themselves and of each other.[50] Evangelical French and
British missionaries set the curriculum they studied. While there is no
denying that many missionary schools in Burma and elsewhere provided
excellent education and filled much needed lacunae, it is also true that
the overarching purpose of these schools was proselytizing.
(Proselytizing was high on the agenda of all European colonizers, as
the 'plunder of goods [could be] justified by the gift of Christianity'.[51])

The Fourth Princess's children say that in the stories the Fourth
Princess narrated about the past she never maligned or criticized the
First Princess; it was only for the Second Princess that unkind words
were reserved. What brought about this change of heart towards her
eldest sister is difficult to say. The Fourth Princess was well aware of
her own overriding influence in the family. She very often spelt out to
her children that she had had 'the power . . . a voice . . . a very strong
voice' in family affairs.[52] Perhaps she now realized what a prominent
role *she* had played in her family's attitude towards her eldest sister;
perhaps she had been sensitized by her own unhappiness. Her children
remember that their mother occasionally wrote to the First Princess,
although details of what she wrote are not known.[53]

Perhaps it was release from the oppressively cocooning environment
of her adult years in Ratnagiri—an environment that had sadly
become irreversibly and overwhelmingly suffused with unhealthy
acrimony—that allowed a much gentler and kinder facet of the Fourth
Princess's personality to conspicuously emerge. Her children remember
her as an affectionate, caring and lenient mother. Prince Taw Phaya recalls:

> We never ate what the servants cooked. She always cooked for us . . . I
> used to be very close to her. I remember when I was only about eight

or nine years old, we used to go for pilgrimages across the Moulmein Thanlwin River, towards the other bank and go up the hill where there was a famous pagoda. I used always to be sort of her guide and caretaker. I used to take her hand and lead her over the steps . . . [54]

He has memories of his mother sitting on the large verandah at the back of their home in Moulmein. She would sit there almost every day in the afternoons. She would dry her hair on this verandah, in the gentle breeze and sunlight. He adds that she had a 'head bath about once a month and normal bath once a week or something'.[55]

The Fourth Princess's youngest son, Prince Taw Phaya Galae, recalls that perhaps due to the outbreaks of plague in Ratnagiri, his mother had developed a paranoia of infections, and

was so worried that when anyone of the family members had allergic manifestations of the skin, she carefully applied methylated spirit and skin ointments . . . Once I suffered from itchiness over my thighs. My mother applied alcohol very hard on my thighs. And because of this over application, I got skin abrasions and there is still a scar.[56]

Her daughter, Princess Hteik Su Phaya Gyi, says that the children called the Fourth Princess 'Ashin Phaya' and their father 'Kodaw'—royal terms the British disapproved of—for this was what they had heard the numerous visitors in Mandalay deferentially call their parents. (Ko Ko Naing called the Fourth Princess 'Suphaya'.) According to her, her mother was a 'very good housewife. She did not scold the servants.' She indicates that her mother cooked Indian food regularly and well, 'so up to my children, down to my grandchildren, [we] all love Indian food'. When home all six children slept with their mother, while their father slept on a different bed: 'So we all tried to grab the spot right next to my mother!'[57]

Although the Fourth Princess's niece (the Third Princess's daughter) did not spend much time with her aunt, she repeats what her mother probably told her about this sister:

She was a gifted person . . . was a fine artist who could draw and paint, besides making beautiful sprays of flowers out of wax, cloth, paper and even cork . . . she was a good cook and perhaps [because] of the influence of English companions [was able to] bake cakes and prepare

a full course English dinner. Knowing English she learnt home
nursing and first aid. She was quite musical and played the concertina
besides the violin and the harmonica! She married beneath her and I
am sorry to say . . . [her husband] managed to break the fine spirit of
a strong minded woman . . .[58]

The Fourth Princess's children remember their father as a strict
disciplinarian, and their mother as always standing up for them.[59] Ko
Ko Naing 'had a separate cane for each of the children—each with the
name of the child written on it, and if one does something wrong all
six have to line up and he judged the case . . . it was military-like
training.' Once, a prince who had come to visit them gave Princess
Hteik Su Phaya Gyi, who was under twelve at the time, a gold chain.
She immediately put it around her neck. As jewellery was not permitted
in school, when it was time for her to go back, her father took it away.
Upset, she complained to one of her school nuns. From the nun, to
the mother superior, from the mother superior to the deputy
commissioner, a Chinese whisper conveyed a twisted version of facts:
'Her father grabbed the chain from his daughter's neck.' Ko Ko Naing
was ordered by the commissioner to explain his behaviour. Furious
with his daughter for having discussed personal matters in school, he
whipped her legs till she bled.[60]

  Frightened by the continued anger directed by her husband at her
eldest daughter, the Fourth Princess initiated discussions for Princess
Hteik Su Phaya Gyi's marriage with the Sawbwa of Nyaungshwe's
nephew (this nephew would go on to become Burma's first president).
According to U Than Swe, betrothal at such a young age was not
unusual, nor was it uncommon to send such a young girl (including
royal ones) away to live in a distant palace: 'Our Burmese custom—
you send your daughters to the palace . . . before puberty . . . they will
be offered as a princess . . . she will be well looked after and only when
she becomes mature they will get married . . .'[61] (At the time the
British annexed Upper Burma and abolished its monarchy, they allowed
the Shan sawbwas (chieftains) to continue to run their fiefdoms,
under British suzerainty of course, but with minimal internal
interference. So the sawbwas pretty much continued their courts in
the traditional manner.) Princess Hteik Su Phaya Gyi overheard

servants in her house discussing her proposed betrothal, the meaning of which, at that time, she could not comprehend. But she did understand—a maid obligingly clarified matters for her—what it signified. She realized that she was going to be plucked from her home, separated from her parents and siblings, and be sent to live *forever* with people she did not know. She remembers being petrified at the thought.[62] But she was never sent to the Nyaungshwe *Haw* (palace), because before the details of her betrothal could be finalized, her mother, sadly, suddenly and unexpectedly, died.

On 3 March 1936, just two months short of her forty-ninth birthday, the Fourth Princess passed away. It was never conclusively determined what she died of, and speculation on the subject ranges from poisoning, to cancer, to small pox, to pneumonia. Prince Taw Phaya Galae feels his mother died of smallpox,[63] as does U Than Swe who says she died before the eruption of the distinctive smallpox blisters.[64] Says Prince Taw Phaya:

> No! Our mother did not die of cancer or smallpox. My assumption is she may have died of pneumonia. Reason—a week or so before her demise she had [a] warm [head] bath in the afternoon and after[wards], sat on the back verandah where it was very windy being the month of March. She must have caught a chill and did not bother to treat it. Two days after her bath she ran a [high] temperature and lay in bed. The Parsee family doctor was away in Yangon, so an Indian doctor was summoned—however, she was dead the next evening.[65]

The children, who were in school, were informed of their mother's death, and were permitted to return home immediately.[66]

On the morning of her death, the Fourth Princess had indicated that she was feeling hot. Knowing of her fondness for the soft drink Vimto, this was given to her to help cool her down. When she died that evening, traces of this brownish drink trickled out of her mouth, leading the servants to whisper that she had been poisoned. The suspicion was compounded by Ko Ko Naing's actions right after her death. A no-nonsense man, he realized that the Fourth Princess's body would have to be kept at home for months and the quicker he acted the better it would be:

In Myanmar's culture whenever a pongyi or prince or princess died the
funeral [took] a long time. The body had to be preserved and only 3
or 4 months afterwards the cremation [took] place. So for the Fourth
Princess they had to wait for the money from the British for the
funeral expense, and they had to invite all their relatives from Mandalay
and they had to do all the royal procedures, so Ko Ko Naing [knew
that] he had to keep the body 3 or 4 months, so in front of the
servants he opened the Fourth Princess's abdomen and removed the
inner contents and buried that in the compound.[67]

The government had always disapproved of Ko Ko Naing for they
knew he was a staunch patriot (apart from anything else, he had been
guilty of introducing his children to Burmese history and literature
during their holidays[68]). They also disapproved of him because they
believed he had supported the Fourth Princess in her efforts to
reclaim her father's kingdom.[69] (Says Prince Taw Phaya Galae, 'My
father was a good companion to my mother for her anti-colonial
activities. He made visits to Sayadawgyis and political leaders whom
my mother was not allowed to visit . . .'[70]) They eyed him suspiciously
because he was an alchemist. They knew that there was tension in his
marriage, and on learning of the Fourth Princess's sudden demise, of
the brown liquid that had appeared around her mouth right after her
death,[71] and of Ko Ko Naing's subsequent very odd behaviour (getting
rid of the evidence, they thought), they had the earthen pot containing
the Fourth Princess's innards dug up and sent to the National Health
Laboratory in Rangoon for examination. No trace of any poison was
ever found.[72]

The body of the Fourth Princess, preserved with the chemicals with
which her husband had filled her abdominal cavity, lay in her home for
the next few months, while Ko Ko Naing lobbied hard to have it sent
to Mandalay to be placed in a mausoleum in the Golden Palace.[73] The
Third Princess travelled down from Maymyo to pay homage to her
dead sister, whom she had not seen in the past few years. It was a very
emotional visit; she broke down on seeing her sister's body, and being
aware of her unhappy marriage and of the rumours of poisoning, she
accused Ko Ko Naing, who was sitting nearby at the time, of having
played a role in her death.[74] The Second Princess and her husband
attempted to come, but were not permitted to do so by the

H.M. Queen Supayalat's scene of death in Rangoon in 1925.

The epitaph on Queen Supayalat's tomb in Rangoon. Photograph by author 2009.

government.[75] How the First Princess reacted to her youngest sister's death is not known.

As the government did not permit the Fourth Princess's body to be taken to Mandalay, or even to Rangoon to be near that of her mother's, about five months after she died the Fourth Princess was entombed in Moulmein (on 23 August 1936; Prince Taw Phaya thinks this is the date of the entombment, but is not absolutely sure).[76] Prince Taw Phaya Galae says that her funeral 'was attended by thousands and thousands of monks and citizens'.[77] 'The whole town turned up, because this was the first time an elaborate royal funeral was being held in Moulmein,' clarifies Prince Taw Phaya.[78] He continues,

> If you ever manage to go to Moulmein, as soon as you cross the Salween [now called Thanlwin] river bridge you will see the gilded pagoda on the background hill of Moulmein town. Our mother is entombed on the road leading to Kyaik Than Lun Pagoda. The view from atop the hill is quite picturesque, with the town below, the Thanlwin river, a few ships, boats moving, the island Balu-gyun in the distance . . .[79]

After the Fourth Princess's death, Ko Ko Naing regretted the harshness with which he had treated her, says one of his children.[80] The government offered him a reduced pension, which he refused. Although there is no record as to why he did so, it is believed that his strong nationalistic feelings, his ever-increasing anti-British sentiment, his innate set of moral codes, and a robust ego are what prevented him from accepting anything directly from the British government.[81] Besides, a thrifty man, he had for years saved a portion of the Fourth Princess's pension, and therefore had something to fall back on.[82] The Fourth Princess's children, however, all continued to receive an education allowance of Rs 100 each per month, which they had been receiving since their seventh birthdays.[83]

Princess Hteik Su Phaya Gyi says that her mother's death heralded the end of negotiations for her betrothal to the Sawbwa of Nyaungshwe's nephew. Therefore, she honestly admits, her sorrow was very guiltily mixed with a flood of relief.[84] For Prince Taw Phaya, who was a few days short of twelve when his mother died, there was no silver lining to the terribly dark cloud that completely engulfed him:

Our mother—what should I say—she was all goodness for us, loving, kind, lenient, softening the strictness our father imposed on us. A pillar of strength, even with servants galore, when her children got sick, she would look after us herself . . . From a very young age I was her constant companion, running errands and doing little jobs to lighten her work . . . And being a Saturday born like her father the King [she] had a soft spot for me. I thought my world had collapsed when she left us.[85]

19

THE FIRST PRINCESS

In early July 1920, Gopal waited on the sandy shores of Ratnagiri to receive the First Princess and their daughter Tu Tu[1]—it had been over a year since he had seen them. There is no official record of this reunion because, unlike when the First Princess first arrived in Ratnagiri in 1886 or left it in 1919, on this occasion there were no reporters or government officials. She was, after all, returning as a private citizen.

Gopal had rented a small house for them on the outskirts of Ratnagiri, on the Kolhapur–Ratnagiri Road not far from King Thibaw's tomb.[2] The First Princess was well aware that Gopal had said he could never marry her and would arrange for a separate house for her. What she was unprepared for, however, and what came as a shock to her, was that her new home was a sparsely furnished small cottage, the guest cottage of another bungalow. The stupendous contrast between this and the Royal Residence greatly dismayed the First Princess. So, in denial and escorted by Gopal, she marched off to the collector's office to ask for permission to stay in her old home. Someone there pointed out to her, perhaps politely but certainly firmly, that this was out of the question. He elaborated that the Royal Residence was to be put to other use and besides, the question of her staying anywhere at government expense did not arise.[3]

In August 1920 the First Princess received a pension of Rs 200 (with around Rs 5 deducted as income tax). The smallness of it astonished her. It shouldn't have, for she had clearly been told that this was all she would get if she chose to return to Ratnagiri. Her lack of comprehension of her situation was obvious in a letter she wrote to the government. The letter, dated 20 August 1920, began: 'I, First Princess Thisu Myat Paya Gyi of Burma, respectfully beg . . .' It wasn't to defy the government that she continued calling herself 'Princess'; the tone of the rest of the letter was too humble for that.[4] While she had been growing up in Ratnagiri, her parents had continually reinforced that just because they were no longer in power did not mean they were no longer royals. Although painfully aware that her status in society had greatly diminished after her affair with Gopal and the birth of their daughter, how could the signing of a declaration, any declaration, change the truth of her pedigree?

In this letter, the First Princess appealed for a higher monthly pension, arguing that since her mother was no longer meeting her expenses she 'should get Rs 200 as my dress allowance, plus Rs 200 or more as my maintenance allowance in all Rs 400 or more . . .' It didn't take long for the government to turn down her request and point out to her that since she was an unmarried daughter of the late ex-King Thibaw, Rs 200 was all she could expect, and that the government could not be held responsible if she was unable to manage on this amount. It was also pointed out to her that she had returned to Ratnagiri at her own request, and had signed a declaration renouncing her royal status.[5]

It took a year for the First Princess to send another letter to the government asking them again to increase her pension. Her letter was now long and detailed, in the form of a memorial.[6] It is evident that she and Gopal had got considerable help drafting it. In this memorial, for the first time, the First Princess spelt out that 'as she could not pull on well with the other members of the family [she] was obliged to return to Ratnagiri'. She did not elaborate on this statement but she did indicate that she intended to spend the rest of her life in Ratnagiri. And again, as if unaware of or unable to comprehend the significance of the declaration she had signed in Rangoon, she pleaded that 'an adequate increase be made in her present allowance befitting her position as a Princess of the Royal House of Burma' and that a 'separate provision be made for special grants for Diwali and other festivals'. She went on to suggest that if the government could not increase her allowance, then she 'be given something in consideration of the use and occupation by the Government of the palace built by her late father Ex-King Thebaw at Ratnagiri which she cannot occupy not having sufficient means at her command to do so'.[7] Although she knew that the Royal Residence was by now being used as the home of the collector and assistant collector of Ratnagiri, she seems to have been unaware that it had never actually been owned by her father, but had been paid for, built and owned by the government as her father's glorified prison.

A short note informed the First Princess that the detailed memorial she had so laboured over and had so pinned her hopes on was not even going to be put up for consideration to the powers that be.[8] This terse note seems to have had an epiphanic effect on the First Princess, and it was perhaps now that the enormity of her decision to renounce her royal status and return to Ratnagiri dawned on her. No more records of any pleas from her to the government can be located; with her not writing any more letters, she, as it were, just dropped from the government's radar. After having spent almost all her life as a virtual prisoner, secluded from the rest of world, with the constant presence of police/political officers and collectors, their total absence had to have been disconcerting and must have added to her growing sense of abandonment. Compounding her distress must have been the fact that the Ratnagiri she had known from the blurring distance of the Royal Residence actually had a totally different complexion now that she was living in it as a private citizen.

Ratnagiri, a small town, comprised an insular, conservative and deeply patriarchal society. Most people, including Gopal, lived in joint-family units, which were hierarchal and consisted of people spanning several generations.[9] Although the family unit was large, it was not the custom among Hindus to have more than one wife, although it was not unheard of if a wife bore no sons. Socialization was mainly within the family unit, and occasionally with members of the same caste.[10] A woman's primary function was to be a good wife, and qualities such as chastity and modesty were the most valued. Most women were not educated beyond a few years of schooling, if that, and were married young so that their husband's family could mould more easily their nascent personalities.[11] Women had no social freedom and did not even leave their homes to shop.[12] Laxmibai, Gopal's wife, 'like other women of her generation was rarely seen by male non-family members. Any interaction was from behind curtains.'[13] Shakuntaladevi (Gopal and Laxmibai's daughter-in-law) says that although Laxmibai was simple and plain-looking, she was kind and loving, and she and Gopal got along well. However, because of the First Princess's presence in Gopal's life, 'there was a definite sadness in Laxmibai, but she never talked about it'.[14]

Gopal's conservative joint family could not be expected to and did not welcome the First Princess on her return. In fact, there was never any interaction between them and her. Tu Tu also had no contact, during her childhood, with her father's family.[15] Although there was no stigma on Gopal for the child born to him out of wedlock, to some in Ratnagiri it appeared as if Gopal had 'no attachment to the child born of this affair'.[16] Nor was there any taint on Gopal for his involvement with the First Princess. Rather, embellished and romanticized stories lionizing Gopal circulated, stories as to how much 'the princess loved Gopal and wanted to stay with only him, whether he was rich or poor, servant or king, married or unmarried'.[17] Many in Ratnagiri 'were proud that Gopal had brought home a princess—there was nothing in that to be ashamed of', but they were not so generous in their attitude towards the First Princess.[18] In this deeply traditional, male-dominated society that valued the virtuous unsullied woman, she was viewed as a woman of loose morals and no character.[19]

It didn't help matters that word had been spread by the collector's office (around the time of her return to Ratnagiri) that the First Princess was now no longer a princess but a private citizen. (The government's objective in doing this was to spell out its lack of responsibility for her, in an attempt to minimize her capacity to raise debt.)[20] Although the citizens of Ratnagiri had the same difficulty as the First Princess in comprehending how a person once royal could now not be, they nonetheless got the message that her position had altered. The perception that she was a woman of no reputation (with even the government dissociating itself for reasons not explained and therefore not understood), compounded by the prevailing social norms and structure in Ratnagiri at the time, led to the First Princess's isolation. Other than Gopal, there was nobody who welcomed her back, there was nobody whom she could visit, and there was hardly anybody who visited her.[21] And so, far away from her own family, cast loose by the government, disregarded in the town she had chosen to spend the rest of her life, she was now totally dependent on Gopal, for who else was there for her and her young daughter?

Gopal's joint family was very important to him, and all his life he never neglected them.[22] Gopal had brought up his brother Atmaram, many years younger than him, after the death of their parents. The brothers were very attached to each other and Atmaram, his wife and five children lived with Gopal. Also living with Gopal was his widowed sister. Gopal and Laxmibai had had a son who had died in his teens. Another son, Chandrakant, was born to them in 1924, a few years after the First Princess's return. Chandrakant, a legitimate child, a coveted son, was the apple of his father's eye. Gopal spent every night in his joint family home.[23] Every morning, after donning his standard all-white outfit of a dhoti, coat and turban, and after drinking a whole urn of freshly produced cow's milk, he, a deeply religious man, would visit three temples including the Kaal Bhairav Mandir (of which he became the chief trustee from 1932 until his death). He then ran various errands and returned to his joint-family home for his lunch—sometimes of fish, which was his favourite—and a short afternoon nap.[24]

Gopal's family had large land holdings—around 200 acres of land—in four villages around Ratnagiri.[25] (The government was confident that a fair portion of these holdings had been acquired with amounts Gopal had received from the king and the First Princess over the

years.[26]) Most of this land was agricultural, and Gopal frequently
spent the late afternoons visiting his paddy fields and mango orchards,
to ensure all was well. Although uneducated, Gopal was literate and it
was he who maintained the land records and collected the rent. Over
the years, Gopal, a soft-spoken man, well liked and well respected in
the extended Shivrekar—Sawant family, got busier and busier as he
presided over all festivities of his caste. Gopal also became a member
of the Ratnagiri Municipal Corporation.[27]

It was generally in the evenings that he would cycle over to the First
Princess's house, and spend perhaps half-an-hour to an hour with
her.[28] Since there were no streetlights in Ratnagiri during the First
Princess's lifetime, he always left well before dark.[29] Although the
First Princess had been told that she would have to live separately, this
definitely could not have been what she had anticipated. After all,
Gopal had begged her not to go, and had then pleaded with her to
return. She, having promised him she would, had kept her word. But
Gopal never honoured his end of the bargain, whether it had been
explicitly spelt out or not, of dividing his time fairly between his two
families. When she had lived in the Royal Residence he had often
spent nights with her, and this is what she must have expected would
continue.

Although Gopal's family was land-rich they were not cash-rich; very
few families in Ratnagiri were. Gopal, therefore, could not have given
the First Princess anything substantial to supplement her pension; he
just didn't have that kind of liquidity, not with a large joint family to
support.[30] But it appears that the question of a contribution to the
First Princess was not what Gopal ever had in mind. Although Gopal
could have helped the First Princess live the best she could on her
pension, this was not the choice he opted for: he felt entitled to
appropriate some of it himself. There can be no doubt that Gopal's
attraction for the First Princess had always been, in large part,
mercenary, and sadly this did not change now.

Gopal took some of the First Princess's money to pay her rent and
to buy the things she needed, but it also appears that he siphoned off
most of it for himself. Gopal had earned Rs 15 a month when he had
been a gatekeeper at the Royal Residence,[31] a little more when he became

a driver, and compared to prevalent salaries in Ratnagiri at the time, the First Princess's pension could not have looked too small to him. It certainly was enough for her and her daughter to have lived, if not royally, at least comfortably. She could have had a much nicer house, afforded a live-in servant or two, and definitely lived a lot better than she did. Long-time residents of Ratnagiri opine that Rs 200 in the 1920s, '30s and '40s was a fair sum to live on, especially for a family comprising just two people.[32] The history of their relationship must have prepared the First Princess for the eventuality that Gopal would pocket some of her pension. Perhaps she was prepared, even willing, to give some of it to him. However, it is unlikely that she anticipated how grasping he would be, how much he would take, and as a consequence how frugally she would have to live. Her royal upbringing, in spite of the exile, had not prepared her for thrifty living. She simply did not know how to penny pinch and budget. Now, suddenly impoverished and with absolutely no one to turn to, the distraught First Princess quickly sank into depression for had there not been enough misery on her plate already?

In Burma, the common expression 'karma is the womb that bore me' signifies how deeply rooted in the Burmese psyche is the belief that a person's actions in earlier lives shapes his destiny in this one.[33] As a Buddhist, as a believer in karma, the First Princess probably felt that she was paying for her past sins,[34] sins perhaps not only of past lives, but also of this one. To atone for her past, and to help her through the present, she turned to religion with fervour, reposing all her trust in a higher being. There was no one else for her to turn to. For the rest of her life people would see her pacing up and down, her hands clasped behind her back, her lips moving in prayer. When seated, she would tell her beads. As an act of merit, she would share her meagre rations with any poor person passing by; sometimes all she had to give was 'half a slice of bread'. The townspeople, seeing her piety and her distress, viewed her with newfound compassion and sympathy.[35]

Although sorry for her, they never reached out to her.[36] The First Princess, on her part, not having gone through any 'normal' process of socialization while growing up, not having received any education to stretch her mind and broaden her interests, and not having any depth of knowledge of either the language or culture of the people of Ratnagiri, was ill equipped to make any appropriately friendly overtures, or to find any way of integrating herself. Not that it would have been easy to do so—in this rigid society she was too much of an oddity, a piece that just did not fit.

The First Princess had no more children after her return. Tu Tu, before the family's exile had ended, had spent one or two years at the local missionary girls' school. It was reported that she was 'bright' and was 'doing well' in school.[37] Although a loving and devoted mother, overwhelmed with the position she found herself in, and perhaps not realizing its importance, the First Princess paid no attention to Tu Tu's education after their return to Ratnagiri. She taught her how to cook, she taught her how to sew, and she taught her how to make paper flowers, but she did not teach her how to read and write, nor did she send her to school.[38] Gopal also did nothing to ensure that his daughter got even some basic education. Certainly he was in a position to have insisted upon it and paid for it. The result of two literate parents ignoring her schooling was that Tu Tu grew up illiterate. She also grew up wounded by her father's rejection, and enveloped by her mother's sense of grief and shame. This deeply influenced the person she would later become.

In 1930, ten years after their return from Burma, when Tu Tu was twenty-four years old, she married Shankar Yeshwant Pawar. After her marriage, Tu Tu settled in a home not far from her mother's and quickly got busy with her own life. Although she visited her mother frequently, her visits were not lengthy ones.[39]

During the 1930s and early 1940s, the First Princess, now living truly all alone, turned to local young children for some companionship. Some of these children, now adults in their seventies and eighties, still have vivid though limited memories of her. One gentleman, who used to see her regularly, recalls that every evening 'she used to hand out biscuits to kids and biscuits were rare in Ratnagiri in those days'. He remembers she would invite him and his friends into her home, which consisted of three very bare rooms with a chair or two, a stool and a cupboard. He does not remember a bed and says she slept on the floor. For an hour or so every evening the boys would play boisterously in her house, shattering the deafening silence that usually permeated it, and inadvertently providing her with a measure of distraction and a semblance of belonging. Although she and the boys had nothing much to say to each other, he recalls her attempts to talk to them in her foreign-accented, broken Marathi which was not always easy to follow. He says she called Gopal 'Shivrekar' (as did many in Ratnagiri), and she would tell the children, 'Shivrekar has taken my money and gone.' He describes how she waited 'every evening at her door for Shivrekar. When she would see him coming she would chase the kids away, saying in Marathi "Shivrekar *alle*! Shivrekar *alle*!" (Shivrekar's come! Shivrekar's come!).'[40] It was clear she wanted the children gone before Gopal reached her door; it was clear she sought and needed his company.

Another gentleman who used to, as a young boy, walk by the First Princess's house everyday recalls her 'regal bearing', and says that she was 'very beautiful'.[41] (Her home had no curtains, two windows with wooden bars and a front door that remained almost always open.[42]) He remembers a threadbare carpet, and a few old pieces of crockery and cutlery, relics of days gone by. He noticed she ate mainly rice with *amti*, or some other curry, which she was always happy to share. She would call out to every poor person she saw walking past, to hand them something to eat.[43] (People in Ratnagiri knew Gopal 'lived quite well', and that the First Princess 'lived in poverty', but many believed that Gopal took the First Princess's money only 'to get all her things for her'; that her poverty was due to an inadequate government pension and because she 'gave away a lot' on a daily basis.[44]) A Ratnagiri resident says he often saw the First Princess and Gopal sitting peacefully together, mainly in the evening, sometimes during the day. He believes that Gopal and the First Princess were victims of circumstances and of the era they lived in, that Gopal's actions were governed by the dictates of his caste, and that he really loved her.[45] Another Ratnagiri resident, who also saw her regularly, feels this was not the case. He thinks that Gopal's relationship with the First Princess was based on 'lust not love', for how could it be anything else when they could not even communicate effectively since her Marathi was not very good and his Burmese was non-existent?[46]

Over the years the First Princess had some communication with her

own family, although never with her mother. She exchanged letters, in
an amalgamation of Marathi and Hindi, with a few Burmese and Goan
words thrown in, with the Second Princess. In these letters, the First
Princess did mention her financial problems, she did state she was not
getting her full pension, but it seems she never mentioned why.
Perhaps too ashamed to let her sister know that she was living so
impoverished and lonely a life, right at the end of a letter acknowledging
receipt of a money order the Second Princess had sent her, the First
Princess wrote in broken Marathi, '*Hamko miha taakraat nahi*', meaning,
'I have no complaints.'[47] (See Appendix II.) The grim details of her
sister's plight were conveyed to the Second Princess by news reports
that were beginning to surface by 1938–39.[48] Greatly distressed, she
wrote to the collector's office in Ratnagiri requesting an enquiry and
intervention.[49] Although a cursory enquiry was made, the government
curtly replied to the Second Princess that she should not waste any
more of its time unless 'something amiss has actually taken place'.
Something amiss *was* taking place; the collector's office had to have
realized that the First Princess's standard of living was not commensurate
with what they were paying her 'regularly every month'.[50] But this was
never further investigated; she was now, after all, a private citizen.

A real enigma is the correspondence between the First and Fourth
Princesses. Something must have made the Fourth Princess write to
the First Princess for it seems hard to imagine the First Princess
initiating the correspondence. In one of her letters to the First
Princess, the Fourth Princess mentioned her own financial difficulties.
In response, the First Princess, with unbelievable generosity, 'sent all
her allowance, Rs 200, in a tin packed with mango preserve'. One of
the Fourth Princess's sons, Prince Taw Phaya, remembers picking up
this parcel himself at the Moulmein post office. This was 'just before
our mother died, say about 1935'.[51] Was it to tangibly demonstrate to
a self-righteous, critical sister that she was all right, or was it out of
innate kindness that the First Princess helped her sister financially
when she could ill afford to do so? This generosity in all probability
added to the Rs 3,000 debt the First Princess accumulated over the
years.[52] Unfortunately, none of the correspondence between these two
sisters exists today, but the Fourth Princess's children mention that
the two princesses occasionally wrote to each other in Marathi.[53]

The trickle of Burmese people and goods that had taken place during the royal family's long exile in Ratnagiri completely dried up once they left, and it appears nothing from Burma,[54] other than the occasional letter from the Fourth Princess, was ever sent by anyone to the First Princess, and nobody from Burma ever visited her.[55] Then all of a sudden, one morning in October 1938, a Burmese reporter arrived at her home and told her that he wished to interview her. Without any hesitation the First Princess refused, saying she wanted nothing to do with anyone Burmese, and firmly shut her door.[56] The reporter—thoroughly taken aback by her attitude—questioned (with the help of his interpreter) people passing by about her. They told him what little they knew including that they often saw her sitting 'in a dark corner' of her house all by herself, an image that stayed with the reporter and haunted him for years afterwards.[57] The reporter now 'begged her to let [him] in as [he] had come a long way from Burma to see her'.[58] Prince Taw Phaya Galae (one of the Fourth Princess's sons) describes the interaction that purportedly followed between the reporter and the First Princess:

> 'Princess, you can do whatever you like—you can hit me, kick me, abuse me, whatever, but you must let me in.' Then, when she opened the door a crack, he forced himself in and saw the princess crying.
> 'My life has been lost. So what do you want to know?' she said.
> 'We want to let the Burmese people know you are in such a position.'
> 'The *Burmese* people,' she responded, 'Do they still remember me?'[59]

The reporter spent an hour interviewing the First Princess. She confessed that she harboured 'bitter' feelings towards the Burmese; the reporter, realizing that this bitterness was born out of a feeling of abandonment, reassured her that she had not been forgotten in Burma and that people were lobbying with the government to try and get her finances improved. The First Princess built up quite a rapport with this reporter, and corresponded with him after his visit. He interviewed her again in 1940, and two articles based on these interviews were published in Burma.[60]

The reporter described the First Princess as 'a very simple person' with 'very limited knowledge of the modern times and the modern world'. He said that her house was 'no better than a hut'. Although the Ratnagiri coastline is very picturesque, he wrote, the First Princess 'dared not venture out of her hut as she was afraid that people might notice her poor and humble state and so she was suffering alone . . .' Rather poignantly one of the articles had a photograph of the First Princess with the following caption: 'The First Daughter was too poor and her dress was torn and shabby so she gave an old photograph to this reporter and did not allow him to take a photograph . . .'[61]

The princess told the reporter the tragic truth of how little of her pension she actually got for her own use: 'Sawant [Gopal] took out the First Daughter's monthly pension of Rs 200, but the First Daughter only got Rs 8 for house rent and Rs 20 to 30 for household expenses. And so the First Daughter had to live in a state of great poverty but she made no complaints about her husband for his ill treatments and on his part Sawant just neglected her . . .' She also told the reporter that her financial condition was such that 'sometimes she had to skip her meals', and that moneylenders, to whom she was in debt, were continually 'scolding her, and that she no longer wished to be alive'.[62]

The reporter was so moved by the First Princess's deplorable condition that he begged her to come back with him to Burma. She replied that 'this was out of the question because she did not wish to depart from the graveyard of her father. She also could not leave her daughter and her three grandchildren.' Later in the same interview she told the reporter that although 'she wished to return to Burma, she was much afraid that the Burmese people might have bitter feelings towards her for being the wife of an Indian commoner and so she refused to come back'.[63]

By the mid-forties the First Princess, who had enjoyed good health most of her life, weakened considerably. By now the townspeople, who had never really known or understood her, increasingly looked upon her as an eccentric.[64] Some of her mannerisms had always seemed peculiar to them—for example, every time she fed a poor person she 'would raise her arms and eyes upwards'.[65] There was a logical explanation for this, but due to cultural barriers, was not understood by the people who witnessed it. Just as her mother, Queen Supayalat, had fed pongyis in Rangoon, the First Princess fed poor people passing by primarily as an act of charity. According to Burmese custom, whenever you do a good deed it is customary to share the merit you get for having done it. Therefore, as 'her father and mother are dead and are in *nat-pyi-san* and *nat-ywa-san* (respectively)—Burmese belief king and queen go to heaven—so she looks up, raises her arms, her eyes, and shares her good deeds with her parents'.[66]

One Ratnagiri resident remembers the First Princess as a 'calm and quiet lady' who became rather odd towards the end.[67] She constantly murmured and muttered to herself.[68] Another Ratnagiri resident says that in her later years she became unpredictably aggressive and sometimes threw stones at people for no apparent reason.[69] One of the First Princess's grandsons says that his *aji* (grandmother in Marathi) went distinctly mad towards the end of her life, and he remembers her shaking the bars of the windows in her house, her face distorted with anger, yelling in Marathi at people passing by to go away and not come near her. He was very young when his grandmother died, and sadly this is his overwhelming memory of her.[70] According to one of Tu Tu's daughters, Tu Tu and the First Princess 'had a big fight towards the end of her mother's life. Her mother was strange and they fought over something. Tu Tu then didn't want to go back.'[71] Tu Tu did go back— many Ratnagiri residents, and Tu Tu's daughter, Malti, say that she continued to visit her mother almost daily until her mother's death— but it was not an easy relationship towards the end.[72]

Sometime possibly in late 1946, or early 1947, the Shirkes, the owners of the cottage the First Princess stayed in most of her life (and which one of their descendants takes pains to point out that although a cottage, had had a cement roof, not a tin one; a tin one would have made the cottage like an oven in summer, and very noisy in the monsoons[73]), decided to redevelop their entire property, and asked Gopal to relocate the First Princess.[74] Gopal shifted the First Princess to a property he owned himself.[75] He, it is said, took some trouble to make the new residence cozier than her earlier home had been. This one had curtains and a cot. He knew the First Princess did not have much longer to live and 'people from Burma may come when she died, and he did not want them to see how she had lived'. A resident of

Ratnagiri says that this was not because Gopal had been mean-hearted in the past. No, not at all. He just hadn't had the money or the ability to give her a better life. Now that she was dying he didn't want her demeaned in front of her own people, so he made a special effort to prevent this.[76] However, her new home was located even further from town than her first one had been—far enough for all the boys who used to stop by regularly, to no longer be able to do so.[77] Also, although better appointed, her new home was not a grand one; rather, it was a humble structure, so basic that when she died Gopal converted it into a cowshed.[78]

Almost twenty-seven years after returning to Ratnagiri, the First Princess died on the night of 3 June 1947, at the age of sixty-seven. It is not known if anyone was with her at the time of her death, or what exactly she died of. Her funeral was held on 5 June, after the arrival of three Burmese Buddhist priests.[79] From the description of her funeral cortege and the ceremonies held at the time of her cremation, it appears that it was only in death that the First Princess fleetingly came alive for the officialdom and townspeople for whom she had ceased to exist during her life, for an internal government memo indicates:

> The procession went through the main streets of Ratnagiri to the cremation ground, the daughter of the Princess being the Chief Mourner. On its way to the cremation ground, the body was garlanded by the President of the Muslim League, and by other leading merchants and institutions of Ratnagiri. At the entrance to the cremation ground a guard of honour was presented by the Armed District Police. After the body was placed on the Pier, the District Magistrate and other leading citizens made suitable speeches. The Police band was employed throughout; a salute was fired and the Last Post sounded.[80]

The government felt that the Third Princess should be asked if she wished for the ashes of her sister to be brought back to Burma. But it was then decided—seemingly without reference to the Third Princess— that perhaps it would be better to entomb the First Princess's remains in Ratnagiri, next to that of her father.[81] The British government stored her ashes in the Ratnagiri treasury in a wooden box, pending a final decision. At some stage the Indian government did construct—at the cost of Rs 5,000—a tomb for the First Princess's mortal remains right next to that of her father. (Both tombs share a common wall.) Under the plaque on her tomb, a small square aperture was created to enable the insertion of her ashes once the question of whether the entombment was to be in India or Burma was resolved; however her ashes were *never* deposited in her tomb. Over the years Tu Tu intermittently lobbied to get her mother's ashes entombed,[82] but it appears the matter just slipped through the cracks of the system. (The time of the First Princess's death was in very close proximity to the time of both Indian and Burmese independence, leading to a change of guards with far more pressing issues on hand.) The aperture is, to this day, unsealed. The Ratnagiri treasury has indicated that they have no record today of her ashes,[83] and all attempts to trace them have so far been unsuccessful. Her mortal remains have either been misplaced or lost over the years. Tragically, even after her death, there has been no end to her betrayal . . .

After a lifetime in exile and captivity, at the age of forty years, the government abruptly released the First Princess into a bewildering world, with which she was ill equipped to deal. The government—that had for so many years interfered in almost every aspect of her life—suddenly thought it fit to let her go with no checks and balances to ensure her transition, and with no safety net to haul her in if things panned out badly. True she had pleaded for her freedom, but the British were well aware of the compulsions that propelled her towards this choice, and clearly saw the calamity lurking around the corner, eager and ready to engulf her. Severely judged and cruelly betrayed by all, the First Princess lived a life of poverty, monotony and loneliness so achingly intense that she was finally edged into numbing insanity. Death was her salvation, for death not only released her, but perhaps also led her to a life thereafter where she found much greater happiness and peace than she had had in this one. Certainly she believed this was possible; certainly she heroically struggled against all odds to tot up the requisite merits to try and ensure this.

20

THE FIRST PRINCESS'S DAUGHTER

O n her arrival in Rangoon in 1919, Tu Tu, then twelve and a half
years old, was exposed to the prejudices of the extended Burmese
royal family, a family imbued with deeply traditional values and
attitudes, a family that considered the purity of their lineage so
important that half-brothers and sisters married each other to preserve
its sanctity. It is not known if Tu Tu was ever directly taunted, or
whether the disapproval was by way of innuendos and whispers. At any
rate, both mother and daughter keenly felt the contempt. As an adult
Tu Tu had bitter memories of her days in Burma;[1] her mother had been
disconcerted enough not to want to stay on anywhere in Burma, even
in a separate home.[2] Certainly in Rangoon the queen had not treated
Tu Tu with any affection and visiting royal relatives in all likelihood
took their cue from her. Many years later, in interviews given by Tu Tu
to various journalists she repeatedly referred to her grandmother as a
'*kardankaal*', a Marathi word meaning 'a frightful ogress'.[3] She continued,

however, to have fond memories of her grandfather, King Thibaw, and said he was 'a very good person, and very kind to the local people'.[4]

Tu Tu's life was not happy or easy even after she returned to Ratnagiri. Here, she was viewed as an illegitimate child of no caste, a difficult title to wear in a very conservative, insular town where people bathed when the shadow of a Dalit (a person of the 'untouchable' caste) fell on them.[5] Her own father viewed her with indifference, and contributed nothing, financially or otherwise, to her upbringing.[6] Her mother was socially isolated and deeply depressed. Apart from her parents Tu Tu had no family in Ratnagiri, did not go to school, and lived in a sparsely populated area on the outskirts of the town. All this led to Tu Tu *longing* to belong.

In 1930 Tu Tu married Shankar Yeshwant Pawar. Shankar had been a motor car driver in the Royal Residence (and a colleague of Tu Tu's father, Gopal) and his duties had included walking the royal family's dogs.[7] A valued palace servant, he had been asked to accompany the family back to Burma as a *hamal* (a run-around boy).[8] There is no record to show why or when Shankar returned to Ratnagiri, but he appears to have returned in the early 1920s.[9] Perhaps he returned around the same time as the First Princess and Tu Tu. Details of their courtship and marriage are not known, although Tu Tu's children say their parents fell in love while still at the Royal Residence in Ratnagiri. It is also not known whether the First Princess attended her daughter's wedding (it is known that she did not oppose it), but Gopal objected to the marriage, did not attend it, did not contribute towards its cost, and gave no gift to his daughter on the occasion. He disapproved of Shankar because he belonged to a caste lower than his own.[10]

For Tu Tu, Shankar's marriage proposal was a lifeline thrown her way, for it enabled her to legitimize her status and integrate into Ratnagiri society. She learnt to speak Marathi like a native;[11] she cooked mainly Maharashtrian food; and she brought up her children as locals.[12] People who knew her say Tu Tu was totally Maharashtrian in her mannerisms and in the customs she followed.[13] Short, plump, not pretty like her mother, she stood apart only because of her Burmese facial features, and because she rarely wore a sari. Instead she wore a long skirt and a hip-length blouse with short, puffed sleeves, all of which she stitched on her own. However, she insisted that her daughters regularly wear saris, once they were old enough to. She wanted them to blend in, she said, as once they married 'they would have to go into local people's homes'.[14]

Tu Tu now called herself, for legal purposes, Baisubai Shankar Pawar.[15] She renounced Buddhism and adopted her husband's religion, Hinduism, with all the enthusiasm of a new convert. Following his lead she worshipped Dattaguru, a local Hindu deity.[16] Years later, when asked about her religion, she denied being a Buddhist and appeared to resent being questioned about it. 'Oh I don't know, I'm a Hindu,' she said.[17] One of Tu Tu's sons would later tell a journalist that Tu Tu 'hardly knew anything about the Buddhist religion or about the Konbaung dynasty'.[18] It is evident she wanted a *complete* break from her past.

Tu Tu and Shankar began their married life in a rented home on Nachane Road on the outskirts of Ratnagiri, about a kilometre or two from her mother's residence. Their home was a tiny hut on about thirty-four *guntha*s (totaling just under an acre) of agricultural land.[19] Shankar's family, upset with his choice of a bride of no caste, refused to have anything to do with Tu Tu. The couple therefore stayed as a nuclear family.[20] Tu Tu must have been hurt by yet another rejection, but it appears she did not talk about it. She and Shankar had nine children, seven of whom lived to be adults: two daughters (Pramilla and Malti) and five sons (Dighambar, Shrikant, Chandrakant or Chandu, Suresh and Narayan).[21]

Unlike Tu Tu, Shankar was literate and his children say that *annah*, as they called him, regularly pored over the newspaper while chewing a paan.[22] About four years older than Tu Tu, Shankar was a gentle and warm man who unfortunately gradually became an alcoholic.[23] In spite of his addiction, Shankar did hold a job most of his life,[24] but sadly, he squandered away much of his salary on drinking binges,[25] and it was Tu Tu who had to eke out a living, in addition to looking after her perpetually growing family and her lonely ageing mother.

Tu Tu's daughter Malti says that her *ahee* (mother) got up every morning between 3 and 4 a.m. She cooked for her family, and packed lunch for her husband.[26] She then made scented paper flowers and decorations, which her children carried to the market to sell. People from Ratnagiri and the neighbouring villages would buy these ornamentations for use at weddings, in temples, and at shrines in their homes.[27] She also stitched (and sold) quilts, and vests and caps for babies, all by hand, as she had no sewing machine.[28] She raised ducks and goats for sale.[29] And, with her children's help, she grew and harvested paddy on the land on which she lived.[30] People in Ratnagiri say that Tu Tu was never ashamed or embarrassed to do any kind of work. They remember her setting out, basket on hip, to salvage discarded scraps from around town to recycle; they remember her collecting cow dung to pat into cakes to sell as fuel. She disregarded exclamations of 'Look at the princess now making cow dung cakes!' and soldiered on. According to one of her ex-neighbours Tu Tu had two strains of genes: royal and worker. The worker genes were apparent in the hard work she relentlessly put in every day; the royal genes were apparent in her regal bearing and her generosity, which reminded people of her mother, the First Princess, and her grandfather, King Thibaw.[31] Tu Tu did not let a harsh and impoverished existence kill her innate generosity and kindness.

Perhaps because she had felt unloved and stigmatized as a child, Tu Tu had tremendous compassion for unwanted babies. Numerous unwed mothers, from in and around Ratnagiri, would silently leave their newborns on Tu Tu's doorstep, secure in the knowledge that she would take the baby in and look after it. Estimates vary—for she never kept count—but it is thought that Tu Tu rescued around eighteen babies.[32] Four she kept and raised herself (two boys: Rajkumar and Babloo, and two girls: Tara and Chandra); the rest she gave up for adoption to childless couples.[33] A local Brahmin family abandoned their baby after being told by a soothsayer that the infant was 'unlucky'. Tu Tu raised this baby herself, as no one else would have her.[34] According to one of her adopted children—Tara—Tu Tu was a very loving mother, and she confidently adds that she was Tu Tu's favourite child.[35] Another of Tu Tu's daughters, Malti, says that Tu Tu was always kinder and gentler with her adopted children, as if perpetually trying to compensate them for the injustice they had endured.[36]

Stories abound in Ratnagiri of Tu Tu's benevolence and zeal to help.

Apart from babies, Tu Tu also adopted numerous stray and wounded dogs.[37] She helped arrange many low-cost marriages for girls from economically disadvantaged backgrounds.[38] She taught impoverished homebound women to make paper flowers. This skill, which helped her earn much of her own income, she generously shared for no fee and with no thought of the competition she was creating for herself.[39] As a result of her endless humanitarian work, Tu Tu became a well-known and well-loved figure in town and people often referred to her as the Mother Teresa of Ratnagiri.[40]

As Shankar could not be counted on for anything, Tu Tu sometimes found her responsibilities overwhelming. So, occasionally, in the evening, she would set off with her children and goats for a nearby hillock and sit and gaze into the distance. Once a month she, with an entourage of her children, would go for the 9 p.m. show at Lata Talkies to catch a Marathi movie.[41] Sometimes she needed to be just by herself, and would wander off aimlessly.[42] Once in a while people would see her sitting on the roadside, smoking a beedi.[43] Although Tu Tu's cheerful, friendly personality enabled her to make acquaintances easily (and at least one very good friend—they 'were as close as sisters'[44]), she did not find it easy to confide in anyone. She talked a lot, but said very little, says someone who knew her.[45] And everyone who was familiar with Tu Tu noticed that she did not like to speak of her past even with her own children. Although she dearly loved them all, she was so absorbed by the relentlessness of her struggle and, as one long-term Ratnagiri resident puts it, was so 'in her own world', that like her mother she tragically paid no attention to their education. It wasn't just a lack of attention, but as her children grew up, she needed and asked for their help for her daily activities and chores. As a result school was not a priority and none of her children studied beyond middle school (the seventh standard).[46]

Tu Tu went to stay with her mother for her first few deliveries, but with her rapidly increasing brood, and with no support at all in her own home, it became increasingly difficult for her to do so.[47] Always a concerned mother, and well aware of her daughter's expanding family and impoverished life, the First Princess badly wanted to help her daughter financially, and searched for ways to do so. She told the

Burmese reporter who visited her that she was very keen 'to provide for her daughter and grandchildren but she was not able to do so . . .' She begged him to find out about Burmese laws that governed pensions of 'relatives of Kings', and whether her daughter Tu Tu was eligible.[48]

It is said that the First Princess never saw Tu Tu's marital home.[49] While it is true that the First Princess hardly, if ever, went out,[50] and in all probability herself chose not to visit her daughter's home, it also appears that Tu Tu never pressurized her mother to come stay with her, or even to occasionally come by. Sadly—for this could have dramatically changed the First Princess's life—for various reasons, neither mother nor daughter was comfortable with the idea. Perhaps it was her always drunk husband, perhaps it was her inhibition at letting her mother see her very changed life-style, perhaps it was the prominent Dattaguru shrine in her home that made Tu Tu reluctant to have her mother come over. Or perhaps she chose to adhere to an old Hindu custom where protocol did not permit a mother to visit her married daughter's home. Although Tu Tu did not live in a joint family, although it is highly unlikely that Shankar would have objected to the First Princess's visits, Tu Tu tightly embraced her newfound Hindu identity, and her daughters say that she refused to visit them in their marital homes.[51]

Additionally, Tu Tu had plenty of demons of her own to battle, and heavy burdens of her own to carry. Although many years later she would describe her mother as 'a very good and kind person',[52] there were undercurrents in their relationship that complicated it. Tu Tu may have held her mother at least partially responsible for the very difficult childhood she had had. Certainly she had been profoundly impacted by the choices her mother had made, and perhaps as an adult she judged her mother like everyone else—the very parochial environment in which she lived defining her sense of right and wrong. So, for myriad reasons, Tu Tu just did not have the kind of space in her life for her mother that her mother so desperately needed.

After Tu Tu's marriage, she was not in frequent touch with her father, Gopal.[53] He visited her twice a year, when he went to his fields that lay opposite her home. He would then sit with Tu Tu for a short while.[54] Occasionally, he gave her small amounts of money: 'Even Rs 5 went a long way then.'[55] After Gopal's wife Laxmibai's death in 1957, she visited her father in his home once in a rare while.[56] Gopal was not an involved grandfather, and Tu Tu's children don't have many memories of him. They never visited his home; during his bi-annual visits to their home—one of them remembers that he had a distinct limp—he sometimes gave them a silver rupee coin.[57]

As a politically active Ratnagiri resident, Gopal made some enemies. In 1950, on the festival of Phalgun Poornima, acid was thrown on his face, and he lost vision in one eye. On another occasion, someone physically attacked him.[58] Apart from these unfortunate disruptions, Gopal led a full and busy life right up to his death. In the words of Gopal's grandson, Vilas:

> My grandfather was alert till the end. Eight days before he died he sat down while out walking, as he felt giddy. Going out was his weakness. My father told him not to go out, that he'd get whatever he wanted. On 7 September 1972, my father gave him tea, and my grandfather told him to go collect rent. My grandfather passed away soon after my father left, around 9 a.m.[59]

In his will, Gopal made no mention at all of Tu Tu.[60] According to a long-term Ratnagiri resident, 'Sons always got landed property. Daughters never inherited property. They would get things like jewellery, money etc. at the time of their marriage.'[61] But Tu Tu had got nothing at the time of her wedding either, and Gopal could not have forgotten that it was from *her* mother that he had continually taken money, some of which he had used to buy a part of his land holding. He must also have been aware that Tu Tu lived in rented property, which was under litigation.

In spite of the fact that Shankar had never been of much support to his family, financially or otherwise, and although his alcoholism was a constant source of sorrow for Tu Tu, she loved him.[62] According to one of her daughters-in-law, Tu Tu and Shankar were 'very happily married, he was an affectionate man'.[63] It appears the family just accepted Shankar for what he was, and when he passed away in 1976 his death was deeply mourned.[64] All his children were adults by the time he died, and most were married (all marriages had taken place with no dowry being either taken or given).[65]

Tu Tu's large family provided her with noisy affection and an intricate web of relationships. Like a matriarch, she dominated family get-togethers and continued, almost to the end, to have a strong presence and 'a commanding voice'.[66] Many of her grandchildren remember her as a caring grandmother. Her granddaughter Sangeeta recalls learning how to make delicious Burmese dishes, paper flowers and decorations from her.[67]

Sometimes, particularly towards the end of her life when really hard pressed for money, Tu Tu could be seen on the streets of Ratnagiri 'begging for alms'.[68] Sometimes she asked for just a beedi that she so loved to smoke.[69] A journalist reminisces that once when he had gone to interview her, she immediately sat up and struck a regal pose in her very humble surroundings. He also recalls, for he interviewed her more than once, that as her memory gradually faded, she frequently blanked out mid-conversation and sometimes got unpredictably irritable and abusive. He remembers Chandrakant (Chandu), her responsible, loving son, noticing that he had noticed and gently pointing out to him that her memory loss and occasional rude behaviour was surely to be expected after *all* she had had to endure in her long and difficult life?[70]

Right through her adult life Tu Tu had had no contact with her Burmese relatives, and never spoke about them.[71] Her aunts, with whom she had spent almost fourteen years of her life, had, after her early years, not been involved or loving, and they seem to have had no contact with her after her return to Ratnagiri. Even the First Princess's most concerned sister, the Second Princess, 'didn't speak or make any mention of Tu Tu', not even in her own home to her own family.[72]

In 1993 (when Tu Tu was eighty-seven years old) some of the Fourth Princess's children came to Ratnagiri to perform the last rites of their grandfather and grandaunt, rites which had earlier not been performed. Tu Tu met her cousins for the first time during this visit and one of the Fourth Princess's daughters, Princess Hteik Su Phaya Gyi remembers: 'My brother Taw Taw [Prince Taw Phaya Galae] said sit next to Tu Tu, she is your older sister. So I went and sat with her. She held my hand, she looked at me, you know. And she put her two hands on my face . . . oooooouuuuu, they were rough.'[73] Rough due to years of hard manual work of the kind her cousins could not even begin to imagine. Prince Taw Phaya remembers that Tu Tu kept repeating 'Phaya Gyi Phaya'—the name she called her mother; other than this her cousins discovered that Tu Tu remembered no Burmese whatsoever.[74] As she knew no English either, communication between the cousins ended before it had even had a chance to begin.

Ever since the late 1950s, a constant source of tension in Tu Tu's and her family's life was litigation over the property where they lived. The case was convoluted, and Shankar, Tu Tu and their son, Chandu, spent years fighting for the family to be permitted to stay on and cultivate the property.[75] This prolonged dispute cost the already impoverished family a lot of money,[76] and it also cost them a lot of heartache. By 1999 Tu Tu and her family lost various appeals and were ordered to vacate their home. (Tu Tu's family had flouted tenancy laws due to ignorance and financial desperation.[77] But many also feel that over the years the case had been mishandled, and that the family certainly could have, under the Bombay Tenancy and Agricultural Land Act, 1948, held on to at least part of the property.[78])

To enforce the eviction, a posse of five policemen and one lady constable arrived unannounced a few days before Diwali in 1999 and physically dragged the then ninety-three-year-old Tu Tu and her family out, and threw their possessions off the property. Demolition of the house began that very instant, with the roof and the Dattaguru shrine being destroyed in the family's presence. A devastated Tu Tu refused to budge and stayed next to her broken hut for three nights, after which she was cajoled by her family to move into Chandu's home.[79]

Tu Tu, at various stages in her life, had appealed to the government for financial help. (Although the Political Pension Act in 1940 in Burma granted a pension of Rs 600 per month to each grandchild of King Thibaw,[80] Tu Tu, his first grandchild, was granted nothing.[81]) Like her mother, she believed that the Royal Residence in Ratnagiri belonged rightfully to her family and that the government had appropriated it without any compensation. She felt that as King Thibaw's granddaughter, she was entitled to some help—financial, housing—from the government and it frustrated her that this help never came, and that she had to live in poverty in a small hut almost all her life. When even this inadequate hut was cruelly snatched from her, she sentimentally pleaded that she be allowed, for old time's sake, to spend just one day in the Royal Residence that had been her childhood home. 'After spending a day in the Palace I will die happily,' she said to a journalist. But the Indian government, for various bureaucratic reasons, was unable to grant this request to the dying woman who had given so much of herself to the town of Ratnagiri.[82]

Tu Tu died on 24 October 2000, at the age of ninety-four, in the garage cum residence where her son Chandu still lives with his family.[83] According to Chandu, his mother, who came to live with him exactly three days before Diwali in 1999, died exactly three days before Diwali in 2000. Hindu death rites were followed, her body was cremated, and her ashes were immersed in the sea off the coast of Ratnagiri.[84] Like her grandmother and her aunts, Tu Tu had shared a deep bond with her dogs. One of her ex-neighbours told Malti that the stray dogs Tu Tu had fed and looked after before her eviction had uncannily sensed her impending death and had howled ceaselessly for over an hour just before she died.[85]

21

THE SECOND PRINCESS

The government believed that 'by marrying commoners the political importance of the princesses would disappear',[1] so when the Second Princess married a non-royal, the British expected that she and her husband would quietly settle down and fade into obscurity. However, the collector of Ratnagiri quickly noticed that though the Second Princess did 'not share her father's exalted notions of a still existent royal status',[2] Kin Maung Lat (later more commonly known as Lat*thakin*; many Burmese nationalists joined the Do-bama Asi-ayone movement and entitled themselves *thakin*, which means master) had 'lordly notions as to the position of the princess and himself . . .'[3]

Latthakin, with his wife's support, vociferously objected to their limiting monthly allowance and, since the couple's move to Calcutta in March 1917, letters had flown back and forth on the issue. In August 1920 an allowance of Rs 500 per month was finally decided upon, much to the couple's chagrin.[4] Although this was an increase from the Rs 300 earlier indicated,[5] it was a far cry from what the couple felt entitled to. Latthakin refused to accept the revised pension, and it is said that over the years the more practical Second Princess signed for it behind his back.[6]

The government initially expected that once the ill-will in Burma over the Second Princess and Latthakin's marriage died down, the couple would relocate to their homeland.[7] But this never happened. When the Second Princess and Latthakin finally left Calcutta on 1 March 1920, it was not for Burma, but for the small north-eastern Indian town of Kalimpong. It is here that they chose to settle.

Set in the foothills of the Himalayas, straddling a ridge, Kalimpong had (and still has) panoramic views of green valleys and snowcapped peaks. Perched at an altitude of about 1,250 metres, the climate was moderate throughout the year. Until 1865 Kalimpong had been a part of the Kingdom of Bhutan; now it was part of British India. The borders of Sikkim and Nepal were just a stone's throw away, and Tibet was also conveniently close (a mere thirty miles). From these four neighbouring Himalayan countries there came a constant flow of traders and travellers. Buddhist monasteries, both Tibetan and Bhutanese, attracted an eclectic mix of foreign scholars, monks and curious visitors. Due to the town's picturesque location and its salubrious climate, artists, writers, tourists and missionaries visited it; some stayed on and made it their home. For the Second Princess and Latthakin, Kalimpong was an inspired choice: a town steeped in varied ethnicities, cultures and religions (including their own), in which it would be relatively easy to settle. Also, on a more mundane level, the cost of living in Kalimpong was considerably lower than it had been in Calcutta, making it much more affordable. Another bonus was that in this town the Second Princess wasn't the only royalty—Rani Chuni Wangmo, the sister of the King of Sikkim, after her marriage to Raja Sonam Tobgye Dorji of Bhutan, had settled here with her husband (their daughter, Kesang Choden, later married the third King of Bhutan). And importantly, this town was remote. It was far enough from the people of their past to enable the couple to reinvent themselves if they chose to do so. In this town they could *really* begin a new life. And they certainly did.

Details of the couple's very early years in Kalimpong are not clearly known but it appears that they quickly assimilated into its life and society. The Second Princess's monthly allowance was sufficient for them to live rather well. They continually supplemented it with loans to live even better. Not many years after their arrival—nobody knows exactly when—residents of Kalimpong began to refer to Latthakin as 'Burma Raja' (prince of Burma), and the Second Princess as 'Rani Saab' (princess).[8] Stories circulated as to how King Thibaw had 'handpicked' Latthakin to marry his second daughter;[9] how had the kingdom not been colonized, Latthkin would most likely have been its king. Not only had he married King Thibaw's daughter but he himself, declared Latthakin, was the king's nephew (the king sister's son, to be precise[10]), a person of royal blood, and therefore an acceptable successor. A resident of Kalimpong, the well-known English Buddhist monk, Sangharakshita, recalls in his memoirs that Latthakin spoke often of King Thibaw, and about the glorious days in the Golden Palace, and although his excitement and enthusiasm was abundantly evident, since he 'spoke rather rapidly, and tended to jump breathlessly from one topic to another', what he actually said could barely be comprehended by Sangarakshita or by anyone else.[11]

Latthakin was a friendly, outgoing man, and it appears he quite effortlessly carried off the persona of 'Burma Raja'. An 'intensely Burmese' man, Latthakin always dressed in rich silk pasoes and jackets, topped with a dramatic matching silk gaung baung (Burmese-style turban) on his head. He also 'sported a pair of fierce handlebar moustaches of truly regal dimensions'.[12] It was his personality, and not that of the Second Princess's, that enabled the couple to figure prominently in Kalimpong's social life.[13] One of the first homes they rented was a very commodious bungalow called Springburn with a beautiful view and a large garden.[14] It was from here that Latthakin launched the couple's social life: '[H]e and the Rani gave lavish tea, lunch and dinner parties to their friends in Kalimpong . . . The first time Ma attended such a party she came back starry eyed. The opulence of the house, the gracious hospitality of the Raja and Rani . . .'[15] Prominent residents of Kalimpong entertained the couple, including Raja and Rani Dorji, who would invite them to cocktails and receptions. Formal invitations addressing the couple as 'Prince & Princess' would arrive for these occasions.[16] Latthakin also befriended

Kalimpong's numerous visitors. These included Prince Peter, a member of the Greek royal family and a scholar of Tibetan culture; the well-known artists Dr Roerich and Kanwal Krishna;[17] and the Scottish missionary Dr Graham who was not really a visitor as he had settled in Kalimpong.[18]

A well-read man, Latthakin subscribed to Burmese and Indian newspapers and publications, from which he clipped and stored articles of interest to him. He took correspondence courses including one with the Pelman Institute in Delhi for training of the 'Mind, Memory and Personality'. He became a member of the National Geographic Society, Washington DC.[19] Passionate about solving crossword puzzles, he often consulted his four-volume Webster's dictionary,[20] which was part of his large and varied library. Each of his books was carefully stamped 'Latthakin Home Library'.[21] The Second Princess, by contrast, was 'semi-literate' and her reading was limited to Buddhist prayer books.[22] An uxorious husband, Latthakin tried to involve his disinterested wife in his various intellectual pursuits. He, with a friend, established a lodge of the Theosophical Society and tried, unsuccessfully, to persuade the Second Princess to attend its weekly meetings with him.[23] A meticulous diary keeper, he encouraged his wife to keep one too. Pocket-sized diaries from Mandalay were sent for, and in these the Second Princess wrote her name in Burmese and English on the first page, and almost daily made one-line entries in Burmese about mundane household matters.[24] (See Appendix II.) Latthakin helped his wife draft numerous letters, including one to Sir Harcourt Butler, the governor of Burma, supporting Sayadaw U Ottama, a revered Burmese monk imprisoned by the British.[25]

When Queen Supayalat passed away in November 1925, the Second Princess asked the government to fund her and her husband's trip to Rangoon for the funeral. The government refused, and in protest the couple set off on foot.[26] But, as Latthakin pithily put it, their 'physical bodies did not follow [their] spirit'. After resting in Kankipong for about two and a half months, they turned home. While in Kankipong, possibly needled by Latthakin's persistent letters, the government sent an emissary to placate the couple.[27]

Annoyed with the government on various issues, a year later Latthakin

wrote to the viceroy of India requesting that either the government
accede to his stated demands (that both the king and queen be
entombed in Mandalay) or permit him 'to fight a duel with Sir
Harcourt Butler'![28] Eccentric and colourful, there is no doubt that
Latthakin was also charismatic. In Kalimpong he was popular and
sought after. In Burma he won some recognition for his numerous
letters and articles that highlighted his virulently anti-British stance,
his patriotism and his loyalty to the Burmese royal family. Over the
years, seduced by the image Latthakin so effectively projected of
himself, in the minds of many people lines got blurred, memories
faded, and Latthakin metamorphosized into a royal: a prince. King
Thibaw had once written that his daughter would not be permitted to
'marry in such a low caste as this man [Latthakin] belongs';[29] King
Thibaw's grandson, the Fourth Princess's son, Prince Taw Phaya
Galae, many years later wrote an article entitled 'Latthakin, the Great
Patriot' in which he waxed eloquent about the man who had married
his aunt. Unfortunately, it was published after the Second Princess's
and Latthakin's deaths, and therefore this stamp of approval by a
prominent member of the Burmese royal family came too late to
provide any sense of vindication to the couple.[30]

Not only could Latthakin not interest his wife in his intellectual
pursuits but he was also unsuccessful in involving her in his other
activities and hobbies. He was deeply interested in yoga and
meditation.[31] Painting was also something he seriously pursued (with
some lessons from the artist Kanwal Krishna), and large oil canvases
depicting Mount Kailas and other landscapes dotted his home.[32] One
of his other passions was hunting; he had a large collection of guns
and rifles and was reputed to have been an excellent marksman.[33] He
would often go on hunting expeditions, including tiger hunts, in the
lush jungles around Kalimpong, and there still exist photographs of
him sitting or standing triumphantly over his kills. The Second
Princess rarely joined him; she objected to hunting on religious
grounds. Very occasionally, she would go along with him, at his
insistence, 'just for a picnic'.[34] One of Latthakin's diary entries, dated
5 November 1930, sketchily describes one such outing: 'Both went to
Nazeok. Princess by *Dolai* [palanquin] & self and servants on foot and

returned here on the 12th instant ... 8 servants accompanied us ...
There was duck shooting.'[35]

Latthakin always referred to his wife as 'Princess', and always treated
her as such. He never forgot who she was, even if this was because he
never forgot his own elevated position. Also, in spite of their differences
both in terms of intellect and interests, theirs was a marriage that
worked harmoniously and beautifully. According to someone who
lived with them for many years, 'They were very attached to each other
and were always cooing together like two pigeons. They couldn't do
without each other.' If one of them left the room, the other would
soon follow in search.[36]

Although happy together, due to the lifestyle they adopted, the
couple was always short of money. The Second Princess, less egotistical
and more practical than her husband, signed for her pension payments
without his knowledge and vaguely explained away the source of her
liquidity.[37] This was not difficult to do as Latthakin was aware of the
loans that they were forever raising, that from time to time some of
their possessions were being sold, and that not too small an income
was being generated from the sale of milk produced by the numerous
cows they owned.[38] Besides, 'although very well read, Latthakin was
not very worldly', so he also readily bought explanations from his wife
of the kind, 'Madanlal, who is like your son, says it is his duty to help
us out financially',[39] and other unlikely ones, never pressing for
details. He was, however, well aware that the government had paid
Rs 3,000 for his hospitalization in 1927, that it had settled some of
the couple's loans, and that it paid their house rent directly to their
landlords.[40]

While the Second Princess financially supported her husband's
varied hobbies, and although she dutifully signed long letters frequently
penned by him on a variety of subjects, it was religious prayers and
rituals that took up most of her time. She rose early every morning
and sent her servants off to pluck flowers from her garden and from
around town: '[S]he used to use *buckets* of flowers for her daily puja.'
She was also a good cook, and made both Indian and Burmese food
equally well. The Second Princess was not social, and almost never
went out—she went very reluctantly with Latthakin only when he

insisted. And although the parties they threw at home were lavish and admired, during these parties, though not ungracious, she generally sat silently on her own. Very occasionally she enjoyed the company of a few neighbours but she was really most comfortable holding court with her household retainers, all of whom left her royal presence walking respectfully backwards.[41]

One of these retainers was a Nepali boy, Jaiman. It is uncertain as to what the boy's exact function in the household was (his children categorically state that he was never the couple's servant). Perhaps he ran errands for the couple, and performed odd jobs, in return for food and accommodation. When Jaiman was old enough to wed, the Second Princess and Latthakin helped arrange his marriage to a Nepali woman, Satyamaya, and he and his wife continued to stay in the couple's compound. On 28 January 1932, a son named Premlall Jan was born to Jaiman and Satyamaya, and having been unable to have a child of their own, the Second Princess and Latthakin adopted the boy at birth. They affectionately called him A Lu Gyi (when older, he was called by the more respectful name Maung Lu Gyi).[42] There was now a new purpose in the Second Princess's life, and she became a besotted mother. Maung Lu Gyi was adored, pampered and brought up like a little prince.[43]

Maung Lu Gyi's birthdays were always celebrated. The house was filled with flowers, a special prayer was said, a party was thrown, poor children were fed, and the staff was tipped.[44] Maung Lu Gyi remembers his initiation into Buddhism as a young boy: his head was shaved, he wore a pongyi robe, and he participated in a special ceremony followed by a feast. He recalls that unlike the other little boys, he never went to school unescorted: '[M]orning a servant would come with me to school and would have to remain there till noon until another servant would come there with my lunch, and then the morning servant would go home and the lunch servant would stay and bring me home.' He remembers how the Second Princess always covered up for him if he did anything he shouldn't have, and even at night she wouldn't let him out of her sight: '[S]he was very affectionate, till her death she used to sleep along with me only.'[45]

In spite of the extra attention and tuitions that Maung Lu Gyi was given, he was never a good student.[46] Latthakin—a concerned father—

spent many hours with him in his home library sharing his books and showing him maps and pictures in an attempt to spark some interest of an academic kind. But he was not successful in doing this; Maung Lu Gyi, without his parent's knowledge, frequently bunked school,[47] and according to Sangharakshita, associated with the wrong crowd.[48] After completing his schooling Maung Lu Gyi worked as his parents' secretary cum assistant.[49]

In 1935, the landlord of Springburn asked the Second Princess to either buy it (for Rs 18,000) or vacate it. Reluctant to shift, anxious to have their own home, and not having received any reply to their numerous appeals for funding over the years, Latthakin shot off yet another letter to the government. This letter was long, and it bristled with indignation:

> It is high time we were given an adequate sum . . . to enable us to live according to our position as children of King of Burma and independent of the petty annoyances to which we are now constantly subjected. This is our right, our due, and cannot be regarded as the granting of a favour. To be free from charity of the Government and from the degradation of receiving the miserly pittance is our desire and is not a very big thing to grant . . .[50]

There was no reply to this letter, and in January 1936, Latthakin shot off another letter pointing out that the government had given the king of Burma only seven days to respond to an ultimatum which concerned a matter as earth shattering as the future of his kingdom, whereas Latthakin had given the government enough time to respond to 'a small personal matter' and there had been no response. As a protest, because 'the limit of toleration has now been reached', Latthakin said 'we shall not renew our gun license as usually [is] done in December and January the latest'.[51] The government did not ignore this threat like they had his letters; there was a price to pay for this act of defiance.

Sometime in 1936, the Second Princess, her family and entourage shifted from Springburn to Arcadia. Located on about six acres of land, at the end of a long winding uphill driveway, the house commanded a panoramic view of distant mountains and the shimmering Teesta River set in an emerald green valley.[52]

In the early hours of a cold January morning in 1937, the sub-
divisional officer of Kalimpong arrived at Arcadia with a band of
twelve policemen to confiscate Latthakin's extensive hunting gun
collection for which he had not renewed licenses. After a tense stand-
off, Latthakin handed over his guns, but insisted that they be broken
in his presence. He said he would claim damages from the government
to purchase new ones.[53] (The government, not surprisingly, never
reimbursed him.)

Years later, Latthakin narrated this whole gun confiscation incident
to Sangharakshita, but with an additional bit of information that
provides a fascinating insight into his attitude towards his wife. He
matter-of-factly said that his reaction had been to fortify his home
and defend it by shooting anyone who got too close. He indicated that
'First he would have shot the princess, then he would have shot as
many policemen as he could before *they* shot *him*. That was the
important thing. The princess must not be touched: she was
sacrosanct . . .' Luckily none of this came to pass, as two of Latthakin's
friends (Madanlal, a lawyer, and Gopal who had worked as Latthakin's
manager at some stage,[54]) effectively mediated to calm down the
situation. As Sangarakshita puts it, 'the princess [therefore] survived
to be shot by her protector on some other occasion'![55] Whether the
Second Princess was ever informed about *this* nuance of the incident
remains unknown.

In the early 1940s the couple shifted again, this time to Tapoban.
This home had an impressive Burma teak staircase that connected the
upper and lower floors. It was on the landing of the upper floor, in an
alcove with a large window and a breathtaking valley view, that Latthakin
installed his library. Tapoban had a private clay tennis court spectacularly
located just near the edge of a precipice,[56] and it was here that
Latthakin frequently 'played tennis . . . with his friends. Tea was
served at the court. The menu consisted of cucumber sandwiches,
cakes and pastry in true British style.'[57]

While he may have enjoyed entertaining British style, for many years
the government had labelled Latthakin as 'dangerously anti-British'.[58]
Maung Lu Gyi says his father was *very* anti-British.[59] Around 1945, at
a time of heightened patriotic fervour as Burma inexorably marched

towards her independence (the Allies had just helped oust the Japanese and the British had reoccupied Burma), Latthakin's already strong anti-British sentiment intensified. Much to the amusement of locals, he put up a sign on the Tapoban gate declaring 'Europeans and dogs not allowed'.[60]

An incident that followed—in all probability apocryphal or at the least highly exaggerated—was related by Maung Lu Gyi to Prince Taw Phaya Galae (the Fourth Princess's son). Prince Taw Phaya Galae described, with unabashed admiration, the occurrence in an article he later wrote: One day an Englishman, the deputy commissioner of the area, came to visit Latthakin for some official business. The gate at Tapoban was closed as usual, and the gatekeeper pointed to the sign that had provided so much entertainment in town. Furious at this impertinence, the deputy commissioner warned the gatekeeper that he would crash his jeep through the gate unless it was immediately opened. The flustered gatekeeper rushed in to consult Latthakin who ordered him to return to his post. Seeing no move to let him in, the deputy commissioner reversed, revved his engine and made a dash for the gate. Just at that moment a single shot was heard and 'a bullet pierced through the hat of the Deputy Commissioner making a hole ... The Deputy Commissioner took off his hat and examined it. He then glanced at my [father] who was standing upstairs. My [father] waved at him and made a gesture signaling him to turn back.' The infuriated deputy collector reversed his jeep once more and accelerated towards the gate. This time bullets smashed the windshield on the passenger side of the jeep. The deputy collector now beat such a hasty retreat that his punctured hat was blown off his head and out of the window. The hat was retrieved and proudly kept as a trophy by Latthakin for many years.[61] The consequences of Latthakin's bravado— and there *must* have been consequences—are unfortunately neither reported in the article nor remembered by his son.

Sometime in 1946 or 1947 the couple shifted again. They moved to Panorama, a bungalow with its own small guesthouse.[62] While they were staying here, India and Burma got their independence from Britain: India on 15 August 1947 and Burma some months later, on 4 January 1948. Latthakin and the Second Princess had wanted this very much, but paradoxically Independence signalled the nemesis of the life the couple had known. After Independence, the monthly allowance that the Second Princess had been receiving ceased abruptly (the house rent, however, continued to be paid by the government directly to the landlord). With no allowance the couple's life inevitably and dramatically altered. (It was probably at this stage that Latthakin was informed that his wife had been accepting her pension without his knowledge all these years—a bit of information he apparently reacted to disbelievingly and furiously.) The couple, to meet their daily expenses, had to frequently sell and pawn many of their possessions. Gulabi (Maung Lu Gyi's sister who lived with the couple, but was never adopted by them) recalls a beautiful gold and ivory broach with dangling pearls that the Second Princess had received as a wedding present. She vividly remembers it being pawned for Rs 60. 'When the money comes I'll get it back,' the Second Princess had told Gulabi— but she never could.[63]

Latthakin now withdrew from Kalimpong's social life.[64] He said to his good friend Sangharakshita years later that since he could no longer reciprocate invitations, he preferred not to accept any.[65] Slowly all but his closest friends faded away.[66] The couple stopped celebrating their own and Maung Lu Gyi's birthdays, reduced their staff strength, and began looking for a more affordable home.[67] And a desperate Latthakin shot off numerous letters (signed by his wife) to the newly formed Burmese government reminding it of the wealth that had once been King Thibaw's, including ruby mines, oil fields and much, much more, and indicating that the government must now compensate the king's descendants for these priceless assets. In November 1948, the Second Princess wrote a letter to the prime minister of India, Pandit Jawaharlal Nehru, in which she briefly introduced herself, and requested for the help of the Indian government in reclaiming some of her father's assets.[68] But the money they dreamt about and appealed so hard for never materialized.

The couple was no longer young, and the Second Princess— although still always immaculately dressed in silk tameins and short silk jackets and carefully groomed with her hair pulled back in a tight knot on her head—now had a pronounced stoop. According to

Sangharakshita, who lived for a few months in their guesthouse, every time he visited their home the Second Princess, if her husband was not around, would press him to immediately inform various people of her dire need for money. Or so he thought, for he was never sure what exactly it was that she was trying to say, because 'on occasions on which she confided in me in this way the Princess's customary whisper sank so low, while the mixture of Hindi and Nepali in which she spoke became so rapid and intense, that it was virtually impossible for me to make out what she was saying'.[69]

What the poor Second Princess was trying to do was to raise loans behind her husband's back. To save him the indignity of knowing the extent of their loans, she pretended that it was nats (spirit-beings) that came to her aid when things got really tough. Latthakin once confided in Sangharakshita that 'the princess was not just a devout Buddhist, not just an advanced meditator: she possessed magical powers of a high order. Whenever they were really short of money . . . all that the princess had to do was to make offerings to the [nats] and they gave her money, usually in the form of hundred rupee notes.' These notes appeared overnight on her altar, he indicated, tucked under her Buddha statues. The money actually of course came from another source—Marwari money lenders whom the Second Princess surreptiously met while her husband was otherwise occupied.[70]

The government, from early 1951, completely stopped paying all allowances, including house rent, to the Second Princess. (The Gratuity Law for Royal Relatives newly passed in Burma excluded all royal relatives residing permanently outside Burma.)[71] By early 1952 their financial situation forced the couple to vacate Panorama and move to its much smaller guesthouse.[72]

According to an article written by U Than Swe, the Burmese embassy in Delhi was sympathetic to the couple's plight and sometimes helped them out. He says that the Burmese prime minister, U Nu, asked the Burmese ambassador to India, U Kyin, to visit the couple in Kalimpong to urge 'the Royal Couple to come back to Burma . . . [and] to provide them with cash of 10,000 rupees'. U Kyin visited the couple in May 1952 and he later recalled a relatively well-appointed home of plush sofas, Persian carpets, satin curtains, antique chandeliers and silver spears, swords and daggers ornamenting a few walls.[73]

The Second Princess entered the room some time after Latthakin, and the ambassador noticed that she sat down so close to her husband that he had to shift slightly to accommodate her. She refused to personally take the sealed envelope containing the gifted money, and gestured that it be put on the carpet on which they were all seated. She then asked that the loans she had taken from the Burmese embassy be calculated and deducted. When told that the prime minister had specified that no deductions be made, she was adamant that she could not accept the entire amount. It is evident that conducting herself in a manner that kept her pride intact was more important to her than taking the money she so badly needed. It was calculated that she owed the embassy Rs 7,000; this was reluctantly removed by the ambassador (after a bit of high drama wherein the Second Princess summoned her son with a candle and matches to burn the Rs 7,000 she felt she could not keep!), and the Second Princess accepted the balance.[74]

What amazed the ambassador even more was the time warp in which the couple seemed to live. Although well read and up to date on current events, when discussing the couple's return to Burma, Latthakin refused to accept that Burma was 'really' independent, appeared deeply suspicious, and asked the ambassador for proof! The Second Princess added that even if Burma was now truly independent 'there will be English spies for sure who might harm us' just as there had been English spies in the palace before her father's deposition. The ambassador soon realized that it was futile arguing with the couple on this subject; that 'their feelings were too deeply rooted in past bitter experiences'. It appears that the matter ended with this visit; there were no more government overtures, formal or informal, to try to persuade the couple to return to Burma.[75] However, at some stage after 1952, the Burmese government did restart paying the Second Princess a monthly pension of Rs 500.[76]

By 1952–53 various health problems besieged both the Second Princess and Latthakin. The Second Princess suffered from giddiness brought on by high blood pressure. Latthakin, who had asthma, was diagnosed with heart trouble (angina pectoris).[77] According to a family friend, although he could no longer hunt or follow some of his other passions 'he never gave up smoking his aromatic Burma cheroots.

He was getting older, frailer and mellower by the day . . .' He had taken
to spending more and more of his time meditating in a small gazebo
on the Panorama property, which he had had capped with a typically
Burmese hti.[78] (This hti-capped gazebo, now somewhat decrepit,
stands to this day.[79])

On the night of 10 January 1955, after a short bout of bronchitis,
Latthakin passed away.[80] As soon as he heard of this the next morning,
Sangharakshita rushed over to the Panorama. Here he found the
Second Princess 'sitting in the sun, in the little garden beside the
guest cottage, smoking a cigar and having her long grey hair combed
by the maidservant'. Latthakin's death had come as a profound shock
to her (according to Gulabi she never got over it); in denial she
indicated to Sangharakshita that he 'would find Raja Sahib inside the
cottage'.[81]

It was Sangharakshita, with the help of Madanlal Pradhan, who
made arrangements for the funeral, and who arranged a sum of
Rs 2,000 from the Kalimpong treasury for funeral expenses (a
distressed Maung Lu Gyi had indicated that there were only a few
rupees in the house). As soon as a jeep containing four lamas arrived
from the Tharpa Choling Gompa (a Tibetan monastery in Kalimpong)
to begin preparing the body for cremation, the Second Princess,
always deeply suspicious of strangers, insisted that nobody but
Sangharakshita touch her husband's mortal remains. After some gentle
persuasion, it was agreed that Sangharakshita would supervise what
the lamas did. Once the preparations were completed, Latthakin's
body was put onto a vehicle, and a sizeable cortege formed to accompany
it to the Tibetan crematorium. Just as the cortege was about to leave,
a still dry-eyed Second Princess urgently whispered to Sangharakshita,
'Raja Sahib must be cremated with sandalwood logs. Nothing but
sandalwood logs. Members of the Burmese Royal family cannot be
cremated with anything else.' Although this was not possible—the
cost would have been too prohibitive—packets of sandalwood powder
were sprinkled onto his funeral pyre. Maung Lu Gyi lit his father's
pyre, and Latthakin's mortal remains were cremated to the sound of
Pali *suttas* (Buddhist discourse) recited by Sangharakshita and others.[82]

It seems it was only after the funeral that reality finally sank in and, according to Gulabi, an inconsolably desolate Second Princess 'would just keep wandering around the house and we children tried to distract her. We couldn't leave her alone even for a moment. There always had to be someone with her, and it was like looking after a young child.' Shortly after Latthakin's death his sister, Khin Khin Latt, who the Second Princess had not seen for many years (Khin Khin Latt and her husband Dr Thein Maung—Burma's first ambassador to Japan—used to visit the couple for short holidays when they had lived in Springburn and Arcadia) came to take her brother's ashes away for entombment in Burma.[83]

On 8 February 1955, two of the Fourth Princess's sons, Prince Taw Phaya and Prince Taw Phaya Galae, arrived to condole with an aunt they had previously never met: the aunt the Third and Fourth Princesses had told them was 'sort of an outcast'.[84] They also came hoping to persuade this estranged aunt to return with them to her homeland.[85] But she refused. After all, as was to be expected, says Prince Taw Phaya, 'she was more attached to her Gurkha people than to us'. The Second Princess's attachment to her dogs was another reason why she refused to return, he adds, because she would have had to leave some of them behind. He says, 'From the queen to our mothers, they were very fond of dogs because they said dogs are more loyal and faithful than people.'[86]

Gulabi recalls that the meeting between the Second Princess and her nephews was not an effusive one. The Second Princess was a reserved and private person, who did not easily interact with people she was unfamiliar with. Although she did enquire about her sister, the Third Princess, it was Maung Lu Gyi who shared with his cousins stories of the past.[87]

Now acutely conscious of her own mortality and wanting to ensure that whatever little she owned went only to her son, the Second Princess signed a declaration transferring all her worldly possessions to Maung Lu Gyi. Poignantly, all she had to leave to him were her household belongings. She owned no assets of the kind she and Latthakin had continually hoped for; she had no bank balance, no jewellery and no landed property.[88]

A few months after Latthakin's death, the Second Princess and her entourage vacated the Panorama guesthouse and moved to a small bungalow called Vikchu Kothi. She indicated to Maung Lu Gyi that she was now keen to return to Burma but was afraid 'there would be enmity as many felt she should not have adopted "a Nepali fellow" instead of some blood relative. She felt some harm would be done to [him]'. What occurred to assuage this fear is not known, but in March 1956, a visiting Burmese pongyi convinced the Second Princess to return to Burma and offered to travel back with her. So, accompanied by the pongyi, Maung Lu Gyi, his birth mother and a servant, the Second Princess set off for Calcutta en route to Rangoon. The rest of Maung Lu Gyi's family was to follow at a later date.[89]

In Calcutta the Second Princess stayed in the austere residential rooms attached to the Burmese Buddhist temple on Eden Hospital Road. As the weather was hot, and the Second Princess was intolerant to heat, ice was procured to chill her drinking water. It was probably the contaminated ice, Gulabi feels, which caused the Second Princess's severe indigestion. Temple pongyis helped Maung Lu Gyi transport his mother to P.G. Hospital. Due to their poor financial situation, the Second Princess had to occupy a bed in the many-bedded general ward of the hospital. Here she lay, for four or five days, ill, and surrounded by strangers for whom she had always harboured so much distrust and suspicion. Very weak and poorly attended to by the overworked hospital staff, it was here that she died at 11.30 a.m. on 4 April 1956, at the age of almost seventy-five. Her funeral was arranged by the Burmese consul general in Calcutta, and she was cremated that very evening.[90]

Her ashes were handed over to her son. For many years Maung Lu Gyi kept the ashes in his home, below an altar dedicated to Lord Buddha. However, as he got older and frailer, both he and his sister Gulabi were anxious that the princess's remains be sent to Burma to be entombed near those of her beloved husband, or if his gravesite could not be located, near those of her mother.[91] Once the Burmese government's permission was received, U Soe Win (the Fourth Princess's grandson) personally came to collect the ashes. On 25 February 2008, after a brief emotional ceremony at Maung Lu Gyi's home, the urn was taken to the Burmese consulate. Here Maung Lu Gyi formally handed it over to U Soe Win.[92]

On 2 May 2008, not too many days after the Second Princess's epitaph had been erected on the northern perimeter of Queen Supayalat's tomb (in preparation for the insertion of her ashes), Cyclone Nargis struck and knocked it down. Says Prince Taw Phaya, tongue-in-cheek, 'The old Queen in disgust kicked down the plaque of her disobedient daughter!!'[93] And remembering the queen's fiery spirit this is not too difficult to imagine! The Second Princess's tombstone was re-erected, and on 19 November 2008, with no further disruptions, natural or supernatural, the Second Princess's ashes finally were entombed in her mother's mausoleum.[94]

22

THE THIRD PRINCESS

It is said that the Third Princess was the most charming and popular of the four princesses.[1] Unlike her other sisters she was cheerful, talkative, affable and trusting, thereby endearing herself to many including, so dearly, her own mother. As King Thibaw's daughter, she often attracted attention. Shortly after her return to Burma she drew a crowd at a shrine she visited, and when she spoke people were taken aback by her accented Burmese. Her intonation, like that of her sisters, was Indianized and different, and remained so all her life.[2] Many called her Madras Suphaya since Madras was the city of her birth.[3]

On the occasion of the Mandalay Centenary Festival, she gave an interview to a well-known Burmese writer (Journal Kyaw Ma Ma Lay). When asked what her feelings on arriving in Burma in 1919 had been, the Third Princess's reply was: 'I was so frightened to see the very big trees. There were no such trees in Ratnagiri. I started thinking that Burma was too frightful a place with trees reaching up to the sky . . .'[4] It was not just age and a faded memory that elicited this ingenuous response in 1959; from the time of her return it was noticed that years of isolation and lack of any formal education had bestowed on her a surreal aura of innocence that made her seem out of touch with reality.

It was probably her simplicity and lack of exposure, says her son-in-law, that led to her falling in love with Prince Hteik Tin Kodaw Gyi, a young, handsome ladies' man, very many years her junior.[5] After their dramatic elopement in 1921, their initial years of marriage were busy and happy ones. On their return to Rangoon, Prince Hteik Tin Kodaw Gyi efficiently supervised the queen's home and helped look after the endless stream of visitors and pongyis.[6] The Third Princess gave birth to a daughter, Hteik Su Gyi Phaya (later known as Princess Rita), on 20 May 1924. Her life was now occupied with attending her mother's audiences, and looking after her newborn child; the sudden death of the queen in 1925 signalled the end of her cosseted life.

After her mother's death, the Third Princess applied for permission to shift to Mandalay, and she was allowed to do so probably by late 1926 or early 1927. In Mandalay the government generously granted her a plot of land to enable her to build her own home.[7] (This house is now the Mandalay General Hospital's civil surgeon's official residence. It is not known how and when the Third Princess lost it, but she probably had to sell it at some stage to settle the debts she was forever accumulating.[8]) The favour of the grant of a plot of land was never extended to any of the other daughters of King Thibaw. According to Prince Taw Phaya (the Fourth Princess's son) the Third Princess was favoured as she was never perceived as a threat, was thought of as the 'harmless one', and was liked by all the government officials that dealt with her. The Fourth Princess, on the other hand, when she was finally permitted to shift to Mandalay, was provided with a rented home, and was 'watched warily by the government'.[9] (Ironically, the First and Second Princesses, born in Mandalay, never saw the city again; the Third and Fourth Princesses, born in India, both lived in Mandalay for a while.)

In a memorial she wrote to the government, the Third Princess indicated that in Mandalay she was forced to spend lavishly 'to maintain her prestige and dignity as a daughter of the late King Thibaw whose capital was Mandalay'. She indicated that numerous people of all stations and ranks, subjects of her late father, called on her and she was obliged to entertain them and this 'necessarily meant a great drain on the small pension of Rs 750 allowed by His Majesty's Government and as a consequence your memorialist was compelled to resort to friends and money-lenders both large and small according to circumstances'.[10] (Like the Fourth Princess, she was given a pension of Rs 750 and a house allowance of Rs 250 a month, a festival allowance of Rs 500 per annum, and grants for ceremonies like marriage, cradling and earboring, and for medical expenses and school fees.[11])

The Third Princess lived beyond her pension and ran up debts not only in an attempt to maintain a certain lifestyle, which she felt was expected of her, but also on account of her husband's extravagance. Prince Hteik Tin Kodaw Gyi had no occupation, and lived a life of pleasure: 'A real wastrel . . . he went out in Mandalay taking credit and buying things . . . Cars were for 3 or 4 thousand [rupees]. He brought a brand new car, drove it up to Maymyo and overturned it!'[12] After living for about two years in Mandalay, the Third Princess and her family shifted to a rented bungalow on the Mandalay–Lashio Road in Maymyo, but it was in Mandalay itself that the Third Princess's marriage had begun to crumble. While they had been living with the queen, Prince Hteik Tin Kodaw Gyi had treated the Third Princess deferentially. After the queen's death, he began to assert himself, but it is unlikely that the Third Princess objected to this. She probably realized that this was bound to have happened sooner or later. What greatly upset her, though, was that 'slowly slowly, he got a bit big for his shoes and he started having affairs'.[13]

Queen Supayalat might have viewed Prince Hteik Tin Kodaw Gyi as an inconsequential minor prince, but he was still royalty. He was also young, virile and handsome. According to Prince Taw Phaya:

[In] those days princes had their liberty with women . . . women used to go run after him and he used to have fun with them . . . even in the house there were these girls, the servant girls and he used to go have fun with them . . . being a very simple-minded person the Third Princess stayed by herself, and he was having fun all along. And with a thousand rupees coming in every month those days . . .[14]

Although simple and not wise in the ways of the world, the Third Princess soon realized what was going on. And probably for the first time in her life, she felt terribly alone: her mother and youngest sister were no longer available to comfort her and ameliorate her problems. Prone to hysteria and fits, these intensified with her distress. Then, one morning in 1929, the Third Princess's marriage suddenly and completely unravelled. In Prince Taw Phaya's words:

> Tension was building up since 2/3 years . . . the last straw was when he brought his paramour and kept her in a house just a street or two away from the Princess's house and stayed away for days . . . Early one morning he came back, so the Princess said, 'Why don't you stay away for good?' at which Prince Hteik Tin Kodaw Gyi grasped the front of her jacket and threw her on the floor. She picked herself up, took her 6-year-old daughter by the hand, got a *gharry* [horse cart] and went to the newly married English Sub Div Officer Mr Oxbury's house and told her story. Prince Hteik Tin Kodaw Gyi was ordered to leave Maymyo within 24 hours, and the Princess was hospitalized as she had had a nervous breakdown. Her troubles did not end there: one night the Treasury Officer U Shwe Hman, drunk, came and banged on her ward door and started shouting her name. The Princess ran out of the back door and called the English matron who drove the treasury officer away and reported to the Mandalay district commissioner. When she returned home the new S.D.O. Mr Noyce used to visit her too often for comfort, and there were also other people visiting her. Eventually the D. C. of Mandalay had 2 police men posted outside her house with 'No admission' stuck on the gate . . . The commissioner of Mandalay division, Mr A.G. Gilliat was very fond of the simple innocent Third Princess and her small daughter Rita and used to visit them whenever he came up to Maymyo, and whenever he came he used to go down on his knees in front of the Princess . . . (sheiko) . . . and say, 'I am your most obedient and faithful servant.' He knew U Mya U (a lawyer) so he asked U Mya U to take care and look after the Princess beguiled by suitors and creditors . . .[15]

The Third Princess and Prince Hteik Tin Kodaw Gyi divorced under Buddhist law in 1930.[16] But there was the matter of the considerable debt that Prince Hteik Tin Kodaw Gyi had run up. The Third Princess assumed responsibility for his debt, realizing that her ex-husband would never be in a position to repay it, and not wanting herself to be under the constant tension of legal suits. She did this because she was advised to,[17] but for the rest of her life she would behave generously towards the man who had treated her in such a cavalier and shabby manner.

Some royal family descendents believe that the government precipitated the separation and divorce, that perhaps reconciliation could have taken place[18] had Prince Hteik Tin Kodaw Gyi not been so abruptly and totally banished from Maymyo.[19] They believe that since the prince was viewed as anti-British, the government had always disliked him.[20] While living with the queen he had had the opportunity to meet and interact with many nationalists, and in Maymyo, people like Thakin Kodaw Hmaing (the great patriot and writer who had been a supporter of Queen Supayalat) and Thakin Aung San (later called General or Bogyoke Aung San) visited his home.[21] Additionally, since Prince Hteik Tin Kodaw Gyi was of royal blood, and his wife was King Thibaw's daughter, the couple was viewed as potentially 'a very good symbol—a national rallying point' (although the Third Princess was never politically active).[22] Therefore, as soon as an opportunity presented itself the government grabbed it, physically removed him, and encouraged the Third Princess to divorce him.[23] Without the pension, and with the Third Princess no longer his wife, the government was confident that Prince Hteik Tin Kodaw Gyi's influence would diminish considerably.

After his divorce Prince Hteik Tin Kodaw Gyi was a broken man and took to drinking heavily. Seeing his sorry state many nationalists banded together and arranged his marriage to Daw Mama Gyi. She had a stabilizing influence on him; the couple settled in Mandalay, and he spent the rest of his life with her. Like the Third Princess, Prince Hteik Tin Kodaw Gyi had no more children.[24] Financially not well off and prohibited from travelling to Maymyo, he occasionally sent his wife to the Third Princess with a request for money. The Third Princess attempted to help to the extent she could. She also sometimes sent their daughter to visit him.[25] Princess Rita did not particularly miss her father's presence; even as a young girl she strongly identified with her mother and held her father's mistreatment of her against him.[26]

Prince Hteik Tin Kodaw Gyi now concentrated his energies on a strongly nationalistic, anti-British movement, a movement whose followers titled themselves Thakin. This movement was called Do-bama Asi-ayone (We the Burmese). Prince Hteik Tin Kodaw Gyi was one of its founding members, and became a mascot for the organization, attracting crowds around the country due to his princely status and charisma.[27]

A romantic relationship soon developed between the Third Princess and the lawyer entrusted by the government to look after her, U Mya U.[28] U Mya U had been separated from his wife for many years, and had a married daughter who lived in Rangoon.[29] He was about nineteen years older than the Third Princess—almost as much older as her first husband had been younger![30] U Mya U was trained as a civil engineer, and had also studied law in England. He practised law. He was editor of the law journal *Burma Law Notes*, and was a strong advocate for the improvement of the educational system in Burma.[31] He obligingly helped the Third Princess through her multitude of legal wrangles ranging from her divorce to her problems with numerous creditors. U Mya U also owned the bungalow the Third Princess had rented since her arrival in Maymyo.[32]

When the Third Princess and U Mya U decided to marry, the Fourth Princess objected. According to Prince Taw Phaya, the reason was that U Mya U

> was a lady's man like her [the Third Princess's] former husband . . . he had so many affairs with other women but being educated was more discreet in his ways . . . besides he was still legally married to his first rich wife who had sent him to England for his law degree. Although they had lived separately for over 10 years, in the eyes of the people the Third Princess [would be] the lesser wife, a condition most decent women would like to avoid . . . In the good old days there were very few cases of marriage[s] breaking up as most women tolerated their husbands taking other wives, some even lived together . . .[33]

It appears that the Fourth Princess, like her mother, did not believe in divorce: when you married, you married 'till death'. This was one of the conditions the queen had asked Ko Ko Naing to agree to before his marriage with the Fourth Princess.[34]

In spite of her sister's disapproval, the Third Princess and U Mya U got married some time in 1931.[35] According to Prince Taw Phaya, 'the Princess was a nice juicy piece of meat with a monthly pension of Rs 1000 so the old man swallowed her with the promise of taking care of her and guarding against the loan sharks'.[36] Regarding their marriage ceremony, Prince Taw Phaya Galae says 'the marriage expenses were borne by the British government . . . it was a very grand ceremony . . .'[37] The ceremony was held in Rangoon in U Mya U's younger brother's home, was well attended by high-ranking British officials and eminent citizens of Rangoon, and 'was more a western style ceremony with the Princess holding a bunch of flowers, and [she and] U Mya U sitting at each end of a Chesterfield settee'.[38]

Although the Third Princess lived a happier life with U Mya U than she had with her earlier husband (her fits and attacks of hysteria were treated and gradually completely stopped), this was no blissful marriage.[39] A jealous U Mya U resented the very close attachment between mother and daughter, and as a result, the stepfather and stepdaughter didn't get along. He was domineering, and tried to take control of his wife's pension and restrict her expenditure.[40] He retired not long after the marriage (he had been about sixty-four at the time); it was, therefore, the Third Princess who looked after all household and other expenses.[41] 'Once you're idle and there is nothing to do,' says Prince Taw Phaya, one thing leads to another and U Mya U occasionally 'had fun with the servant girls'.[42] Although aware of this, the Third Princess tried to make the best of her second marriage. Her extended royal family, however, never took to U Mya U. They viewed him as very pro-British, were suspicious of him since he had studied law in England, and believed that he 'knew how to manipulate the British mind'. They felt the British had encouraged and arranged the marriage between the Third Princess and their own man,[43] the 'British agent'. Their loyalty therefore remained firmly with Prince Hteik Tin Kodaw Gyi.[44]

It appears that U Mya U was not very successful in containing his wife's expenses. The Third Princess felt entitled to a certain lifestyle, which she had been brought up to think of as her due. Also, she, more than any of her sisters, had been the spoilt darling of her mother. On at least one occasion she even requested her sister, the Second Princess (with whom she hardly ever corresponded, and who got about half the pension she herself got), for a loan![45] Her young nieces and nephews (the Fourth Princess's children), on the few occasions they visited her, were taken aback at the ease with which she spent her money. One incident stands out vividly in Prince Taw Phaya's mind: '[W]e [were] in school as boarders. And we [would] have a leg of a chicken, it [was] rather rare. But when we came to visit her, she used to take the breast of a chicken, tear it into half and feed the dogs!'[46]

Like the Fourth Princess's children, Princess Rita was boarded in a missionary school. The school (St Joseph's Convent) wasn't far from the Third Princess's home, and greatly missing her little daughter, she would visit the school almost every day; in fact, it is said that she almost lived in the convent herself! The nuns at the school were fond of her, and welcomed these visits. The Third Princess often sat conversing with one of them until her daughter had a recess or a free period. She frequently took Burmese or Indian food that she had cooked for the nuns to share.[47]

On 1 May 1938, when Princess Rita was nearly fourteen, her earboring ceremony was held in her home. Prince Hteik Tin Kodaw Gyi was not permitted by the government to attend the ceremony, nor was his name mentioned on the invitation. The ceremony was an elaborate affair, for which the government sanctioned Rs 3,000.[48] *The Illustrated Weekly of India* reported: 'With a needle of pure gold, tipped with a diamond, Hteik Su Gyi Paya [Princess Rita], daughter of Ashin Hteik Su Myat Paya, the Third Princess of Burma, had her ear bored recently in surroundings reminiscent of the old regime. A cannon fired a salute, the royal drums (*seedaw*) rolled . . .'[49] (See Appendix II.)

The Third Princess and U Mya U lived in Maymyo for most of the year. As prominent citizens of Maymyo, they sometimes received official visitors. When Pandit Nehru visited Maymyo in the 1930s, he was entertained in their garden. Prince Taw Phaya says that U Mya U knew Nehru, as U Mya U had been 'involved in politics before 1930 together with the Third Princess's first husband Prince Hteik Tin Kodaw Gyi . . . In the 1930s the Indian Congress was the torch for Myanmar politicians, and these two famous Indian leaders—Gandhi and Shri Nehru—were revered and admired by budding Myanmar politicians'.[50]

During the winter months, to escape the Maymyo cold, the family would shift down to Sagaing (across the river from Mandalay) where U Mya U owned a rest house. Once, sometime in the 1930s, while they were in Sagaing, the couple was invited to a reception in Mandalay in honour of the visiting viceroy of India. When the viceroy entered the room, as was the custom, everyone stood up—everyone that is except the Third Princess. The additional district commissioner shook the Third Princess's chair to indicate what was expected of her, but she glanced up at him, and insouciantly ignored his suggestion. 'So it [the incident] passed away. Of course the Burmese people were quite pleased that their Princess kept her seat,' says Prince Taw Phaya.[51]

Over the years the Third Princess (with her husband's help) wrote numerous letters to the press and to the government. When the government indicated that they would pay her medical bills only in exceptional circumstances, her response is interestingly indicative of how she viewed herself:

> The word 'substantial' is a relative term, and a sum of money which may be regarded as substantial from the point of view of a commoner, cannot be so regarded when viewed from the height of a person of my position . . . It is regrettable that the Government should have required me to submit to the ignominy of having to prove exceptional circumstances in submitting medical bills, and thus to make me cease forwarding medical bills because the Government is well aware that honour and prestige are dearer to me than life.[52]

During World War II, Japan occupied Burma for around three years from early 1942. The monthly allowance payable to members of the royal family was discontinued. During this period, the Third Princess and her family relocated to U Mya U's rest house in Sagaing. It was here, in July 1943, that U Mya U suddenly passed away after a serious bout of indigestion, at the age of seventy-six.[53] Although the Third Princess grieved U Mya U's death (he had, after all, been a companion of sorts for twelve years) she wasn't exactly devastated.[54] While she had not come across as unhappy during her second marriage (she was 'a jolly type';[55] the marriage was a stable one; she had known worse) it appears that it was not from this marriage that she had drawn her happiness. A passing remark she made some years later to Prince Taw Phaya Galae made him realize that after years of being weighed down in relationships where she had felt controlled and dominated, she now felt unyoked and free.[56] But this feeling was to come afterwards; right after U Mya U's death, 'suitors, swindlers and hangers-on' hounded the Third Princess and Princess Rita, and made their lives miserable.[57]

Hearing of their plight, Thakin Kodaw Hmaing told the Fourth Princess's eldest son, Prince Taw Phaya Gyi, that he needed to take on his aunt and cousin's responsibility, that he should marry Princess Rita and move in with the Third Princess. Prince Taw Phaya Gyi, who was in love with someone else, refused to do so. However, he and Prince Taw Phaya rushed to Sagaing to see what else could be done. Shortly after their arrival, the Third Princess reminded Prince Taw Phaya that he and Princess Rita had been 'betroth[ed] from the cradle' by their grandmother, Queen Supayalat.[58] ('You see', says Prince Taw Phaya, 'the story is like this: I am Saturday born . . . Rita was Tuesday born . . . The King was Saturday born. The Queen was Tuesday born . . . So when [Rita] was born . . . the old Queen she said, "Ah! Why don't these two children, when they grow up, we get them married?"'[59] [In Burma, the day of the week that a person is born is of great significance because it is believed that this influences the person's character.]) Everyone had forgotten about this; in fact, sometime earlier Princess Rita had almost been married off to a sawbwa. Prince Taw Phaya recounts that 'these Sawbwas [Shan chieftains] used to come and try and make matches between the descendants of the king [and] their descendants'. He and Princess Rita both decided to honour their late grandmother's wish, 'so the princess, myself, Rita and a few servants took the train . . . and went down to Rangoon and stayed and got engaged in [Thakin] Kodaw Hmaing's house'. On 4 May 1944 the couple married in Princess Rita's father's house—a big house near the Mandalay Ice Factory. (The Third Princess had been very ill with typhoid just before the wedding, which is why Prince Hteik Tin Kodaw Gyi had volunteered to host his daughter's wedding. He had prospered during Japanese occupation as in 'those days all these [anti-British] politicians were given nice houses by the Japanese. Commandeered and given.')[60]

The Third Princess, her daughter and her new son-in-law now all lived together in Sagaing. Prince Taw Phaya recalls a memorable visit by 'an old doddering monk in his mid-eighties—a royal court official who came to seek the Third Princess's hand. I nearly chewed his head off and drove him out'. He recounts another visit by someone from the old palace days, one of Queen Supayalat's old maids of honour. He remembers her being 'horrified when she saw Rita and myself eating together with the Third Princess . . . since then the Third Princess was served alone . . .' Prince Taw Phaya decided that some of the other old customs of the palace should also be observed in his home due to the Third Princess's presence, including the custom of royalty talking in a dignified and quiet manner. He adds, however, that the Third Princess would often forget this rule and shout amazingly loudly at her mischievous grandchildren![61]

Towards the end of World War II, in March 1945, the Allies shelled and bombed the Golden Palace, which was being used as a supply depot by the Japanese. As British officers stood on the covered steps of Mandalay Hill and watched the action through their binoculars, a dense cloud of smoke rose high above what had once been the beautiful, intricately carved old teak-wood buildings of the palace. In the face of the intense attack, the Japanese abandoned the palace grounds; the British marched in, reoccupied it and hoisted the Union Jack.[62] By a bizarre quirk of fate, the grandson of Lord Dufferin (who had been the viceroy of India during Britain's war with King Thibaw, and after whom the Golden Palace had been rechristened 'Fort Dufferin' after British occupation) was killed during the attack and 'the news of his courageous death in action was received by the people of Mandalay with great regret and sympathy, and to the inhabitants of the Golden City, it was a noble act of expiation for the conquest of Mandalay by his illustrious grandfather, Viceroy of India'.[63] On hearing of the destruction of the Golden Palace, the Third Princess was overcome with sadness;[64] after all that had been taken from her family, now even the once magnificent palace that had so visibly symbolized the power and wealth of their past was destroyed. The moat and the vast fortification walls survived, but these impressive sentries now encircled nothing but smouldering destruction, and served only to evoke a glory that had once been.

The war over, the Third Princess's family moved back to Maymyo in March 1946, and the princess spent the rest of her life here.[65] With her loving daughter and son-in-law, and their growing brood of children (eight children born between 1945 and 1956) living with her, she was never alone or lonely. One of her grandsons remembers her as a very involved grandmother, to the extent that she was like a second mother to them all. He recalls her being 'very good hearted' and 'very simple'.[66] Although the Third Princess could barely speak English, she would sing English lullabies (learnt no doubt in Ratnagiri from the Fourth Princess's English companions) to put her beloved grandchildren to sleep![67]

In Maymyo the Third Princess chose to spend her time 'in prayers, meditation and rosary, cooking, gardening and listening to tales brought in by nuns, servants and hangers-on'. She prayed twice a day in the traditional manner as taught to her by her parents. Like her parents and sisters, she believed not only in the teachings of the Buddha, but also in the propitiation of nats, and observed both nat and Buddhist festivals. And like her sisters she was an excellent cook. Says Prince Taw Phaya, 'The Third Princess used to make strawberry jam and send it to the English Governor's wife whenever they came up for their summer stay. She was always so pleased whenever I enjoyed her cooking . . .'[68]

His mother-in-law lavished a lot of care and attention on him, and was firm that her daughter do the same. Says Princess Rita, 'My husband [got] all the privileges of the Burmese male. My mother insisted on her nephew cum son-in-law having special treatment like a room of his own, and meals waited on by the wife . . .'[69] According to Prince Taw Phaya, his mother and her sister looked a lot alike,

except the Third Princess had a mole on the left [side of her] lip. Their expressions and their language and the words they used [were] almost identical. Their voice [was] also very much alike. That is why I tell my other brothers I had a second mother. And she was more loving, she used to take more trouble for me than [for] her daughter when I married Rita. Because I mean she always had only a daughter, no son to love.

Prince Taw Phaya reciprocated her love, and was remarkably sympathetic, understanding and tolerant:

> [The Third Princess] believed ghosts and devils lurked in every nook and corner of the house at night, so Rita had to sleep with her, and servants had to sleep at the foot of the bed. Even after our marriage I slept alone most of the time. Rita used to come [in the] early part of the night, wish me goodnight and go to sleep with the Princess. If Rita lingered a bit longer, the Princess would ring the bell to summon her. Even though there were six grandchildren around, she still wanted Rita beside her.[70]

The only bone of contention between mother-in-law and son-in-law was the Third Princess's addiction to living well beyond her means, on borrowed money. According to Prince Taw Phaya,

> [T]he Third Princess had a whole crowd of creditors, some insulting some suing her. It was sort of a mania in her to take loans, and these loan sharks would come in by the back door and offer her money. After I married Rita I had a hard and quarrelsome time trying to put a stop to this borrowing mania. Finally just 10 years before her demise, her old age and love for her growing family [grandchildren], her borrowing spree stopped.[71]

Burma was re-occupied by the British towards the end of World War II, and it got its independence on 4 January 1948. Just before independence, the happy family had received a shock: the Third Princess's pension had been reduced to Rs 600 a month, and both Princess Rita and Prince Taw Phaya now got nothing. Prince Taw Phaya realized that he had to do something to generate an income as he had a young and rapidly growing family to support. Over the years he dabbled in many businesses, some of which brought him money and some losses. However, it was he who supported his mother-in-law and the rest of his considerable family.[72] (After 1951 the Third Princess's pension of Rs 600 was further reduced, under the newly passed Gratuity Law for Royal Relatives, to Rs 500 per month, which was the amount she drew until her death.[73])

Not long after Burmese independence, in 1949, Thakin Kodaw Hmaing chaired the King Thibaw's Funeral Committee. The Third

Princess was one of its patrons; the Third Princess's ex-husband, Prince Hteik Tin Kodaw Gyi, was made its vice-chairman, and Prince Taw Phaya Galae was appointed its joint secretary. The committee made attempts to bring back King Thibaw's and Queen Supayagalae's remains from India. The matter had been raised in Hluttaw meetings on several occasions, and the government had sanctioned 50,000 kyats for the task. The government in India had apparently agreed to send back the remains, and preparations had been made by the people to pay their respects en route from Rangoon to Mandalay, but for numerous unspecified reasons the arrangements fell through, and the Third Princess and the rest of the royal family were deeply disappointed. Not only because the remains were not to be brought back, but also because King Thibaw's and Queen Supayagalae's last rites were still pending.[74] None of King Thibaw's daughters would live to see these rites performed.

Maymyo is a scenic town where the weather never gets too hot. After Burmese independence, the British practice of shifting the capital to Maymyo in summer continued for some years. When the Sawbwa of Nyaungshwe became the first president of Burma, he, like the rest of the government, shifted to Maymyo for the summer. (The Sawbwa of Nyaungshwe was the nephew of an ardent supporter and confidant of Queen Supayalat, the old Sawbwa of Nyaungshwe, whose title he inherited when his uncle died; he was also the man that Princess Hteik Su Phaya Gyi would have married had her mother, the Fourth Princess, not passed away before the betrothal could be finalized.)

The Third Princess, Princess Rita and Prince Taw Phaya were invited to the first garden party held in the new president's honour in Maymyo. At the reception, as the Sawbwa of Nyaungshwe was greeting invitees, he suddenly saw the Third Princess and instinctively folded his hands and sank to the ground in a sheiko in front of her. His and her family association went back some generations, and his family had always treated hers deferentially. The news of this presidential sheiko ricocheted through government corridors, and the reaction was not favourable. After years of battered and bruised egos, after years of having had to treat their colonial rulers deferentially, officers of the new government wanted and needed to see their new leaders stand tall.

As the president could not be upbraided, the government ensured that the Third Princess was not invited for receptions during his subsequent visits to Maymyo.[75]

In 1953, just after Elizabeth II had been crowned Queen of England, the Third Princess, together with her daughter and the Fourth Princess's children, sent a memorial to the queen requesting for her help in the retrieval of their property. Nothing came of this memorial. The British prime minister's office replied advising them to approach their own government, as all property had already been transferred by the British to the new Burmese government.[76] In spite of the fact that the Third Princess never had the money or property she wanted and felt entitled to, and that she was often deeply in debt, when Princess Rita's father passed away in Mandalay on 11 November 1954, the Third Princess backed Princess Rita's decision not to lay any claim to his property. Says Prince Taw Phaya, 'The compound that he owned was sold by his wife. The Mandalay royalty came up and told Rita look you can claim that. Rita replied that let her enjoy it. Both mother and daughter were very generous. There was always a tiff between Rita and myself for controlling the generosity. Money as well as goods or things.'[77]

During the 1950s the Burmese government had to continually battle various insurgents including communist and ethnic ones. Additionally, the country was not doing well economically. By the late fifties, there were power struggles within the ruling party (the Anti-Fascist People's Freedom League (AFPFL)), civil war was raging in Burma, and the government was increasingly unable to tackle the myriad issues it faced. In 1958, U Nu agreed to temporarily hand over charge to the chief of his Tatmadaw (armed forces), General Ne Win, who formed a caretaker government.[78]

In response to the escalating unrest in Burma, the Fourth Princesses' sons (all devout Buddhists) were urged to start the Association for Buddhism as the National Religion in an attempt to foster peace and harmony. This they did in late 1958. The Third Princess was made its patron, Prince Taw Phaya its vice-president, and Prince Taw Phaya Galae its general secretary. The association urged everyone, from monks to common citizens, to help it in its efforts, and to start

similar associations to spread the teachings of the Buddha.[79] Although
the Third Princess could not have contributed much either in terms
of ideas or effort to the organization, *who* she was made her a highly
suitable patron. Her father, as king, had been the official patron and
protector of Buddhism in the kingdom; her grandfather, King Mindon,
had not only been the patron and protector of the religion but had also
hosted the very important and historic international Buddhist
conference—the Fifth Great Buddhist Synod—in 1871 in Mandalay.
At the end of the conference, the entire Theravada scripture had been
inscribed in Burmese on 729 large marble slabs that had been housed
in the Kuthodaw Pagoda at the foot of Mandalay Hill. This pagoda—
known as the world's largest book—still stands today in testimony to
King Mindon's great piety and effort to popularize his religion.
(According to U Than Swe, the association of Burmese royalty with
Buddhism is so deeply seated in the Burmese psyche that even today
'whenever a pagoda is put up the ceremony is done with umbrellas etc.
to symbolize the presence of royalty'.[80])

General Ne Win's caretaker government was also promoting
Buddhism as the country's religion during this period in an attempt
to tackle the problem of communist insurgency. They hoped to
discredit communism as anti-religion. Since the royal family had
already launched its Buddhist association, the government approached
the family for their help in garnering the public attention needed to
hastily spread the word. A large function to jointly launch the effort
was organized in Shwebo, the town where Alaungpaya, their forefather,
had founded the Konbaung dynasty. In Shwebo, a covered and fenced
stage was erected at Aung Mye (the 'victory ground'), the auspicious
point from where King Alaungpaya had started out for all his battles.
The government let it be known far and wide that the royal family
would be coming, and people from all around the area poured in
through the previous night to reserve a spot for a glimpse of the
family. The Third Princess, Prince Taw Phaya, Prince Taw Phaya
Galae, Princess Hteik Phaya Htwe (the Fourth Princess's youngest
daughter), and two of Prince Taw Phaya's eldest sons attended the
event. As the family approached the stage, girls and women of all ages,
in a truly astounding demonstration of affection, bent forward in the

traditional sheiko, and loosened and laid down their long hair so that
the royal family would not have to walk on the bare ground, 'and we
had to step on their hair and go.' Prince Taw Phaya rather nonchalantly
adds, 'I mean there is always a sentiment for their old kings with the
people.' The government's reaction was not so nonchalant. Taken back
and flustered by the obvious depth of public sentiment for the royal
family, the government took no more chances. They no longer saw the
family as allies for a common cause but as potential competitors for
popular support, and stopped involving them in any further campaigns.[81]

U Than Swe, now in his late sixties, is distantly related to the royal
family and has been fascinated by and has followed its history since his
college days, when he wrote a thesis on the subject. Over the years he
has researched the customs and protocol followed in the royal court,
has met and interviewed descendants, and has written various articles
about the family.[82] He stresses that many people viewed the Third
Princess with deference and awe, and this was reflected in myriad ways:

> In 1959 the whole of the country had to get national registration
> cards—identity card[s]. [In Maymyo] all the people had to line up in
> the town hall and they were all busy . . . an officer came, recognized
> her [the Third Princess, who had joined the queue], and said to her
> 'Princess please go home we will come to your home and do it
> especially for you.'[83]

One of his most memorable encounters, U Than Swe says, was when
he was a teenager and had a chance to meet 'the third daughter of our
last king'. Charmed and fascinated by her, the meeting (which took
place over fifty years ago) is still vividly etched in his mind:

> First I dreamed of meeting this princess, how she is well dressed and
> sitting in a sort of palanquin and all that, but when I saw her, when we
> went to Maymyo you see, say in 1959, she is dressed up in brown, like
> a lady hermit, a *yethayma*. In the Maymyo house in the front part, there
> is a covered corridor joining the main house with the kitchen, and in
> the middle of this corridor she just sits on a sort of a wooden bed, you
> see, not a proper bed, there are jute bags, which are warming on it, as
> it [is] cold in Maymyo. There is a big brass pot of coffee on a lit stove
> near her, and she keeps taking cup by cup and there is some bread and
> chicken rolls, it's meant for her, but she is feeding the dogs the

chicken rolls and bread, and her hands are dirty, and her clothes get dirty as she reaches in to her pocket for money. When the *mohinga* [rice noodles served with various accompaniments] man comes, he has to come every day, she doesn't eat, but all the grandchildren, and the servant's children, go and eat near there. And everyday it costs . . . a lot—[because he overcharges] . . . the mohinga seller comes to kneel in front of the Third Princess. And who ever came, whether the mohinga man, or the fishmonger, they would come and sheiko in front of the princess and she would offer them bread and coffee. She would feed them. All this happened in front of me. They would bow in front of the princess, and use the royal language of the palace, whether they had been trained by her or learnt from elsewhere, I am not sure. I saw the fishmonger saying to the princess—Oh Princess, I am unable to sell any fish today, and I have trouble, I have to go back to my village, which is eleven miles away. So the princess told him to have some coffee and bread and ordered one of her servants to buy all his fish, for as much as it cost.[84]

Around August 1961, the Third Princess, who suffered from a variety of ailments including diabetes, high blood pressure and an enlarged liver, was diagnosed with cancer of the cervix. She was taken to Rangoon for treatment and was admitted to the public ward of the Rangoon General Hospital (a twelve square foot space was screened off to give her some privacy). Aware of who she was, the doctors and nurses were very attentive to her, and for the month she was in hospital, she was given radiation. Her cancer had spread, however, so she was taken home to Maymyo where her family did their best to make her comfortable.[85]

On 21 July 1962, at the age of seventy-six, the Third Princess passed away peacefully at 10.22 p.m. in her home in Maymyo with her devoted family—daughter, son-in-law and her grandchildren—all by her bedside. Says Prince Taw Phaya, 'She did not suffer any pain or discomfort, only a month or two before her end, her memory got fogged and [she] could not remember things although she knew those who were close to her. She died in this house . . .' She was cremated on 24 July 1962 and in accordance with her wishes, an urn containing her ashes was interred in the northern perimeter of her mother's tomb.[86]

23

THE FOURTH PRINCESS'S CHILDREN

The Fourth Princess's six children—two daughters, Princess Hteik Su Phaya Gyi (Princess Tessie) and Princess Hteik Su Phaya Htwe (Princess Margaret), and four sons, Prince Gyi (Prince George), Prince Taw Phaya (Prince Edward), Prince Taw Phaya Nge (Prince Terence) and Prince Taw Phaya Galae (Prince Frederick)—ranged in age from nine to fourteen at the time of her death in 1936. Although their father took a greater interest in their well-being after their mother's death, the government, who had always disliked and mistrusted him, decided to limit his influence over them[1]: 'The moment our mother died we could not go home [for the holidays],' says Prince Taw Phaya. Ko Ko Naing filed a case in the sessions court contesting this, but he knew the case would never be decided in his favour (in fact, it never even came up for hearing). Seeing no point in continuing to live in Moulmein, he relocated to 'one of his houses in the Myanmar quarters in the western part of Rangoon . . . once in Rangoon he became a private money lender and lived comfortably with his three servants . . .' Ko Ko Naing never re-married, nor did he wash his hands off his children. He kept in touch with them, and an eye on them, as best he could, from afar.[2]

So that no other close attachments could be formed, the government decided that the children could not visit any of their royal relatives for their holidays. It's not that invitations from relatives were free flowing, but even the occasional ones were carefully pondered over. Says Princess Hteik Su Phaya Gyi, 'The British kept us apart so that we [would] not later get together . . . united . . . to cause trouble.'[3] In addition, throughout their childhood attempts were made to alienate the children from their Burmese roots. 'See,' points out Prince Taw Phaya Galae, 'the British had planned it very well . . . we were kept as parlour boarders . . . very grand . . . so our closest friends must be white coloured [since almost all parlour boarders were European] . . . Mostly British . . . we must keep away from Burmese friends. That was the rule . . .'[4] Their interaction with Burmese children was therefore limited to the few Anglicized ones in school with them.

Princess Hteik Su Phaya Gyi indicates that permission from the deputy commissioner of Moulmein was necessary even to stay with school friends during holidays.[5] Prince Taw Phaya Galae remembers that he and his siblings would often be farmed out to their schoolteachers during the longer holidays. He adds, rather bitterly, that other descendants of King Mindon were allowed more freedom; only the Fourth Princess's children were singled out for greater supervision because 'we are the direct descendants and the British had a direct interest'.[6]

In spite of the government's best attempts to distance the children from their royal past, they all, like their mother, had a strong sense of their lineage:

> [H]aving to move around with these Europeans and Anglos, when we fight we say 'hey, you are just a white colored fellow, I'm a prince'. So he'll say, 'Yeees, you are a prince but don't forget, you are a slave prince, a slave of the British' . . . And the teachers when we refused to answer or did something that they [didn't] like they say, 'Oh! You're trying to act like Supayalat—that bloodthirsty queen' . . . 'And your grandfather Thibaw he was a drunkard.'

Prince Taw Phaya Galae remembers how he was unable to contest these statements at the time, but how they stung and smouldered deep within him. The Fourth Princess's other children, however, were able to treat these remarks with more equanimity, as an unpleasant but inevitable part of their lives.[7]

The Fourth Princess died just around the time she was planning her daughters' natwin mingala or earboring ceremony and her sons' *shinbyu* or novitiation ceremony (whereupon her sons would become novice monks).[8] She had wanted to celebrate all her children's ceremonies together. Prince Taw Phaya recalls that some years after her death, their father approached the government for an allowance for the ceremonies, but got into a heated argument on the amount sanctioned. The children, as a result, rather unusually, did not go through either of these rites of passage.[9]

On 1 April 1937, Burma was separated from British India (India and Burma were separated for administrative purposes—both still continued to be part of the British Empire). With this change, Burma got a new constitution, Burmese ministers were installed and the people were given more of a say in their own internal matters. In April 1940 the Political Pension Act was passed giving each of the Fourth Princess's children, eighteen and over, an allowance of Rs 600 per month. Only the eldest, Prince Taw Phaya Gyi, qualified for the pension in 1940. (But from 1945, when he married a commoner, the pension was stopped—under the Act a royal who married a commoner was no longer eligible.[10]) The children were now permitted to travel more freely, and they all relocated to Rangoon. Prince Taw Phaya Gyi—who had asked for and been refused permission to study Buddhist scriptures in Ceylon (Sri Lanka)—attended Rangoon University. Along with other sports enthusiasts, he started a sports magazine called *New Life*, introduced weight-lifting matches, and on a very different note, organized Miss Burma beauty pageants![11]

The children did not stay with their father in Rangoon but with Prince Taw Phaya Gyi, who took responsibility for them all. In Rangoon, they continued their education. Princess Hteik Su Phaya Gyi recalls that she enjoyed living with her siblings and that theirs 'was a very happy home'.[12] However, their happiness was short lived.

By 1940, there was increased restlessness in Burma; the changes instituted in 1937 just weren't enough. The country's struggle for independence seemed to be going nowhere, and Britain was unwilling to even give it the status of a dominion that Burmese nationalists had repeatedly been demanding. So, during World War II, Japan was aided by a group of Burmese nationalists to drive the British out of Burma. The Burmese were deceived into believing that the Japanese were helping them gain their independence. The Japanese invasion began towards the end of January 1942, and the destruction caused during the conflict, combined with the Japanese economic policy following occupation, led to rampant inflation and a ruined economy.[13] The Fourth Princess's children, like everybody else in Burma, were greatly impacted; to compound their problems, all allowances to the royal family were now completely stopped by the Japanese government.

As the Allied position in World War II strengthened, Japan wanted the cooperation of Asian countries including Burma, so in August 1943 it ostensibly gave the Burmese the independence it had promised. Burmese ministers were installed but in fact the Japanese oversaw all important decisions and for all practical purposes Burma was still part of the Japanese Empire. The Japanese military police, the Kempeitai, continued to terrorize people, and the Burmese continued to find the Japanese arrogant and unfair in spite of their promises of 'Asiatic brotherhood and co-prosperity'.[14] During Japanese occupation, Prince Taw Phaya Galae was sent to stay with some of his father's relatives in the Delta region. Here he met communist leaders and, rather ironically for a blue-blooded prince, he was taken in by their principles.[15] He says, 'I did not go home for days and studied communism ... So bitter was my feeling towards the British and Fascist Japan that I started to carry out resistance movements in the Delta region. On one occasion ... I tried to attack sentry posts ... so I was arrested by the Kempeitai and was sent to my eldest brother ... Prince Taw Phaya Gyi.'[16] The Japanese had a selfish interest in the Burmese royal family, which was why they did not deal with Prince Taw Phaya Galae in their usual brutal manner, but left it to his eldest brother to discipline him. Prince Taw Phaya Gyi proceeded to 'thrash the communist ideas out of his [brother's] head', and appointed him as his assistant, and

Prince Taw Phaya Galae remained with Prince Taw Phaya Gyi throughout the Japanese occupation.[17]

According to Prince Taw Phaya Galae, as Japan had no popular support in Burma, it decided to exploit the Burmese obsession with its royalty, and designated Prince Taw Phaya Gyi as the future king.[18] Prince Taw Phaya Galae, being his assistant, was appointed heir-apparent.[19] Prince Taw Phaya Gyi was initially opposed to being designated as the future king by the hated Japanese. Says U Than Swe, '[W]hen the Japanese offered the crown he refused it at first ... But Ko Ko Naing [said] accept it, and help the Burmese people. To help our people as much as he can, he accept[ed] it.'[20] Prince Taw Phaya Galae also points out that the notorious Japanese Kempeitai arm-twisted his brother into accepting the offer.[21] Just like the puppet Burmese government they had earlier instituted, the Japanese were trying to put into place a puppet Burmese king in a futile attempt to appease the people.

In March 1945, under Bogyoke Aung San's able leadership, the Burma Defence Army (established by the Japanese to fight alongside its army) rose in rebellion against the Japanese and, with Allied help, the Japanese were driven out by May 1945. Burma was reoccupied by the British, who envisioned a period of reconstruction, followed by granting of dominion status to Burma after an unspecified number of years. But Bogyoke Aung San and other Burmese leaders wanted total independence quickly, and were vociferous in voicing their demand.[22] Prince Taw Phaya Galae says that it was at this stage that Home Minister Sir Paw Tun (from 1937 the Burmese were represented in the British government in Burma; this practice was continued by the British after Japanese occupation ended) approached his eldest brother with the proposal that if Prince Taw Phaya Gyi agreed 'to join hands with the British Government to suppress Aung San, I [Sir Paw Tun] will take care of the matter that Prince Taw Phaya Gyi should become King-designate'. A shocked Prince Taw Phaya Gyi, who wanted his country's independence as much as any of his most patriotic countrymen, and who saw in Bogyoke Aung San the means to this cherished end, categorically refused. Sir Paw Tun asked him to reconsider and accept the offer that was being made by the British 'out of goodwill'. Prince Taw Phaya Gyi, a man of principle, indignantly replied, 'I would rather be a vagrant than be a king elected by the British and that's my answer, Sir Paw Tun . . . As a man of wisdom you may have heard of the adage "A lion even though dying of hunger does not eat grass."'[23]

Not only did the British have plans for Prince Taw Phaya Gyi, says his youngest brother Prince Taw Phaya Galae, but they had plans for all the Fourth Princess's children:

> Tessie [Princess Hteik Su Phaya Gyi], the second eldest, she was very good at painting, so she'll be sent to the Sorbonne University in Paris for that. And then comes the brother in Maymyo, Prince Taw Phaya. He wanted to become an engineer. So he'll be sent to England . . . I'm a very good talker, so they wanted me to become a barrister. And my youngest sister Margaret [Princess Hteik Su Phaya Htwe], she likes sports, so she will be trained there. And Terence [Prince Taw Phaya Nge], my third brother, he calls himself Napoleon of Burma, he likes fighting, so the British planned to send him to Sandhurst Military Academy. See the British had planned it very well . . .

So deeply distrustful were the Fourth Princess's children of the British, that what could have been marvellous opportunities for quality education were viewed with deep suspicion, and summarily rejected. 'We would have become puppets!' says Prince Taw Phaya Galae with great confidence, even so many years later (in 2005).[24]

Not long after the re-occupation of Burma by the British, Bogyoke Aung San approached Prince Taw Phaya Gyi to work with him in the government. But the prince had by then established a sports association, set up a gymnasium, and was concentrating on organizing a Burmese Olympic team. He indicated that while Bogyoke Aung San would always have his support, he himself 'had turned his back on politics'. Some politicians and others periodically approached Prince Taw Phaya Gyi to become the king-designate, but he shunned all these approaches leading Bogyoke Aung San to comment:

> I have to admire these royal relatives. I am not a man obsessed with the monarchy as others. But I despise the act of the British who dethroned our Burmese king. The meaning of independence will be complete if we can reestablish the dynasty. We can switch to the Presidency if we

no longer want a monarchy. Now the public is still expecting a future king, and these royal relatives [Prince Taw Phaya Gyi and his brothers] are the sole heirs of the throne. I can't do anything if these relatives don't want back the throne. But they must not make any complaints after the establishment of a republic.[25]

Prince Taw Phaya Gyi and his brothers must have realized that once Burma was an independent republic, it would be difficult to restore the monarchy. Why then did they miss opportunities that came their way? U Than Swe says that the brothers would have liked 'a plebiscite for the people to decide, only then would [one of them] step in as king'. Prince Taw Phaya Gyi had been criticized for accepting the Japanese offer, and they felt that a referendum was the only way for the monarchy to be re-established without a loss of face or dignity, because only then could one of them have become a respected king;[26] without that all-important prestige, as the old Burmese saying goes, a king has 'nothing but his umbrella'.[27] Prince Taw Phaya adds that there was another important reason why none of them pushed for the throne: there was escalating resistance by 'communists and socialists . . . these chaps have guns, and one bullet is enough to keep you quiet'.[28]

Many in Britain were by now sympathetic to the Burmese desire for independence and this was reflected in the British press. By late 1946 the last British governor, Sir Hubert Rance, set about establishing a much more participatory government by forming a cabinet with himself and nine Burmese, including Bogyoke Aung San, as members. In January 1947, Bogyoke Aung San met British Prime Minister Attlee in London for discussions. According to Prince Taw Phaya Galae, Bogyoke Aung San did raise the issue of reinstituting the monarchy with one of King Thibaw's descendants, 'but the British refused to discuss the matter. They even advised Bogyoke not to raise the matter among the Burmese people' to avoid complicating matters.[29] The Aung San–Attlee Agreement was signed at the conclusion of these discussions, which among other things, gave the Burmese cabinet the same status as any dominion cabinet had, and promised Burma independence with the option not to join the Commonwealth, if that's what it wanted.[30] Many leaders in Burma felt Bogyoke Aung San had not been tough enough with the British; dissension ruled, and a new opposition party was born. However, Bogyoke Aung San had popular support and his party (the AFPFL) resoundingly won the general elections for the constituent assembly in April 1947.

With Burmese leaders repeatedly pressing for independence, with Britain's own economy devastated as a result of World War II, and with the attitude towards colonialism changing the world over including in Britain, negotiations began in earnest between the Burmese and the British government. Burma asked for full independence, without joining the Commonwealth (unlike its neighbour India, whose freedom movement Burma closely followed). Very unfortunately, the man who hated imperialism of any kind 'whether British or Japanese or Burmese',[31] and who so successfully and charismatically led his country towards its independence, did not live to see it. On 19 July 1947, during a cabinet meeting, Bogyoke Aung San, along with some of his fellow cabinet members, was brutally murdered in an assassination orchestrated by a political opponent. U Nu (who at that time was Bogyoke Aung San's deputy) stepped into his place, formed a new cabinet, and on 4 January 1948, at exactly 4.20 a.m. (a time deemed auspicious by astrologers) he became the first prime minister of newly independent Burma. Sao Shwe Thaik (the Sawbwa of Nyaungshwe) became the country's new president. Burma, a republic, was now rechristened the Union of Burma.

Although shocked and saddened by the loss of Bogyoke Aung San (he is often known as the father of modern Burma), Prince Taw Phaya Gyi and the rest of his family fully backed U Nu. U Nu was a deeply religious man and a devout Buddhist; the royal family regarded him as a very moral man, and was sure that 'they would not be overlooked' by him. It therefore came as a big shock to them, and to the extended Burmese royal family, when the newly formed Burmese government stopped monthly allowances for all of them except the Third Princess (these had been restarted by the British after they had reoccupied Burma). The Fourth Princess's family believed that this situation was temporary, that as things settled down in their newly independent country, the government would turn its attention to them. After all, it wasn't possible that their own government would overlook them, when the British had provided for them for so long. They made no representation at this stage, as they felt none was necessary. But they were to be disappointed; the younger members of the royal family were henceforth expected to fend for themselves.[32]

Prince Taw Phaya Gyi

In April 1945,[33] Prince Taw Phaya Gyi (who by now had a BA degree) married his sweetheart Susan, an attractive, languorous woman.[34] After independence, he joined the civil supplies as a petrol-rationing officer. He, however, continued with his sports activities under the banner of the National Sports Association, an association in which he involved his brothers and sisters. Prince Taw Phaya recalls that his brother's '"national fitness group" was the first of its kind in the country where young girls wore short skirts and played games and sports, much to the horror of old fogies!'[35]

In early April 1948 Prince Taw Phaya Gyi accompanied Cook of Steel Brothers on a car journey to Upper Burma (to visit Prince Taw Phaya and family in Maymyo; Cook was going to visit his own family). They arrived at 4 p.m. in the town of Pyinmana, which, in those days, was overrun by communist insurgents. Although friends of Prince Taw Phaya Gyi in Pyinmana tried to persuade him to stay the night, he and Cook decided not to. Both felt safe: they were travelling in a reinforced station wagon. Besides, Prince Taw Phaya Gyi felt confident that he would be able to talk his way out of any nasty situation, should it arise. A few miles outside Pyinmana, one of their car tyres got punctured. A passing Chinese gentleman generously offered to tow them to the next town. As the two vehicles were passing through an embanked patch of the road, insurgents fired heavily upon them. No questions were asked, no dialogue or explanation was possible, and very tragically Prince Taw Phaya Gyi's short and promising life ended on 9 April 1948 when he just twenty-six years old. Both he and Cook

died on the spot. Arrangements were made for Prince Taw Phaya Gyi's
body to be escorted from Pyinmana to Rangoon. Here a simple
Buddhist ceremony was held, and his ashes were entombed on the
southern side of Queen Supayalat's tomb. Thakin Kodaw Hmaing—
family friend, philosopher and guide—supervised the funeral. Says
Prince Taw Phaya Galae, 'Sayagyi Thakin Kodaw Hmaing, who in his
mind had designated Prince Taw Phaya Gyi as a future king, was much
disappointed.'[36]

   The family was shattered. Prince Taw Phaya Gyi left behind his
young, pregnant wife and a two-year-old son. He left behind siblings
for whom he had become a father figure. After the loss of their mother
so many years earlier, this was another terrible blow, a life altering
moment for all of them.[37] The family received a condolence letter
from the Communist Party condemning the tragic incident, and
indicating that the party had executed Bo Kyar whom they held
responsible for the murder.[38] A still-grieving Princess Hteik Su Phaya
Gyi indicates that this letter brought them no solace at all.[39]

Princess Hteik Su Phaya Gyi

Princess Hteik Su Phaya Gyi (Princess Tessie aka Daw Su Su Khin),
the Fourth Princess's second eldest child, is described by one of her
brothers as having been, as a young adult, 'a Bohemian . . . interested
in art, music, culture . . . a good pianist, a fashion buff . . . always
made up and painted . . . mediocre in her studies but a good painter
and artist'.[40] She was studying in the tenth grade at the time of the
Japanese invasion, and this heralded the end of her education. During
evacuation, Princess Hteik Su Phaya Gyi fell in love with Susan's
brother, Maung Maung Khin, and they decided to get married.[41] Just
like her grandmother and mother, Princess Hteik Su Phaya Gyi had
her children in fairly quick succession (she had six, one died young).
She recalls, in her clipped quaint British accent, that her 'very jovial'

brother, Prince Taw Phaya Galae, used to tease her about her constant pregnant state saying, '[W]hen a mosquito bites, you get pregnant!' and, rather impishly, she goes on to explain that at night '[W]hen a mosquito bites you, you are awake [so] you make love—that is the story!'[42]

Although in the beginning her marriage was a happy one, she was 'a petite good looking girl'[43] and she received a lot of male attention. This increasingly incensed her husband, transforming him into a very jealous and possessive man. 'I think I followed my mother's footstep [in an unhappy marriage]. They say it is retribution because our ancestors killed ... the whole family,' she says,[44] referring to the massacre of the royals in 1879.

Ironically, Princess Hteik Su Phaya Gyi's ability to speak English comfortably—thanks to her enforced missionary boarding school days—was what enabled her to find jobs with facility. For much of her working life she was employed by foreign embassies and organizations, including American, Australian and German. She earned relatively well all her life, but could not save anything.[45] She had a large family, and besides, like many in her family, she was extravagant in her ways.[46] Her husband also worked and supported the family until his death in 1984. Upon her retirement (after the nationwide pro-democracy uprising on 8 August 1988—commonly known as the 8.8.88 protests—which was brutally suppressed by the Junta), Princess Hteik Su Phaya Gyi continued capitalizing on her strength. English, she knew, was not being adequately taught in the nationalized Burmese schools, and she realized that there was a growing market of students wanting to learn the language. She gave private tuitions in students' homes, travelling to and fro on public transportation, and earned a modest living. Over the last few years, however, as her ailments have increased, the number of her tuitions has dwindled, and as she has nothing put away to fall back on, times have been very hard for her. She feels she is the worst off of her immediate relatives, and says, 'In our Myanmar Proverb we have a saying ... "Dozing has no shame; Starvation has no shame; Lust has no shame" ... I think I have come down to the second line, which I now face. Life is most cruel when one is facing poverty ...'[47]

She regrets that only two of her daughters have done all right financially. Her sons still struggle. She says her youngest son, Aung Khin, '[A]lways lived with me . . . An artist, he has the mother's blood. Doesn't earn well as an artist. My eldest son and he are the only ones [who] sell knick-knacks on the pavement—they don't choose jobs.'[48] She blames fate for all her problems including the sudden death of her beloved youngest son, who passed away after a cerebral haemorrhage in October 2008. Like all her siblings she is a staunch Buddhist and prays regularly for herself and for others.[49]

Prince Taw Phaya and Princess Rita

As suggested by Queen Supayalat shortly after his birth, Prince Taw Phaya (Prince Edward aka U Tun Aung), the Fourth Princess's third child, married his first cousin, the Third Princess's daughter, Princess Rita. Amazingly, or perhaps not so amazingly, just as foretold by their grandmother, their marriage was a very happy one. Says Princess Hteik Su Phaya Gyi, 'He and Rita were very affectionate. He arrives in Rangoon at about 12 or something like that and he writes a *long* letter and he goes to the general post office to post that letter to her. We talk about it very often . . . how much he loves Rita . . .'[50]

From the time he had been eight years old Prince Taw Phaya had 'tinkered with clock, cycles and electricity' to the extent that his eldest brother used to scream in fright and frustration, '[Y]ou bloody fool, you'll kill yourself with an electric shock'; after Burmese independence when the royal family's allowances were stopped, he looked around for a business in which he could use some of his mechanical skills. He found a disused oil and flour mill, which he rented and ran. Since neither he nor his partner knew anything about the business, they lost heavily. In 1951, he joined his brother, Prince Taw Phaya Galae, who had set up in Rangoon an import–export business named Thibaw Commercial Syndicate Co. Ltd. They, with some financial help, set up an office 'with meager facilities that comprised two chairs, a table, a hired typewriter and a bicycle'. It was decided that their three other siblings would also get a share of the profit the company made. In 1952, the family made a 'nice nest egg' as a result of a very profitable rice tender the company undertook. Says Prince Taw Phaya, 'With money in hand blood suckers came round Prince Taw Phaya Galae and gave him hare brained ideas which I saw as sure failures. I tried to stop him but of no avail so I gathered what share I had and returned to Maymyo in August 1952.'[51]

Back in Maymyo with a substantial bank balance, Prince Taw Phaya purchased a large new home located on Forest Road and surrounded by three acres of land.[52] (It is in this home that the Third Princess and Princess Rita died,[53] and where Prince Taw Phaya lived until late 2008.) He greatly upgraded his lifestyle; according to his brother, he got his suits tailored in Hong Kong,[54] and according to his sister, 'Prince Taw Phaya was the only one of us who could afford to ride a Mercedes in the 1950s!'[55]

To maintain the new lifestyle, for he knew the nest egg would not last forever, he looked around for business opportunities. By early 1953 he was dabbling in construction business, and again made quite a bit of money. Then, at his brother's request, he rejoined him in Thibaw Commercial Syndicate Co. Ltd, and injected some capital into the dying business.[56] In 1955, Prince Taw Phaya and Prince Taw Phaya Galae made a trip to Japan to negotiate a contract with a large Japanese company to import building materials, steel railings, etc. The deal was signed. However, the brothers did not have the advantages of larger players, and could not compete when tenders for reconstruction (financed by the Japanese as part of war reparation) were floated in Burma. They now looked for other opportunities, and their business sluggishly chugged along, providing some income for the family.[57]

It may be recalled that in 1958, U Nu had temporarily handed over charge of the government to the chief of his armed forces, General Ne Win, who had restored a semblance of law and order in the country over the next one and a half years. In 1960 the reins of the government had been handed back to U Nu, after he convincingly won the general elections. But the situation did not remain stable for long—old

simmering conflicts had resurfaced and Burma was once again caught
up in a civil war. The army, in the meantime, had been stealthily
planning a takeover; on 2 March 1962, General Ne Win staged a coup;
U Nu, the Sawbwa of Nyaungshwe, and other ministers were arrested;
Burma was declared a socialist state to be run by the military through
a 'revolutionary council' headed by a coterie of generals. Led, of
course, by General Ne Win.

General Ne Win now lost no time in dissolving the parliament,
shelving the constitution, disbanding courts of law, sacking experienced
civil servants, nationalizing all businesses (big or small, foreign or
local), expelling all Western agencies and institutes, whether aid or
educational, banning all opposition parties, and issuing a manifesto
called 'The Burmese Way to Socialism'.[58] One of the casualties of the
nationalization was Thibaw Commercial Syndicate Co. Ltd, the business
that had intermittently provided all the Fourth Princess's children
income for over a decade.[59] Like countless other people in Burma at
the time, Prince Taw Phaya and Prince Taw Phaya Galae had to find
another way to earn a living in an increasingly hostile and constantly
changing environment.

In November 1964 the British government, to demonstrate its
goodwill both towards the Burmese government and people, handed
over to General Ne Win numerous articles of both historical and
financial value, which had been seized from the Golden Palace after
the defeat of King Thibaw in 1885. The Mandalay Regalia, as this
collection was called, was described by *The Times* (London) as 'the
most important single collection of Burmese art in existence . . .' It
included one of the emblems of Konbaung kingship—the four-edged
dagger, the Than Lyet, which had at one time been owned by the
founder of the dynasty, Alaungpaya.[60] On his return to Burma with
these rare treasures, General Ne Win 'descended the aircraft steps like
a returning conqueror, triumphantly bearing the great sword of
Alaungpaya . . .'[61] The returned regalia was housed in the National
Museum in Rangoon, and descendants of King Thibaw were not given
even one keepsake, in spite of the fact that many of the articles it
comprised had once belonged personally to their grandfather. (It was
probably around this time that old photographs of the royal family

while they had been in India, and of the early years after their return to Burma, were suddenly 'taken away by the military for a museum' and were never returned. Of some family members had copies, of many they didn't.[62])

In the early 1970s Princess Rita wrote numerous letters to David Symington (who had contacted her as he was penning a book on the family's stay in Ratnagiri; he had been the collector of Ratnagiri about ten years after the family left it). In many of her letters she described the trouble her family was facing since the nationalization of their business. In one letter she thanked him for a gift of a parcel of clothes saying, 'God bless you, as since 1962 we have not had new outfits.' She went on to write, 'Before all this trouble in Burma, I used to buy books and magazines all the time and did not care for films or clothes! A freak! We read lighter novels now as a form of escapism from the grim side of life here.' In another letter, she described her daily life: 'I am too busy from dawn to dusk cooking, cleaning and washing up for 12 people! Just a humdrum life of a housewife who cannot afford to indulge in dreams or memories!'[63]

Prince Taw Phaya and Princess Rita had five sons and three daughters together; two of them died in childhood. After a very happy marriage of fifty-eight years, Princess Rita died of heart thrombosis in 2002.[64] Prince Taw Phaya misses her, and fondly remembers her:

> Rita was a very intelligent girl, always at the top of her classes . . . She was rather willful and stubborn at times, but a kind, generous, devoted wife and mother. She stood up for the oppressed and cruelty against humans and animals. It's a pity she left us . . . She was a very good correspondent, she used to contribute short articles to the English magazine 'The Lady' about [Burmese] monthly festivals until the Government said—all articles and memos must go through them— that ended her writing . . .[65]

Princess Rita is remembered as 'a lady of culture' by a history professor and author who personally interacted with her.[66]

Today Prince Taw Phaya is in his late eighties, and his health is not what it used to be.[67] He is a well-built man, and he has an imposing and regal presence. He is also a man of much grace, warmth and wit, and is a good raconteur. He writes long, detailed friendly letters, deliberately throwing in occasional Hindi expressions (for instance *'hum ka na-seep'* meaning 'my luck' and *'kalas ho-gi-ya'* meaning 'all finished'[68]) in testimony to a legacy that resulted from his mother's and aunt's long years in India.

Prince Taw Phaya Nge

Prince Taw Phaya Nge (Prince Terence), the Fourth Princess's fourth child, was, according to his brother, 'another athlete, a good forward footballer and a good sprinter, a prankster often on the mat ...' During Japanese occupation he joined the Burma Defence Army. In early 1946, he wished to be ordained as a monk, so the Third Princess supplied him with robes and put him under the care of a sayadaw. Word spread that there was a prince monk in the monastery and an unusual number of people came to visit, some out of curiosity, some to pay their respects. Prince Taw Phaya Nge soon realized that in spite of his devotion to his new profession, and no encouragement on his part, women suppliant for his attention were constantly visiting the monastery. So—after a failed attempt to get away from the opposite sex by moving to another small monastery deep within a jungle—he left for Rangoon. Here he de-robed and joined the government as deputy director of religious affairs. He had a distinguished career of about five years during which he led delegations to Laos, Thailand, Cambodia and China, and simultaneously completed his BA and BL degrees. He then, unfortunately, had to leave the government under a cloud, because a monk working under him absconded with some of the department's funds. Prince Taw Phaya Nge, like his eldest sister, now turned to teaching English to earn a living, and this he did successfully for a number of years.[69]

After about seven years of his first marriage, his son died due to what Prince Taw Phaya Nge and his family felt was 'the sloven[ly] and negligent ways of the wife'. He divorced her, and married a girl from his Moulmein school days. Off and on he would answer a spiritual calling, become a short-term monk, and escape from the real world for some weeks or months (it is not uncommon for religiously devout Burmese men to still do this). His last tryst with monkhood began in December 1994 when he went away to a monastery not far from his childhood home in Moulmein. It ended on 21 April 1995, when he passed away there at the age of seventy.[70]

Prince Taw Phaya Galae

It was the Fourth Princess's youngest son, Prince Taw Phaya Galae (Prince Frederick aka U Aung Zae; affectionately called Taw Taw by his family and friends), who was the most politically active and the most anti-British of all his siblings. Prince Taw Phaya describes him as 'the politician, orator and organizer'. In his younger days Prince Taw Phaya Galae 'was very lively[,] always falling off trees, breaking his arm and injuring his knee'.[71] One such fall, not long after his mother's death, led to a particularly serious injury to his right leg. Doctors in Moulmein recommended amputation; Ko Ko Naing voiced his opposition very strongly and demanded that his son be transferred to the Rangoon General Hospital. Here, doctors were able to save Prince Taw Phaya Galae's leg. The stay in Rangoon impacted him deeply because 'the British had separated him from the Burmese people; when he broke his leg when he was around ten years old and had to stay in hospital for a couple of years he deal[t] with Burmese people in hospital. Then the first feeling of patriotism [was] awaken[ed] in his heart.' On his return to Moulmein, his first nationalistic act was to refuse to respond to the name 'Frederick'. He also decided to wear the traditional Burmese pasoe (or longyi) in place of trousers to school. These decisions resulted in numerous conflicts with his teachers.[72] Prince Taw Phaya Galae emphasizes that it was his experiences in school that led him to harbour deeply anti-colonial, anti-British sentiments: 'We really hated them because they have humiliated us very much.'[73] It also led him, many years later, to turn to politics as a way to fight injustice.

During Japanese occupation Prince Taw Phaya Galae attended a Japanese Buddhist school in Rangoon from where he completed his education. Here he met Khin May, then seventeen. They fell in love and got married in October 1945,[74] and had one daughter, Devi Thant Cin. After Burmese independence and the ensuing lawlessness, Prince Taw Phaya Galae, who from his teenage days had been an ardent admirer and supporter of Thakin Kodaw Hmaing, was inspired by him to work towards promoting dialogue and peace. At some stage in the 1950s he formed an abiding friendship with Ludu Daw Ahmar—a highly respected intellectual, writer and critic of the military government—with whom he shared a leftist political ideology.[75]

In November 1958, on the seventy-third anniversary of Pardawmu day (commemorated annually, it marks the day when King Thibaw and his family were taken away on exile), Prince Taw Phaya Galae gave up his royal title and took the common name Thant Cin (which he later changed to Aung Zae).[76] In 1959, when the Mandalay Centenary Festival was celebrated and some attention was being focused on the monarchy, the prince brought out a book he had written entitled *King Thibaw: The Inside Story*. A devout Buddhist, he attributed the family's misfortunes mainly to fate, to karma (and of course to the British!).[77] Politics, and the history of his family, had always been of considerable interest to him, and after the 1962 nationalization of all businesses, he concentrated on these areas. He contributed articles regularly to various magazines voicing his views. One of the articles he wrote was about the famous missing, priceless Nga Mauk ruby[78] and he ceaselessly—almost up to his death—tried to trace it. On his visiting card he called himself 'History Research Scholar, Writer'. He was an active member of a host of varied associations and organizations including the World Peace Organization, Afro-Asian Solidarity Association, Union of Burma Exporters' Federation and the U Ottama Memorial Committee,[79] and channelled his energies to help the common man in whatever way he could.[80]

Many affectionately called Prince Taw Phaya Galae 'The Red Prince' due to his leftist leanings.[81] One of his nephews narrates that his egalitarian philosophy led him to abhor the ubiquitous sheiko; he would discourage people from adopting this position, and to those who nonetheless sank before him, he would quip 'has something been lost—what are you looking for on the ground?'[82] By 1963, so disturbed was he with the state of economic, social and political affairs in Burma, that he began to actively oppose the military regime.[83] The military leadership, not surprisingly, did not appreciate this, and he often had to go into hiding.[84] On two occasions he was jailed: from 1968 to 1970, and again from 1989 to 1993.[85] His sister, Princess Hteik Su Phaya Gyi, jokes that he was so outspoken that he always had to keep his bedroll packed and ready because they could come to get him anytime![86]

Since the days of British rule, students in Burma had been politically active and colleges and universities were spawning grounds for youth voicing discontent and demanding change. Thakin Kodaw Hmaing and Ludu Daw Ahmar had both been part of student movements. Following in the footsteps of his two icons, Prince Taw Phaya Galae associated himself with the well-known uprising on 8.8.88. (This uprising gave birth to a new Burmese leader, Aung San Suu Kyi, daughter of Bogyoke Aung San. Affectionately called 'The Lady' in Burma, Aung San Suu Kyi is a source of deep inspiration, comfort and hope for the people of her country.)

In 1988, Prince Taw Phaya Galae became the patron of the Mandalay-based Ma-Na-Ta (the National Political Front),[87] which had the objective, as the Junta saw it, of carrying out 'anti-government activities' and 'inciting unrest in the country'.[88] The Ma-Na-Ta was told to disband and was declared illegal,[89] and for his patronage of this organization, and for his support to student leaders during the 1988 demonstrations, Prince Taw Phaya Galae was arrested and jailed in 1989. Realizing that the 8.8.88 uprising had been precipitated largely due to economic reasons, the government now allowed limited private sector development and foreign investment. This enabled Prince Taw Phaya Galae to start a rice export business after his release from jail in 1993. He called his new business National International Commercial Enterprise (N.I.C.E.). (His eldest grandson manages this business today.)[90]

In 1998 (at the age of seventy-two) Prince Taw Phaya Galae began

giving English tutorials in his home.[91] Queen Supayalat had years
earlier justified accepting pension from the hated British government
because she felt they owed her; perhaps Prince Taw Phaya Galae had
the same justification for using English as a way to earn a living.
Certainly he saw no contradiction between his self-professed dislike of
the British and his use of their language as a means to earn a
livelihood. Over the years, he built up a large and loyal student base,
and his students say they learnt a lot more from him than just a
language. He was a kind, popular and inspirational teacher, who talked
to them on a variety of subjects and urged them not to be satisfied
with just academic knowledge. He charged his students what he felt
was a fair rate; for those who could not afford to pay, he waived his
fees.[92] His wife feels he gave away much more than they could afford.
Although she never complained, and always stood by him, once, in a
moment of despair (for financial shortage was such an integral part of
her life) she is said to have commented, 'Oh, Prince Taw Phaya Galae
is like a little sparrow, everybody comes and picks out all the feather[s]
and now he is featherless . . .'[93]

For many years, the prince battled ill health. His lungs, never strong,
had taken a severe battering during his first stint in jail. In addition, he
suffered from chronic urinary tract infections. On the morning of 18
June 2006, after hospitalization in the intensive care unit of Rangoon
General Hospital for approximately two weeks, Prince Taw Phaya
Galae passed away of heart failure. He was just a few weeks short of
his eightieth birthday.[94] As his body lay in a glass coffin, with four
golden umbrellas at each corner in a nod to his royal ancestry, people
from all walks of life, including writers, politicians, business people,
academicians and his students and friends, came to pay their respects.[95]
Prince Taw Phaya Galae was cremated and his ashes were entombed on
the southern perimeter of Queen Supayalat's mausoleum. A flurry of
magazine and newspaper articles were written in his memory including
by Ludu Daw Ahmar, whom he had loved and idolized for over fifty
years. She wrote an article entitled 'Oh! How I Yearn for Our
Comrade Taw Taw'. She ended it by saying, 'Taw Taw never wavered
from his belief throughout his life . . . Taw Taw, may you rest in peace
and watch your comrades still struggling with their hardships from
your new better world.'[96]

Princess Hteik Su Phaya Htwe

The Fourth Princess's youngest child, Princess Hteik Su Phaya Htwe (Princess Margaret), was 'a saucy young brat that drove the nun in charge of small girls in the Moulmein convent to tears'. A very pretty girl, in 1947 she stood second in the Miss Burma beauty contest (organized by her brother's group of associates). After independence, she joined the National Fitness Council as a coordinator. In this capacity, she travelled around the country demonstrating exercises and games. Her father, Ko Ko Naing, went blind around 1951, and after he suffered a debilitating stroke in 1956, Princess Hteik Su Phaya Htwe moved in with him (he lived on a plot next to Queen Supayalat's tomb—the government had granted him this plot in June 1947, to enable him to maintain his mother-in-law's tomb[97]), and nursed him until his death in September 1959.[98]

After her father's death, Princess Hteik Su Phaya Htwe rejoined the National Fitness Council, where she attracted a lot of male attention: she had good looks, charm and a royal background. In order to escape one married man's persistent attentions, she ran away to Maymyo for an extended stay with her aunt and brother, but the determined love-struck man followed her. This greatly perturbed the Third Princess who, at that time, was dying of cancer. She resolved that something drastic had to be done to drive away this very unsuitable suitor, and she decided that her niece and her grandson (Prince Taw Phaya's eldest son) should marry. The difference in the proposed partners' ages was never an important consideration for the Third Princess— her own husbands had been either much younger or much older than her—so she brushed aside the fact that her niece was thirty-four years old whereas her grandson was just seventeen. Seeing that Princess Hteik Su Phaya Htwe was 'quite fond of [her] mischievous' grandson, that her grandson liked his aunt ('a very kind, very simple person who wore no make up' he recalled many years later[99]), and as both of them were of royal lineage, the Third Princess was convinced it was a good match. Her grandson's parents, Prince Taw Phaya and Princess Rita, did not disagree. In May 1962, Princess Hteik Su Phaya Htwe and Prince Richard (U Tun Kyaw) were married; two months later the Third Princess passed away, secure in the knowledge that she had done the right thing for her family.[100]

After his marriage, Prince Richard completed his schooling and joined the Government Technical College from where he got a diploma in engineering. He went on to become a specialist in marine and cold storage, and for many years worked on foreign ships. He communicated adequately in English, was highly thought of, and was able to earn a good living—good enough for him to be able to send a regular monthly contribution to his parents in Maymyo, after he and his wife settled in Rangoon.[101]

Princess Hteik Su Phaya Htwe taught English to young children and concentrated on bringing up their only child, a son, born in 1964. In the beginning their marriage, says her brother (and father-in-law), 'was more of an elder person guiding a young one. However, when the husband became more experienced, [Princess Hteik Su Phaya Htwe] took a back seat'.[102] Her sister says that the couple had many very happy years together:

> [H]e looked after her very well . . . They were very affectionate—just like the father Prince Taw Phaya and Rita were very affectionate . . . her [Princess Hteik Su Phaya Htwe's] life was beautiful. When she was going out, he used to grind the sandalwood for her, iron her clothes, and he [would ask] what longyi are you going to wear and he [would] iron that . . . everything [was] laid out. Very good husband . . .[103]

In the early 1990s, the princess developed a heart condition, which caused her to somewhat slow down. She was in her sixties now; her husband was in his forties. Their age difference, it appears, was suddenly noticeable and significant. Perhaps this is what led to Prince Richard's romantic involvement with a much younger woman whom he met at the office of the Korean shipping line where he was employed. It all started quite gradually and harmlessly. Myint Myint Aye lived with her grandfather. She was bullied at office; Prince

Richard felt sorry for her. She was 'always in need of help'; he helped her out whenever he could. She got close to his family, often visiting his home, and 'buying things and doing odd jobs for [Princess Hteik Su Phaya Htwe] who was very fond of her'.[104] It therefore hurt the princess all the more when she discovered that the girl she liked and trusted, 'a laywoman', was having an affair with her husband. And her grief knew no bounds when her husband of over three decades took Myint Myint Aye as his second wife[105] in 1993.[106]

For Myint Myint Aye, Prince Richard was such 'a good catch',[107] so any pangs of guilt were suppressed. Besides, the law and the cultural milieu supported her. Says U Than Swe, '[A] male can marry [as many times] as he likes so long as he can support. This is our Buddhist law.'[108] Years ago, Queen Supayalat had decreed that the old custom of multiple wives had to go, and her descendants—her grandsons and great grandsons—had all been monogamous, in spite of what custom and law still allowed. Besides, Princess Hteik Su Phaya Htwe was a beloved member of the family, so the family was very upset. Prince Taw Phaya unequivocally voiced his anger at his son. However, he eventually accepted his son's new wife and Prince Richard took Myint Myint Aye with him to Maymyo to pay homage to his parents.[109]

Prince Richard tried to be fair, as best he could, in the circumstances. He set up a separate home for Myint Myint Aye, and he spent four nights a week with her, and three nights a week (over the weekend) with Princess Hteik Su Phaya Htwe, who continued to stay in their old home with their son and his family. But this was small consolation for the princess; she 'was heart-broken ... She'd rather die than continue living because of the second wife'.[110] Princess Hteik Su Phaya Htwe now cut off her long hair, dressed like a yogi,[111] and according to an unverified rumour, stopped taking her heart medication. One morning in June 2003, as she sat reading a newspaper, she collapsed as a result of a brain haemorrhage, and passed away a few days later.[112] She was seventy-six at the time. Myint Myint Aye tried to attend her funeral, but the family 'drove her out ... she had to go out crying and ... now they sort of just ignore her'.[113]

When they were growing up, the Fourth Princess had repeatedly told her children that the mortal remains of King Thibaw and Queen Supayagalae had been forcibly entombed without the necessary *tharanagaon* ceremony (last rites; a ceremony accorded to *every* Buddhist Burmese after his or her death).[114]

A sense of deep indignation and regret was shared by all of King Thibaw's descendants in Burma, and by many other Burmese who were aware of this omission: 'You see we regard[ed] our kings as future Buddhas. Although Thibaw [was] weak, he [was] well learned in [the] scriptures and we pitied him that even in his death he did not have this special religious ceremony,' says U Than Swe.[115] Over the years, Prince Taw Phaya and Prince Taw Phaya Galae had made several attempts to visit Ratnagiri, but it was only in December 1993—'108 years after Pardawmu day, seventy-seven years after the demise of King Thibaw, and forty-five years after Burmese independence'—that they were able to make this trip, and were finally able to set this long-standing omission right.[116]

The family arrived in Ratnagiri at 1 a.m. on 12 December. They stayed at the Landmark Hotel (which, they noticed, to their delight, was on Thebaw Palace Road—something they believed had to be more than a coincidence, had to be 'the wish of the spiritual world'). Later that morning they paid a visit to Tu Tu. They were all meeting her for the first time. Perhaps they expected some familial resemblance, some similarities of custom, but they were taken aback to see that their cousin, 'looked like an old Indian woman from an Indian family'. They were dismayed to find that Tu Tu and her family 'were living very poorly, just like beggars' in a tiny unkempt hut, housing an image of a god they did not recognize. Communication between them and Tu Tu was difficult, and aided by the few Hindi words that the Fourth Princess's children knew, and by their helpful but not very fluent driver who acted as interpreter, the cousins could exchange some very basic information. Tu Tu's cousins were shocked to discover that this granddaughter of King Thibaw, who had spent the first twelve and a half years of her life in her royal grandparents' home, had not even a hint of Burmese 'patriotism or national spirit'. While departing, as they gifted Tu Tu Rs 5,000 and paid their respects to her, Prince Taw Phaya Galae says that they had 'to remind [themselves] that she was actually [their] cousin'.[117]

In the afternoon (due to financial constraints the family would stay in Ratnagiri for just over thirty hours), the descendants visited the Royal Residence—they are adamant that it *cannot* be called a palace[118] (although ironically enough, archival material shows that the king, queen and Fourth Princess all referred to their home in Ratnagiri as 'palace' in many of their letters)—and wandered through it. Although very disappointed that it was in a dilapidated and dirty condition, the visit rekindled memories of stories their mother and aunt had told them so many years ago.[119] Standing on the terrace, Princess Hteik Su Phaya Gyi recalled her mother saying:

> Queen Supayalat used to look out from this verandah and *long* for her home. So when I went there and saw this place, I had tears in my eyes, it was very very sad. The sun [was] setting on one side of the [sea], and a little boat [was] passing and I said, 'Oh! That is how my grandmother felt, no?'[120]

As they shared these memories with one another, all of them 'felt anguish and sorrow'[121] for the long years of exile King Thibaw and his family had had to endure, for all their family had once had, and lost.

Before the end of the day, the family also visited King Thibaw's and the First Princess's adjacent tombs. They discovered to their horror that the orifice of the First Princess's tomb had not been sealed, and, on enquiry were informed that the box containing her ashes still lay in the collector's office. They noticed that the epitaph on her tomb—written in Burmese—had carelessly been cemented upside down.[122] Turning their attention to their grandfather's tomb, they 'all felt very painful and sorry to see the tomb of King Thibaw in such a state'. The tomb was covered with moss, and small plants sprouted from the numerous crevices that criss-crossed it. All types of debris—including excreta—littered the tomb's small enclosure. They realized, to their deep regret, that they had neither the ability to get the necessary permissions (Burmese and Indian), nor the wherewithal to arrange for the transportation of the mortal remains of their grandfather and aunt back to Burma. They also did not have the financial resources to renovate the tomb. All they were in a position to do was perform the tharanagaon ceremony and leave.[123]

The ceremony was held on Monday, 13 December 1993 (or, according to the Burmese calendar, on the eighth waning day of Tazaungmon 1355). The ceremony began at 7 a.m., and was attended by seven white-clad descendants of the Fourth Princess (all her five surviving children and two of her grandchildren), the Burmese consul (who had escorted them, at the Burmese government's expense, from Bombay), and the three drivers that had driven the entourage from Bombay to Ratnagiri.[124] Neither Tu Tu nor any of her children were invited (Princess Hteik Su Phaya Gyi says this was to avoid a crowd in the small tomb enclosure, and to effect the ceremony as respectfully and quietly as possible).[125]

Sayadaw U Kawwida of the Calcutta Burmese Buddhist Temple performed the tharanagaon ceremony (the family had hoped to bring the sayadaw from the Mya Taung monastery—the queen's monastery in Mandalay—for the purpose, but they could not afford the travel expenses that this would have entailed).[126] During the ceremony, which was both very emotional and momentous for the family, one of King Thibaw's grandchildren read out that they had all come to perform 'this historic task' for the late king, junior queen, and for the First and Second Princesses. Prince Taw Phaya Galae stated that as King Thibaw, Queen Supayagalae and the princesses 'were true citizens of Mandalay, we offered them Mandalay htoumoun, moon cakes, kayekaya, jaggery and pickled tea leaves . . .'

Right at the end, after the yeizet-cha or water pouring ritual, the 'note of merit sharing' was read out:

> We, the grandchildren and great grandchildren of the second ruler of the Yadanabon Naypyidaw [Mandalay, Abode of Kings] and the donor of the Mya Taung Pagoda, King Thibaw and the Chief Queen Supayalat, are devout Buddhists who believe in karma.

We are offering Buddha and his sanghas with *soon* and other items of food on behalf of all our Royal ancestors including the deceased King Thibaw and the Chief Queen Supayalat who contributed much for the establishment of Buddhism, Buddhist literature and Buddhist culture in Burma.

For all the meritorious deeds we have done, we pray that we have the ability to contribute more for the welfare of our country and the citizens; we also wish for the welfare of all living beings in the *samsara*, and we pray that we would one day attain *nirvana*.

We would like to share merits with all our Royal ancestors including our grandfather, King Thibaw ruler of the Yadanabon Naypyidaw, and our grandmother, Chief Queen Supayalat, who in their time had done their best for the development of Buddhism, Buddhist literature and Buddhist culture in our land. We would also like to share our merits with our grandmother, the lesser Queen Supayagalae, Ashin Hteik Su Myat Phaya Gyi [the First Princess], Ashin Hteik Su Myat Phaya Lat [the Second Princess], Ashin Hteik Su Myat Phaya [the Third Princess], Thakin Prince Hteik Tin Kodaw Gyi [the Third Princess's divorced husband], Ashin Hteik Su Myat Phaya Galae [the Fourth Princess] and husband Ko Ko Naing, and our eldest brother Prince Taw Phaya Gyi.

We would like to share our merits with all the celestial beings, *zawgyis* [alchemists with supernatural powers], persons with supernatural powers, and those living beings seen and unseen around the tomb. We would like to share our merits with all forms of life in this universe.

Let's share all our merits! Let's share all our merits! Let's share all our merits!

Thadu! Thadu! Thadu! [Well done! Well done! Well done!][127]

EPILOGUE

Should the question of restoration of Burmese monarchy ever come up now there are bound to be many contestants, as there are many descendants today of sons and daughters of long deceased Konbaung kings. Although technically 'any royal can claim the throne', it is the grandsons and great grandsons of King Thibaw who have the greatest claim on the Lion Throne, says U Than Swe.[1] This does not simplify matters because it's not a question of who has the highest claim, Prince Taw Phaya says, because 'in Burmese history, whoever has the strength, *he* becomes king'.[2]

Far away in England lives a man who calls himself 'HRH the Prince Shwebomin the Crown Prince of Burma'. A slight, middle-aged, distinguished-looking gentleman, he reveals that he has the all-important peacock seal in his possession; that his mother is a descendant of King Pagan, but on the night of occupation of the Golden Palace, the treasury was burnt down and with that all proof of his ancestry vanished. He passionately argues that King Mindon snatched the throne from King Pagan, that King Thibaw should never have been king, that he does not 'recognize' King Thibaw and his descendants.[3] U Than Swe, however, pooh-poohs Prince Shwebomin's claims. Whether anyone recognizes King Thibaw as the rightful king or not cannot take away from the fact that he *was* the king, he says emphatically. He also says that Prince Shwebomin's facts are all mixed up, that his possession of the peacock seal is totally meaningless: 'In Burmese royal culture that seal is not important. He has copied from the Chinese culture. In the Chinese, when the emperor died the dowager queen would seize the seal because the one who has the seal is the heir [possession of the seal signified having the 'Mandate from Heaven']. In our culture the seal is not important.' So saying he reiterates the important insignias of Burmese royalty: a white ceremonial umbrella, a crested headdress, a yak tail hair whisk (fan), the Than Lyet (four-edged dagger) and royal footwear. Shouldn't an aspiring king of Burma know at least this, he asks, with a dismissive laugh?[4]

IN RATNAGIRI

Although there is nobody alive in Ratnagiri today who has personally met King Thibaw, one can meet people whose grandfathers knew him as his lawyer, washerman, moneylender or grocer. Stories about him and his family have been passed down as folklore, as have some of his possessions, though sadly none of King Thibaw's descendants today owns anything that once belonged to him. Rumour has it that in town still are many pieces of jewellery that were gifted or pawned by the king over the years.[5] The grandson of King Thibaw's lawyer, for instance, has the large emerald ring and other items that were gifted to his grandfather for his housewarming ceremony in 1908.[6]

'Thebaw Palace' stands at the end of a road now called 'Thebaw Palace Road', and is today a museum that holds a handful of dusty unmemorable memorabilia. The Royal Residence, as the descendants prefer to call it, after various avatars including as a technical training institute, and after many years of neglect, is now a protected monument and is maintained by the government.[7] Although the building is still run down, it continues to stand majestically on a promontory that does not have many other structures on it. Development in Ratnagiri over the years has not obstructed the spectacular view the building commands. Its large rooms, although mouldy, decaying and in places encrusted with pigeon droppings, are deeply atmospheric and evocative of the lives once lived within their walls.

Queen Supayalat had said long ago that her husband's and sister's tomb was located in a 'nasty unconsecrated place';[8] if she could see the tomb today she would be truly devastated. When constructed in 1919, the location had been serene and isolated—'in the midst of a forest';[9] now, most unfortunately, King Thibaw and Queen Supayagalae's tomb, as also the First Princess's *still* empty tomb, are hemmed in on all sides and overlooked by a shabby, two-storeyed housing colony.[10] After many years of neglect and disrepair, the tombs, like the Royal Residence, are now protected monuments looked after by the government.[11] (There has been talk on and off about shifting the remains of the last Mughal emperor, Bahadur Shah Zafar II, from Rangoon—where he had died during British-imposed exile—to India, and the remains of King Thibaw and Queen Supayagalae from Ratnagiri to Burma, but nothing has come of it yet.)

Those in Ratnagiri who remember the First Princess, refer to her as 'Phaya' (perhaps this is what Gopal called her). The small home where she stayed for many lonely years no longer exists. The house where the First Princess died is now government-owned—the government having acquired large tracts of Gopal's land over the years. It today houses a small, musty, archaic-looking office. The home where Tu Tu spent over sixty-six years of her life and from which she was forcibly evicted is still in the half-broken condition it was rendered into in 1999. The entire plot remains vacant and is overgrown with weeds. Two wild cobras guard it, says her son Chandu, and menacingly rear their hoods when anybody ventures near the hut. But, he adds, once when *he* went to pay his obeisance at the partially demolished Dattaguru shrine, they did not challenge him. This is significant to him; he dreams that his old home may one day be restored to the family, but accepts that this is improbable and in the meanwhile, has decided not to tempt fate again![12]

Ratnagiri remains a sleepy provincial town, with a population of around 170,000. It is still known mainly for its agricultural produce (including the alphonso mango) and for its fishing industry. Connected by railroad with the rest of India only in 1996, it has few major industries, and therefore employment and business opportunities are limited.[13] All of Tu Tu's children have been constrained by this lack of prospects, by their minimal education, and by the absence of any financial resources. Though most of them are leading lives far fuller and happier than their grandmother did, none of them has been able to quite shake off the shackles of their impoverished and education-deprived past. This aspect of the First Princess's life, most regrettably, continues to echo in the lives of most of her descendants. Like their father, Shankar, many of Tu Tu's sons have struggled with alcoholism.[14] Some of her sons work as vehicle drivers or mechanics, like Shankar and Gopal did, and this legacy has been passed down to even some of Tu Tu's grandsons.[15] Some of the First Princess's female descendants work as domestic help or part-time cooks and this, not surprisingly, is a topic of conversation in town: 'Guess what, Thibaw Rajah's great great granddaughter is washing dishes in my house!'[16] According to Tu Tu's son, Digambhar, *'Naam bada par sab kangal'* (The name may be big but we are all impoverished).[17]

Chandu, Tu Tu's most responsible child, was the one closest to his mother.[18] He runs his own small garage in which he repairs and services vehicles. However, his has always been a hand to mouth existence.[19] More than any of his other siblings, says a long-time Ratnagiri resident, Chandu is of the same mould as his royal ancestors. He is generous and helpful. Two of his brothers, recovering alcoholics, stay with him. His kindness is not restricted to his family—he is always willing to lend a hand to anyone who needs it.[20] Now there is a definite awareness in his family of the importance of education: in Chandu's house hangs a large poster of Goddess Saraswati, the Hindu goddess of knowledge. Under this poster sits and studies Purnima, Chandu's very bright and pretty thirteen-year-old granddaughter who has been awarded a Rotary scholarship in recognition of her outstanding grades.[21]

One of Tu Tu's granddaughters, Jayshree (Jayu), lives in a really tiny one-room chawl in Mumbai. She has studied only up to the fourth standard and regrets this. She works hard both as a part-time maid washing dishes in several homes and as a cook in a food stall, to try and ensure that her two cheerful young children, Prachi and Udayan, complete their education. Prachi is now attending college. Very ironically, the college application of this great great great granddaughter of the last king of Burma was strengthened by the fact that she belongs to what the government of India calls the 'OBC' or 'Other Backward Class', which includes people from socially and economically disadvantaged communities.[22]

In 2004 one of Gopal's grandson's constructed a bungalow for himself that he called 'Laxmi–Gopal' in loving tribute to his grandparents.[23] In stark and sad contrast, the First Princess is barely remembered by her grandchildren. Perhaps her mental instability towards the end of her life overshadowed their earlier impressions of a loving grandmother, and weakened their bond with her. And with Tu Tu not wanting to visit the past, no other memories of her were reinforced or passed down. Her descendants seem to have no interest at all in their Burmese lineage. All they know is that King Thibaw, the exiled king of Brahmadesh (Burma in many Indian languages, including Marathi), whose very grainy and small photograph hangs high up on one of Chandu's walls, was an ancestor. Perhaps in deference to this ancestor, once every few years Chandu's family buys tickets to visit the Royal Residence, like any visitor to Ratnagiri might.[24] All of the First Princess's descendants are devout Hindus, and to the casual observer this family is no different from any other typically Maharashtrian family. However, once in a while, a great great grandchild of the First Princess is born with such distinctly Burmese features—like Sakshi, Chandu's young granddaughter—that a startling and vivid hark back to the faded past is inevitable.

IN CALCUTTA

During an interview towards the end of his life, an ailing Maung Lu Gyi gazed misty-eyed out of the window of his small rented one-room apartment, a stone's throw from Calcutta's Burmese Buddhist Temple, as he remembered his devoted parents and gently shook his head at opportunities missed.[25] His sister, Gulabi, sharper and more incisive in her analysis of the situation, says that the Second Princess had adored her brother to such an extent, had molly-coddled and protected him so much, that he had never really had a chance to grow up. He was frozen in a childlike state, she says, and was ill-equipped for life and its knocks.[26]

His mother's death in April 1956 devastated Maung Lu Gyi, and shattered any dream he may have harboured of settling in the land of his royal ancestors. Without his mother's presence to ease him into some kind of a life in Burma, he had no choice but to return to Kalimpong. The Second Princess's pension ceased immediately after her death, and Maung Lu Gyi hurriedly sold much of their household effects and had to give up their rented home. The entire family, including Maung Lu Gyi, now moved to a small house his birth mother owned as 'there was nowhere else to go'.[27]

In 1959 Maung Lu Gyi shifted to Calcutta where he lived for eighteen years in a room attached to the Burmese Buddhist Temple. In Calcutta, he got himself a job with the Burmese consulate (as personal assistant to the Burmese consul general), and married Bina Devi, a girl he had known in Kalimpong. He worked at the consulate until it closed down in 1988, after which he was employed by Hotel Majestic (where his parents had briefly stayed in 1938) as a receptionist cum cashier until his retirement in 1998.[28] After his retirement he was eligible for a very small pension of a few hundred rupees, had negligible savings, and found it very difficult to make both ends meet. Maung Lu Gyi and his wife had no children of their own and informally treated a young woman from Kalimpong as their daughter. He was financially aided by his 'daughter' and by his sister, Gulabi. (Gulabi, very protective of her brother, has always tried to be there for him and look after his interests.[29])

On 18 December 2008, a couple of weeks after being informed that his mother's ashes had *finally* been entombed in Queen Supayalat's tomb (he had handed the urn over to U Soe Win in February 2008), he passed away peacefully in his sleep at his home in Calcutta. He was seventy-six years old at the time.[30]

Gulabi, like her brother, gets teary-eyed when remembering the Second Princess and Latthakin, who she says played a greater role in her upbringing (although she was not adopted by them) than her real parents. Educated only up to the fourth grade, married by the couple when she was barely sixteen, she and her husband continued living with them until the Second Princess's death. She has lived in Calcutta since 1962, is now a widow, and runs a small beauty parlour in the

same building where she resides. Gulabi has lovingly kept an old
Burma teakwood chest of the Second Princess and Latthakin's papers
as a memento of the magical years she had spent with them.[31]

IN MANDALAY

According to one of her grandsons, the monastery (Mya Taung) that
Queen Supayalat had had built as a work of merit just before the exile
was 'burnt down by an incendiary bomb fired by British troops in
April 1942 . . . before they evacuated Mandalay'. A brick monastery
was rebuilt in its place.[32] (It is said that the monks of the queen's
monastery played a prominent role in the Saffron Revolution of
September 2007. Triggered by the spiralling prices of everyday goods,
peaceful anti-government demonstrations, led by monks, were held in
various parts of Burma.)

The Golden Palace was destroyed in March 1945. The original
fortified walls and the beautiful many-tiered pyatthats on it still
stand, as do some masonry structures including King Mindon and
Sinbyumashin's tombs. Reconstruction of the palace started in 1989—
news reports say using forced labour—but the newly built palace does
not have the intricate detailing and the imposing grandeur of the past.
However, it does give an idea of how the buildings once lay. To get an
idea of what the palace *was*, a visit to the Shwenandaw Kyaung is
essential. This used to be King Mindon's apartment, and this is where
he died. After his death, King Thibaw thought that his father's ghost
haunted the building, so he had it dismantled, shifted and reassembled
beyond the walls of the Royal Golden City, in the town of Mandalay.
This exquisite building—used for years as a monastery—therefore
survived, and is all that remains today of the original teakwood palace
buildings.

Other than two granddaughters of Prince Taw Phaya[33] none of King
Thibaw's descendants lives in Mandalay today. However, many other
Konbaung descendants still do. According to U Than Swe,

> In Mandalay there are some royalty that are quite well off . . . some are
> nearly beggars. I saw the great grandson of a prince. He has to live near
> his great grandfather's tomb, with a roof connected with the tomb. He

[can't afford anything else] . . . Some princes were educated by the British in India, and when they returned to Burma, they [got good jobs], but the British says you can get a salary or a pension. The pension was higher than the salary, so they put away the work and enjoy the pension . . . when the government changes [at the time of Burmese independence] they become like this . . . helpless.[34]

IN MAYMYO

Prince Taw Phaya, King Thibaw and Queen Supayalat's only living grandson, continues to live in Maymyo. Maymyo (now called Pyin U Lwin) remains a time-forgotten relic of British times, in spite of its large military presence. In late 2008, Prince Taw Phaya sold the large rambling house on Forest Road that he had bought in his heyday, and now lives in a smaller and more modern home.[35]

Pictures of the royal family dot his living room's walls, and are the only objects in it to hint at his royal ancestry. He is very well informed about his family history and strongly identifies with his royal roots, but he has never been anti-British. He says that in their day-to-day lives none of his children considers themselves royalty, in spite of the fact that as young children they had their grandmother, the Third Princess, constantly around, and Prince Taw Phaya's home followed some old royal customs. He laughs and says, 'No, they have to be reminded!' And reminded they are. He relates an incident that evokes a parallel with the last Emperor of China who spent his last few years working as a humble gardener:

> My second son was a district police officer—DSP—and when he left the job and retired, he went and worked in some ex-army officer's garden—in Madaya, some 28 miles north of Mandalay. There was a big plantation and he used to work there and stay with this ex-army officer. He was doing gardening—cleaning the ground and manuring the trees. When news leaked out that this was the great grandson of King Thibaw, people used to come in the evening and sit and listen to what he had to say. And pay their respects before they go back . . . There is always a sentiment when Burmese royalty is concerned, especially in the villages.[36]

Prince Taw Phaya now lives with his two daughters, and three granddaughters—'a harem of five women' as he playfully puts it.[37] He says, '[W]ith Rita gone ... I cannot raise a finger, [his eldest daughter Princess Anne-Marie] will be beside me to take over whatever I intend to do. God bless her.' He also indicates that his eldest son [Prince Richard] 'sends a substantial monthly contribution so I'm quite comfortable'. He spends his time watching a bit of television, and finds football matches particularly absorbing. Apart from interactions with his family, his life today is pretty much a solitary one; he does not encourage too many visitors.[38] Recently, however, he consented to meet a Reuters correspondent, and during the interview he said, 'I'd be mad to want to become a king now. With these chaps, I don't think I'd get very far.' He ended this interview with his usual brand of irreverent humour: 'If somebody farts in a house, they know who it is.'[39]

IN MOULMEIN

The monks of the pagoda where the Fourth Princess's tomb lies look after it, regularly maintaining and whitewashing it.[40] On the perimeter of her tomb are the ashes of two of her children, Prince Taw Phaya Nge and Princess Hteik Su Phaya Htwe.[41] The large rented home on West Cantonment Road, in which she lived and died during her exile to Moulmein, still stands. It has been converted into a school, and carries a prominent sign over its entrance, 'The Fourth Princess Hall'.[42]

IN RANGOON

The rented house on 23 Churchill Road, where the queen stayed for the last six years of her life, no longer exists. In its place stands an extension of the Sangha Hospital. The road is now known as Kominkochin Road.[43]

Periodically, the queen's tomb is repaired and whitewashed by her descendants; periodically there is talk of relocating her remains to Mandalay. Over the years the ashes of Queen Supayalat's family have been added to the perimeter of her tomb. The queen's tomb faces east (the most auspicious direction of the Burmese compass). On the north side are entombed the ashes of the Second Princess, the Third Princess and Princess Rita. On the south side are entombed the ashes of Ko Ko Naing, Prince Taw Phaya Gyi and Prince Taw Phaya Galae.[44] Near the queen's tomb lie the tombs of Thakin Kodaw Hmaing, U Thant (a former secretary general of the United Nations), and Daw Khin Kyi (wife of Bogyoke Aung San; a noted social worker and politician, whose ill-health led to her daughter, Aung San Suu Kyi, returning to Burma in 1988). None of these tombs is a protected monument, and neither tourists nor locals are encouraged to visit any of them.[45]

Just as Prince Taw Phaya Gyi had tried to do so many years ago, today his son, U Soe Win, who is based in Rangoon, attempts to hold the family together.[46] (U Soe Win recently retired as deputy director general, Protocol Department, in the Ministry of Foreign Affairs; he is now director, International Affairs, of the Myanmar Football Federation.[47] He shares his father's and uncle's love for sport, especially football.)

Prince Taw Phaya Galae's widow, Khin May, continues to live in the small ancestral home that stands near Queen Supayalat's tomb. A small-built, amiable, chatty woman, she and Prince Taw Phaya Galae had a long and happy marriage of sixty-one years. A prominent picture of Prince Taw Phaya Galae graces a small table in the living room, along with a photograph of the four princesses. Two vases of fresh flowers and two candles have been placed on the table forming a kind of altar. On the wall hang paintings of King Thibaw and Queen Supayalat, of the Fourth Princess and Ko Ko Naing, of Thakin Kodaw Hmaing, and a photograph of Ludu Daw Ahmar posing with Khin May. After Prince Taw Phaya Galae's death, his daughter Devi and her family moved in with Khin May. Like her father, Devi also writes articles in various magazines, and has brought out her own magazine 3G, but her emphasis is solely on the environment.[48]

Princess Hteik Su Phaya Gyi—King Thibaw and Queen Supayalat's only surviving granddaughter—is now almost ninety. For years she has told everyone not to call her 'Princess', not to call her by her royal title Princess Hteik Su Phaya Gyi, but by the common name she has taken, Daw Su Su Khin, since 'I don't live like a princess. I'm walking on the streets.'[49] Short and petite, Princess Hteik Su Phaya Gyi is about the same height as her grandmother was. She carries herself with great confidence, speaks slowly and precisely, and is sharp and witty. She does not hesitate to voice her opinions. In her one glimpses Queen Supayalat. Princess Hteik Su Phaya Gyi is very pleased when likened to her strong, imperious grandmother.[50] But unlike her grandmother, mother and youngest brother, she has never had any interest whatsoever in politics. Unlike them she does not hate the British, and this she says had led to endless arguments with her youngest brother.[51] Princess Hteik Su Phaya Gyi, however, justifies her position by saying,

> [T]he difference between the British government and the Burmese government: the British were our enemies, but the Burmese are not our enemies. We are the same kind. But the difference! People say, 'Oh! You talk good about the British in spite of them taking your grandparents, and taking the country and making it into slavery'— they all say that . . .

Of course, the British shouldn't have robbed her grandparents of the kingdom, she says, but that done and over with, in her opinion, the British looked after the descendants quite well; the betrayal was by her own government, after independence.[52]

For Queen Supayalat the British were anathema: white outside dark inside, to paraphrase what she once so memorably said. She blamed all her losses on them, and spent her life shunning all things British, including its language. Most of her grandchildren decided long ago to let go of the hatred and the anger, to move on from the negativity of the past.[53] All her grandchildren in Burma were Anglicized; the missionary boarding schools they had been forced to attend having done their jobs well in this regard. Throughout their lives they informally referred to each other by their missionary-given Christian names.[54] They ate with cutlery, not with their hands, points out one of them to demonstrate the extent of their Anglicization.[55] And most of them disliked the overpowering smell of ngapi—the ubiquitous fermented fish paste that flavours almost all Burmese meals—leading one of their spouses to sharply and repeatedly comment: 'A Burmese Prince *should* be able to stand the smell of the favourite [condiment] of the Burmese . . .'[56] They all conversed easily in English; in fact they all *thought* in English, and spoke to each other in English.[57] Four of Queen Supayalat's grandchildren made a living teaching the language their grandmother had refused to learn. Although proud of their ancestry, although well aware that many people in Burma still have lingering respect for the royal family, her two surviving grandchildren know too well that their family's moment has come and gone. Stories of the past, as told to them by the Third and Fourth Princesses, live on in their memories but any hope of a royal future died many, many years ago.

Appendix I

Timeline

HISTORIC

1752–1885	133 years of Konbaung rule
1824–26	First Anglo-Burmese war
1852–53	Second Anglo-Burmese war
1857	King Mindon shifts capital of Kingdom of Ava from Amarapura to Mandalay
1866	Rebellion staged by two of King Mindon's sons; attempt made on King Mindon's life; Crown Prince Kanaung killed
15 September 1878	Thibaw declared heir-apparent
1 October 1878	Death of King Mindon
1878–85	Thibaw—king of the Kingdom of Ava
November 1878	Supayalat becomes queen
15–17 February 1879	Massacre of royals
6 October 1879	British Resident withdrawn from Mandalay
December 1882	Burma rejects proposed treaty with Britain
August 1883	King Thibaw's representatives arrive in France
September 1884	Mandalay jailbreak massacre
15 January 1885	France–Burma treaty is signed
May 1885	Bonvillian returns to Mandalay with a young French wife

June/July 1885	Proof of Mandalay's agreements with the French reaches British hands
August 1885	Hluttaw rejects the Bombay-Burma Trading Company's appeal; levies a large fine on it
3 October 1885	Mandalay refuses arbitration in Bombay-Burma Trading Company case
22 October 1885	Date of British ultimatum to King Thibaw
31 October–1 November 1885	Ultimatum discussed in Hluttaw
7 November 1885	King Thibaw issues a proclamation to all his subjects announcing the impending war
14 November 1885	Third Anglo-Burmese war commences
28 November 1885	The British flotilla arrives in Mandalay, and King Thibaw informally surrenders to Colonel Sladen
29 November 1885	King Thibaw formally surrenders to General Prendergast; the king and his family are put on a steamer sailing for Rangoon
1 January 1886	Proclamation announcing Burma as part of the British Empire is issued
12 February 1886	Lord Dufferin's ignominious reception by the Hluttaw
13 February 1886	Lord Dufferin recommends annexation of Burma
26 February 1886	Upper Burma is made part of the Indian Empire
16 December 1916	Death of King Thibaw in Ratnagiri
18 April 1919	Queen Supayalat and family arrive in Rangoon
1 April 1937	British Burma is separated from British India
1942–45	Japanese occupation of Burma
August 1943	Japan ostensibly gives Burma her independence
March 1945	Bogyoke Aung Sang leads a rebellion against the Japanese
March 1945	The Golden Palace, Mandalay, is shelled and destroyed by the Allies (as it had been occupied by the Japanese)

May 1945	The Japanese are driven out of Burma; Britain reoccupies Burma
January 1947	Aung San–Attlee Agreement signed
April 1947	Bogyoke Aung San's party (AFPFL) wins a resounding victory
19 July 1947	Bogyoke Aung San and some of his cabinet ministers are assassinated
4 January 1948	Burma gains her independence from Britain; U Nu becomes the first prime minister of independent Burma
March 1948	Lion Throne (the one from the Hluttaw) returned to Burma
1958–60	The Ne Win caretaker government in power
1959	Centennial celebrations of the formation of Mandalay
2 March 1962	Military coup in Burma led by General Ne Win
November 1964	The British government hands over the Mandalay Regalia to General Ne Win
8 August 1988	8.8.88 uprising in Burma
May 1990	Aung San Suu Kyi's National League for Democracy wins Burmese elections; the military refuses to relinquish its power
November 2005	Capital of Burma shifted from Yangon (Rangoon) to Naypyidaw
September 2007	Saffron revolution in Burma
May 2008	The devastating typhoon, Nargis, hits Burma; national referendum held for a new constitution
May 2009	The 150th year anniversary celebrations of the founding of Mandalay
November 2010	General elections in Burma
March 2011	A new 'civilian' government installed with Thein Sein as president
April 2012	By-elections for parliament held; Aung San Suu Kyi wins a seat (her party, National League for Democracy, wins forty-three of the forty-five seats contested)

FAMILY

Part I: Before the Exile

I January 1859	Birth of Thibaw
13 December 1859	Birth of Supayalat
9 September 1879	Queen Supayalat gives birth to a son and possible heir; he dies six months later
5 September 1880	Queen Supayalat gives birth to a daughter—the First Princess
Mid-1881	King Thibaw's involvement with Mi Khingyi
11 August 1881	Queen Supayalat gives birth to a daughter—the Second Princess
March 1882	Yanaung is murdered
April 1882	Mi Khingyi is killed
March 1884	Sinbyumashin conspires to marry her youngest daughter, Supayagalae, to the Myngun Prince, and have King Thibaw overthrown
March/April 1884	King Thibaw takes Supayagalae as wife
24 November 1885	British shelling of Myingyan, the sound of which is heard by Queen Supayalat in Mandalay
28 November 1885	The British arrive in Mandalay; King Thibaw surrenders to Colonel Sladen
29 November 1885	King Thibaw formally surrenders to General Prendergast; the king and his family are put on a steamer sailing for Rangoon

Part II: During the Exile

5 December 1885	The royal family arrives in Rangoon
10 December 1885	The royal family sails for Madras, India
14 December 1885	The royal family arrives in Madras
7 March 1886	Queen Supayalat gives birth to a daughter—the Third Princess
10 April 1886	The royal family leaves for Ratnagiri
16 April 1886	The royal family arrives in Ratnagiri

25 April 1887	Queen Supayalat gives birth to a daughter—the Fourth Princess
22 June 1888	Sinbyumashin and Supayagyi arrive in Ratnagiri
January 1890	Supayagyi returns to Burma
Early 1891	Sinbyumashin returns to Burma
Mid-1892	King Thibaw hires a solicitor, Mr Edgelow
October 1895	Ex-King Thebaw's Act passed
1 January 1896	King Thibaw is permitted to manage his own household
Mid-1898	All King Thibaw's assets now belong to the government
27 February 1900	Sinbyumashin passes away in Rangoon
Early 1900s	Queen Supayalat's mental and physical health deteriorates
August 1906	King Thibaw's allowance increased to Rs 100,000 a year (including contribution to Reserve Fund)
26 November 1906	Birth of Tu Tu (the First Princess and Gopal Bhaurao Sawant's daughter)
1906	The government for the first time raises the question of the princesses' marriage with the king
June 1907	The government sanctions Rs 125,711 for the construction of a home for the royal family
November 1910	The Royal Residence in Ratnagiri is occupied; housewarming ceremony is held
28 June 1912	Death of Queen Supayagalae
5 March 1914	Earboring ceremony of the princesses
12 October 1916	The Second Princess runs away from the Royal Residence
16 December 1916	Death of King Thibaw
5 February 1917	Funeral ceremony of King Thibaw; temporary entombment in Royal Residence compound
20 February 1917	Marriage of the Second Princess to Kin Maung Lat (later known as Latthakin)
February 1918	Royal family's pension significantly reduced

September 1918	Government of British Burma agrees to take back, for the present, only the First and Third Princesses
November 1918	Shortly after the end of World War I, the government of British Burma gives its permission for the royal family to return to Burma
15 January 1919	The queen petitions the viceroy of India that he allow it to be publicly announced in India and Burma that the Fourth Princess is the head of the family
January 1919	The government of British Burma refuses permission for the mortal remains of King Thibaw and Queen Supayagalae to be brought back to Burma
14 February 1919	The government attempts to open King Thibaw and Queen Supayagalae's coffins
March 1919	The government of British Burma indicates that the family cannot return to Burma unless they agree to the permanent entombment of King Thibaw and Queen Supayagalae's remains in Ratnagiri
15 March 1919	The Queen and the Fourth Princess agree to the permanent entombment of King Thibaw's and Queen Supayagalae's remains in Ratnagiri
19 March 1919	Entombment of King Thibaw and Queen Supayagalae's mortal remains
1 April 1919	The government of British Burma wires permission that the royal family can now be permitted to leave for Burma.

Part III: After the Exile

10 April 1919	Queen Supayalat and family leave Ratnagiri
18 April 1919	The royal family arrives in Rangoon
1 March 1920	The Second Princess and Latthakin leave Calcutta to settle in Kalimpong
29 June 1920	The First Princess and her daughter Tu Tu leave Rangoon to settle in Ratnagiri

1 July 1920	The Fourth Princess marries Ko Ko Naing
1921	The Third Princess elopes and marries Prince Hteik Tin Kodaw Gyi
6 May 1922	The Fourth Princess's first child born—Prince Taw Phaya Gyi
5 April 1923	The Fourth Princess's second child born—Princess Hteik Su Phaya Gyi
22 March 1924	The Fourth Princess's third child born—Prince Taw Phaya
20 May 1924	The Third Princess's daughter born—Princess Rita
17 July 1925	The Fourth Princess's fourth child born—Prince Taw Phaya Nge
24 November 1925	Death of Queen Supayalat in Rangoon
17 December 1925	Queen Supayalat entombed; day declared a national holiday by the government
30 July 1926	The Fourth Princess's fifth child born—Prince Taw Phaya Galae
Late 1926 or early 1927	The Third Princess and family shift to Mandalay
20 August 1927	The Fourth Princess's sixth child born—Princess Hteik Su Phaya Htwe
Late 1927 or early 1928	The Fourth Princess and family shift to Mandalay
Late 1928 or early 1929	The Third Princess and family shift to Maymyo
1929	The Third Princess's marriage unravels; the government banishes her husband, Prince Hteik Tin Kodaw Gyi from Maymyo
1930	The Third Princess divorces her husband, Prince Hteik Tin Kodaw Gyi
1930	Tu Tu (the First Princess's daughter) marries Shankar Yeshwant Pawar
1931	The Third Princess marries U Mya U
1930 and 1931	The Fourth Princess writes letters to the government of British Burma, India and England asking for the return of her father's kingdom
28 January 1932	Maung Lu Gyi born to Jaiman and

	Satyamaya, and adopted by the Second Princess and Latthakin
May 1932	The Fourth Princess and family leave for their exile to Moulmein
3 March 1936	Death of the Fourth Princess in Moulmein
1 May 1938	Earboring ceremony of Princess Rita (the Third Princess's daughter)
October 1938	Journalist from Burma visits the First Princess
1940	Journalist who visited the First Princess in 1938 visits her again
April 1940	Political Pension Act comes into force entitling each grandchild of King Thibaw's (over eighteen years of age) to Rs 600 per month (no pension is ever given to the First Princess's daughter or to the Second Princess's adopted son)
1942–46	The Third Princess lives in Sagaing (during Japanese occupation of Burma)
July 1943	U Mya U (the Third Princess's second husband) passes away
4 May 1944	Prince Taw Phaya (the Fourth Princess's son) and Princess Rita (the Third Princess's daughter) marry
3 June 1947	Death of the First Princess
4 January 1948	Burma gains her independence; royal family's pension is stopped (except the Third Princess's)
12 April 1948	The Fourth Princess's son, Prince Taw Phaya Gyi, is killed by communists
1948	Prince Taw Phaya Galae (the Fourth Princess's son) starts Thibaw Commercial Syndicate Co. Ltd in Rangoon
1951	Gratuity Law for the Royal Relatives passed (only the Third Princess now qualifies for pension)
10 January 1955	The Second Princess's husband, Latthakin, passes away
March 1956	The Second Princess leaves Kalimpong to return to Burma via Calcutta

4 April 1956	Death of the Second Princess in Calcutta; funeral held on the same day
Late 1958	The Fourth Princesses' sons start the Association for Buddhism as the National Religion
September 1959	Death of the Fourth Princess's husband, Ko Ko Naing
2 March 1962	Military coup in Burma followed by nationalization of all private businesses including Thibaw Commercial Syndicate Co. Ltd
21 July 1962	Death of the Third Princess
7 September 1972	The First Princess's companion, Gopal Bhaurao Sawant (Shivrekar), dies
1976	Tu Tu's husband, Shankar Pawar, passes away
13 December 1993	Tharanagaon ceremony for King Thibaw is performed in Ratnagiri
21 April 1995	Prince Taw Phaya Nge (the Fourth Princess's son) passes away
24 October 2000	Tu Tu (the First Princess's daughter) passes away
27 November 2002	Princess Rita (the Third Princess's daughter) dies of a heart thrombosis
21 June 2003	Princess Hteik Su Phaya Htwe (the Fourth Princess's daughter) passes away of cerebral haemorrhage
18 June 2006	Prince Taw Phaya Galae (the Fourth Princess's son) passes away
25 February 2008	Maung Lu Gyi (the Second Princess's son) hands over the Second Princess's ashes for entombment in his mother's tomb
October 2008	Princess Hteik Su Phaya Gyi's youngest son, Aung Khin, dies
19 November 2008	The Second Princess's ashes entombed in Queen Supayalat's tomb
18 December 2008	Maung Lu Gyi (the Second Princess's son) passes away

APPENDIX II

LETTERS, DIARY ENTRIES AND AN INVITATION

အလှူရှိများ ကနည်း လမ်းအတိုင်း ပို့ဆောရန်

 သုံ့ပိုင်အုပ် ရွှေ်မင်းသီဆော ရှင်မှာ မန္တလေး မှာ တပါ၊ တညင့်ရှိသော ကျွနုပ်အဂဲမ
တော်ဘညှ် မတ်လ ၊ ၁ ၊ ရက်နေ့ ကနတ်ကွန်ဘဘညှ်ဖြစ် ၊ ၁၅ ၊ ရက်မှာ အဖြိုတော်
မျ ဖြညှ် ကျွနုပ် တိုဖြဏ္ဍ မဖ်းတိုဖ္ဂ နရည်းလမ်းတုံးခံမှာ တက်နိုင်အင်္ဂါ ကျူဇ္ဇ
တောက်ပန်ဖြ ဖြစ်ပါသညှ် ကျွနုပ်အဲညှ် ဝွာ လရည်း မတ္တား နှိုင်တွေ့ လရည်းမတွေ့
နှိုလရည် ကိုဝမ်း နရည်းလျသညှ် ပှ္ကျွနုပ်ဖြ အဂဲမတော်ဘသညှ်လမ် ဆုံးသွားပြိ
ဖြစ်၍ လက်ကျန်ဒွ္ဇ က ဒွေ ၅ဝဝ၀ ထုပ်ကြ ဂျ လှ္ပါ ဘညှ်အကြောင်း ကျွနုပ်
ကျူဇ္ဇ ရှုဘ္ပ်ကြောင်း ကြေားနန် အဲ များ ပဒ်ရ ကြောင်း အ ရုရှိ အသိ ပဖြစ်၍ ခံလှ္
လောက်ဆ သာလ စရည်ဒွ္ဇတော်က လ တိုင်း နှုပ်ရဲ့ဘဲရ ဖြနျှ် ကျနဒွ္ဇ နဖို့ဇ္ဂို
နန်တော်ဂြိုး ဇ္ဇသာ ရှ်ဖလံ လောက်သညှ် ကိုင့်ဘသညှ်ဖြစ်၍ မဆျမ်း မသာခ်နေ ရ မည်
အပြ္ဇ ကျ လရည် တစ်ခ ရဘာ ရှ်တော့ လသညှ် ထိုကြောင် လ စရည် ဒွေ တော်က မ နိုင်
ဘ ဒွေ ၅ဝဝဝ ထုပ်ကိုဆို ဂြ ဖြို ပ ရည်ဇ္ဇ ကြောင်း ကြာ လိုက်သညှ်

ဗြင်္သ ရှုပ် ဇ္ဇ်

Letter signed by King Thibaw in March 1911 requesting for Rs 5,000 from the Reserve Fund as his contribution towards his sister's funeral. PD 1911, no. 198, p. 415, The Maharashtra State Archives, Mumbai.

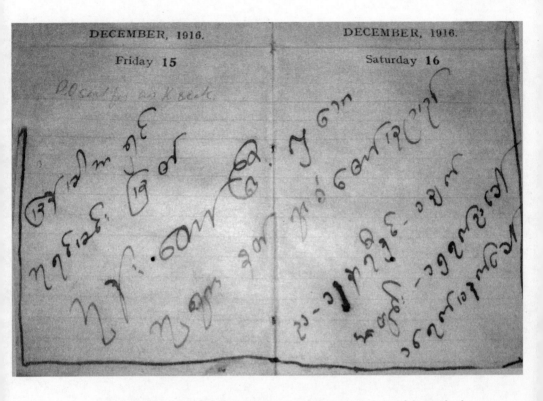

Diary entry made by Kin Maung Lat (Latthakin) upon King Thibaw's death.
Translation: Our great Burmese Majesty passed away between midnight and 1 a.m. on
15th night/16th morning. Courtesy Kamal Chandarana (Gulabi).

Palace
Ratnagiri
25th Feb 1919

1) I understand all that was said
by Mr Brendon yesterday about bringing
Poongyis, band, and umbrellas from
Burma. I refuse the Poongyis, on
arrival, to intomb the coffins, if
that is still the determination.
I refuse to give up the key of my
husband's tomb.

(2) I solemnly affirm that the body
of my husband and my sister
are in the coffins which are in
the tomb in the Palace compound
in Ratnagiri.

(& Queen's signature

Ashin Thisu Myat Payaglay
the IV Princess

Received today.
B A Brendon
nagiri
5th Feb 1919.   Collector of Ratnagiri

*Letter dated 25 February 1919 signed by Queen Supayalat and the Fourth Princess.
PD 2093-II/1920, p. M207, The Maharashtra State Archives, Mumbai.*

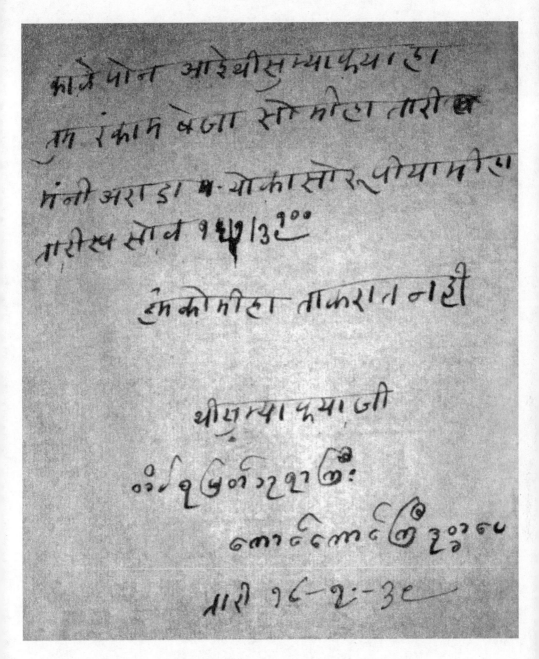

The last page from a letter the First Princess wrote to the Second Princess in 1939.
Courtesy Kamal Chandarana (Gulabi).

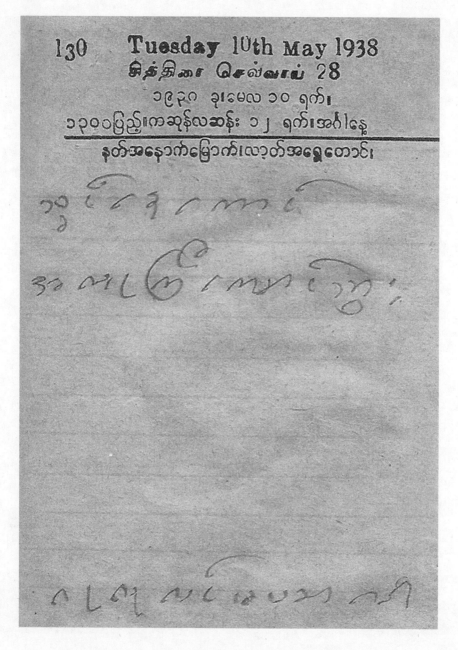

A page from a 1938 diary belonging to the Second Princess. Translation: Thakin is fine.
A Lu Gyi (Maung Lu Gyi) went to school. Gulu (?) couple came over.
Courtesy Kamal Chandarana (Gulabi).

Ashin Hteik Su Myat Paya
(Her Highness the Third Princess of Burma)
and
U Mya U, F.R.G.S. Bar-at-Law

request the pleasure of the Company of

Ashin Hteik Su Myat Paya Lat + K. M. Lat Thakin.

at the Ear-boring Ceremony of their daughter

Hteik Su Gyi Paya (Princess Rita)

at their residence, Maymyo

on Sunday, the 1st May, 1938

at 11 a.m

Refreshments
and
Musical Entertainments.

*Invitation for Princess Rita's earboring ceremony sent by the Third Princess to
the Second Princess in 1938. Courtesy Kamal Chandarana (Gulabi).*

APPENDIX III

FLOOR PLANS, RATNAGIRI

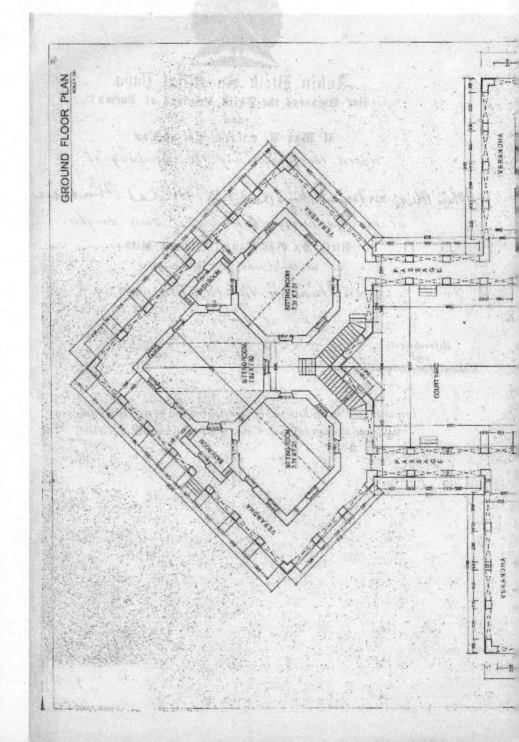

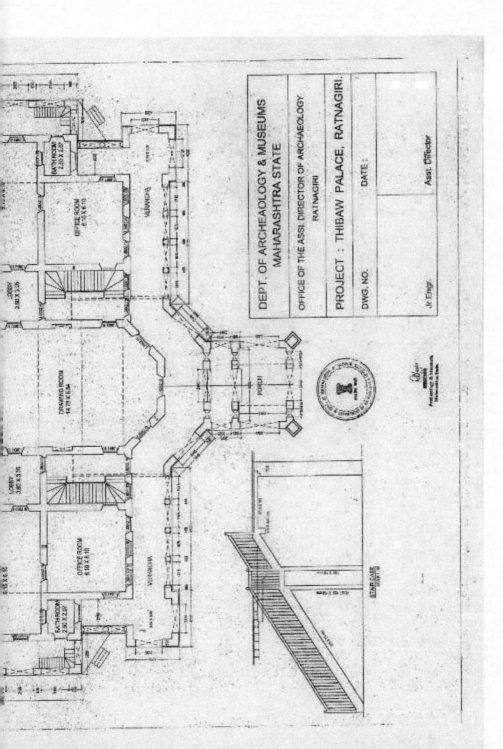

DEPT. OF ARCHAEOLOGY & MUSEUMS
MAHARASHTRA STATE

OFFICE OF THE ASSI DIRECTOR OF ARCHAEOLOGY
RATNAGIRI

PROJECT : THIBAW PALACE, RATNAGIRI.

DWG. NO.   DATE :

Jr. Engr.   Assi. Director

Floor plan of the ground floor of the Royal Residence, Ratnagiri. Courtesy Directorate of Archaeology and Museums, Maharashtra, Mumbai.

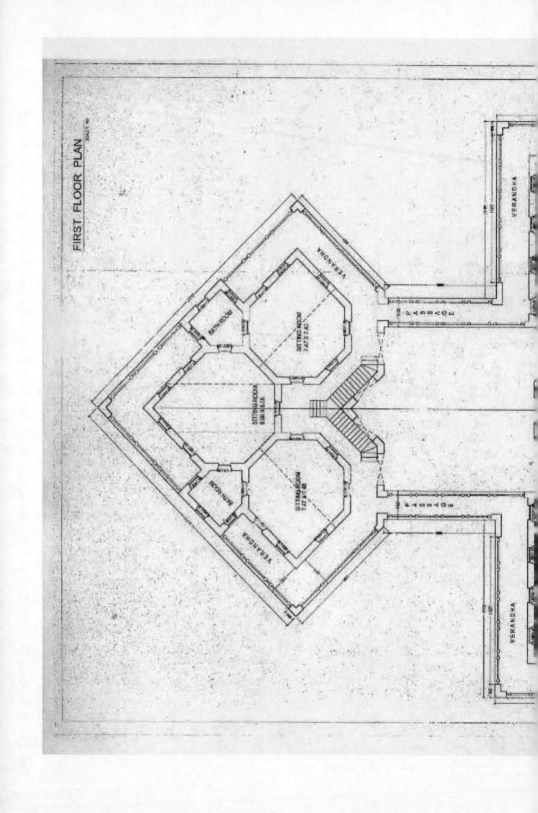

FIRST FLOOR PLAN

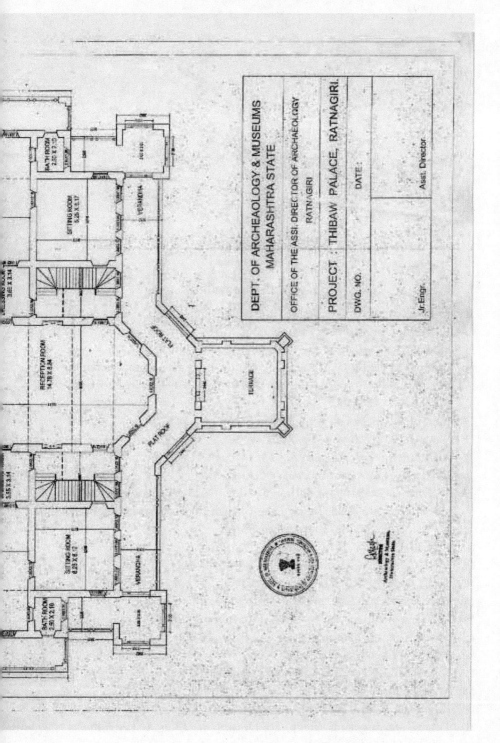

Floor plan of the first floor of the Royal Residence, Ratnagiri. Courtesy Directorate of Archaeology and Museums, Maharashtra, Mumbai.

NOTES

PART I: BEFORE THE EXILE

1. Thibaw and Supayalat

1. F. Tennyson Jesse, *The Lacquer Lady*, pp. 85–86.
2. E.C.V. Foucar, *Mandalay the Golden*, pp. 50–51.
3. Shway Yoe, *The Burman*, p. 458.
4. Princess Hteik Su Gyi Phaya's (Rita) letters to Mr Symington dated 22 December 1970 and 23 March 1971, British Library, London, MSS Eur D 1156/7.
5. John Ebenezer Marks, *Forty Years in Burma*, pp. 218–19.
6. Shway Yoe, *The Burman*, pp. 467–48.
7. Marks, *Forty Years in Burma*, p. 224.
8. Jesse, *The Lacquer Lady*, pp. 105–06.
9. U Than Swe's letter to author dated 12 May 2007, translated for author from the Burmese into the English by Than Htay; interview with U Than Swe on 2 December 2006.
10. Ibid.
11. Interview with U Than Swe on 2 December 2006.
12. Ibid.
13. Jesse, *The Lacquer Lady*, pp. 108–09.
14. Interview with U Than Swe on 2 December 2006.
15. Shway Yoe, *The Burman*, p. 456.
16. Jesse, *The Lacquer Lady*, p. 119.
17. C.L. Keeton, *King Thebaw and the Ecological Rape of Burma*, p. 19.
18. W.S. Desai, *Deposed King Thibaw of Burma in India, 1885–1916*, p. 2.
19. 'Mindon's Heirs', *The Nation* supplement, 26 August 1962.
20. Foucar, *Mandalay the Golden*, p. 86; Desai, *Deposed King Thibaw of Burma in India, 1885–1916*, p. 2.

21. H. Fielding, *Thibaw's Queen*, pp. 38–39.

22. Foucar, *Mandalay the Golden*, pp. 87–88.

23. Ibid., pp. 89–90; interview with U Than Swe on 2 December 2006.

24. Foucar, *Mandalay the Golden*, pp. 89–90.

25. Paul J. Bennett, *Conference under the Tamarind Tree: Three Essays in Burmese History*, p. 75.

26. Maung Htin Aung, *The Stricken Peacock: An Account of Anglo-Burmese Relations 1752–1948*, pp. 68–69.

27. Keeton, *King Thebaw and the Ecological Rape of Burma*, p. 21.

28. Foucar, *Mandalay the Golden*, p. 91.

29. Jesse, *The Lacquer Lady*, pp. 124–25.

30. Bennett, *Conference under the Tamarind Tree*, pp. 74–75.

31. Foucar, *Mandalay the Golden*, pp. 95–96.

32. 'Mandalay in 1878–9: The Letters of James Alfred Colbeck, Originally Selected and Edited by George H. Colbeck in 1892', SOAS Bulletin of Burma Research, vol. 1, no.2, Autumn 2003, ISSN 1479–8484, pp. 69–73.

33. Ibid.

34. Than Tun, ed., *The Royal Orders of Burma, A.D. 1598–1885*, vol. 9, A.D. 1853–85, pp. 237–40.

35. Ibid.

36. Shway Yoe, *The Burman*, p. 466.

37. Fielding, *Thibaw's Queen*, p. 39.

38. Jesse, *The Lacquer Lady*, pp. 135–36.

39. Fielding, *Thibaw's Queen*, pp. 30–31.

40. *Mandalay Palace*, The Directorate of Archaeological Survey, Ministry of Union Culture, Revolutionary Government of the Union of Burma, 1963, p. 14.

41. Shway Yoe, *The Burman*, pp. 466–67.

42. Jesse, *The Lacquer Lady*, p. 138.

43. Ibid., pp. 146–57.

44. Fielding, *Thibaw's Queen*, pp. 44–45.

45. Michael Charney's email to author dated 9 November 2010.

46. Jesse, *The Lacquer Lady*, p. 157.

47. Fielding, *Thibaw's Queen*, p. 46.

48. Marks, *Forty Years in Burma*, p. 136.

49. Interview with U Than Swe on 24 November 2006.

50. Mi Mi Khaing, *Burmese Family*, p. 74.

51. Jesse, *The Lacquer Lady*, pp. 158–59.

52. Ibid., pp. 160–02.

53. Keeton, *King Thebaw and the Ecological Rape of Burma*, p. 93; 'Mandalay in 1878–9: The Letters of James Alfred Colbeck, Originally Selected and Edited by George H. Colbeck in 1892', SOAS Bulletin of Burma Research, vol. I, no. 2, Autumn 2003, p. 77.

54. U Than Swe's letter to author dated 30 December 2007; U Than Swe, *Records of the Royal Audiences*, ch. 9, translated for author from the Burmese into the English by Than Htay. (References: Bayluwa Saya Tin, 'A Genius in Burmese Orchestra' and 'Gitalinkaradipani or Basic Music'; U Maung Maung Tin, *Konbaung Chronicles*, vol. 3.)

2. First Year of the Reign

1. Terence R. Blackburn, *The British Humiliation of Burma*, p. 86.
2. Keeton, *King Thebaw and the Ecological Rape of Burma,* p. 18.
3. Thant Myint-U, *The Making of Modern Burma*, pp. 157–58 (KBZ, vol. 3, pp. 570–79; MMOS, vol. 2, pp. 241–46); Bennett, *Conference under the Tamarind Tree*, pp. 76–77.
4. Michael W. Charney, *Powerful Learning*, p. 243.
5. Thant Myint-U, *The Making of Modern Burma*, pp. 159–60 (MMOS, vol. 2, pp. 251–52).
6. Foucar, *Mandalay the Golden*, p. 100.
7. Jesse, *The Lacquer Lady*, p. 240.
8. Bennett, *Conference under the Tamarind Tree*, p. 77.
9. Keeton, *King Thebaw and the Ecological Rape of Burma*, p. 27.
10. Charney, *Powerful Learning*, p. 244.
11. Bennett, *Conference under the Tamarind Tree*, p. 81.
12. Fielding, *Thibaw's Queen*, p. 55.
13. Marks, *Forty Years in Burma*, p. 295.
14. Interview with U Sein Maung Oo on 21 November 2006.
15. V.C. Scott O'Connor, *Mandalay and Other Cities of the Past in Burma*, p. 22.
16. Interview with U Sein Maung Oo on 21 November 2006.
17. Foucar, *Mandalay the Golden*, pp. 107–09
18. Fielding, *Thibaw's Queen*, p. 49.
19. Interview with U Than Swe on 24 November 2006.
20. Keeton, *King Thebaw and the Ecological Rape of Burma*, pp. 28–30; Foucar, *Mandalay the Golden*, p. 109.
21. Interview with U Than Swe on 2 December 2006; Thant Myint-U, *The Making of Modern Burma*, p. 161 (KBZ, vol. 3, pp. 505–10).
22. Jesse, *The Lacquer Lady*, pp. 184–85.

23. Foucar, *Mandalay the Golden*, pp. 111–12.

24. Thant Myint-U, *The Making of Modern Burma*, p. 162.

25. Maung Htin Aung, *The Stricken Peacock*, pp. 57, 70–71.

26. Keeton, *King Thebaw and the Ecological Rape of Burma*, pp. 23–25.

27. Thant Myint-U, *The Making of Modern Burma*, p. 162.

28. Maung Htin Aung, *The Stricken Peacock*, pp. 72–73.

29. Foucar, *Mandalay the Golden*, pp. 114–15.

30. Jesse, *The Lacquer Lady*, p. 266.

31. Kirkman Finlay, *An Account of a Journey from Rangoon by Train and Steamer to Mandalay* (a handwritten journal), MS/380016, SOAS Library, London.

32. Keeton, *King Thebaw and the Ecological Rape of Burma*, p. 27.

33. Blackburn, *The British Humiliation of Burma*, p. 83.

34. Keeton, *King Thebaw and the Ecological Rape of Burma*, p. 49.

3. Life at the Palace

1. *Mandalay Palace*, The Directorate of Archaeological Survey, Ministry of Union Culture, Revolutionary Government of the Union of Burma, 1963, p. 31.

2. Ibid., p. 13.

3. Shway Yoe, *The Burman*, p. 481; *Mandalay Palace*, The Directorate of Archaeological Survey, Ministry of Union Culture, Revolutionary Government of the Union of Burma, 1963, pp. 19–20.

4. Charney, *Powerful Learning*, p. 249; Elizabeth Moore, 'The Reconstruction of Mandalay Palace: An Interim Report on Aspects of Design', Bulletin of the SOAS, vol. 56, no. 2, p. 348.

5. *Mandalay Palace*, The Directorate of Archaeological Survey, Ministry of Union Culture, Revolutionary Government of the Union of Burma, 1963, pp. 10, 17–18.

6. Ibid., pp. 10, 22.

7. Ibid., p. 9.

8. Shway Yoe, *The Burman*, pp. 529–47.

9. George Orwell, *Burmese Days*, p. 296.

10. O'Connor, *Mandalay and Other Cities of the Past in Burma*, p. 84.

11. *Mandalay Palace*, The Directorate of Archaeological Survey, Ministry of Union Culture, Revolutionary Government of the Union of Burma, 1963, p. 24.

12. Ibid., pp. 12, 25–27.

13. Interview with U Than Swe on 24 November 2006.

14. *Mandalay Palace*, The Directorate of Archaeological Survey, Ministry of Union Culture, Revolutionary Government of the Union of Burma, 1963, pp. 24–27, 33–34.
15. Ibid., pp. 28–33.
16. Fielding, *Thibaw's Queen*; Jesse, *The Lacquer Lady*.
17. *Mandalay Palace*, The Directorate of Archaeological Survey, Ministry of Union Culture, Revolutionary Government of the Union of Burma, 1963, pp. 29-30.
18. Interview with U Sein Maung Oo on 21 November 2006; interview with U Than Swe on 24 November 2006.
19. *Mandalay Palace*, The Directorate of Archaeological Survey, Ministry of Union Culture, Revolutionary Government of the Union of Burma, 1963, p. 30.
20. Ibid., p. 25.
21. Fielding, *Thibaw's Queen*, pp. 19, 65–66.
22. 'The War in Upper Burmah', *The Times of India*, 19 December 1885.
23. *Mandalay Palace*, The Directorate of Archaeological Survey, Ministry of Union Culture, Revolutionary Government of the Union of Burma, 1963, pp. 21–23.
24. Interview with U Than Swe on 24 November 2006.
25. Shway Yoe, *The Burman*, p. 286.
26. Fielding, *Thibaw's Queen*, pp. 71–72.
27. Shway Yoe, *The Burman*, pp. 286–309.
28. Jesse, *The Lacquer Lady*, pp. 173, 310.
29. Shway Yoe, *The Burman*, pp. 70–71.
30. Fielding, *Thibaw's Queen*, pp. 72–73.
31. Jesse, *The Lacquer Lady*, pp. 263–66.
32. 'The Queen of Burmah', *The New York Times*, 21 May 1882 (reproduced from *Fraser's Magazine*).
33. Fielding, *Thibaw's Queen*, pp. 60–63.
34. 'Royal Palace of Mandalay', *The New York Times*, 4 June 1882 (reproduced from *Fraser's Magazine*).
35. Princess Hteik Su Gyi Phaya's (Rita) letter to Mr Symington dated 22 December 1970, British Library, London, MSS Eur D 1156/7.
36. Jesse, *The Lacquer Lady*, pp. 234–35.
37. Fielding, *Thibaw's Queen*, pp. 206–07.
38. Shway Yoe, *The Burman*, p. 467.
39. Foucar, *Mandalay the Golden*, pp. 28, 128.
40. Ibid., pp. 33, 236.
41. Ibid., p. 39.

42. Shway Yoe, *The Burman*, p. 464.

43. Fielding, *Thibaw's Queen*, pp. 97–98.

44. U Sein Maung Oo's letter to author dated 13 October 2005.

45. Interview with Princess Hteik Su Phaya Gyi on 26 February 2005; Jesse, *The Lacquer Lady*, p. 140 (quotation).

46. Foucar, *Mandalay the Golden*, p. 67.

47. Interview with U Than Swe on 2 December 2006.

48. Jesse, *The Lacquer Lady*, p. 267.

49. Fielding, *Thibaw's Queen*, p. 94.

50. Ibid., p. 93; interview with Princess Hteik Su Phaya Gyi on 26 February 2005; Jesse, *The Lacquer Lady*, pp. 174, 266.

51. Fielding, *Thibaw's Queen*, pp. 96–97.

52. Interview with Prince Taw Phaya on 30 November 2006 .

53. Interview with Prince Taw Phaya Galae on 27 February 2005; telephone conversation with U Than Swe in February 2009.

54. Shway Yoe, *The Burman*, p. 593; interview with U Sein Maung Oo on 15 February 2009.

55. Fielding, *Thibaw's Queen*, p. 69.

56. Thant Myint-U, *The Making of Modern Burma*, pp. 170–71.

57. Fielding, *Thibaw's Queen*, p. 96.

4. Supayalat, the Queen

1. Thant Myint-U, *The Making of Modern Burma*, pp. 75, 171–76.

2. Foucar, *Mandalay the Golden*, p. 122.

3. Thant Myint-U, *The Making of Modern Burma*, pp. 171, 107 , 142–44.

4. Mi Mi Khaing, *Burmese Family*, p. 86.

5. Thant Myint-U, *The Making of Modern Burma*, p. 163.

6. Charney, *Powerful Learning*, p. 251.

7. Ibid., p. 45. (Koenig, *Burmese Polity*, p. 91.)

8. *Mandalay Palace*, The Directorate of Archaeological Survey, Ministry of Union Culture, Revolutionary Government of the Union of Burma, 1963; Fielding, *Thibaw's Queen*; Jesse, *The Lacquer Lady*.

9. Fielding, *Thibaw's Queen*, p. 137.

10. Keeton, *King Thebaw and the Ecological Rape of Burma*, p. 109.

11. Ibid., p. 88.

12. U Than Swe's letter to author dated 3 May 2005; interview with U Than Swe on 26 February 2005.

13. Prince Taw Phaya 's letter to author dated 5 December 2007.

14. U Than Swe's letters to author dated 3 May 2005 (including

quotations) and 30 December 2007; Yi Yi, 'Life at the Burmese Court under Konbaung Kings', *Journal of the Burma Research Society (JBRS)*, vol. 44, pt 1, June 1961, pp. 89–99.

15. Desai, *Deposed King Thibaw of Burma in India, 1885–1916*, p. 94, fn. 1.
16. Keeton, *King Thebaw and the Ecological Rape of Burma*, p. 90.
17. Fielding, *Thibaw's Queen*, p. 110.
18. 'Some of Theebaw's Crimes', *The New York Times*, 14 May 1882 (reproduced from *London Daily News*).
19. Interview with U Than Swe on 24 November 2006.
20. Jesse, *The Lacquer Lady*, pp. 251–52; Foucar, *Mandalay the Golden*, p. 131.
21. Fielding, *Thibaw's Queen*, pp. 107–08.
22. Keeton, *King Thebaw and the Ecological Rape of Burma*, pp. 90–91. (J.G. Scott and J.P. Hardiman, *Gazetteer of Upper Burma and the Shan States*, pp. 87–88.)
23. Prince Taw Phaya's letter to author dated 5 December 2007.
24. Foucar, *Mandalay the Golden*, p. 132.
25. Jesse, *The Lacquer Lady*, p. 252.
26. Keeton, *King Thebaw and the Ecological Rape of Burma*, p. 91. (Scott and Hardiman, *Gazetteer of Upper Burma and the Shan States*, pp. 87–88.)
27. Interview with U Than Swe on 24 November 2006.
28. Fielding, *Thibaw's Queen*, pp. 80–81.
29. Ibid., p. 44.
30. Interview with Tin Maung Aye on 19 February 2009.
31. Jesse, *The Lacquer Lady*, p. 254.
32. Fielding, *Thibaw's Queen*, pp. 109–10.
33. Keeton, *King Thebaw and the Ecological Rape of Burma*, p. 92.
34. Jesse, *The Lacquer Lady*, p. 247.
35. Keeton, *King Thebaw and the Ecological Rape of Burma*, pp. 92–94. (Rawlings (?) to Bernard's secretary, 19 March 1882, nos 125–46, and 20 March 1882, nos 125–46, pp. 6–7.)
36. Ibid., p. 95.
37. Fielding, *Thibaw's Queen*, pp. 117–18.
38. Interview with Prince Taw Phaya on 20 February 2009.
39. Interview with Tin Maung Aye on 19 February 2009.
40. Fielding, *Thibaw's Queen*, pp. 120–21.
41. Interview with U Than Swe on 24 November 2006; O'Connor, *Mandalay and Other Cities of the Past in Burma*, p. 23.
42. Fielding, *Thibaw's Queen*, pp. 147–73.
43. U Than Swe's letter to author dated 30 December 2007.

44. Keeton, *King Thebaw and the Ecological Rape of Burma*, p. 131.
45. Fielding, *Thibaw's Queen*, pp. 185–92.
46. Ibid., p. 192.

5. Rumblings of War

1. Bernard Porter, *The Lion's Share: A Short History of British Imperialism, 1850–1995*, p. 136. (Faber, *The Vision and the Need: Late Victorian Imperialist Aims*, p. 64.)
2. Maung Htin Aung, *The Stricken Peacock*, p. 16. (W.S. Desai, *History of the British Residency in Burma, 1826–40*, p. 129.)
3. Shway Yoe, *The Burman*, p. 394.
4. Porter, *The Lion's Share*, p. 46.
5. Marks, *Forty Years in Burma*, p. 54.
6. Finlay, *Account of a Journey from Rangoon by Train and Steamer to Mandalay*; MS/380016, SOAS Library, London.
7. Thant Myint-U, *The Making of Modern Burma*, pp. 163–64.
8. Fielding, *Thibaw's Queen*, p. 7.
9. 'The Sun-descended King', *The New York Times*, 9 April 1880.
10. 'Mandalay Massacres: Upper Burma during the Reign of King Theebaw', *Rangoon Gazette Press*, April 1884, p. 19, British Library, London, MSS Eur E 290/18.
11. Blackburn, *The British Humiliation of Burma*, p. 82.
12. 'Theebaw's Wife and Baby', *The New York Times*, 25 November 1883 (from *The Times of India*).
13. 'Theebaw's Taxes', *The New York Times*, 21 May 1882 (Rangoon letter to the *London Daily News*).
14. 'Some of Theebaw's Crimes', *The New York Times*, 14 May 1882.
15. Interview with U Than Swe on 2 December 2006.
16. Maung Htin Aung, *The Stricken Peacock*, pp. 39–40. (Burney's letter dated 18 July 1838; cf. Dorothy Woodman, *The Making of Burma*, The Cresset Press, London, 1957, p. 115.)
17. Charney, *Powerful Learning*, pp. 181–82.
18. Keeton, *King Thebaw and the Ecological Rape of Burma*, p. 157.
19. Bennett, *Conference under the Tamarind Tree*, p. 57.
20. Alfred P.C. Lyall, *The Life of the Marquis of Dufferin and Ava*, pp. 397–98.
21. A.T.Q. Stewart, *The Pagoda War: Lord Dufferin and the Fall of the Kingdom of Ava*, p. 46.
22. Keeton, *King Thebaw and the Ecological Rape of Burma*, pp. 103–29.
23. Ibid., p. 129.

24. Interview with Prince Taw Phaya Galae on 27 February 2005 (including quotation); Keeton, *King Thebaw and the Ecological Rape of Burma*, p. 131; ('Rangoon' (Allahabad), *Pioneer Mail*, 9 January 1883, pp. 62–63.)

25. 'Mandalay Massacres: Upper Burma during the Reign of King Theebaw'; *Rangoon Gazette Press*, April 1884, British Library, London, MSS Eur E 290/18.

26. Keeton, *King Thebaw and the Ecological Rape of Burma*, pp. 134–35. ('The Mandalay Massacre', *The Times of India* (Bombay), 18 October 1884.)

27. Keeton, *King Thebaw and the Ecological Rape of Burma*, pp. 134–37. ('The Mandalay Massacre', *The Times of India* (Bombay), 18 October 1884 and 1 November 1884.)

28. Lyall, *The Life of the Marquis of Dufferin and Ava*, pp. 397–98.

29. Jesse, *The Lacquer Lady*, pp. 261, 281–84, 294–99.

30. Ibid., pp. 299–300.

31. Keeton, *King Thebaw and the Ecological Rape of Burma*, p. 173.

32. Ibid., p. 173.

33. Jesse, *The Lacquer Lady*, pp. 303–05.

34. Maung Htin Aung, *The Stricken Peacock*, p. 82.

35. Keeton, *King Thebaw and the Ecological Rape of Burma*, pp. 217–24.

36. Fielding, *Thibaw's Queen*, pp. 205–12.

37. FD 1886, Secret E Pros, August 1886, nos 528–52, no. 531, National Archives of India, New Delhi.

38. Desai, *Deposed King Thibaw of Burma in India, 1885–1916*, p. 112.

39. Maung Htin Aung, *The Stricken Peacock*, p. 87.

40. Desai, *Deposed King Thibaw of Burma in India, 1885–1916*, pp. 7–8, 115.

41. Keeton, *King Thebaw and the Ecological Rape of Burma*, p. 246. (Encl 4 in no. 158, Bernard to Kinwun, 22 October 1885; in C. 4614, pp. 252–54.)

42. Keeton, *King Thebaw and the Ecological Rape of Burma*, p. 242.

43. Ibid., p. 254. (General news column, *Englishman* (Calcutta), 18 November 1885, pp. 4–5.)

44. Jesse, *The Lacquer Lady*, p. 310.

45. Fielding, *Thibaw's Queen*, p. 223.

46. Keeton, *King Thebaw and the Ecological Rape of Burma*, p. 255.

47. Fielding, *Thibaw's Queen*, p. 225.

48. Jesse, *The Lacquer Lady*, p. 310.

49. Fielding, *Thibaw's Queen*, pp. 225–29 (including quotation); Keeton, *King Thebaw and the Ecological Rape of Burma*, p. 256.

50. Fielding, *Thibaw's Queen*, pp. 226–27; Keeton, *King Thebaw and the Ecological Rape of Burma*, p. 256

51. Fielding, *Thibaw's Queen*, pp. 226–27.

52. Jesse, *The Lacquer Lady*, p. 311.

53. Fielding, *Thibaw's Queen*, pp. 228–29.

54. Keeton, *King Thebaw and the Ecological Rape of Burma*, p. 257.

55. Fielding, *Thibaw's Queen*, p. 230.

56. 'Mandalay in 1878–9: The Letters of James Alfred Colbeck, Originally Selected and Edited by George H.Colbeck in 1892', SOAS Bulletin of Burma Research, vol. 1, no. 2, Autumn 2003, ISSN 1479-8484, p. 74.

57. Keeton, *King Thebaw and the Ecological Rape of Burma*, p. 256.

58. Fielding, *Thibaw's Queen*, pp. 230–31.

59. Jesse, *The Lacquer Lady*, pp. 311–12

60. H.R.H. The Fourth Princess, Daughter of the Late H.M. King Thi Baw and His Crowned Queen, *Private Affairs*, p. 5.

61. Fielding, *Thibaw's Queen*, pp. 229–33.

62. Jesse, *The Lacquer Lady*, p. 313.

63. Terence R. Blackburn, *Actors on the Burmese Stage: A Trilogy of the Anglo-Burmese Wars*, vol. 3, p. 65.

64. 'Interview with King Theebaw's Brother in Calcutta', *The Times of India*, 5 November 1885.

65. Fielding, *Thibaw's Queen*, pp. 235–39; Keeton, *King Thebaw and the Ecological Rape of Burma*, p. 258.

66. Fielding, *Thibaw's Queen*, pp. 236–41.

67. Jesse, *The Lacquer Lady*, p. 311.

68. Fielding, *Thibaw's Queen*, p. 241.

69. Keeton, *King Thebaw and the Ecological Rape of Burma*, p. 258.

70. Thant Myint-U, *The River of Lost Footsteps*, p. 17.

71. Keeton, *King Thebaw and the Ecological Rape of Burma*, pp. 261–64.

72. 'Last of the Burmese Kings, Mr Noyce Reminiscences', *New Burma*, 6 December 1935.

73. 'Interview with King Theebaw's Brother in Calcutta', *The Times of India*, 5 November 1885.

74. Desai, *Deposed King Thibaw of Burma in India, 1885–1916*, pp. 8, 117–18.

75. Keeton, *King Thebaw and the Ecological Rape of Burma*, p. 259. ('The Burma Crisis', *Englishman* (Calcutta), 9 November 1885, p. 4.)

6. The War and the Lies

1. Shway Yoe, *The Burman*, pp. 497–506; Fielding, *Thibaw's Queen*, p. 141.

2. Thant Myint-U, *The Making of Modern Burma*, p. 170.

3. Keeton, *King Thebaw and the Ecological Rape of Burma*, pp. 275–76.

4. Ibid., p. 275.

5. Foucar, *Mandalay the Golden*, p. 189.

6. Keeton, *King Thebaw and the Ecological Rape of Burma*, pp. 276–77.

7. Maung Htin Aung, *The Stricken Peacock*, pp. 89–90.

8. 'Burmah' (1886). 'Correspondence relating to BURMAH since the Accession of King Theebaw in October 1878: Presented to Both Houses of Parliament by Command of Her Majesty', Classmark EY/18342, SOAS Library, London, pp. 230–31.

9. Keeton, *King Thebaw and the Ecological Rape of Burma*, pp. 278–79.

10. 'The Burmese War', *The Times*, 1 December 1885.

11. Foucar, *Mandalay the Golden*, p. 193.

12. 'The Burmese War', *The Times*, 1 December 1885.

13. Shway Yoe, *The Burman*, p. 500.

14. Fielding, *Thibaw's Queen*, pp. 243–45.

15. Foucar, *Mandalay the Golden*, p. 183.

16. Fielding, *Thibaw's Queen*, pp. 262–63.

17. Foucar, *Mandalay the Golden*, p. 195.

18. Fielding, *Thibaw's Queen*, pp. 264–65.

19. Keeton, *King Thebaw and the Ecological Rape of Burma*, p. 281; Fielding, *Thibaw's Queen*, pp. 266–67.

20. Keeton, *King Thebaw and the Ecological Rape of Burma*, p. 282. (Grattan Geary, *Burma, After the Conquest*, pp. 214–16.)

21. Than Tun, ed., *The Royal Orders of Burma, A.D. 1598–1885*, vol. 9, A.D. 1853–85, p. 312.

22. Ibid.

23. 'The War in Upper Burmah', *The Times of India*, 19 December 1885.

24. Fielding, *Thibaw's Queen*, pp. 266–67.

25. Ibid., pp. 267–70.

26. Keeton, *King Thebaw and the Ecological Rape of Burma*, pp. 281–82.

27. Ibid., p. 282. (Geary, *Burma, After the Conquest*, pp. 214–16.)

28. Foucar, *Mandalay the Golden*, p. 200.

29. Keeton, *King Thebaw and the Ecological Rape of Burma*, p. 282.

30. 'The Burmese War', *The Times*, 2 December 1885.

31. Foucar, *Mandalay the Golden*, p. 200.

32. 'The Burmese War', *The Times*, 2 December 1885.

33. Ibid.

34. 'The War in Upper Burmah', *The Times of India*, 19 December 1885.

35. Keeton, *King Thebaw and the Ecological Rape of Burma*, p. 283. (H.E. Staton, *The Third Burmese War*, p. 31.)

36. Keeton, *King Thebaw and the Ecological Rape of Burma*, pp. 283–84. (Geary, *Burma, After the Conquest*, p. 217.)
37. 'The Burmese War', *The Times*, 2 December 1885.
38. Thant Myint-U, *The Making of Modern Burma*, p. 192. (Burma Military Procedings, no. 885.)
39. Keeton, *King Thebaw and the Ecological Rape of Burma*, p. 286. (F.T. Jesse, *The Story of Burma*, p. 75.)
40. 'The Burmese War', *The Times*, 2 December 1885.
41. Keeton, *King Thebaw and the Ecological Rape of Burma*, p. 284.
42. Ibid., pp. 277–78. (H.N.D. Prendergast, 'Burman Dacoity and Patriotism and Burman Politics', *Blackwood's Edinburgh Magazine* (Edinburgh), new series, vol. 5, January–April 1893, p. 276.)
43. Thant Myint-U, *The River of Lost Footsteps*, p. 19.

7. The Defeat and Exile

1. 'The War in Upper Burmah', *The Times of India*, 19 December 1885.
2. Foucar, *Mandalay the Golden*, p. 205.
3. 'The Burmese War', *The Times*, 4 December 1885
4. 'The War in Upper Burmah', *The Times of India*, 19 December 1885.
5. Blackburn, *The British Humiliation of Burma*, p. 101.
6. Fielding, *Thibaw's Queen*, pp. 282–84.
7. Ibid., pp. 284–86.
8. Foucar, *Mandalay the Golden*, p. 206.
9. Fielding, *Thibaw's Queen*, pp. 186–87.
10. 'The War in Upper Burmah', *The Times of India*, 19 December 1885; FD 1886, Secret E Pros, August 1886, nos 528–52, no. 531, National Archives of India, New Delhi.
11. 'The Burmese War', *The Times*, 4 December 1885.
12. Edmond Charles Browne, *The Coming of the Great Queen: A Narrative of the Acquisition of Burma*, pp. 175–76.
13. Fielding, *Thibaw's Queen*, pp. 287–88.
14. FD 1886, Secret E Pros, August 1886, nos 528–52, no. 531, National Archives of India, New Delhi.
15. Foucar, *Mandalay the Golden*, pp. 208–09.
16. 'The Burmese War', *The Times*, 4 December 1885.
17. Sladen Collection, British Library, London, MSS Eur E 290/65 (Rough 1885 Diary kept by Colonel Sladen).
18. Keeton, *King Thebaw and the Ecological Rape of Burma*, p. 287. ('The War in Burma', *Englishman* (Calcutta), 4 December 1885.)

19. 'The Burmese War', *The Times*, 4 December 1885.

20. FD 1886, Secret E Pros, August 1886, nos 528–52, no. 531, National Archives of India, New Delhi.

21. Browne, *The Coming of the Great Queen*, p. 176.

22. 'Interview with King Theebaw's Brother in Calcutta', *The Times of India*, 5 November 1885.

23. 'The War in Upper Burmah', *The Times of India*, 19 December 1885.

24. 'The Burmese War', *The Times*, 4 December 1885.

25. FD 1886, Secret E Pros, August 1886, nos 528–52, no. 531, National Archives of India, New Delhi.

26. Blackburn, *The British Humiliation of Burma*, pp. 112–13.

27. Jesse, *The Lacquer Lady*, p. 318.

28. FD 1886, Secret E Pros, August 1886, nos 528–52, no. 531, National Archives of India, New Delhi.

29. Stewart, *The Pagoda War*, p. 97. (White–Mrs White, 7 December 1885, WP.)

30. 'The War in Upper Burmah', *The Times of India*, 19 December 1885.

31. *Mandalay Palace*, The Directorate of Archaeological Survey, Ministry of Union Culture, Revolutionary Government of the Union of Burma, 1963, p. 31; O'Connor, *Mandalay and Other Cities of the Past in Burma*, p. 96.

32. Ibid., p. 96.

33. Charney, *Powerful Learning*, pp. 258–61.

34. Ni Ni Myint, *Selected Writings*, pp. 1–2.

35. 'Second Princess to the Additional Secretary to the Government of the Union of Burma, Rangoon.' Letter dated 15 December 1948, courtesy Kamal Chandarana (Gulabi).

36. Sladen Collection, British Library, London, MSS Eur E 290/50 (Rough 1885 Diary kept by Colonel Sladen).

37. Ibid.

38. 'The Burmese War', *The Times*, 5 December 1885.

39. H.R.H. The Fourth Princess, Daughter of the Late H.M. King Thi Baw and His Crowned Queen, *Private Affairs*, p. 13.

40. Prince Taw Phaya Galae's letter to author dated 20 July 2005.

41. Interviews with U Than Swe on 26 February 2005 and 24 November 2006.

42. Sladen Collection, British Library, London, MSS Eur E 290/65 (Rough 1885 Diary kept by Colonel Sladen).

43. Browne, *The Coming of the Great Queen*, p. 179.

44. 'The Burmese War', *The Times*, 5 December 1885.

45. Thant Myint-U, *The River of Lost Footsteps*, p. 21.

46. Browne, *The Coming of the Great Queen*, pp. 179–81.

47. Ibid., pp. 180–82.

48. Blackburn, *The British Humiliation of Burma*, p. 104.

49. 'The War in Upper Burmah', *The Times of India*, 19 December 1885.

50. Browne, *The Coming of the Great Queen*, pp. 182–83.

51. Ibid., pp. 183–85.

52. 'The War in Upper Burmah', *The Times of India*, 19 December 1885.

53. Keeton, *King Thebaw and the Ecological Rape of Burma*, p. 288. (Scott and Hardiman, *Gazetteer of Upper* Burma, vol. I, pt I, p. 113.)

54. Browne, *The Coming of the Great Queen*, p. 185; Foucar, *Mandalay the Golden*, p. 215.

55. Keeton, *King Thebaw and the Ecological Rape of Burma*, p. 288. (Mortimer Durand, *The Life of Field Marshal Sir George White*, vol. I, pp. 315–19. Excerpts from White's letters.)

56. Browne, *The Coming of the Great Queen*, p. 185.

57. 'Last of the Burmese Kings, Mr Noyce Reminiscences.'

58. Interview with U Than Swe on 24 November 2006.

59. Maung Htin Aung, *The Stricken Peacock*, p. 92.

60. Interview with U Than Swe on 24 November 2006 (including quotation); Maung Htin Aung, *The Stricken Peacock*, p. 92; U Than Swe, *Lecturer U Thet Tin Attends a Royal Audience*.

61. 'Last of the Burmese Kings, Mr Noyce Reminiscences.'

62. 'The Burmese War,' *The Times*, 4 December 1885.

63. 'The War in Upper Burmah', *The Times of India*, 19 December 1885.

64. Browne, *The Coming of the Great Queen*, pp. 186–87.

65. Telephone interview with U Than Swe in February 2009.

66. 'The War in Upper Burmah', *The Times of India*, 19 December 1885.

67. Keeton, *King Thebaw and the Ecological Rape of Burma*, pp. 289–90. ('The Burma Expedition', *Pioneer Mail* (Allahabad), 8 December 1885, p. 591.)

68. Keeton, *King Thebaw and the Ecological Rape of Burma*, p. 290.

69. 'The War in Upper Burmah', *The Times of India*, 19 December 1885.

70. Fielding, *Thibaw's Queen*, pp. 292–93.

PART II: DURING THE EXILE

8. The Royal Family in Madras

1. Browne, *The Coming of the Great Queen*, p. 187.

2. 'Last of the Burmese Kings, Mr Noyce Reminiscences.'

3. FD 1886, Secret E Pros, January 1886, nos 284–332, no. 286, National Archives of India, New Delhi.
4. Blackburn, *The British Humiliation of Burma,* p. 82.
5. 'Last of the Burmese Kings, Mr Noyce Reminiscences.'
6. H.R.H. The Fourth Princess, Daughter of the Late H.M. King Thi Baw and His Crowned Queen, *Private Affairs,* p. 5.
7. FD 1886, Secret E Pros, January 1886, nos 284–332, nos 286, 287, 291, 292, National Archives of India, New Delhi.
8. Ibid., nos 284–332, nos 294, 297.
9. Ibid., nos 284–332, no. 286.
10. Ibid., nos 284–332, no. 311.
11. PD vol. 50, 1911, p. 383, The Maharashtra State Archives, Mumbai.
12. FD 1886, Secret E Pros, January 1886, nos 284–332, no. 284, National Archives of India, New Delhi.
13. Ibid., nos 284–332, nos 285, 298.
14. Ibid., no. 289.
15. Ibid., nos 289, 298.
16. Ibid., no. 301.
17. Ibid., nos 299, 302.
18. Ibid., no. 316.
19. Ibid., no. 298.
20. Desai, *Deposed King Thibaw of Burma in India, 1885–1916,* p. 34, (IFDP July 1886, Secret E, no. 265).
21. FD 1886, Secret E Pros, January 1886, nos 284–332, no. 316, National Archives of India, New Delhi.
22. Ibid., nos 284–332, no. 319.
23. Ibid., nos 813–29, no. 818.
24. Ibid., no. 815.
25. Ibid., nos 284–332, no. 328.
26. Ibid., July 1886, nos 458–85, no. 478.
27. Ibid., no. 459.
28. Ibid.
29. Ibid., nos 458–85, no. 477.
30. Ibid., nos 470, 472, 473, 475.
31. PD vol. I, no. 43/1898, compl. 464, The Maharashtra State Archives, Mumbai; Desai, *Deposed King Thibaw of Burma in India, 1885–1916,* pp. 45–46.
32. FD 1886, Secret E Pros, January 1886, nos 284–332, no. 324, National Archives of India, New Delhi.
33. Ibid., nos 813–29, no. 815.

34. U Thein Maung, *A Collection of Ratnagiri Articles*, translated for author from the Burmese into the English by Than Htay.

35. FD 1886, Secret E Pros, July 1886, nos 458–85, nos 476, 479, National Archives of India, New Delhi; Desai, *Deposed King Thibaw of Burma in India, 1885–1916*, p. 29.

36. FD 1886, Secret E Pros, January 1886, nos 284–332, no. 324, National Archives of India, New Delhi.

37. Ibid., nos 813–29, no. 815.

38. Series I/1(A), 1961, 1886, 220, pt I, p. 3, National Archives Department of Myanmar, Yangon.

39. FD 1886, Secret E Pros, January 1886, nos 284–332, no. 329, National Archives of India, New Delhi.

40. Ibid., July 1886, nos 458–85, nos 474–75.

41. Ibid., no. 479.

42. Ibid., no. 461.

43. Ibid., May 1886, nos 32–36, no. 35; Series I/1(A), 1961, 1886, 220, pt I, p. 165, National Archives Department of Myanmar, Yangon.

44. Series I/1(A), 2684, 1888, 31P, pp. 19–23, National Archives Department of Myanmar, Yangon; Series I/1(A), 2668, 1888, 3P, National Archives Department of Myanmar, Yangon.

45. FD 1886, Secret E Pros, January 1886, nos 813–29, not numbered, letter dated 19 January 1886, National Archives of India, New Delhi.

46. Ibid., nos 813–29, no. 821.

47. Ibid., July 1886, nos 458–85, no. 469.

48. Ibid., January 1886, nos 813–29, not numbered, letter dated 19 January 1886.

49. Ibid., May 1886, nos 48–50, nos 49, 48.

50. Ibid., July 1886, nos 458–85, nos 461–85.

51. Ibid., no. 463.

52. Ibid., January 1886, nos 284–332, no. 324.

53. Ibid., July 1886, nos 458–85, no. 472.

54. Ibid., January 1886, nos 813–29, not numbered, letter dated 19 January 1886.

55. Ibid., July 1886, nos 458–85, no. 469.

56. Ibid., May 1886, nos 223–25, no. 223.

57. Ibid.

58. Ibid., July 1886, nos 458–85, nos 470, 474.

59. Ibid., no. 478.

60. Series I/1(A), 1961, 1886, 220, pt I, pp. 120–21, p. 59, National Archives Department of Myanmar, Yangon.

61. FD 1886, Secret E Pros, February 1886, nos 216–21, National Archives of India, New Delhi.

62. Ibid., July 1886, nos 458–85, no. 471.

63. Ibid., no. 480.

64. Ibid., nos 480, 482, 484.

65. Ibid., June 1886, nos 141–44, no. 142.

66. Ibid., July 1886, nos 458–85, no. 483.

9. Burma without a King

1. 'Burmah' (?), *The Times,* 17 December 1885.

2. FD 1886, Secret E Pros, July 1886, nos 458–85, no. 460, National Archives of India, New Delhi.

3. Shway Yoe, *The Burman,* pp. 485–89.

4. Desai, *Deposed King Thibaw of Burma in India, 1885–1916,* p. 20. (IFDP January 1886, Secret E, no. 516.)

5. D.E.G. Hall, *Burma,* p. 143.

6. Thant Myint-U, *The River of Lost Footsteps,* p. 24.

7. Keeton, *King Thebaw and the Ecological Rape of Burma,* p. 300.

8. Thant Myint-U, *The River of Lost Footsteps,* p. 25.

9. Thant Myint-U, *The Making of Modern Burma,* p. 195.

10. Keeton, *King Thebaw and the Ecological Rape of Burma,* p. 307.

11. Thant Myint-U, *The Making of Modern Burma,* p. 195.

12. Marchioness of Dufferin and Ava, *Our Viceregal Life in India: Selections from My Journal 1884–1888,* vol. I, pp. 292, 306–07.

13. Keeton, *King Thebaw and the Ecological Rape of Burma,* p. 315. ('Burmah', *The Times,* 15 February 1886.)

14. Maung Htin Aung, *The Stricken Peacock,* p. 92.

15. Keeton, *King Thebaw and the Ecological Rape of Burma,* p. 316.

16. Maung Htin Aung, *The Stricken Peacock,* pp. 92–93.

17. FD 1887, External A Pros, September 1887, nos 181–210, no. 205, National Archives of India, New Delhi.

18. FD 1886, Secret E, December 1888, nos 173–75, no. 174, National Archives of India, New Delhi.

19. Marchioness of Dufferin and Ava, *Our Viceregal Life in India,* vol. I, pp. 319–27.

20. Ibid., pp. 322–25.

21. V & A Museum, Museum no. IM 10–1909, Breast cloth or stole, Yinzi or *tabet.*

22. 'The Hidden Treasures at Mandalay, Burmah', *The Illustrated London News,* 14 April 1894.

23. Interview with U Than Swe on 2 December 2006.
24. FD 1886, Secret E Pros, August 1886, nos 105–11, National Archives of India, New Delhi.
25. 'King Theebaw's Treasures, Some of the Loot from His Mandalay Palace Exhibited', *The New York Times*, 10 October 1886 (from *The London Telegraph*).
26. *The Times of India*, 16 April 1886, p. 5.
27. G.E. Harvey, *History of Burma*, p. 328.
28. Charles William Lambert, *The Missionary Martyr of Thibaw: A Brief Record of the Life and Consecrated Missionary Labours of Charles William Lambert in Upper Burma*, p. 66.
29. Thant Myint-U, *The River of Lost Footsteps*, pp. 24, 30; Thant Myint-U, *The Making of Modern Burma*, pp. 199, 200.
30. Foucar, *Mandalay the Golden*, p. 222.
31. *Mandalay Palace*, The Directorate of Archaeological Survey, Ministry of Union Culture, Revolutionary Government of the Union of Burma, 1963, p. 15.
32. Maung Htin Aung, *The Stricken Peacock*, p. 95.
33. Interview with U Than Swe on 24 November 2006.
34. 'A Song Composed in Honour of Hteik Su Myat Phaya Lat' (anthology of poems), *Dagon Magazine*, n.d., courtesy U Than Swe, translated for author from the Burmese into English by Than Htay.
35. Lambert, *The Missionary Martyr of Thibaw*, p. 71.
36. Thant Myint-U, *The River of Lost Footsteps*, p. 162.

10. The King in Ratnagiri

1. Desai, *Deposed King Thibaw of Burma in India, 1885–1916*, p. 33.
2. 'Theebaw in Rutnagherry', *The Times of India*, 19 April 1886.
3. PD 56/1892, p. 324, The Maharashtra State Archives, Mumbai.
4. 'Theebaw in Rutnagherry.'
5. Ibid.
6. Ibid.
7. Ibid.
8. *Gazetteer of the Bombay Presidency*, Ratnagiri and Savantvadi Districts, vol. 10, pp. 176, 364–66.
9. FD 1886, Secret E, November 1886, nos 279–88, no. 280, National Archives of India, New Delhi.
10. Ibid.
11. Ibid.

12. Ibid., not numbered, letters dated 7 August 1886 and 9 October 1886.

13. Series 1/1(A), 1961, 1886, 220, pt 1, p. 18, National Archives Department of Myanmar, Yangon.

14. Ibid., pt 2, pp. 14–20.

15. Desai, *Deposed King Thibaw of Burma in India, 1885–1916*, p. 39. (IFDP February 1887.)

16. FD 1887, Secret E, June 1887, nos 165–70, no. 166, National Archives of India, New Delhi.

17. Interview with Manik Lad in early 2009; FD 1886, Secret E Pros, November 1886, nos 378–92, no. 379, National Archives of India, New Delhi.

18. PD 56/1892, p. 504, The Maharashtra State Archives, Mumbai.

19. PD vol. 1, no. 44/1896, p. 164, The Maharashtra State Archives, Mumbai.

20. Desai, *Deposed King Thibaw of Burma in India, 1885–1916*, p. 35. (IFDP November 1886, Secret E, nos 370, 381, 382, 392.)

21. FD 1886, Secret E Pros, November 1886, nos 378–92, no. 379, National Archives of India, New Delhi.

22. FD 1887, Secret E Pros, May 1887, nos 221–23A, K.W. no. 1, National Archives of India, New Delhi.

23. Ibid., August 1887, nos 435–38, not numbered, letter dated 30 June 1887.

24. Series 1/1(A), 2684, 1888, 31 P, pp. 30–31, National Archives Department of Myanmar, Yangon.

25. Ibid., pp. 34–35.

26. PD 56/1892, p. 43, The Maharashtra State Archives, Mumbai.

27. Series 1/1(A), 1962, 1886, 220, pt 2, pp. 62–67, National Archives Department of Myanmar, Yangon.

28. PD 56/1892, pp. 345–46, The Maharashtra State Archives, Mumbai.

29. PD vol. 1/1899, no. 43, pp. 109, 111, The Maharashtra State Archives, Mumbai.

30. PD 56/1892, pp. 11–45, The Maharashtra State Archives, Mumbai.

31. PD vol. 1/1899, no. 43, pp. 109, 111, The Maharashtra State Archives, Mumbai.

32. Interview with Prince Richard on 16 February 2009; Prince Taw Phaya Galae, *From Yadanabon to Ratnagiri*, translated for author from the Burmese into the English by Than Htay.

33. PD 56/1892, pp. 502–09, The Maharashtra State Archives, Mumbai.

34. PD vol. 1, no. 50/1893, p. 46, The Maharashtra State Archives, Mumbai.

35. Desai, *Deposed King Thibaw of Burma in India, 1885–1916*, p. 47.
36. U Than Swe, *Records of the Royal Audiences*, ch. 12, translated for author from the Burmese into the English by Than Htay. (Reference: *Sarphat Thu* journal, vol. 2, nos 17, 18, 19, 2001.)
37. FD 1889, Secret E Pros, May 1889, nos 572–79, p. 6, National Archives of India, New Delhi.
38. PD 56/1892, pp. 11–45, The Maharashtra State Archives, Mumbai.
39. Ibid., p. 15.
40. PD vol. 34/1895, p. 26, The Maharashtra State Archives, Mumbai; PD 56/1892, pp. 177–78, The Maharashtra State Archives, Mumbai.
41. Series I/IA, 2728, 1888, 109P, National Archives Department of Myanmar, Yangon.
42. PD 56/1892, pp. 501–02, The Maharashtra State Archives, Mumbai.
43. FD 1889, Secret E Pros, May 1889, nos 572–79, not numbered, letter dated 16 March 1889, no. 573, National Archives of India, New Delhi.
44. Desai, *Deposed King Thibaw of Burma in India, 1885–1916*, pp. 43, 88 .
45. PD vol. 1, no. 50/1893, pp. 289–95, The Maharashtra State Archives, Mumbai.
46. Ibid.
47. PD 56/1892, pp. 289–383, The Maharashtra State Archives, Mumbai.
48. Desai, *Deposed King Thibaw of Burma in India, 1885–1916*, p. 50.
49. PD vol. 1, no. 44/1896, pp. 7–8, The Maharashtra State Archives, Mumbai.
50. Desai, *Deposed King Thibaw of Burma in India, 1885–1916*, p. 52.
51. PD vol. 1, no. 44/1896, pp. 7–8, The Maharashtra State Archives, Mumbai.
52. Ibid., pp. 7–9.
53. PD vol. 34, 1895, pp. 251, 325, 329–32, The Maharashtra State Archives, Mumbai.
54. Ibid., pp. 325–26.
55. PD vol. 1, no. 44/1896, p. 99, The Maharashtra State Archives, Mumbai.
56. PD dept vol. 1, no. 43/1899, p. 129, The Maharashtra State Archives, Mumbai.
57. Desai, *Deposed King Thibaw of Burma in India, 1885–1916*, pp. 50–55.
58. PD vol. 1, no. 43/1898, compl. 464, pp. 164–65, The Maharashtra State Archives, Mumbai.
59. Ibid., pp. 75–79, 81–82.
60. PD vol. 1, no. 43/1898, compl. 464, p. 164, The Maharashtra State Archives, Mumbai.

61. Ibid., p. 206.

62. Ibid., pp. 283–85.

63. Ibid., p. 347.

64. PD vol. I, no. 42/1900, p. 109, The Maharashtra State Archives, Mumbai; PD vol. 4/1906, no. 108, p. 110, The Maharashtra State Archives, Mumbai.

65. Interview with Nanasahib Gandhi on 19 July 2004.

66. Interview with Dr (Mrs) Gore on 20 July 2004.

67. PD vol. I, no. 43/1899, pp. 113, 115, The Maharashtra State Archives, Mumbai.

68. PD Abstract of Proceedings, May 1910, p. 1,149, The Maharashtra State Archives, Mumbai.

69. PD 201, 50/1911, p. 431, The Maharashtra State Archives, Mumbai.

11. The Royal Family in Ratnagiri

1. Interview with U Aung Win and others in February 2009; U Than Swe's letter to author dated 12 May 2009.

2. Ibid.

3. FD 1887, Secret E Pros, May 1887, nos 221–23A, no. 223, National Archives of India, New Delhi.

4. Series I/I (A), 2684, 1888, 31P, pp. 8–10, 26–28, 32–33, National Archives Department of Myanmar, Yangon.

5. FD 1889, Secret E Pros, July 1888, nos 346–69, National Archives of India, New Delhi.

6. Ibid., no. 364.

7. Ibid., May 1889, nos 572–79, no. 573.

8. Ibid., July 1888, nos 346–69, no. 354.

9. Ibid., May 1889, nos 572–79, no. 573; Desai, *Deposed King Thibaw of Burma in India, 1885–1916*, p. 43. (Bom G.R. Pol. Dept, Collector Candy to GOI, 30 July 1888.)

10. Series I/I (A), 2684, 1888, 31P, pp. 43–44, pp. 8–10, National Archives Department of Myanmar, Yangon.

11. FD 1890, Secret E Pros, July 1890, nos 16–34, no. 30, National Archives of India, New Delhi.

12. Ibid., no. 29.

13. Series I/I (C), 8895, 31P, pp. 1–3, National Archives Department of Myanmar, Yangon.

14. FD 1890, Secret E Pros, July 1890, nos 16–34, no. 32, National Archives of India, New Delhi.

15. PD vol. I, no. 50/1893, pp. 107–08, The Maharashtra State Archives, Mumbai.

16. Ibid., no. 42/1900, p. 41.

17. Interview with U Than Swe on 24 November 2006; PD dept vol. I, no. 42/1900, p. 41, The Maharashtra State Archives, Mumbai.

18. Interview with U Than Swe on 24 November 2006; PD dept vol. I, no. 42/1900, p. 53, The Maharashtra State Archives, Mumbai.

19. Ibid., p. 59.

20. Interview with U Than Swe on 24 November 2006.

21. Ibid.; Sao Sanda, *The Moon Princess: Memories of the Shan States,* p. 27.

22. PD dept vol. I, no. 42/1900, p. 169, The Maharashtra State Archives, Mumbai.

23. U Sein Maung Oo's letter to author dated 13 October 2005.

24. Ibid.

25. U Than Swe, *Records of the Royal Audiences,* ch. 12, translated for author from the Burmese into the English by Than Htay.

26. PD vol. I, no. 36/1897, pp. 225–26, The Maharashtra State Archives, Mumbai; U Than Swe, *Records of the Royal Audiences,* ch. 1, translated for author from the Burmese into the English by Than Htay. (References: The royal audience attended by the *Bandoola* journal reporter U Maung Galay; Desai, *Deposed King Thibaw of Burma in India, 1885–1916.*)

27. Princess Hteik Su Gyi Phaya's (Rita) letter to Mr Symington dated 12 December 1970, British Library, London, MSS Eur D 1156/7.

28. Interview with Prince Taw Phaya on 20 February 2005.

29. Princess Hteik Su Gyi Phaya's (Rita) letter to Mr Symington dated 17 August 1971, British Library, London, MSS Eur D 1156/7.

30. U Than Swe, *Records of the Royal Audiences,* ch. 12, translated for author from the Burmese into the English by Than Htay. Telephone interview with Prince Taw Phaya on 1 March 2010; Princess Hteik Su Gyi Phaya's (Rita) letter to Mr Symington dated 23 March 1971, British Library, London, MSS Eur D 1156/7.

31. PD 56/1892, pp. 549–54, The Maharashtra State Archives, Mumbai.

32. PD vol. I, no. 50/1893, pp. 137–39, 169, The Maharashtra State Archives, Mumbai.

33. U Than Swe, *Records of the Royal Audiences,* ch. 12, translated for author from the Burmese into the English by Than Htay; interview with Prince Taw Phaya on 30 November 2006.

34. U Than Swe, *Records of the Royal Audiences,* ch. 12, translated for author from the Burmese into the English by Than Htay.

35. PD miscell. 1907, vol. 23, no. 115, compl. 687, p. 171, The Maharashtra State Archives, Mumbai.

36. Xerox of an old invitation that has survived the years, courtesy Anil Joshi, Ratnagiri.

37. Anil Shrikhande, 'This Is the Way King Thiba of Burma Lived in Ratnagiri', *Saptahik Manohar*, 18–24 June 1978, translated for author from the Marathi into the English by Aksharmaya.

38. Ibid.

39. Interviews with S.S. Salgaonkar on 17 July 2004 and 19 July 2004.

40. Interview with Anil Birje on 16 July 2004.

41. PD vol. 4/1906, no. 108, p. 113, The Maharashtra State Archives, Mumbai; PD miscell. 1907, vol. 23, no. 115, compl. 687, p. 171, The Maharashtra State Archives, Mumbai.

42. U Than Swe, 'Ledi Panditta in the Chief Queen's Presence'.

43. PD miscell. 1907, vol. 23, no. 115, compl. 687, p. 171, The Maharashtra State Archives, Mumbai.

44. Series I/I(A), 1962, 1886, 220, pt 2, pp. 14–20, National Archives Department of Myanmar, Yangon.

45. U Than Swe, 'Lecturer U Thet Tin Attends a Royal Audience'.

46. U Thein Maung, *A Collection of Ratnagiri Articles*, translated for author from the Burmese into the English by Than Htay.

47. Interview with Prince Taw Phaya Galae on 27 February 2005.

48. PD dept. vol. 1, no. 43/1899, pp. 115, 257–58, The Maharashtra State Archives, Mumbai.

49. Desai, *Deposed King Thibaw of Burma in India, 1885–1916*, p. 60. (IFDP September 1906, Extl-A, no. 3.)

50. Interview with Prince Taw Phaya Galae on 27 February 2005; Prince Taw Phaya Galae, *From Yadanabon to Ratnagiri*, translated for author from the Burmese into the English by Than Htay.

51. Series I/I(A), 4025, 1888, 2M, pp. 7–13, National Archives Department of Myanmar, Yangon; interview with U Than Swe on 2 December 2006.

52. U Than Swe, *Records of the Royal Audiences*, ch. 12, translated for author from the Burmese into the English by Than Htay.

53. PD vol. 4/1906, no. 108, p. 113, The Maharashtra State Archives, Mumbai.

54. Interview with U Than Swe on 24 November 2006.

55. U Than Swe, *Records of the Royal Audiences*, ch. 12, translated for author from the Burmese into the English by Than Htay.

56. PD vol. 1, no. 44/1896, p. 99, The Maharashtra State Archives, Mumbai.

57. U Than Swe, *Records of the Royal Audiences,* ch. 12, translated for author from the Burmese into the English by Than Htay.
58. Interview with Prince Taw Phaya on 30 November 2006.
59. Princess Hteik Su Gyi Phaya's (Rita) letter to Mr Symington dated 22 December 1970, British Library, London, MSS Eur D 1156/7.
60. Interview with Prince Taw Phaya on 30 November 2006.
61. PD 2093-2/1920, p. M115, The Maharashtra State Archives, Mumbai; PD 1496/1919, pp. M43–M47, The Maharashtra State Archives, Mumbai.
62. U Than Swe, *Records of the Royal Audiences,* ch. 12, translated for author from the Burmese into the English by Than Htay.
63. Interview with Prince Taw Phaya Galae on 27 February 2005.
64. Princess Hteik Su Gyi Phaya's (Rita) letter to Mr Symington dated 12 December 1970, British Library, London, MSS Eur D 1156/7.
65. PD vol. 50/1911, p. 419, The Maharashtra State Archives, Mumbai.
66. Interview with Prince Taw Phaya on 30 November 2006; telephone interview with Prince Taw Phaya on 1 March 2010.
67. Princess Hteik Su Gyi Phaya's (Rita) letters to Mr Symington dated 23 March 1971 and 22 December 1970, British Library, London, MSS Eur D 1156/7.
68. Ibid.
69. U Thein Maung, *A Collection of Ratnagiri Articles,* translated for author from the Burmese into the English by Than Htay.
70. Princess Hteik Su Gyi Phaya's letter to Mr Symington dated 23 March 1971, British Library, London, MSS Eur D 1156/7.
71. PD vol. 50/1911, p. 421, The Maharashtra State Archives, Mumbai.
72. Interview with Prince Taw Phaya on 30 November 2006.
73. U Than Swe, *Records of the Royal Audiences,* ch. 1, translated for author from the Burmese into the English by Than Htay.
74. Interview with Princess Hteik Su Phaya Gyi on 23 November 2006.
75. PD vol. 4/1906, no. 108, pp. 113, 115, The Maharashtra State Archives, Mumbai.
76. Desai, *Deposed King Thibaw of Burma in India, 1885–1916,* p. 62. (IFDP July 1907, no. 7.)
77. PD vol. 50/1911, p. 311, The Maharashtra State Archives, Mumbai.
78. PD 2093-1/1920, p. M304, The Maharashtra State Archives, Mumbai.
79. PD no. 115/1909, compl. 190, p. 477, The Maharashtra State Archives, Mumbai.
80. U Thein Maung, *A Collection of Ratnagiri Articles,* translated for author from the Burmese into the English by Than Htay.

81. PD-A of P, June 1910, pp. 1, 569–70, The Maharashtra State Archives, Mumbai.
82. U Than Swe, *Records of the Royal Audiences,* ch. 12, translated for author from the Burmese into the English by Than Htay.

12. The Princesses Grow Up

1. PD vol. 4/1906, no. 108, p. 71, The Maharashtra State Archives, Mumbai.
2. Ibid., pp. 110–14.
3. Ibid., pp. 112–15.
4. Ibid., pp. 110–15.
5. Ibid.
6. PD miscell. 1907, vol. 23, no. 115, compl. 687, p. 3, The Maharashtra State Archives, Mumbai.
7. PD vol. 50/1911, p. 207, The Maharashtra State Archives, Mumbai; PD miscell. 1907, vol. 23, no. 115, compl. 687, p. 171, The Maharashtra State Archives, Mumbai; Desai, *Deposed King Thibaw of Burma in India, 1885–1916,* p. 62 .
8. Proceedings of the FD, July 1907, no. 77, National Archives of India, New Delhi.
9. PD 2093-2/1920, p. M592, The Maharashtra State Archives, Mumbai.
10. PD no. 89/1908, p. 423, The Maharashtra State Archives, Mumbai.
11. PD miscell. 1907, vol. 23, no. 115, compl. 1602, p. 393, The Maharashtra State Archives, Mumbai.
12. Proceedings of the PD, April 1907, pp. 891–92, The Maharashtra State Archives, Mumbai.
13. Ibid., p. 892.
14. FD Notes, External-A Proceedings, July 1907, nos 78–82, no. 79 (enclosure 3), National Archives of India, New Delhi.
15. PD miscell. 1907, vol. 23, no. 115, compl. 1602, pp. 409–15, The Maharashtra State Archives, Mumbai.
16. Ibid., p. 411.
17. FD Notes, External-A Proceedings, July 1907, nos 78–82, no. 78, National Archives of India, New Delhi.
18. Interview with U Than Swe on 24 November 2006.
19. Ibid.
20. Desai, *Deposed King Thibaw of Burma in India, 1885–1916,* p. 62
21. PDC no. 128/1912, compl. 2045, p. 425, The Maharashtra State Archives, Mumbai; Desai, *Deposed King Thibaw of Burma in India, 1885–1916,* p. 63

22. U Sein Maung Oo's letter to author dated 13 October 2005.

23. Interview with U Than Swe on 24 November 2006.

24. Interview with Prince Taw Phaya Galae on 27 February 2005.

25. Proceedings of the FD, July 1907, no. 76, National Archives of India, New Delhi. PD 930/1921, pp. M1, M2, The Maharashtra State Archives, Mumbai; Desai, *Deposed King Thibaw of Burma in India, 1885–1916*, p. 62; PD no. 115/1909, compl. 190, p. 423, The Maharashtra State Archives, Mumbai.

26. Proceedings of the FD, July 1907, no. 76, National Archives of India, New Delhi; Thebaw Palace, Ratnagiri (print out collected at Thebaw Palace); *Maharashtra State Gazetteer*, 1962, p. 794.

27. *Mandalay Palace,* The Directorate of Archaeological Survey, Ministry of Union Culture, Revolutionary Government of the Union of Burma, 1963, pp. 12, 25–27.

28. PD vol. 4/1906, no. 108, p. 114, The Maharashtra State Archives, Mumbai; Plans of Thebaw Palace, Department of Archaeology and Museums, State of Maharashtra.

29. PD no. 115/1909, compl. 190, p. 505, The Maharashtra State Archives, Mumbai; PD 1496/1919, p. M197, The Maharashtra State Archives, Mumbai.

30. Interviews with Bapusaheb Parulekar on 19 July 2004 and 27 November 2004.

31. Interview with U Than Swe on 24 November 2006.

32. PD no. 115/1909, compl. 190, p. 423, The Maharashtra State Archives, Mumbai.

33. PD vol. 50/1911, pp. 41, 77, The Maharashtra State Archives, Mumbai.

34. PD Abstract of Proceedings, January 1910, p. 213, The Maharashtra State Archives, Mumbai; PD Abstract of Proceedings, November 1910, no. 192/2, p. 3,045, The Maharashtra State Archives, Mumbai.

35. U Than Swe, *Records of the Royal Audiences*, ch. 12, translated for author from the Burmese into the English by Than Htay.

36. Princess Hteik Su Gyi Phaya's (Rita) letter to Mr Symington dated 22 December 1970, British Library, London, MSS Eur D 1156/7.

37. Interview with Prince Taw Phaya Galae on 27 February 2005.

38. Thebaw Palace, Ratnagiri (print out collected at Thebaw Palace).

39. PDC vol. 128/1912, compl. 1366, The Maharashtra State Archives, Mumbai.

40. PD Abstract of Proceedings, June 1910, p. 1,569, The Maharashtra State Archives, Mumbai.

41. Prince Taw Phaya Galae, *From Yadanabon to Ratnagiri*, translated for author from the Burmese into the English by Than Htay. (Ne Win Myint, *Wild Crow and Other Short Stories*.)

42. PD vol. 50/1911, p. 383, The Maharashtra State Archives, Mumbai.

43. PD miscell. 1907, vol. 23, no. 115, compl. 1602, p. 393, The Maharashtra State Archives, Mumbai.

44. Series 1/1(A), 1961, 1886, 220 pt. I, p. 18, National Archives Department of Myanmar, Yangon.

45. Prince Taw Phaya Galae, *From Yadanabon to Ratnagiri*, translated for author from the Burmese into the English by Than Htay. ('The Burmese Dance and Musical Troupe in Ratnagiri, India', *The Kyemon Daily*, 1 September 1994.)

46. U Than Swe, *Records of the Royal Audiences*, ch. 12, translated for author from the Burmese into the English by Than Htay.

47. PD vol. 50/1911, p. 419, The Maharashtra State Archives, Mumbai.

48. Ibid., p. 383.

49. Ibid., pp. 381–87.

50. Ibid., pp. 421–23.

51. Ibid.

52. Ibid., pp. 41–42.

53. PD 1911, no. 198, p. 413, The Maharashtra State Archives, Mumbai.

54. Ibid., pp. 414–15.

55. Desai, *Deposed King Thibaw of Burma in India, 1885–1916*, p. 66.

56. PD vol. 50/1911, p. 97, The Maharashtra State Archives, Mumbai.

57. Ibid., pp. 127–29.

58. Ibid., p. 183.

59. U Thein Maung, *A Collection of Ratnagiri Articles*, translated for author from the Burmese into the English by Than Htay.

60. Proceedings of the FD, May 1911, no. 5 (enclosure), National Archives of India, New Delhi.

61. Proceedings of the FD, March 1912, no. 12 (enclosure), National Archives of India, New Delhi.

62. Proceedings of the FD, May 1911, no. 5 (enclosure), National Archives of India, New Delhi; Proceedings of the FD, March 1912, no. 13 (enclosure), National Archives of India, New Delhi.

63. PD vol. 50/1911, p. 651, The Maharashtra State Archives, Mumbai.

64. PDC no. 204-2/1917, pp. M49–51, The Maharashtra State Archives, Mumbai.

65. Proceedings of the FD, August 1912, Secret G, nos 1–7, nos 1-4, National Archives of India, New Delhi.

66. PD 2093-2/1920, p. M49, The Maharashtra State Archives, Mumbai.
67. U Than Swe, *Records of the Royal Audiences*, ch. I, translated for author from the Burmese into the English by Than Htay.
68. Interview with Kamal Chandarana (Gulabi) on 5 June 2005.
69. Princess Hteik Su Gyi Phaya's (Rita) letter to Mr Symington dated 22 December 1970, British Library, London, MSS Eur D 1156/7.
70. PDC 128/1912, compl. 2045, pp. 419–21, The Maharashtra State Archives, Mumbai.
71. PD miscell. 1913, vol. 118A, compl. 615, pp. 357–58, The Maharashtra State Archives, Mumbai.
72. Interview with U Than Swe on 26 February 2005.
73. PD miscell. 1913, vol. 118A, compl. 615, p. 371, The Maharashtra State Archives, Mumbai.
74. Ibid., pp. 369, 371, 411, 425, 439; PDC vol. 128/1912, compl. 1366, pp. 325–27, The Maharashtra State Archives, Mumbai.
75. PDC 311/1914, pp. M9, M19, M61, The Maharashtra State Archives, Mumbai; PD miscell. 1913, vol. 118A, compl. 615, pp. 439, 440, The Maharashtra State Archives, Mumbai; PDC vol. 128/1912, compl. 1366, pp. 305, 306, 325–27, The Maharashtra State Archives, Mumbai.
76. Notes on photographs of earboring ceremony gifted by U Than Swe to author; interview with U Than Swe on 2 December 2006.
77. Princess Hteik Su Gyi Phaya's letter to Mr Symington dated 22 December 1970, British Library, London, MSS Eur D 1156/7.
78. Telephone interview with Princess Hteik Su Phaya Gyi on 3 March 2010.
79. Notes on photographs of earboring ceremony gifted by U Than Swe to author; interview with U Than Swe on 2 December 2006.
80. Princess Hteik Su Gyi Phaya's letter to Mr Symington dated 22 December 1970, British Library, London, MSS Eur D 1156/7.

13. The Frustrations and the Squabbles

1. Princess Hteik Su Gyi Phaya's (Rita) letters to Mr Symington dated 23 March 1971 and 12 December 1970, British Library, London, MSS Eur D 1156/7.
2. Princess Hteik Su Gyi Phaya's (Rita) letter to Mr Symington dated 23 March 1971, British Library, London, MSS Eur D 1156/7.
3. FD Notes 1913, Secret G, May 1913, nos 5–10, no. 6, National Archives of India, New Delhi.

4. PD no. 230, pt I/1915, pp. M245–M248, The Maharashtra State Archives, Mumbai; PDC no. 204-1/1917, pp. M19–M20, The Maharashtra State Archives, Mumbai.

5. PD no. 230, pt I/1915, p. M93, The Maharashtra State Archives, Mumbai.

6. Ibid., pp. M253–M254.

7. PD 198/1916, p. M65, The Maharashtra State Archives, Mumbai.

8. Interviews with three of the Fourth Princess's children.

9. PDC 204-2/1917, p. M282, The Maharashtra State Archives, Mumbai.

10. Ibid., p. M6.

11. PDC vol. 128/1912, compl. 715, pp. 245–47, The Maharashtra State Archives, Mumbai; PDC no. 204-2/1917, p. M47, The Maharashtra State Archives, Mumbai.

12. Ibid., pp. M5–M12.

13. Interview with Prince Taw Phaya on 20 February 2005.

14. PDC 204-2/1917, pp. M276–M277, The Maharashtra State Archives, Mumbai; PD 1496/1919, p. M101, The Maharashtra State Archives, Mumbai.

15. PD 492/1918, p. M24, The Maharashtra State Archives, Mumbai; PDC no. 204-2/1917, pp. M467, M469, M471, The Maharashtra State Archives, Mumbai.

16. James Halliday (aka David Symington), unpublished manuscript, British Library, London, MSS EUR D 1156/10.

17. PDC 204-2/1917, pp. M277, The Maharashtra State Archives, Mumbai.

18. James Halliday (aka David Symington), unpublished manuscript, British Library, London, MSS EUR D 1156/10.

19. Interviews with U Than Swe on 26 February 2005 and 24 November 2006; U Than Swe, *Records of the Royal Audiences*, ch. 2, translated for author from the Burmese into the English by Than Htay. (References: Interview with U Sein Maung Oo; Desai, *Deposed King Thibaw of Burma in India, 1885–1916*; Dagon Khin Khin Lay, *Our Female Artists*.)

20. PDC 204-2/1917, pp. M5–M12, The Maharashtra State Archives, Mumbai.

21. Ibid.

22. Ibid.

23. PDC 204-1/1917, p. M43, The Maharashtra State Archives, Mumbai.

24. PDC 204-2/1917, pp. M5–M12, The Maharashtra State Archives, Mumbai.

25. Ibid.

26. U Than Swe, *Records of the Royal Audiences*, ch. 2, translated for author from the Burmese into the English by Than Htay.
27. PDC 204-2/1917, pp. M5–M12, The Maharashtra State Archives, Mumbai.
28. Ibid., pp. M43–M59.
29. Ibid., p. M24.
30. Interview with U Than Swe on 24 November 2006; U Than Swe, *Records of the Royal Audiences*, ch. 2, translated for author from the Burmese into the English by Than Htay.
31. Interview with Anil Joshi on 19 May 2011.
32. PDC 204-2/1917, pp. M39–40, M37, The Maharashtra State Archives, Mumbai.
33. Ibid., p. M37.
34. Ibid., pp. M39–40.
35. Ibid., pp. M43–M59.
36. Ibid.
37. Ibid.
38. Ibid.
39. Ibid., pp. M77, M55.
40. Ibid., p. M40; U Than Swe, *Records of the Royal Audiences*, ch. 2, translated for author from the Burmese into the English by Than Htay.
41. Telephone interview with Princess Hteik Su Phaya Gyi on 3 March 2010.
42. PD no. 198/1916, pp. M151–M154, The Maharashtra State Archives, Mumbai.
43. PDC 204-2/1917, pp. M93–M95, M103–105, The Maharashtra State Archives, Mumbai.
44. Desai, *Deposed King Thibaw of Burma in India, 1885–1916*, p. 72.

14. Death of the King and the Ensuing Unrest

1. PD 204-2/1917, p. M283, The Maharashtra State Archives, Mumbai.
2. PDC no. 204-1/1917, p. M43, The Maharashtra State Archives, Mumbai; PD no. 198/1916, pp. M158, M163, The Maharashtra State Archives, Mumbai.
3. Ibid., p. M71.
4. PDC no. 204-1/1917, p. M41, The Maharashtra State Archives, Mumbai; U Than Swe, *Records of the Royal Audiences*, ch. 2, translated for author from the Burmese into the English by Than Htay.
5. PDC no. 204-1/1917, p. M41, The Maharashtra State Archives, Mumbai.

6. Interview with Prince Taw Phaya Galae on 27 February 2005; Prince Taw Phaya Galae, *From Yadanabon to Ratnagiri*, translated for author from the Burmese into the English by Than Htay.

7. PDC no. 204-1/1917, p. M41, The Maharashtra State Archives, Mumbai.

8. James Halliday (aka David Symington), unpublished manuscript, British Library, London, MSS EUR D 1156/10.

9. Interview with U Sein Maung Oo on 26 February 2005.

10. Interview with Prince Taw Phaya on 30 November 2006.

11. PDC no. 204-1/1917, p. M41, The Maharashtra State Archives, Mumbai.

12. PD 2093-2/1920, p. M618, The Maharashtra State Archives, Mumbai.

13. PDC no. 204-1/1917, pp. M51–M58, The Maharashtra State Archives, Mumbai.

14. Ibid., pp. M19–M22.

15. PDC no. 204-2/1917, p. M591, The Maharashtra State Archives, Mumbai.

16. PDC no. 204-1/1917, p. M33, The Maharashtra State Archives, Mumbai.

17. PD no. 2093-2/1920, pp. M591–592, The Maharashtra State Archives, Mumbai.

18. PDC no. 204-1/1917, p. M84, The Maharashtra State Archives, Mumbai.

19. Ibid., p. M47.

20. Ibid., p. M42.

21. PD no. 204-2/1920, p. M407, The Maharashtra State Archives, Mumbai.

22. PDC no. 204-2/1917, p. M277, The Maharashtra State Archives, Mumbai.

23. Ibid., p. M278.

24. Ibid., p. M201.

25. Ibid., p. M269.

26. PD no. 204-1/1917, pp. M187–M188,The Maharashtra State Archives, Mumbai.

27. PDC no. 204-2/1917, p. M117, The Maharashtra State Archives, Mumbai.

28. Ibid., pp. M289, M290.

29. Ibid., p. M287.

30. Ibid., p. M109.

31. Ibid., p. M121.

32. Ibid., p. M278.

33. Ibid., pp. M121–M122.

34. Ibid., pp. M181, M206.

35. Ibid., p. M278.

36. Prince Taw Phaya Galae, *From Yadanabon to Ratnagiri*, translated for author from the Burmese into the English by Than Htay.

37. PD no. 2093-2/1920, pp. M155–M160, The Maharashtra State Archives, Mumbai.

38. PD no. 204-2/1917, pp. M111, M113, The Maharashtra State Archives, Mumbai (information from photographs).

39. Ibid., p. M278.

40. PD no. 2093-2/1920, p. M191, The Maharashtra State Archives, Mumbai.

41. PDC no. 204-1/1917, p. M63, The Maharashtra State Archives, Mumbai.

42. PD no. 2093-2/1920, p. M111, The Maharashtra State Archives, Mumbai.

43. Desai, *Deposed King Thibaw of Burma in India, 1885–1916*, pp. 74–75.

44. PDC no. 1917/204-2, pp. M275–M276, The Maharashtra State Archives, Mumbai.

45. Ibid., pp. M275–M279.

46. Ibid., p. M275.

47. Ibid., pp. M275–M276.

48. PDC no. 204-1/1917, pp. M155–M159, The Maharashtra State Archives, Mumbai.

49. U Than Swe, *Records of the Royal Audiences*, ch. 12, translated for author from the Burmese into the English by Than Htay.

50. PDC no. 204-1/1917, p. M159, The Maharashtra State Archives, Mumbai.

51. Proceedings of the PD, May 1917, pp. 755–56, The Maharashtra State Archives, Mumbai.

52. PD 204-2/1917, p. M396, The Maharashtra State Archives, Mumbai.

53. Ibid., p. M375.

54. Ibid., p. M396; PD 2093-2/1920, p. M606.

55. PD 204-2/1917, p. M396, The Maharashtra State Archives, Mumbai.

56. Ibid., pp. M281–M284.

57. Ibid., pp. M357, M398.

58. PDC no. 204-1/1917, p. M217, The Maharashtra State Archives, Mumbai.

59. PD no. 204-2/1917, p. M445, The Maharashtra State Archives, Mumbai.

60. PDC no. 204-1/1917, pp. M241–242, The Maharashtra State Archives, Mumbai.

61. PD 204-2/1917, p. M469, The Maharashtra State Archives, Mumbai; PD no. 492/1918, p. M23, The Maharashtra State Archives, Mumbai.

62. Proceedings of the PD, July–August 1917, pp. 1,335–336, The Maharashtra State Archives, Mumbai.

63. Ibid.

64. PD 492/1918, p. M37, The Maharashtra State Archives, Mumbai.

65. Proceedings of the PD, July–August 1917, pp. 1,336–337, The Maharashtra State Archives, Mumbai.

66. PD 2093-2/1920, pp. M111–M116, M596, The Maharashtra State Archives, Mumbai.

67. Ibid., p. M596.

68. PD 2093-1/1920, pp. M77–M79, The Maharashtra State Archives, Mumbai.

69. PD 2093-2/1920, p. M596, The Maharashtra State Archives, Mumbai.

70. PD 204-2/1917, pp. M323, M333–M335, The Maharashtra State Archives, Mumbai.

71. Ibid., pp. M393–M394.

72. Ibid., p. M433.

73. Ibid., p. M415.

74. Ibid., p. M394.

75. Ibid., pp. M393–M394.

76. Ibid., pp. M394–M395.

77. Ibid., pp. M431–M437.

78. PD 2093-2/1920, p. M593, The Maharashtra State Archives, Mumbai.

79. Ibid., p. M607.

80. Ibid., pp. M596–M598, M604–M605.

81. Ibid., p. M111.

82. Ibid., p. M605.

83. PD 2093-1/1920, p. M191, The Maharashtra State Archives, Mumbai.

84. PD 2093-2/1920, p. M608, The Maharashtra State Archives, Mumbai.

85. PD no. 1496/1919, p. M15, The Maharashtra State Archives, Mumbai.

86. PD 2093-2/1920, p. M607, The Maharashtra State Archives, Mumbai.

87. Ibid., pp. M607–M611.

88. Ibid., p. M617.

89. Ibid., p. M610.

90. PD no. 492/1918, pp. M23, M37, The Maharashtra State Archives, Mumbai.

91. PD no. 1496/1919, pp. M4, M7, The Maharashtra State Archives, Mumbai.
92. Ibid., pp. M4–M5.
93. PD 2093-2/1920, p. M606, The Maharashtra State Archives, Mumbai.
94. Desai, *Deposed King Thibaw of Burma in India, 1885–1916*, pp. 152–54. (The Collector's File, 1918.)
95. PD 2093-2/1920, p. M112, The Maharashtra State Archives, Mumbai.
96. PD 2093-1/1920, pp. M185–M186, The Maharashtra State Archives, Mumbai.
97. PD 2093-2/1920, p. M612, The Maharashtra State Archives, Mumbai.
98. Interview with U Than Swe on 24 November 2006.
99. Ibid.
100. PD 2093-2/1920, p. M611, The Maharashtra State Archives, Mumbai.
101. PD no. 1496/1919, pp. M29–M30, The Maharashtra State Archives, Mumbai.
102. PD 2093-1/1920, p. M617, The Maharashtra State Archives, Mumbai.
103. PD no. 492/1918, p. M23, The Maharashtra State Archives, Mumbai.
104. PD 2093-1/1920, pp. M77–M79, The Maharashtra State Archives, Mumbai.
105. Ibid., pp. M269–M270, The Maharashtra State Archives, Mumbai.
106. PD 2093-2/1920, pp. M618, The Maharashtra State Archives, Mumbai.
107. PD 2093-1/1920, pp. M85, M285, The Maharashtra State Archives, Mumbai.
108. PD 2093-2/1920, p. M618, The Maharashtra State Archives, Mumbai.

15. Prelude to the End of the Exile

1. PD 2093-2/1920, p. M115, The Maharashtra State Archives, Mumbai.
2. PD 1496/1919, pp. M43–47, The Maharashtra State Archives, Mumbai.
3. PD 2093-2/1920, p. M271, The Maharashtra State Archives, Mumbai.
4. Ibid., p. M75.
5. Ibid., pp. M363–M364.
6. PD 1496/1919, pp. M43–M47, The Maharashtra State Archives, Mumbai.
7. PD 2093-2/1920, pp. M111–M116, The Maharashtra State Archives, Mumbai.
8. Ibid., pp. M49–M51.
9. PD 1496/1919, pp. M59–M61, The Maharashtra State Archives, Mumbai.

10. Ibid., pp. M43–M47.

11. PD 2093-1/1920, p. M347, The Maharashtra State Archives, Mumbai.

12. PD 1496/1919, p. M91, The Maharashtra State Archives, Mumbai.

13. PD 2093-2/1920, pp. M49–M51, The Maharashtra State Archives, Mumbai.

14. PD 2093-1/1920, p. M623, The Maharashtra State Archives, Mumbai.

15. Ibid.

16. PD 2093-2/1920, pp. M55–M57, The Maharashtra State Archives, Mumbai.

17. Ibid.

18. Ibid., pp. M93–M95.

19. Ibid., pp. M273–M281.

20. Ibid.

21. Ibid.

22. PD 1496/1919, pp. M63–M67, The Maharashtra State Archives, Mumbai.

23. PD 2093-2/1920, pp. M147–M149, M169–M173, The Maharashtra State Archives, Mumbai.

24. Ibid., pp. M169–M173, M191.

25. Ibid., pp. M625, M627.

26. Ibid., p. M183.

27. Ibid., p. M625.

28. Ibid., pp. M169–M173.

29. H.R.H. The Fourth Princess, Daughter of the Late H.M. King Thi Baw and His Crowned Queen, *Private Affairs*; Prince Taw Phaya Galae, *From Yadanabon to Ratnagiri*, translated for author from the Burmese into the English by Than Htay.

30. PD 2093-2/1920, p. M191, The Maharashtra State Archives, Mumbai.

31. Xerox copy of Queen Supayalat's signed will, courtesy U Than Swe.

32. PD 2093-2/1920, pp. M155–M160, The Maharashtra State Archives, Mumbai.

33. Ibid., pp. M111–M116.

34. PD 1496/1919, pp. M59–M61, The Maharashtra State Archives, Mumbai.

35. Ibid., pp. M59–M61.

36. PD 2093-2/1920, pp. M7–M9, The Maharashtra State Archives, Mumbai.

37. PD 1496/1919, pp. M59–M61, The Maharashtra State Archives, Mumbai.

38. PD 2093-2/1920, pp. M634–M635, The Maharashtra State Archives, Mumbai.

39. Ibid., pp. M363–M364, M471.

40. Ibid., pp. M191.

41. Ibid., pp. M93–M95.

42. Ibid., pp. M193–M197.

43. Ibid., pp. M197, M651; PD 1496/1919, p. M121, The Maharashtra State Archives, Mumbai.

44. Ibid., pp. M79–M83.

45. PD 2093-2/1920, pp. M627–M628, The Maharashtra State Archives, Mumbai.

46. Ibid., pp. M627–M628.

47. Ibid., p. M207.

48. Ibid., pp. M627–M628.

49. PD 1496/1919, pp. M89–M95, The Maharashtra State Archives, Mumbai.

50. PD 2093-2/1920, p. M235, The Maharashtra State Archives, Mumbai.

51. Ibid., pp. M632–M634.

52. Ibid., p. M641.

53. PD 1496/1919, pp. M121–M123, The Maharashtra State Archives, Mumbai.

54. PD 2093-2/1920, p. M297, The Maharashtra State Archives, Mumbai.

55. PD 1496/1919, pp. M125–M126, The Maharashtra State Archives, Mumbai.

56. PD 2093-2/1920, p. M651, The Maharashtra State Archives, Mumbai; actual inscription on the tomb.

PART III: AFTER THE EXILE

16. The Homecoming

1. PD 2093-2/1920, pp. M646–M648, The Maharashtra State Archives, Mumbai.

2. U Sein Maung Oo's letter to author dated 13 October 2005.

3. PD 2093-2/1920, pp. M273–M281, The Maharashtra State Archives, Mumbai.

4. Ibid., p. M113.

5. Ibid., pp. M646–M648.

6. Ibid., p. M646.

7. Ibid., pp. M489, M646–M648.

8. Ibid., pp. M7–M9.

9. Ibid., pp. M646–M648.

10. Ibid., pp. M385–M389, M646–M648, M297,

11. Rajmohan Gandhi, *Mohandas*, pp. 224–25.

12. PD 2093-2/1920, pp. M646–M648, The Maharashtra State Archives, Mumbai.

13. Desai, *Deposed King Thibaw of Burma in India, 1885–1916*, p. 85.

14. PD 2093-2/1920, pp. M385–389, The Maharashtra State Archives, Mumbai.

15. Ibid., p. M648.

16. Ibid., p. M385–389.

17. Ibid., p. M489.

18. Ibid., p. M648.

19. Interview with U Than Swe on 2 December 2006.

20. Interview with Prince Taw Phaya Galae on 27 February 2005. (He attributed the quotation to Ludu Daw Ahmar.)

21. Foucar, *Mandalay the Golden*, p. 223.

22. U Than Swe, *Records of the Royal Audiences*, ch. 3, translated for author from the Burmese into the English by Than Htay. (References: U Maung Maung Tin, *Chronicles of the Konbaung Dynasty*, vol. 3; interviews with U Sein Maung Oo and Mintat Hteik Tin Taw Lay.)

23. Foucar, *Mandalay the Golden*, p. 223.

24. Interview with U Sein Maung Oo on 26 February 2005; interview with Prince Taw Phaya on 30 November 2006.

25. PD 1133/1920, p. M3, The Maharashtra State Archives, Mumbai.

26. U Than Swe, *Records of the Royal Audiences*, ch. 1, translated for author from the Burmese into the English by Than Htay.

27. Interview with Prince Taw Phaya on 20 February 2005.

28. U Than Swe, *Records of the Royal Audiences*, chs 2 and 8, translated for author from the Burmese into the English by Than Htay.

29. U Than Swe, *Records of the Royal Audiences*, translated for author from the Burmese into the English by Than Htay.

30. Foucar, *Mandalay the Golden*, p. 223.

31. PD 1133/1920, p. M1, The Maharashtra State Archives, Mumbai.

32. Ibid., p. M2.

33. Ibid.

34. Interview with U Than Swe on 2 December 2006.

35. PD 1133/1920, pp. M3–M4, The Maharashtra State Archives, Mumbai.

36. Ibid., p. M3.

37. Ibid., pp. M1–M8.
38. Ibid., p. M8.
39. Ibid., p. M7.
40. Ibid., p. M2.
41. Interview with Prince Taw Phaya Galae on 27 February 2005.
42. PD 1133/1920, pp. M1–M4, The Maharashtra State Archives, Mumbai.
43. PD 204-2/1917, p. M59, The Maharashtra State Archives, Mumbai.
44. PD 1133/1920, p. M6, The Maharashtra State Archives, Mumbai.
45. Ibid., p. M27.
46. Ibid., pp. M1–M4.
47. Ibid., p. M7.
48. Ibid., p. M6.
49. Ibid., pp. M29, M27.
50. Ibid., pp. M27, M43.
51. Interview with U Than Swe on 2 December 2006.

17. Queen Supayalat

1. Interview with U Than Swe on 24 November 2006.
2. Interview with Prince Taw Phaya on 20 February 2005.
3. Interview with U Sein Maung Oo on 21 November 2006.
4. Interview with U Than Swe on 24 November 2006.
5. Interview with Prince Taw Phaya on 30 November 2006.
6. 'Thebaw's Daughter Married', *The Times of India*, 5 July 1920.
7. Interview with U Than Swe on 24 November 2006; Desai, *Deposed King Thibaw of Burma in India, 1885–1916*, p. 154.
8. Interview with Princess Hteik Su Phaya Gyi on 23 November 2006.
9. Interview with U Than Swe on 24 November 2006.
10. Prince Taw Phaya's letter to author dated 22 May 2005; interview with Prince Taw Phaya on 30 November 2006.
11. Interview with U Than Swe on 24 November 2006; interview with Prince Taw Phaya on 30 November 2006; Series 10/1626, 310 HE. 47, p. 12, National Archives Department of Myanmar, Yangon. (As her pension commenced after her marriage, 1921 is the year of her wedding.)
12. Interview with Prince Taw Phaya on 30 November 2006.
13. PD 2093-1/1920, pp. M269–M270, The Maharashtra State Archives, Mumbai.
14. Interview with U Than Swe on 24 November 2006.

15. Ibid.

16. Prince Taw Phaya's letter to author dated 12 September 2008.

17. U Than Swe, *Records of the Royal Audiences,* ch. 1, translated for author from the Burmese into the English by Than Htay; interview with Prince Taw Phaya on 30 November 2006.

18. U Than Swe, *Records of the Royal Audiences*, ch. 5, translated for author from the Burmese into the English by Than Htay. (References: U Ba Thaw, *A Visit to the Chief Queen*, Myataung centenary booklet, Kyee Pwaryay Publishing House, Mandalay, January 1983; Maung Dagon, *The Living Were Responsible for the Death*; U Thaw Bitaof Heyar Ywama Kyaungni Kyaung, *History of Inlay Phaaung Daw Oo Pagoda*; U Than Swe, *U Hla and Latthakin*, Ludu U Hla, Kyee Pwaryay Publishing House, Mandalay.)

19. Mi Mi Khaing, *Burmese Family*, p. 52.

20. U Than Swe, *Records of the Royal Audiences*, ch. 8, translated for author from the Burmese into the English by Than Htay.

21. Interview with U Than Swe on 2 December 2006.

22. U Than Swe, *Records of the Royal Audiences*, ch. 8, translated for author from the Burmese into the English by Than Htay.

23. Interview with U Than Swe on 2 December 2006.

24. U Than Swe, 'Lecturer U Thet Tin Attends a Royal Audience'.

25. U Than Swe, *Records of the Royal Audiences*, ch. 9, translated for author from the Burmese into the English by Than Htay.

26. Khin Maung Soe, 'The Tragic Queen', *The Irrawaddy*, 2 February 2007; U Than Swe, *Records of the Royal Audiences*, ch. 6, translated for author from the Burmese into the English by Than Htay.

27. U Than Swe, *Records of the Royal Audiences*, ch. 2, translated for author from the Burmese into the English by Than Htay.

28. 'Mindon's Heirs', *The Nation Supplement*, 26 August 1962.

29. U Than Swe, *Records of the Royal Audiences*, ch. 7, translated for author from the Burmese into the English by Than Htay. (References: Desai, *Deposed King Thibaw of Burma in India, 1885–1916*; 'Words of the Elders', Mandalay centenary booklet; Daw Kyan, 'The Downfall of the Burmese Monarchy'; Ludu U Hla, 'History As Told by the Newspapers'; Than Tun, 'Countrywide History', vol. 2.)

30. U Than Swe, *Records of the Royal Audiences*, ch. 6, translated for author from the Burmese into the English by Than Htay.

31. W. Somerset Maugham, *The Gentleman in the Parlour: A Record of a Journey from Rangoon to Haiphong*, p. 33.

32. U Than Swe, *Records of the Royal Audiences*, translated for author from the Burmese into the English by Than Htay.

33. Ibid., ch. 8.

34. Ibid., ch. 1.

35. Ibid., ch. 5.

36. Ibid.

37. Ibid., ch. 9.

38. Ibid., ch. 2.

39. PD 2093-2/1920, p. M618, The Maharashtra State Archives, Mumbai.

40. U Than Swe, *Records of the Royal Audiences*, ch. 4, translated for author from the Burmese into the English by Than Htay. (References: Nagabo Hteik Tin Htwe, 'A History of Rangoon'; interviews with U Sein Maung Oo, Hteik Tin Taw Lay and Myogyi Hteik Tin San.)

41. Ibid., ch. 10, translated for author from the Burmese into the English by Than Htay. (References: Daw Kyan, *The Downfall of the Burmese Monarchy*; U Mya, *A Short History of Burmese Muslims*; U Ba Oo (Shwebo), *Mandalay Centenary and the Biography of Burmese Muslims;* Saya U Pho Che, *Ancient History of Burmese Muslims.*)

42. Ibid., ch. 3.

43. Ibid.

44. Ibid.

45. Ania Loomba, *Colonialism/Postcolonialism*, p. 99.

46. Interview with Prince Taw Phaya Galae on 27 February 2005; Prince Taw Phaya Galae, *From Yadanabon to Ratnagiri*, translated for author from the Burmese into the English by Than Htay.

47. Ibid.

48. Khin Maung Soe, 'Burma's Tomb Raiders', *The Irrawaddy*, 6 November 2006.

49. U Than Swe, *Records of the Royal Audiences,* chs 6 and 7, translated for author from the Burmese into the English by Than Htay.

50. D.E.G. Hall, *Burma*, p. 149.

51. Desai, *Deposed King Thibaw of Burma in India, 1885–1916*, p. 103.

52. Maung Htin Aung, *The Stricken Peacock*, p. 104.

53. U Than Swe, *Records of the Royal Audiences*, ch. 1, translated for author from the Burmese into the English by Than Htay.

54. Maung Htin Aung, *The Stricken Peacock*, p. 104; interview with Prince Taw Phaya Galae on 27 February 2005; 'Ex-Queen of Burma', *The Times*, February 1925, pp. 11, 12.

55. PD 2093-2/1920, pp. M273–M281, The Maharashtra State Archives,

Mumbai; U Than Swe, *Records of the Royal Audiences*, ch. 1, translated for author from the Burmese into the English by Than Htay.

56. Interview with U Than Swe on 2 December 2006.

57. Series 1/15 (D) 2235, 1925, 2P-15, National Archives Department of Myanmar, Yangon.

58. U Than Swe, *Records of the Royal Audiences*, ch. 11, translated for author from the Burmese into the English by Than Htay. (Reference: Zeya,'The Last Burmese Queen I Had Seen', *Ngwe Tar Yi* magazine, no. 54, December 1964.)

59. Ludu Daw Ahmar, *Chief Queen Hteit Su Myat Phaya: The Final Chapter of the Donor of the Mandalay Mya Taung Monastery*, n.d. (An article, courtesy U Than Swe, translated for author from the Burmese into the English by Than Htay.)

60. Desai, *Deposed King Thibaw of Burma in India, 1885–1916*, p. 100.

61. Ludu Daw Ahmar, *Chief Queen Hteit Su Myat Phaya*, translated for author from the Burmese into the English by Than Htay.

62. Series 1/15 (D) 2235, 1925, 2P-15, National Archives Department of Myanmar, Yangon.

63. 'The Passing of Burma's Ex-Queen', *The Rangoon Times*, Christmas number 1926 (information from written material and photographs); Desai, *Deposed King Thibaw of Burma in India, 1885–1916*, pp. 100–01.

64. Ibid., p. 101.

65. Ludu Daw Ahmar, *Chief Queen Hteit Su Myat Phaya*, translated for author from the Burmese into the English by Than Htay.

66. Ibid.

67. Prince Taw Phaya Galae, *From Yadanabon to Ratnagiri*, translated for author from the Burmese into the English by Than Htay.

68. U Than Swe, *Records of the Royal Audiences*, preface, translated for author from the Burmese into the English by Than Htay.

69. 'The Passing of Burma's Ex-Queen.'

18. The Fourth Princess

1. Interview with Prince Taw Phaya on 20 February 2009.

2. Interviews with U Than Swe on 24 November 2006 and 2 December 2006.

3. Princess Hteik Su Gyi Phaya's (Rita) letter to Mr Symington dated 22 December 1970, British Library, London, MSS Eur D 1156/7.

4. H.R.H. The Fourth Princess, Daughter of the Late H.M. King Thi Baw and His Crowned Queen, *Private Affairs*, pp. 28–29.

5. Desai, *Deposed King Thibaw of Burma in India, 1885–1916*, p. 104.
6. Prince Taw Phaya's letter to author dated 5 December 2007.
7. Interview with U Than Swe on 24 November2006.
8. Ibid.
9. Ibid.
10. Interview with Prince Taw Phaya on 30 November 2006; interview with U Than Swe on 2 December 2006.
11. Interview with Princess Hteik Su Phaya Gyi on 26 February 2005.
12. Interview with Prince Taw Phaya on 30 November 2006.
13. Interview with Princess Hteik Su Phaya Gyi on 26 February 2005; H.R.H. The Fourth Princess, Daughter of the Late H.M. King Thi Baw and His Crowned Queen, *Private Affairs*, p. 28.
14. Interview with U Than Swe on 24 November 2006.
15. Maung Htin Aung, *The Stricken Peacock*, p. 120.
16. Prince Taw Phaya's letter to author dated 19 May 2008.
17. Three of the Fourth Princess's children during interviews; interview with U Than Swe on 24 November 2006.
18. Barron, Cheryll, 'Burma: Feminist Utopia?', *Prospect Magazine,* issue 139, 27 October 2007, http://www.prospectmagazine.co.uk/2007/10/burmafeministutopia/.
19. Mi Mi Khiang, *The World of Burmese Women*, p. 16
20. Barron, Cheryll, 'Burma: Feminist Utopia?'
21. Interview with Prince Taw Phaya Galae on 27 February 2005.
22. Prince Taw Phaya's letter to author dated 28 November 2005; interview with Prince Taw Phaya on 30 November 2006.
23. PD no. 1496/1919, pp. M4–M5, The Maharashtra State Archives, Mumbai.
24. Interview with Prince Taw Phaya Galae on 27 February 2005.
25. H.R.H. The Fourth Princess, Daughter of the Late H.M. King Thi Baw and His Crowned Queen, *Private Affairs*, p. 30
26. Interview with Prince Taw Phaya on 30 November 2006.
27. Interview with Prince Taw Phaya on 20 February 2005.
28. H.R.H. The Fourth Princess, Daughter of the Late H.M. King Thi Baw and His Crowned Queen, *Private Affairs*, p. 31
29. Ibid., pp. 29–30.
30. Ibid.; interview with Prince Taw Phaya Galae on 27 February 2005.
31. H.R.H. The Fourth Princess, Daughter of the Late H.M. King Thi Baw and His Crowned Queen, *Private Affairs*, pp. 33–34.
32. Ibid., p. 32.
33. Interview with Prince Taw Phaya on 20 February 2005.

34. Interview with Prince Taw Phaya Galae on 27 February 2005.

35. Interview with Princess Hteik Su Phaya Gyi on 26 February 2005.

36. H.R.H. The Fourth Princess, Daughter of the Late H.M. King Thi Baw and His Crowned Queen, *Private Affairs*, p. 30.

37. U Sein Maung Oo's letter to author dated 13 October 2005.

38. Tint Naing Toe, 'The Fourth Daughter', *The Nan Net Khin Journal*, n.d., translated for author from the Burmese into the English by Than Htay; interview with Prince Taw Phaya on 30 November 2006.

39. Kyaw Hla's letter to Lattakhin dated 6 April 1932, courtesy Kamal Chandarana (Gulabi).

40. Interview with Prince Taw Phaya on 30 November 2006.

41. Interview with Hteik Su Phaya Gyi on 26 February 2005.

42. Kyaw Hla's letter to Latthakin dated 17 May 1932, courtesy Kamal Chadarana (Gulabi).

43. Interview with Hteik Su Phaya Gyi on 26 February 2005 (including quotation); interview with Prince Taw Phaya Galae on 27 February 2005.

44. Interview with Prince Taw Phaya on 30 November 2006.

45. Prince Taw Phaya's letter to author dated 19 May 2008; interview with Prince Taw Phaya on 20 February 2009.

46. Interview with Hteik Su Phaya Gyi on 23 November 2006.

47. Prince Taw Phaya Galae, *From Yadanabon to Ratnagiri*, translated for author from the Burmese into the English by Than Htay.

48. Interview with Princess Hteik Su Phaya Gyi on 26 February 2005.

49. Interview with U Than Swe on 24 November 2006.

50. Interviews with Prince Taw Phaya on 20 February 2005 and 30 November 2006; interview with Prince Taw Phaya Galae on 27 February 2005.

51. Loomba, *Colonialism/Postcolonialism*, p. 99.

52. Interview with Princess Hteik Su Phaya Gyi on 23 November 2006.

53. Interview with Prince Taw Phaya on 30 November 2006.

54. Ibid.

55. Ibid.

56. Prince Taw Phaya Galae, *From Yadanabon to Ratnagiri*, translated for author from the Burmese into the English by Than Htay.

57. Interviews with Princess Hteik Su Phaya Gyi on 26 February 2005 and 23 November 2006.

58. Princess Hteik Su Gyi Phaya's (Rita) letter to Mr Symington dated 22 February 1972, British Library, London, MSS Eur D 1156/7.

59. Interviews with Princess Hteik Su Phaya Gyi on 26 February 2005 and 23 November 2006.
60. Interview with U Than Swe on 24 November 2006.
61. Interviews with U Than Swe on 24 November 2006 and 2 December 2006.
62. Interview with Princess Hteik Su Phaya Gyi on 23 November2006.
63. Interview with Prince Taw Phaya Galae on 27 February 2005.
64. Interview with U Than Swe on 24 November 2006.
65. Prince Taw Phaya's letter to author dated 9 February 2006.
66. Interview with Princess Hteik Su Phaya Gyi on 23 November 2006.
67. Interview with U Than Swe on 24 November 2006 (including quotation); U Than Swe's letter to author dated 17 April 2007; interview with Prince Taw Phaya on 20 February 2009.
68. Interview with U Than Swe on 2 December 2006.
69. Interview with Prince Taw Phaya on 30 November 2006.
70. Prince Taw Phaya Galae, *From Yadanabon to Ratnagiri*, translated for author from the Burmese into the English by Than Htay.
71. Interviews with U Than Swe on 24 November 2006 and 2 December 2006.
72. Prince Taw Phaya's letter to author dated 9 February 2006.
73. Ibid.
74. One of the Fourth Princess's children: anonymity requested.
75. Tint Naing Toe, 'The Fourth Daughter', *The Nan Net Khin Journal*, n.d., translated for author from the Burmese into the English by Than Htay.
76. Prince Taw Phaya's letter to author dated 9 February 2006.
77. Prince Taw Phaya Galae, *From Yadanabon to Ratnagiri*, translated for author from the Burmese into the English by Than Htay.
78. Interview with Prince Taw Phaya on 20 February 2009.
79. Prince Taw Phaya's letter to author dated 19 May 2008.
80. One of the Fourth Princess's children: anonymity requested.
81. Interview with U Than Swe on 24 November 2006.
82. Interview with Princess Hteik Su Phaya Gyi on 26 February 2005; interview with U Than Swe on 24 November 2006.
83. Prince Taw Phaya's letter to author dated 22 May 2005.
84. Interview with Princess Hteik Su Phaya Gyi on 23 November 2006.
85. Prince Taw Phaya's letter to author dated 9 February 2006.

19. The First Princess

1. Interview with U Than Swe on 2 December 2006.
2. Interview with S.S. Salgaonkar on 19 July 2004.
3. Interview with U Than Swe on 2 December 2006; PD 930/1921, pp. M1–M4, The Maharashtra State Archives, Mumbai.
4. PD no. 1049/1920, p. M13, The Maharashtra State Archives, Mumbai.
5. Ibid., pp. M13, M21.
6. PD 1667/1921, pp. M3–M11, The Maharashtra State Archives, Mumbai.
7. Ibid.
8. Ibid., p.M15.
9. V.G. Khobrekar, *Konkan: From the Earliest to 1818 A.D.*, p. 314; Anil Joshi's letter to author dated 14 December 2004 (explaining that social customs described in 'Konkan' book were the same upto 1947).
10. Interview with Dr (Mrs) Gore on 25 November 2004; interview with Mr and Mrs Abhyankar on 26 November 2004.
11. Khobrekar, *Konkan: From the Earliest to 1818 A.D.*, pp. 314, 315; Anil Joshi's letter to author dated 14 December 2004.
12. Interview with Dr (Mrs) Gore on 25 November 2004; Khobrekar, *Konkan: From the Earliest to 1818 A.D.*, p. 315; Anil Joshi's letter to author dated 14 December 2004.
13. Interview with Vijay Salvi on 24 November 2004.
14. Interview with Shakuntaladevi Sawant on 28 November 2004.
15. Ibid.
16. Interview with Vijayrao Salvi on 12 August 2007.
17. Interview with S.S. Salgaonkar on 19 July 2004.
18. Interview with Vijayrao Salvi on 24 November 2004.
19. Interview with Anil Joshi on 26 November 2004; interview with Mr Masurkar on 12 August 2007.
20. PD 1133/1920, p. M43, The Maharashtra State Archives, Mumbai.
21. Interview with Mohan Shirke on 12 August 2007.
22. Interview with Shakuntaladevi Sawant on 28 November 2004.
23. Interviews with Vilas C. Sawant on 19 July 2004 and 11 August 2007; interview with Chandrakant Pawar (Chandu) on 17 July 2004.
24. Interviews with Vilas C. Sawant on 20 July 2004, 26 November 2004 and 11 August 2007; interview with Dr Shinde on 11 August 2007.
25. Interview with B. Parulekar on 19 July 2004; interview with Vilas C. Sawant on 20 July 2004.
26. PD 1133/1920, p. M6, The Maharashtra State Archives, Mumbai.

27. Interviews with Vilas C. Sawant on 20 July 2004 and 11 August 2007.
28. Interview with S.S. Salgaonkar on 19 July 2004; interview with Vijayrao Salvi on 12 August 2007.
29. Interview with Dr (Mrs) Gore on 25 November 2004; interview with Vijayrao Salvi on 12 August 2007; Anil Joshi's email to author dated 22 January 2005.
30. Interview with B.Parulekar on 19 July 2004.
31. U Than Swe, *Records of the Royal Audiences*, ch. 12, translated for author from the Burmese into the English by Than Htay.
32. Interview with Vijayrao Salvi on 24 November 2004; interview with Dr (Mrs) Gore on 25 November 2004.
33. W.C.B. Purser and K.J. Saunders, ed., *Modern Buddhism in Burma. Being an Epitome of Information Received from Missionaries, Officials & Others*, p. 33.
34. Interview with U Than Swe on 2 December 2006.
35. Interview with S.S. Salgaonkar on 19 July 2004.
36. Interview with K.B. Shirke and Rajendra Shirke on 26 November 2004.
37. Proceedings of the PD July–August 1917, p. 1,336, The Maharashtra State Archives, Mumbai.
38. Interview with Chandrakant Pawar (Chandu) on 11 August 2007.
39. Interview with Vijayrao Salvi on 24 November 2004; interview with Chandrakant Pawar (Chandu) on 11 August 2007.
40. Interviews with Vijayrao Salvi on 24 November2004 and 12 August 2007.
41. Interview with S.S. Salgaonkar on 19 July 2004.
42. Interview with Mohan Shirke on 12 August 2007.
43. Interviews with S.S. Salgaonkar on 19 July 2004 and 12 August 2007.
44. Interview with B. Parulekar on 19 July 2004.
45. Interviews with S.S. Salgaonkar on 19 July 2004 and 24 November 2004.
46. Interviews with Vijayrao Salvi on 24 November 2004 and 12 August 2007.
47. The First Princess's letter to the Second Princess dated 18 December 1939, courtesy Kamal Chandarana (Gulabi).
48. Pyizone, 'The Second Daughter Who Made Her Home in Kalimpong', *Yoke Shin Amyoutay Magazine*, 2005, translated for author from the Burmese into the English by Than Htay.

49. The Second Princess's letter to the collector, Ratnagiri, dated 30 January 1939, courtesy Kamal Chandarana (Gulabi).

50. Office of the collector, Ratnagiri, to the Second Princess. Letter dated 25 June 1939, courtesy Kamal Chandarana (Gulabi).

51. Interviews with Prince Taw Phaya on 20 February 2005 and 30 November 2006.

52. 'Shall We Ignore Them?', *Journalgyaw Weekly*, 29 June 1940, translated for author from the Burmese into the English by Than Htay.

53. Interview with Prince Taw Phaya on 30 November 2006.

54. Interview with S.S. Salgaonkar on 19 July 2004.

55. Interview with Prince Taw Phaya on 20 February 2005.

56. 'Heart-breaking Matters', *The Myanma Alin Daily*, 14 November 1938, translated for author from the Burmese into the English by Than Htay.

57. Interview with Prince Taw Phaya Galae on 27 February 2005.

58. 'Heart-breaking Matters.'

59. Interview with Prince Taw Phaya Galae on 27 February 2005.

60. 'Heart-breaking Matters'; 'Shall We Ignore Them?'.

61. Ibid.

62. Ibid.

63. 'Shall We Ignore Them?'

64. Interviews with K.B. Shirke and Rajendra Shirke on 26 November 2004.

65. Interview with S.S. Salgaonkar on 19 July 2004.

66. Interview with U Than Swe on 2 December 2006; letter to author dated 17 April 2007.

67. Interview with B. Parulekar on 19 July 2004.

68. Interview with Vijayrao Salvi on 12 August 2007.

69. Telephone interview with Mohan Shirke on 28 November 2004; interview with Mohan Shirke on 12 August 2007.

70. Interviews with Chandrakant Pawar (Chandu) on 16 July 2004 and 19 July 2004.

71. Interview with Sulabha S. Gijbale (Tara) on 27 November 2004.

72. Interview with Malti More on 25 November 2004; interview with Mohan Shirke on 12 August 2007; interview with Vijayrao Salvi on 24 November 2004.

73. Telephone interview with Rajendra Shirke on 28 November 2004.

74. Interview with Vijayrao Salvi on 27 November 2004.

75. Interview with Vilas C. Sawant on 26 November 2004.

76. Interviews with S.S. Salgaonkar on 19 July 2004 and 27 November 2004.

77. Interview with Vijayrao Salvi on 12 August 2007.

78. A gentleman (an employee) sitting in Udyam Nagar Society Office (the last home of the First Princess). Interview on 27 November 2004.

79. 'Burmese Princess's Death', *The Times of India*, 7 June 1947.

80. Series 10/1 677, 226, HE. 47, pp. 17–18, National Archives Department of Myanmar, Yangon.

81. Ibid., p. 1.

82. Desai, *Deposed King Thibaw of Burma in India, 1885–1916*, p. 95.

83. A. N. Alim, Additional Treasury Office, Ratnagiri Treasury, Ratnagiri. Interview on 25 November 2004; and scan of their 'Strong Room Register' with the help of Tara Subramaniam.

20. The First Princess's Daughter

1. Interview with Sulabha S. Gijbale (Tara) on 12 August 2007.

2. PD 1133/1920, p. M6, The Maharashtra State Archives, Mumbai.

3. Anil Joshi, 'The Pauper Princess Isn't Asking for Much', *Chitralekha*, 15 January 1996, translated for author from the Marathi into the English by Vidula Warawdekar.

4. Interview with Mr Gajabhiye, Director, Directorate of Archaeology and Museum, Mumbai, on 12 April 2005.

5. Interview with Dr (Mrs) Gore on 25 November 2004.

6. Interview with Vijayrao Salvi on 12 August 2007.

7. Interview with Vijayrao Salvi on 24 November 2004; interview with Malti More on 11 August 2007.

8. PD 2093-2/1920, p. M255, The Maharashtra State Archives, Mumbai.

9. S.A. Ajgaonkar, Affidavit dated 16 June 1984, courtesy Chandrakant Pawar.

10. Interview with Chandrakant Pawar (Chandu) on 11 August 2007; interview with Malti More on 11 August 2007.

11. Interview with Vijayrao Salvi on 24 November 2004.

12. Interview with Malti More on 25 November 2004.

13. Interview with Vijayrao Salvi on 24 November 2004.

14. Interview with Malti More on 25 November 2004; interview with Vijayrao Salvi on 24 November 2004.

15. Civil Appeal no. 115 of 1992 in the Court of the District Judge, Ratnagiri, at Ratnagiri, courtesy Chandrakant Pawar.

16. Interview with Malti More on 25 November 2004; interviews with K.B. Shirke and Rajendra Shirke on 26 November 2004.

17. Interview with Mr Gajabhiye, Director, Directorate of Archaeology and Museum, Mumbai, on 12 April 2005.

18. Anil Joshi, 'The Pauper Princess Isn't Asking for Much'.

19. S.A. Ajgaonkar, Affidavit dated 16 June 1984, courtesy Chandrakant Pawar (Chandu).

20. Interview with Chandrakant Pawar (Chandu) on 11 August 2007.

21. Interviews with Chandrakant Pawar (Chandu) on 16 July 2004 and 11 August 2007.

22. Interview with Sulabha S. Gijbale (Tara) on 27 November 2004; interview with Chandrakant Pawar (Chandu) on 11 August 2007.

23. Interview with S.S. Salgaonkar on 19 July 2004; Civil Suit no. 76 of 1957 in the Court of the Civil Judge, Ratnagiri, at Ratnagiri (age of Shankar), courtesy Chandrakant Pawar (Chandu).

24. Interview with Chandrakant Pawar (Chandu) on 11 August 2007.

25. Interview with S.S. Salgaonkar on 24 November 2004.

26. Interview with Malti More on 25 November 2004.

27. Interview with K.B. Shirke and Rajendra Shirke on 26 November 2004.

28. Interview with Malti More on 25 November 2004.

29. Interview with K.B. Shirke and Rajendra Shirke on 26 November 2004.

30. Civil Suit no. 76 of 1957 in the Court of the Civil Judge, Ratnagiri, at Ratnagiri, courtesy Chandrakant Pawar (Chandu); photographs showing family working in the fields, courtesy Chandrakant Pawar (Chandu).

31. Interview with S.S. Salgaonkar on 19 July 2004; interview with Mr and Mrs Kanitker on 26 November 2004.

32. Interview with Urmilla C. Pawar on 17 July 2004; interview with K.B. Shirke and Rajendra Shirke on 26 November 2004.

33. Interview with Sulabha S. Gijbale (Tara) on 27 November 2004.

34. Interview with Malti More on 25 November 2004.

35. Interview with Sulabha S. Gijbale (Tara) on 27 November 2004.

36. Interview with Malti More on 25 November 2004; interview with Sulabha S. Gijbale (Tara) on 12 August 2007.

37. Interview with Vijayrao Salvi on 24 November 2004; interview with Mr and Mrs Kanitker on 26 November 2004.

38. Interview with S.S.Salgaonkar on 19 July 2004.

39. Interview with Mr and Mrs Kanitker on 26 November 2004.

40. Interview with S.S. Salgaonkar on 19 July 2004.

41. Interview with K.B. Shirke and Rajendra Shirke on 26 November 2004; interview with Sulabha S. Gijbale (Tara) on 27 November 2004.

42. Interview with Sulabha S. Gijbale (Tara) on 27 November 2004.

43. Telephone interview with Dr Shinde on 7 August 2005.

44. Interview with Chandrakant Pawar (Chandu) on 24 November 2004; interview with Vijayrao Salvi on 24 November 2004.

45. Interview with K.B. Shirke and Rajendra Shirke on 26 November 2004.

46. Interview with Urmilla C. Pawar on 17 July 2004; interview with K.B. Shirke and Rajendra Shirke on 26 November 2004.

47. Interview with Chandrakant Pawar (Chandu) on 11 August 2007.

48. 'Heart-breaking Matters'; 'Shall We Ignore Them?'

49. Interview with Chandrakant Pawar (Chandu) on 11 August 2007.

50. Interview with K.B. Shirke and Rajendra Shirke on 26 November 2004.

51. Interview with Sulabha S. Gijbale (Tara) on 27 November 2004.

52. Interview with Mr Gajabhiye, Director, Directorate of Archaeology and Museum, Mumbai, on 12 April 2005.

53. Interview with Urmilla C. Pawar on 17 July 2004.

54. Interview with Sulabha S. Gijbale (Tara) on 12 August 2007.

55. Interview with S.S. Salgaonkar on 24 November 2004.

56. Interview with Vilas C. Sawant on 20 July 2004; interview with Shakuntaladevi Sawant on 28 November 2004.

57. Interview with Chandrakant Pawar (Chandu) on 11 August 2007; interview with Sulabha S. Gijbale (Tara) on 12 August 2007.

58. Interview with B. Parulekar on 19 July 2004; interview with Vilas C. Sawant on 20 July 2004.

59. Interview with Vilas C. Sawant on 26 November2004.

60. Interview with Urmila C. Pawar on 17 July 2004.

61. Interview with Dr (Mrs) Gore on 25 November 2004.

62. Interview with Sulabha S. Gijbale (Tara) on 12 August 2007.

63. Interview with Urmilla C. Pawar on 17 July 2004.

64. Interview with Sulabha S. Gijbale (Tara) on 12 August 2007; statement by Chandrakant Pawar in support of Tu Tu's legal case for her property (date of his father's death), courtesy Chandrakant Pawar (Chandu).

65. Interview with Malti More on 25 November 2004.

66. Interview with Suryakant Sathe on 12 August 2007.

67. Interview with Swarupa Sathe (Sangeeta) on 17 July 2004.

68. Telephone interview with Dr Shinde on 7 August 2005.

69. Interview with Mr Masurkar on 12 August 2007.

70. Interview with Anil Joshi on 26 November 2004.

71. Interview with Sulabha S. Gijbale (Tara) on 12 August 2007.

72. Interview with Kamal Chandarana (Gulabi) on 5 June 2005.

73. Interview with Princess Hteik Su Phaya Gyi on 26 Febraury 2005.

74. Interview with Prince Taw Phaya on 20 February 2005.

75. Legal papers pertaining to Tu Tu's rental property case, courtesy Chandrakant Pawar (Chandu).

76. Interview with Mr and Mrs Kanitker on 26 November 2004.

77. Civil Appeal no. 115 of 1992 in the Court of the District Judge, Ratnagiri, at Ratnagiri, courtesy Chandrakant Pawar (Chandu).

78. Interview with S.S. Salgaonkar on 27 November 2004.

79. Interview with Chandrakant Pawar (Chandu) on 11 August 2007.

80. Interview with Prince Taw Phaya on 30 November 2006.

81. Interview with K.B. Shirke and Rajendra Shirke on 26 November 2004; Desai, *Deposed King Thibaw of Burma in India, 1885–1916*, p. 105.

82. Interviews with Anil Joshi on 26 November 2004 and 18 July 2007.

83. Interview with Chandrakant Pawar (Chandu) on 16 July 2004; photograph of Tu Tu on Chandrakant Pawar's living room wall mentions the date of her death.

84. Interviews with Chandrakant Pawar (Chandu) on 16 July 2004 and 11 August 2007.

85. Interview with Malti More on 25 November 2004.

21. The Second Princess

1. PDC no. 204-2/1917, p. M393, The Maharashtra State Archives, Mumbai.

2. Ibid., p. M57.

3. Ibid., pp. M284–M285.

4. The Second Princess's letter dated April 1929 to the viceroy and governor general of Burma, courtesy Kamal Chandarana (Gulabi).

5. PD no. 2093-2/1920, p. M607, The Maharashtra State Archives, Mumbai.

6. Interview with Kamal Chandarana (Gulabi) on 5 June 2005; various letters, courtesy Kamal Chandarana (Gulabi).

7. PDC 1917/204-2, p. M275, The Maharashtra State Archives, Mumbai.

8. Interview with Maung Lu Gyi on 3 June 2005.

9. Monila De, 'Burma Raja', *The Statesman*, 13 December 2002.

10. Telephone interview with Kamal Chandarana (Gulabi) on 14 April 2005.

11. Sangharakshita, *Facing Mount Kanchenjunga*, pp. 133, 135.

12. Ibid., pp. 135, 137.

13. Sangharakshita, *In the Sign of the Golden Wheel*, p. 194; interview with Kamal Chandarana (Gulabi) on 5 June 2005.

14. Ibid.; visit by author to Springburn on 5 June 2005.

15. De, 'Burma Raja'.

16. Card from the Raja and Rani Dorji to Prince and Princess Latthakin, courtesy Kamal Chandarana (Gulabi); interview with Kamal Chandarana (Gulabi) on 5 June 2005.

17. Sangharakshita, *Facing Mount Kanchenjunga*, pp. 132, 144.

18. Latthakin's letter to Dr Graham dated 3 February 1928, courtesy Kamal Chandarana (Gulabi).

19. Interview with Kamal Chandarana (Gulabi) on 5 June 2005; various papers of the Second Princess and Latthakin, courtesy Kamal Chandarana (Gulabi).

20. Sangharakshita, *Facing Mount Kanchengunga*, p. 237.

21. Interview with Kamal Chandarana (Gulabi) on 5 June 2005; various books/papers of the Second Princess and Latthakin, courtesy Kamal Chandarana (Gulabi).

22. Interview with Maung Lu Gyi on 3 June 2005; interview with Kamal Chandarana (Gulabi) on 5 June 2005.

23. Interview with Kamal Chandarana (Gulabi) on 5 June 2005; various papers of the Second Princess and Latthakin, courtesy Kamal Chandarana (Gulabi).

24. Interview with Maung Lu Gyi and Kamal Chandarana (Gulabi) on 25 February 2008; diaries of the Second Princess and Latthakin, courtesy Kamal Chandarana (Gulabi).

25. U Than Swe, *Yoak-Shin Taikabya Magazine*, no. 10, October 2005, translated for author from the Burmese into the English by Mya Mya Kin. (Reference: *Thuriya Magazine*, December 1924.)

26. Latthakin, 'History', courtesy Kamal Chandarana (Gulabi).

27. Latthakin's letter to the viceroy and governor general of India dated 12 December 1927, courtesy Kamal Chandarana (Gulabi).

28. 'Burmese Prince's Unique Challenge!', *The Rangoon Mail*, 18 January 1928.

29. PDC no. 204-2/1917, p. M39, The Maharashtra State Archives, Mumbai.

30. Prince Taw Phaya Galae (Aung Zay), 'Latthakin, the Great Patriot', *Payphuhlwar Magazine*, November 1987, issue no. 78, translated for author from the Burmese into the English by Than Htay.

31. Interview with Kamal Chandarana (Gulabi) on 5 June 2005; interview with Maung Lu Gyi on 3 June 2005.

32. Interview with Kamal Chandarana (Gulabi) on 5 June 2005; Sangharakshita, *Facing Mount Kanchenjunga*, p. 142.

33. Interview with Maung Lu Gyi on 3 June 2005.

34. Interview with Kamal Chandarana (Gulabi) on 5 June 2005; interview with Maung Lu Gyi on 3 June 2005.

35. 1930 diary of Latthakin, courtesy Kamal Chandarana (Gulabi).

36. Interview with Maung Lu Gyi on 3 June 2005; interview with Kamal Chandarana (Gulabi) on 5 June 2005.

37. Telephone interview with Kamal Chandarana (Gulabi) on 22 October 2007; various letters of the Second Princess and Latthakin, courtesy Kamal Chandarana (Gulabi).

38. Lattkakin's letter to the governor of Bengal dated 16 July 1937, courtesy Kamal Chandarana (Gulabi).

39. Telephone interview with Kamal Chandarana (Gulabi) on 22 October 2007.

40. Latthakin, 'History', courtesy Kamal Chandarana (Gulabi).

41. Interview with Kamal Chandarana (Gulabi) on 5 June 2005; interview with Maung Lu Gyi on 3 June 2005.

42. Interview with Kamal Chandarana (Gulabi) on 5 June 2005; telephone interview with Gulabi on 5 June 2010.

43. De, 'Burma Raja'.

44. Interview with Kamal Chandarana (Gulabi) on 5 June 2005.

45. Interviews with Maung Lu Gyi on 3 June 2005 and 25 February 2008.

46. Interview with Kamal Chandarana (Gulabi) on 5 June 2005; interview with Maung Lu Gyi on 3 June 2005.

47. Interview with Kamal Chandarana (Gulabi) on 5 June 2005; interview with Maung Lu Gyi on 3 June 2005.

48. Sangharakshita, *Facing Mount Kanchenjunga*, p. 141.

49. Interview with Maung Lu Gyi on 3 June 2005.

50. Latthakin's letter to the Government of India through the chief secretary to the Government of Bengal dated 6 November 1935, courtesy Kamal Chandarana (Gulabi).

51. Latthakin's letter to the Government of India through the chief

secretary to the Government of Bengal dated 10 January 1936, courtesy Kamal Chandarana (Gulabi).

52. Interview with Kamal Chandarana (Gulabi) on 5 June 2005; visit by author to Arcadia on 5 June 2005.

53. De, 'Burma Raja'; Latthakin's letters to the Government of India through the chief secretary to the Government of Bengal dated 18 January 1937 and 3 November 1938, courtesy Kamal Chandarana (Gulabi).

54. Sangharakshita, *Facing Mount Kanchenjunga*, pp. 127, 132.

55. Ibid., p. 139

56. Interview with Kamal Chandarana (Gulabi) on 5 June 2005; visit by author to Tapoban on 5 June 2005.

57. De, 'Burma Raja'.

58. Latthakin's letter to the Government of India through the chief secretary to the Government of Bengal dated 10 January 1936 (?), courtesy Kamal Chandarana (Gulabi).

59. Interview with Maung Lu Gyi on 3 June 2005.

60. Prince Taw Phaya Galae (Aung Zay), 'Latthakin, the Great Patriot', translated for author from the Burmese into the English by Than Htay.

61. Ibid.

62. Interview with Kamal Chandarana (Gulabi) on 5 June 2005.

63. Ibid.

64. Ibid.

65. Sangharakshita, *Facing Mount Kanchenjunga*, p. 138.

66. Telephone interview with Kamal Chandarana (Gulabi) on 11 November 2005.

67. Interview with Kamal Chandarana (Gulabi) on 5 June 2005.

68. The secretary to the Union Government, Ministry of Home Affairs, Union of Burma, to the Second Princess. Letter dated 3 March 1949, courtesy Kamal Chandarana (Gulabi). The Second Princess's secretary to the president, Union Government of Burma. Letters dated 16 October 1951 and 13 December 1951, courtesy Kamal Chandarana (Gulabi).

69. Sangharakshita, *Facing Mount Kanchenjunga*, pp. 140–41.

70. Ibid., p. 140.

71. The Gratuity Law for the Royal Relatives (1951 Law no. 70), courtesy U Than Swe, translated for author from the Burmese into the English by Than Htay. Additional Secretary, Ministry of Home and Religious Affairs, Union of Burma, to the Second Princess.

Memorandum dated 30 July 1951, courtesy Kamal Chandarana
(Gulabi).

72. Interview with Kamal Chandarana (Gulabi) on 5 June 2005.

73. U Than Swe, 'The Ambassador Who Paid a Visit to the Second
    Daughter', translated for author from the Burmese into the English
    by Than Htay.

74. Ibid.

75. Ibid.

76. The Embassy, Union of Burma, New Delhi, to Imperial Bank of India.
    Letter dated 15 January 1955, courtesy Kamal Chandarana (Gulabi).
    Interview with Kamal Chandarana (Gulabi) on 5 June 2005.

77. Ibid.; various papers of the Second Princess and Latthakin, courtesy
    Kamal Chandarana (Gulabi).

78. De, 'Burma Raja'.

79. Visit by author to Panorama on 5 June 2005.

80. Interview with Kamal Chandarana (Gulabi) on 5 June 2005; interview
    with Maung Lu Gyi on 25 February 2008.

81. Sangharakshita, *In the Sign of the Golden Wheel*, p. 192.

82. Ibid., pp. 193–94.

83. Interview with Kamal Chandarana (Gulabi) on 5 June 2005.

84. Prince Taw Phaya's letter to author dated 21 May 2005; interview
    with Prince Taw Phaya on 30 November 2006.

85. Interview with Prince Taw Phaya Galae on 27 February 2005.

86. Interviews with Prince Taw Phaya on 20 February 2005 and 30
    November 2006.

87. Interview with Kamal Chandarana (Gulabi) on 5 June 2005.

88. The Second Princess. Declaration dated 13 March 1955, courtesy
    Kamal Chandarana (Gulabi).

89. Interview with Kamal Chandarana (Gulabi) on 5 June 2005; telephone
    interview with Gulabi on 22 October 2007; interview with Maung Lu
    Gyi on 3 June 2005.

90. Interview with Maung Lu Gyi on 3 June 2005; interview with Kamal
    Chandarana (Gulabi) on 5 June 2005; telephone interviews with
    Kamal Chandarana (Gulabi) on 1 July 2005 and 11 November 2005.
    The Consul General, Union of Burma, Calcutta Circular, letter dated
    4 April 1956, courtesy Kamal Chandarana (Gulabi).

91. Telephone interview with Kamal Chandarana (Gulabi) on 28 March
    2005; interview with Kamal Chandarana (Gulabi) on 5 June 2005;
    interview with Maung Lu Gyi on 3 June 2005.

92. Author attended the ceremony and handing over of the ashes.

93. Prince Taw Phaya's letter to author dated 12 September 2008.

94. Telephone conversation with U Soe Win on 23 November 2008.

22. The Third Princess

1. Interview with U Than Swe on 24 November 2006.

2. Prince Taw Phaya's letter to author dated 10 July 2005.

3. U Than Swe, *Records of the Royal Audiences*, ch. 1, translated for author from the Burmese into the English by Than Htay.

4. U Than Swe, *Records of the Royal Audiences*, ch. 12, translated for author from the Burmese into the English by Than Htay.

5. Interview with Prince Taw Phaya on 30 November 2006.

6. Ibid.; U Than Swe, *Records of the Royal Audiences*, ch. 1, translated for author from the Burmese into the English by Than Htay.

7. Interview with Prince Taw Phaya on 30 November 2006.

8. Prince Taw Phaya's letter to author dated 5 December 2007.

9. Prince Taw Phaya's letter to author dated 21 May 2005; interviews with Prince Taw Phaya on 20 February 2005 and 30 November 2006.

10. Desai, *Deposed King Thibaw of Burma in India, 1885–1916*, p. 155.

11. Interview with Prince Taw Phaya on 30 November 2006; Desai, *Deposed King Thibaw of Burma in India, 1885–1916*, p. 104.

12. Interview with Prince Taw Phaya on 20 February 2005.

13. Interview with Prince Taw Phaya on 30 November 2006.

14. Ibid.

15. Prince Taw Phaya's letter to author dated 21 May 2005.

16. *The Rangoon Mail*, letter to the editor dated 24 June 1931, written by the Third Princess; Desai, *Deposed King Thibaw of Burma in India, 1885–1916*, p. 154.

17. Interview with U Than Swe on 2 December 2006; Desai, *Deposed King Thibaw of Burma in India, 1885–1916*, pp. 154–55.

18. Interview with U Than Swe on 24 November 2006.

19. Prince Taw Phaya Galae, *From Yadanabon to Ratnagiri*, translated for author from the Burmese into the English by Than Htay.

20. Interview with Prince Taw Phaya on 30 November 2006.

21. Interview with Prince Taw Phaya Galae on 27 February 2005.

22. Interview with U Than Swe on 24 November 2006.

23. Interview with Prince Taw Phaya on 30 November 2006.

24. Interview with U Than Swe on 24 November 2006.

25. Ibid.

26. Prince Taw Phaya's letter to author dated 22 May 2005.

27. Ibid.; Prince Taw Phaya Galae, *King Thibaw: The Inside Story*, translated for author from the Burmese into the English by Than Htay. Princess Hteik Su Gyi Phaya's (Rita) letter to Mr Symington dated 22 December 1970, British Library, London, MSS Eur D 1156/7 .

28. Interview with U Than Swe on 24 November 2006.

29. Ibid.

30. Interview with Prince Taw Phaya on 30 November 2006.

31. U Than Swe's letter to author dated 3 May 2005.

32. Interview with U Than Swe on 24 November 2006.

33. Prince Taw Phaya's letter to author dated 19 May 2008.

34. Interview with U Than Swe on 24 November 2006.

35. Interview with Prince Taw Phaya on 30 November 2006.

36. Prince Taw Phaya's letter to author dated 22 May 2005.

37. Interview with Prince Taw Phaya Galae on 27 February 2005.

38. Prince Taw Phaya's letter to author dated 19 May 2008.

39. Prince Taw Phaya's letters to author dated 22 May 2005 and 10 July 2005.

40. Interview with Prince Taw Phaya on 30 November 2006.

41. Interview with U Than Swe on 24 November 2006.

42. Interview with Prince Taw Phaya on 30 November 2006.

43. Ibid.

44. Interview with Prince Taw Phaya Galae on 27 February 2005.

45. Telegrams dated 22 June 1938, courtesy Kamal Chandarana (Gulabi).

46. Interview with Prince Taw Phaya on 30 November 2006.

47. Ibid.

48. Prince Taw Phaya's letters to author dated 22 May 2005 and 19 May 2008; Princess Rita's earboring invitation card, courtesy Kamal Chandarana (Gulabi).

49. 'Ceremonies Old and New in Burma', *The Illustrated Weekly of India*, 29 May 1938.

50. Prince Taw Phaya's letters to author dated 29 October 2007 and 19 May 2008.

51. Interview with Prince Taw Phaya on 30 November 2006.

52. 'Protest by Third Princess of Burma against Discontinuation of Her Grant of Medical Expenses', *New Burma*, 21 January 1938.

53. Interview with Prince Taw Phaya on 30 November 2006.

54. Interview with Prince Taw Phaya Galae on 27 February 2005.

55. Interview with U Than Swe on 24 November 2006.

56. Interview with Prince Taw Phaya Galae on 27 February 2005.

57. Prince Taw Phaya's letter to author dated 22 May 2005.

58. Interview with Prince Taw Phaya on 30 November 2006.

59. Interview with Prince Taw Phaya on 20 February 2005.

60. Interview with Prince Taw Phaya on 30 November 2006; Prince Taw Phaya's letter to author dated 10 July 2005.

61. Interview with Prince Taw Phaya on 30 November 2006; Prince Taw Phaya's letter to author dated 9 February2006.

62. Blurbs and visuals of film nos JFU 84, 83 and ABY 81, 99, Imperial War Museum, London.

63. Maung Htin Aung, *The Stricken Peacock*, p. 116.

64. Interview with Prince Taw Phaya on 30 November 2006.

65. Ibid.; Prince Taw Phaya's letters to author dated 22 May 2005 and 12 September 2008.

66. Interview with Prince Richard on 16 February 2009.

67. Princess Hteik Su Gyi Phaya's (Rita) letter to Mr Symington dated 23 March 1971, British Library, London, MSS Eur D 1156/7.

68. Interview with Prince Taw Phaya on 30 November 2006; Prince Taw Phaya's letters to author dated 22 May 2005, 10 July 2005 and 19 May 2008.

69. Princess Hteik Su Gyi Phaya's (Rita) letter to Mr Symington dated 22 December 1970, British Library, London, MSS Eur D 1156/7.

70. Prince Taw Phaya's letter to author dated 19 May 2008.

71. Prince Taw Phaya's letter to author dated 28 November 2005.

72. Prince Taw Phaya's letters to author dated 19 May 2008 and 22 May 2005.

73. Interview with Prince Taw Phaya on 30 November 2006; The Gratuity Law for the Royal Relatives (1951 Law no. 70), translated for author from the Burmese into the English by Than Htay, courtesy U Than Swe.

74. Prince Taw Phaya Galae, *From Yadanabon to Ratnagiri*, translated for author from the Burmese into the English by Than Htay; Prince Taw Phaya Galae, *King Thibaw*, translated for author from the Burmese into the English by Than Htay.

75. Interview with U Than Swe on 24 November 2006.

76. Desai, *Deposed King Thibaw of Burma in India, 1885–1916*, pp. 106, 157–63.

77. Interview with Prince Taw Phaya on 30 November 2006.

78. Michael W. Charney, *A History of Modern Burma*, pp. 73–92.

79. Prince Taw Phaya's letter to author dated 19 May 2008; Prince Taw

Phaya Galae, *King Thibaw*, translated for author from the Burmese into the English by Than Htay.

80. Interview with U Than Swe on 2 December 2006.

81. Prince Taw Phaya's letter to author dated 9 September 2007; interview with Prince Taw Phaya on 30 November 2006.

82. U Than Swe's letter to author dated 20 June 2008.

83. Interview with U Than Swe on 24 November 2006.

84. Ibid.

85. Prince Taw Phaya's letters to author dated 22 May 2005, 10 July 2005 and 19 May 2008.

86. Ibid.

23. The Fourth Princess's Children

1. Interview with Prince Taw Phaya Galae on 27 February 2005.

2. Interview with Prince Taw Phaya on 30 November 2006. Letters to author dated 19 May 2008 and 28 November 2005.

3. Interview with Princess Hteik Su Phaya Gyi on 26 February 2005.

4. Interview with Prince Taw Phaya Galae on 27 February 2005.

5. Interview with Princess Hteik Su Phaya Gyi on 26 February 2005.

6. Interview with Prince Taw Phaya Galae on 27 February 2005.

7. Ibid.

8. Interview with Princess Hteik Su Phaya Gyi on 23 November 2006.

9. Interview with Prince Taw Phaya on 30 November 2006.

10. Series 10/1 627, 1947, 311 HE. 47, p. 1, National Archives Department of Myanmar, Yangon.

11. Prince Taw Phaya's letters to author dated 28 November 2005, 19 May 2008 and 4 November 2008.

12. Interviews with Princess Hteik Su Phaya Gyi on 26 February 2005 and 23 November 2006.

13. Maung Htin Aung, *The Stricken Peacock*, pp. 110–13; Hall, *Burma*, pp. 168–73.

14. Ibid., p. 173; Maung Htin Aung, *The Stricken Peacock*, pp. 112–15; Prince Taw Phaya Galae, *King Thibaw*, translated for author from the Burmese into the English by Than Htay.

15. Prince Taw Phaya's letter to author dated 28 November 2005.

16. Prince Taw Phaya Galae, *King Thibaw*, translated for author from the Burmese into the English by Than Htay.

17. Prince Taw Phaya's letter to author dated 28 November 2005.

18. Prince Taw Phaya Galae, *King Thibaw*, translated for author from the Burmese into the English by Than Htay.

19. Interview with U Than Swe on 2 December 2006.

20. Ibid.

21. Prince Taw Phaya Galae, *King Thibaw*, translated for author from the Burmese into the English by Than Htay.

22. Maung Htin Aung, *The Stricken Peacock*, p. 115; Hall, *Burma*, pp. 173–74.

23. Prince Taw Phaya Galae, *King Thibaw*, translated for author from the Burmese into the English by Than Htay.

24. Interview with Prince Taw Phaya Galae on 27 February 2005.

25. Prince Taw Phaya Galae, *King Thibaw*, translated for author from the Burmese into the English by Than Htay.

26. Interview with U Than Swe on 2 December 2006.

27. Thant Myint-U, *The River of Lost Footsteps*, p. 17.

28. Interview with Prince Taw Phaya on 20 February 2009.

29. Prince Taw Phaya Galae, *King Thibaw*, translated for author from the Burmese into the English by Than Htay.

30. Maung Htin Aung, *The Stricken Peacock*, pp. 122–23.

31. Speeches: Aung San of Burma. From his speech, 'An Address to the Anglo-Burmans', delivered at a meeting of the Anglo-Burman Council, at the City Hall, Rangoon, on 8 December 1946, http://aungsan.com/Anglo_Burmans.htm.

32. Prince Taw Phaya Galae, *King Thibaw*, translated for author from the Burmese into the English by Than Htay. Prince Taw Phaya's letter to author dated 19 May 2008. The Gratuity Law for the Royal Relatives (1951 Law no. 70), translated for author from the Burmese into the English by Than Htay, courtesy U Than Swe.

33. Series 10/1 627, 311 HE. 47, p. 1, National Archives Department of Myanmar, Yangon.

34. Prince Taw Phaya's letters to author dated 28 November 2005 and 9 February 2006.

35. Prince Taw Phaya's letters to author dated 22 May 2005 and 28 November 2005.

36. Prince Taw Phaya's letter to author dated 28 November 2005; Prince Taw Phaya Galae, *King Thibaw*, translated for author from the Burmese into the English by Than Htay.

37. Interviews with Princess Hteik Su Phaya Gyi on 26 February 2005 and 23 November 2006.

38. Prince Taw Phaya Galae, *King Thibaw*, translated for author from the Burmese into the English by Than Htay.

39. Interviews with Princess Hteik Su Phaya Gyi on 26 February 2005 and 23 November 2006.

40. Prince Taw Phaya's letter to author dated 28 November 2005.
41. Interview with Princess Hteik Su Phaya Gyi on 26 February 2005.
42. Ibid.
43. Prince Taw Phaya's letter to author dated 28 November 2005.
44. Interviews with Princess Hteik Su Phaya Gyi on 26 February 2005 and 23 November 2006. Princess Hteik Su Phaya Gyi's letter to author dated 30 May 2005.
45. Interview with Princess Hteik Su Phaya Gyi on 26 February 2005.
46. Prince Taw Phaya's letter to author dated 28 November 2005.
47. Interviews with Princess Hteik Su Phaya Gyi on 26 February 2005 and 23 November 2006; Princess Hteik Su Phaya Gyi's letter to author dated 25 January 2006.
48. Interview with Princess Hteik Su Phaya Gyi on 23 November 2006.
49. Interviews with Princess Hteik Su Phaya Gyi on 23 November 2006 and 15 February 2009. Letter to author dated 25 January 2006.
50. Interview with Princess Hteik Su Phaya Gyi on 23 November 2006.
51. Prince Taw Phaya's letter to author dated 22 May 2005; Prince Taw Phaya Galae, *King Thibaw*, translated for author from the Burmese into the English by Than Htay.
52. Interview with Prince Taw Phaya on 20 February 2009.
53. Interview with Prince Taw Phaya on 30 November 2006.
54. Prince Taw Phaya Galae, *From Yadanabon to Ratnagiri*, translated for author from the Burmese into the English by Than Htay.
55. Interview with Princess Hteik Su Phaya Gyi on 23 November 2006.
56. Prince Taw Phaya's letter to author dated 10 July 2005.
57. Ibid.
58. Thant Myint-U, *The River of Lost Footsteps*, pp. 290–92.
59. Prince Taw Phaya's letter to author dated 10 July 2005.
60. 'Rare Treasures Given Back To Burma After 80 Years', *The Times*, 11 November 1964.
61. Andrew Marshall, *The Trouser People*, p. 71.
62. Anonymity requested.
63. Princess Hteik Su Gyi Phaya's (Rita) letters to Mr Symington dated 23 March and 7 January 1971, British Library, London, MSS Eur D 1156/7.
64. Interview with Prince Taw Phaya on 30 November 2006.
65. Prince Taw Phaya's letter to author dated 22 May 2005.
66. Desai, *Deposed King Thibaw of Burma in India, 1885–1916*, preface.
67. Prince Taw Phaya's letters to author dated 29 October 2007 and 5 December 2007.

68. Prince Taw Phaya's letter to author dated 10 July 2005.

69. Prince Taw Phaya's letter to author dated 28 November 2005.

70. Prince Taw Phaya's letters to author dated 28 November 2005 and 12 September 2008.

71. Prince Taw Phaya's letter to author dated 28 November 2005.

72. Interview with Daw Khin May and Daw Devi Thant Cin on 21 November 2006.

73. Interview with Prince Taw Phaya Galae on 27 February 2005.

74. Interview with Daw Khin May and Daw Devi Thant Cin on 21 November 2006.

75. Interview with Prince Taw Phaya Galae on 27 February 2005; Ludu Daw Ahmar, 'Oh! How I Yearn for Our Comrade Taw Taw', *Kalaya Magazine*, December 2006, translated for author from the Burmese into the English by Than Htay.

76. Prince Taw Phaya Galae, *King Thibaw*, translated for author from the Burmese into the English by Than Htay; interview with Daw Khin May and Daw Devi Thant Cin on 21 November 2006.

77. Prince Taw Phaya Galae, *King Thibaw*, translated for author from the Burmese into the English by Than Htay.

78. 'Unity of Opposites', *Kalaya Magazine*, September 2006, translated for author from the Burmese into the English by Than Htay; TWN, 'Writer, Poet, History Researcher Prince Taw Phaya Galae U Aung Zae Passes Away', *The New Spectator Monthly Journal*, September 2006, translated for author from the Burmese into the English by Than Htay.

79. 'Mindon's Heirs', *The Nation Supplement*, 26 August 1962.

80. Prince Taw Phaya Galae, *From Yadanabon to Ratnagiri*, translated for author from the Burmese into the English by Than Htay.

81. http://www.burmanet.org/news/2006/06/20/irrawaddy-obituary-aung-zay-1926-2006/#more-4455

82. Interview with Prince Richard on 16 February 2009.

83. Interview with Prince Taw Phaya Galae on 27 February 2005.

84. 'Burma Last King Thibaw's Grandson Is Dead', *Democratic Voice of Burma*, 18 June 2006.

85. TWN, 'Writer, Poet, History Researcher Prince Taw Phaya Galae U Aung Zae Passes Away'.

86. Interview with Princess Hteik Su Phaya Gyi on 26 February 2005.

87. http://english.dvb.no/print_news.php?id+7296; 'Burma Last King Thibaw's Grandson Is Dead', p. 11.

88. 'The Truth', vol. 8, A Detailed Study of the Statements Published by the Ayeyarwady Publishing House Using the Address of the Chiengmai University, Thailand. Office of Strategic Studies, Ministry of Defence (Myanmar). Translated by The New Light of Myanmar and Daw Kyi Kyi Hla; http://www.myanmar-information.net/truth/truth-8.pdf.

89. http://english.dvb.no/print_news.php?id+7295; 'King Thibaw's Grandson Is Ill'; *Democratic Voice of Burma*, 13 June 2006.

90. 'Grandchild of King Thibaw Passes Away', *The Myanmar Times*, 26 June–2 July 2006.

91. Ibid.

92. Lut Lat Soe, 'Prince Taw Phaya Galae (Aung Zae): A Noble Life and a Noble Death', *Wellness Magazine*, August 2006, translated for author from the Burmese into the English by Than Htay; Su The Moun, 'Portrait of Our Teacher through the Flutter of Wings', *Ma Hae Thi Magazine*, August 2006, translated for author from the Burmese into the English by Than Htay.

93. Interview with Princess Hteik Su Phaya Gyi on 23 November 2006.

94. Lut Lat Soe, 'Prince Taw Phaya Galae (Aung Zae): A Noble Life and a Noble Death', translated for author from the Burmese into the English by Than Htay; Prince Taw Phaya Galae, *From Yadanabon to Ratnagiri*, translated for author from the Burmese into the English by Than Htay; interview with Daw Khin May and Daw Devi Thant Cin on 21 November 2006; interview with Princess Hteik Su Phaya Gyi on 26 February 2005.

95. Lut Lat Soe, Prince Taw Phaya Galae (Aung Zae), 'A Noble Life and a Noble Death', translated for author from the Burmese into the English by Than Htay.

96. Ludu Daw Ahmar, 'Oh! How I Yearn for Our Comrade Taw Taw', *Kalaya Magazine*, December 2006, translated for author from the Burmese into the English by Than Htay.

97. Interview with U Than Swe on 24 November 2006.

98. Prince Taw Phaya Galae, *King Thibaw*, translated for author from the Burmese into the English by Than Htay; 'Prince Taw Phaya Galae Passes Away', *Mahar News Journal*, 22 June 2006; interview with Princess Hteik Su Phaya Gyi on 23 November 2006; Prince Taw Phaya's letters to author dated 12 September 2008 and 4 November 2008; interview with Daw Khin May and Daw Devi Thant Cin on 14 February 2009; interview with Prince Taw Phaya on 20 February 2009.

99. Interview with Prince Richard on 16 February 2009.

100. Prince Taw Phaya's letters to author dated 12 September 2008 and 10 July 2005; interview with Prince Richard on 16 February 2009.

101. Prince Taw Phaya's letter to author dated 29 October 2007.

102. Prince Taw Phaya's letters to author dated 9 February 2006 and 12 September 2008.

103. Interview with Princess Hteik Su Phaya Gyi on 23 November 2006.

104. Prince Taw Phaya's letter to author dated 12 September 2008; interview with Prince Taw Phaya on 30 November 2006.

105. Interview with Princess Hteik Su Phaya Gyi on 23 November 2006; interview with Prince Taw Phaya on 30 November 2006.

106. Interview with Prince Richard on 16 February 2009.

107. Interview with Prince Taw Phaya on 30 November 2006.

108. Interview with U Than Swe on 24 November 2006.

109. Interview with Princess Hteik Su Phaya Gyi on 23 November 2006; interview with Prince Taw Phaya on 30 November 2006.

110. Interview with Princess Hteik Su Phaya Gyi on 23 November 2006.

111. Interview with U Than Swe on 24 November 2006.

112. Interview with Princess Hteik Su Phaya Gyi on 26 February2005.

113. Interview with Prince Taw Phaya on 30 November 2006.

114. Prince Taw Phaya Galae, *From Yadanabon to Ratnagiri*, translated for author from the Burmese into the English by Than Htay.

115. Interview with U Than Swe on 2 December 2006.

116. Prince Taw Phaya Galae, *From Yadanabon to Ratnagiri*, translated for author from the Burmese into the English by Than Htay.

117. Ibid.

118. Interview with Prince Taw Phaya Galae on 27 February 2005.

119. Prince Taw Phaya Galae, *From Yadanabon to Ratnagiri*, translated for author from the Burmese into the English by Than Htay.

120. Interview with Princess Hteik Su Phaya Gyi on 26 February 2005.

121. Prince Taw Phaya Galae, *From Yadanabon to Ratnagiri*, translated for author from the Burmese into the English by Than Htay.

122. Ibid.

123. Ibid.

124. Ibid.

125. Interview with Princess Hteik Su Phaya Gyi on 15 February 2009.

126. Prince Taw Phaya Galae, *From Yadanabon to Ratnagiri*, translated for author from the Burmese into the English by Than Htay.

127. Ibid.

Epilogue

1. Interview with U Than Swe on 2 December 2006; U Than Swe's letter to author dated 17 April 2007.
2. Interview with Prince Taw Phaya on 20 February 2009.
3. 'HRH The Prince Shwebomin The Crown Prince of Burma', October 2006.
4. Interview with U Than Swe on 24 November 2006.
5. Interview with Anil Birje on 16 July 2004; interview with Chandrakant Pawar (Chandu) on 11 August 2007.
6. Interviews with B. Parulekar on 19 July 2004 and 27 November 2004.
7. Interview with Mr Achrekar, Gallery Assistant, Archaeological Survey Office, Ratnagiri, on 27 November 2004.
8. PD 2093-2/1920, pp. M273–M281, The Maharashtra State Archives, Mumbai.
9. U Than Swe, *Records of the Royal Audiences*, ch. 1, translated for author from the Burmese into the English by Than Htay.
10. Numerous visits to the tombs by author (on 27 November 2004, on 11 August 2007, etc.).
11. Interview with Mr Achrekar, Gallery Assistant, Archaeological Survey Office, Ratnagiri, on 27 November 2004.
12. Interview with Chandrakant Pawar (Chandu) on 28 September 2010.
13. Interview with Anil Joshi on 27 November 2004; Anil Joshi's email to author dated 22 January 2005.
14. Interview with S.S. Salgaonkar on 19 July 2004; interview with Chandrakant Pawar (Chandu) on 11 August 2007.
15. Interview with Chandrakant Pawar (Chandu) on 16 July 2004.
16. Interview with Malti More on 25 November 2004; interview with Dr Shinde on 11 August 2007.
17. Interview with Digambar Pawar on 16 July 2004.
18. Interview with S.S. Salgaonkar on 19 July 2004.
19. Interview with Chandrakant Pawar (Chandu) on 24 November 2004.
20. Interview with S.S. Salgaonkar on 24 November 2004.
21. Interview with Chandrakant Pawar (Chandu) on 12 August 2007.
22. Interviews with Jayshree Harishchandra Kule (Jayu) on 18 September 2007 and 11 August 2009.
23. Interview with Vilas C. Sawant on 26 November 2004.
24. Interviews with Chandrakant Pawar (Chandu) on 25 November 2004 and 24 November 2004.

25. Interview with Maung Lu Gyi on 3 June 2005.
26. Interview with Kamal Chandarana (Gulabi) on 28 September 2010.
27. Interview with Maung Lu Gyi on 3 June 2005.
28. Ibid.; interview with Kamal Chandarana (Gulabi) on 5 June 2005.
29. Ibid.
30. Telephone conversation with Kamal Chandarana (Gulabi) on 18 December 2008.
31. Interview with Kamal Chandarana (Gulabi) on 5 June 2005.
32. Prince Taw Phaya's letter to author dated 5 December 2007.
33. Telephone conversation with Prince Taw Phaya on 23 February 2012.
34. Interview with U Than Swe on 24 November 2006.
35. Prince Taw Phaya's letters to author dated 10 July 2005 and 12 September 2008.
36. Interview with Prince Taw Phaya on 30 November 2006.
37. Telephone conversation with Prince Taw Phaya on 27 December 2010.
38. Prince Taw Phaya's letter to author dated 10 July 2005; interviews with Prince Taw Phaya on 20 February 2009 and 30 November 2006.
39. Ed Cropley (Reuter's writer), 'Burma's Last Royal Laments a Crumbling Nation', *The Irrawaddy*, 10 March 2008.
40. Interview with Princess Hteik Su Phaya Gyi on 26 February 2005.
41. Interview with Prince Taw Phaya on 30 November 2006.
42. Interview with U Than Swe on 24 November 2006; Prince Taw Phaya's letter to author dated 5 December 2007.
43. Interview with U Than Swe on 24 November 2006.
44. Visit to Queen Supayalat's tomb by author on 14 February 2009 with Daw Devi Thant Cin.
45. Khin Maung Soe, 'Burma's Tomb Raiders', *The Irrawaddy*, 6 November 2006.
46. Interview with U Soe Win on 24 November 2006; interview with Princess Hteik Su Phaya Gyi on 23 November 2006.
47. U Soe Win's email to author dated 24 January 2011.
48. Interviews with Daw Khin May and Daw Devi Thant Cin on 21 November 2006 and 14 February 2009.
49. Interviews with Princess Hteik Su Phaya Gyi on 26 February 2005 and 23 November 2006.
50. Interview with Princess Hteik Su Phaya Gyi on 26 February 2005.
51. Ibid.

52. Interviews with Princess Hteik Su Phaya Gyi on 26 February 2005 and 23 November 2006.

53. Interview with Prince Taw Phaya on 30 November 2006.

54. Three of the Fourth Princess's children during interviews.

55. Interview with Princess Hteik Su Phaya Gyi on 15 February 2009 (over lunch).

56. Prince Taw Phaya Galae, *From Yadanabon to Ratnagiri*, translated for author from the Burmese into the English by Than Htay.

57. Prince Taw Phaya Galae, *King Thibaw*, translated for author from the Burmese into the English by Than Htay; three of the Fourth Princess's children during interviews.

GLOSSARY

Ashin Nanmadaw Phaya	This was how Queen Supayalat's children addressed her. It means chief queen.
Bei thei	A type of blessing or consecration usually accompanied by the pouring of lustral water. The ceremony is generally done by *ponnas*.
Dah	A Burmese style dagger.
Dhamma	Law or truth (religious); the teachings of Buddha.
Eingshe-min	Heir-apparent to the throne.
Gaung baung	A Burmese style turban.
Hluttaw	Council of State or Royal Council. Also the Supreme Court of the kingdom. (Today the term is used to refer to the parliament of the country.)
Hti	A gilded umbrella-like structure, edged with small bells, mounted at the pinnacle of buildings like pagodas. A gem-encrusted one topped the seven-tier *pyatthat* that stood over the Lion Thone in the Golden Palace, Mandalay.
Kadaw ceremony	A ceremony for paying respect and renewing an oath of fealty to the king.
Kala	Foreigners—all foreigners except the Chinese and Shans were called kala in the Kingdom of Ava. It also meant barbarian. (Today it is used colloquially to refer to people from India.)
Kalamas	In the Kingdom of Ava, foreign women were referred to as kalamas.
Karma	*Kamma* in Pali. The belief that a person's volitional actions shape his/her future.
Kodaw	Literally means 'royal body'. It is a reverential form of address used for male royalty or monks.
Konbaung	A dynasty of Burmese kings who ruled Burma from

	1752 to 1885. The founder of the dynasty was Alaungpaya. With the deposition of King Thibaw in November 1885, Konbaung rule came to an end.
La-hpet	Pickled tea-leaf. A popular snack in Burma, it is generally served with accompaniments.
Leip-bya	Literally meaning butterfly, it refers to the 'butterfly spirit', a concept animistic in origin. The 'butterfly spirit' is how the soul is described when it is not encased in the body.
Longyi	The piece of cloth (also called *pasoe*) worn traditionally by Burmese men in place of trousers.
Maung	Literally means younger brother, but a woman also uses it to address her husband affectionately. It also signifies 'Mister', and is commonly used in front of young men's names.
Mingyi	A senior minister of the Hluttaw—there were four mingyis in all in the Kingdom of Ava.
Mohinga	A very popular Burmese dish. It comprises rice noodles in a fish soup served with various accompaniments.
Nats	Spirit-beings or spirits of nature. It is believed that there are thirty-seven great nats, and numerous other minor ones.
Natwin mingala	Earboring ceremony. Burmese girls had their ears pierced at puberty. The ceremony signified their coming of age, and is now not as commonly held as it was once.
Ngapi	Fermented fish/shrimp paste commonly used as a flavouring in Burmese food.
Nirvana	*Nibbana* in Pali. It means the extinction of the flames of lust, hatred and ignorance, leading to perfect bliss. Colloquially it means freedom from suffering by escaping the cycle of birth and death.
Pali Canons	The scriptures of the Theravada School of Buddhism are known as the Pali Canons.
Parabeik	A white or black tablet made of dried palm leaf. Used for writing/painting upon.
Pardawmu	Refers to the royal procession on the day of exile of King Thibaw. Pardawmu day signifies the day when

the king and family were taken away on exile. Not always on 29 November, it is observed based on the Burmese calendar.

Paritta	Buddhist passages chanted for protection.
Pasoh/pasoe	The piece of cloth (also called longyi) worn traditionally by Burmese men in place of trousers.
Patamabyan	Examination taken by novice monks testing their knowledge of the Buddhist scriptures.
Patamagyo	A person who does very well (stands first) in the Patamabyan examination.
Pawa	Silk scarf used by women to accessorize the jacket traditionally worn over the tamein.
Pongyi	Burmese Buddhist monk.
Ponna	Indian Brahmin priests are called ponnas in Burma.
Poon Dawgyi Paya	Means 'Lord of Great Glory'. This is how Queen Supayalat referred to King Thibaw when talking about him to others. It is also how his children addressed him.
Pwe	The literal translation of pwe is a spectacular feast. Pwe means a traditional Burmese drama performance.
Pyatthat	Five- to seven-tiered, elaborately carved, stepped, wooden spire-like structure.
Sadan/sadone	A Burmese woman's hairstyle of a top knot.
Samsara	Endless cycle of life, of existence, of birth and death.
Sangha	Brotherhood or order of Buddhist monks.
Sawbwa	A Shan chieftain.
Sayadaw	A senior Buddhist monk.
Seedaw/si-daw	Royal drum.
Shan	An ethnic group in Burma, from the Shan Plateau, east of Mandalay. The Shans had their own chiefs (sawbwas), who, until King Thibaw's deposition in 1885, owed allegiance and paid taxes to the king of Burma.
Sheiko	A deep bow, on elbows and knees, with hands folded in front as if in prayer. Traditional Burmese position assumed to show deep respect.
Shinbyu	Novitiation ceremony. Around adolescence it was customary for Burmese Buddhist boys to renounce

the world and become a novice monk (very often just for a very short while). The novitiation ceremony marks this occasion. This custom is still observed by many in Burma.

Soon	Offering of rice/food to monks.
Sutta	A discourse of the Buddha's teachings.
Tabindaing	The princess who was to marry the next king and become the chief queen. Any princess of royal blood could have been declared the Tabindaing princess by the king—not necessarily the first-born daughter.
Tamein	Burmese women wore it in place of a skirt. It was a rectangular piece of cloth that was tied at the waist and reached the feet, with an overlapping slit in the front.
Tatmadaw	Burma's armed forces.
Thadingyut	Festival of Lights. Marks the end of the Buddhist Lent and is celebrated sometime in October (exact date determined by Burmese calendar).
Thakin	Members of the nationalist Do-bama Asi-ayone (We the Burmese Association). Thakin means master and was used by Burmese nationalists to signify that they were masters of their own land, and not slaves of the British.
Than Lyet	A four-edged dagger which had at one time been owned by the founder of the Konbaung dynasty, Alaungpaya. One of the five important emblems of Konbaung regalia.
Thana'kha	A yellowish brown paste, used as a cosmetic and a sun block, made from the ground bark of a flowering shrub (murraya paniculata). Still commonly used by Burmese girls and women.
Tharanagaon	A ceremony that combines animistic and Buddhist elements, and is performed as a last rite after a person's death.
Thingyan	Water Festival. It is celebrated sometime in April (exact date determined by the Burmese calendar) and marks the start of the Burmese New Year.
Wungyi	Ministers of the kingdom, members of the Hluttaw.

Yaung	Long hair tied in a top knot—old customary style for a Burmese man.
Yadanabon Naypyidaw	Mandalay, the 'Abode of Kings' (Yadanabon means a heap of gems).
Yeizet-cha	The yeizet-cha is a ceremony in which water is slowly poured from a small container into a bigger one during religious chanting. The water is then emptied onto the ground, symbolizing the calling upon of Mother Earth to witness a good deed or act of merit. This ceremony is performed to share the benefactor's good deed with all on earth, and to register the good deed in the benefactor's bank of good deeds.
Zawgyi	Alchemist with supernatural powers.

BIBLIOGRAPHY

Books

Armstrong, Karen. *Buddha* (London: Phoenix, Orion Books, 2002).

Aung San Suu Kyi. *Letters from Burma* (London: Penguin Books, 1997).

Banerjee, Anil Chandra. *Annexation of Burma* (Calcutta: A. Mukherjee & Bros, 1944).

Bennett, Paul J. *Conference under the Tamarind Tree: Three Essays in Burmese History* (New Haven: Yale University Southeast Asia Studies, 1971).

Bhattacharya, Swapna (Chakraborti). *India–Myanmar Relations, 1886–1948* (Kolkata: K.P. Bagchi & Co., 2007).

Blackburn, Terence R. *Actors on the Burmese Stage: A Trilogy of the Anglo-Burmese Wars*, vol. 3 (New Delhi: APH Publishing Corporation, 2002).

———. *The British Humiliation of Burma* (Bangkok: Orchid Press, 2000).

Brown, R. Grant. *Burma As I Saw It, 1889–1917* (London: Methuen & Co. Ltd, 1925).

Browne, Edmond Charles. *The Coming of the Great Queen: A Narrative of the Acquisition of Burma* (London: Harrison and Sons, 1888).

Charney, Michael W. *A History of Modern Burma* (Cambridge: Cambridge University Press, 2009).

———. *Powerful Learning: Buddhist Literati and the Throne in Burma's Last Dynasty, 1752–1885* (Ann Arbor: Centers for South and Southeast Asian Studies, University of Michigan, 2006).

Correspondence Relating to Burmah since the Accession of King Theebaw in October 1878: Presented to Both Houses of Parliament by Command of Her Majesty. (London: Eyre and Spottiswoode, 1886).

Cruel and Vicious Repression of Myanmar Peoples by Imperialists and Fascists and the True Story about the Plunder of the Royal Jewels (Myanmar: Media Group of the Committee for Propaganda and Agitation to Intensify Patriotism, Government of the Union of Myanmar, Ministry of Information, Government of the Union of Myanmar, 1991).

Desai, W.S. *Deposed King Thibaw of Burma in India, 1885–1916* (Bombay: Bharatiya Vidya Bhavan, 1967).

Curtis, William Eleroy: *Egypt, Burma, and British Malaysia* (London: Fleming H. Revell Co., 1905).

Marks. John Ebenezer. *Forty Years in Burma* (London: Hutchinson & Co., 1917).

Fielding-Hall, Harold. *Burmese Palace Tales* (Bangkok: White Lotus Co. Ltd, 1997).

———. *The Soul of a People* (London: Macmillan & Co. Ltd, 1898).

———. *Thibaw's Queen* (London and New York: Harper & Brothers, 1899).

Fink, Christina. *Living Silence: Burma under Military Rule* (Bangkok: White Lotus; Dhaka: University Press; London: Zed Books, 2001).

Foucar, E.C.V. *Mandalay the Golden* (London: Dobson Books Ltd, 1963).

Gandhi, Rajmohan. *Mohandas: A True Story of a Man, His People, and an Empire* (New Delhi: Viking, Penguin Books India, 2006).

Gazetteer of the Bombay Presidency: Ratnagiri and Savantvadi Districts, vol. 10 (Mumbai: The Executive Editor and Secretary, Gazetteers Department, Government of Maharashtra, 1996).

Hall, D.E.G. *Burma* (London: Hutchinson's University Library, 1998).

Halton, Elaine Ida. *Lord of the Celestial Elephant* (London: Elaine Halton, 1999).

Harvey, G.E. *History of Burma* (London: Frank Cass & Co. Ltd, 1967).

Jesse, F. Tennyson. *The Lacquer Lady* (New York: The Dial Press, 1981).

———. *The Story of Burma* (London: Macmillan, 1946).

Keeton, C.L. *King Thebaw and the Ecological Rape of Burma* (Delhi: Manohar Book Service, 1974).

Khobrekar, V.G. *Konkan: From the Earliest to 1818 A.D. (A Study in Political, and Socio-economic Aspects)* (Pune: Snehavardhan Publishing House, 2002).

Knox, Thomas W. *The Boy Travellers: Ceylon and India* (New York: Harper & Brothers, 1882).

Lambert, Charles William. *The Missionary Martyr of Thibaw: A Brief Record of the Life and Consecrated Missionary Labours of Charles William Lambert in Upper Burma* (London: Partridge & Co., 1896).

Loomba, Ania. *Colonialism/Postcolonialism* (London & New York: Routledge, 2007).

Lyall, Alfred P.C. *The Life of the Marquis of Dufferin and Ava* (London: Thomas Nelson & Sons, 1905 (?)).

Mandalay Palace, The Directorate of Archaeological Survey, Ministry of

Union Culture, Revolutionary Government of the Union of Burma (Rangoon: Rangoon University Press, 1963).

Marchioness of Dufferin & Ava. *Our Viceregal Life in India: Selections from My Journal, 1884–1888*, vol. I (London: John Murray, 1889).

Marshall, Andrew. *The Trouser People: A Story of Burma in the Shadow of the Empire* (Washington DC: Counterpoint, 2002).

Maugham, Somerset W. *The Gentleman in the Parlour: A Record of a Journey from Rangoon to Haiphong* (London: William Heinemann Ltd, 1930 (?)).

Martin, Steven, Looby, Mic, Clark, Michael, and Cummings. Joe, *Myanmar (Burma)* (Melbourne: Lonely Planet, 2002).

Maung Htin Aung. *Folk Elements in Burmese Buddhism* (Rangoon: Religious Affairs Dept Press, 1959).

———. *The Stricken Peacock: Anglo-Burmese Relations 1752–1948* (The Hague: Martinus Nijhoff, 1965).

Mi Mi Khaing. *Burmese Family* (Bangkok: Ava House, 1996).

———. *The World of Burmese Women* (London: Zed Books, 1984).

Moore, Lucy. *Maharanis: The Lives and Times of Three Generations of Indian Princesses* (London: Viking, Penguin Books, 2004).

Ni Ni Myint. *Selected Writings of Ni Ni Myint* (Yangon: Myanmar Historical Commission, 2004).

O'Connor, V.C. Scott. *Mandalay and Other Cities of the Past in Burma* (Bangkok: White Lotus, Ava Publishing House Ltd, 1996).

Olszewski, Peter. *Land of a Thousand Eyes: The Subtle Pleasures of Everyday Life in Myanmar* (Crows Nest, Australia: Allen & Unwin, 2005).

Oolay. *Ballads of Burma* (Bangkok: Orchid Press, 2000).

Orwell, George. *Burmese Days* (London: Penguin Books and Martin Secker & Warburg Ltd, 2001).

Pascal Khoo Thwe. *From the Land of Green Ghosts: A Burmese Odyssey* (London: Harper Perennial, HarperCollins, 2002).

Pe Maung Tin and Luce, G.H. *The Glass Palace Chronicle of the Kings of Burma* (Rangoon: Rangoon University Press, 1960).

Porter, Bernard. *The Lion's Share: A Short History of British Imperialism 1850–1995* (London: Longman, 1996).

Rawe Htun, trans. San Lwin. *The Modern Buddhist Nun* (Waibargi, North Okkalarpa, Burma: U Tin Shein, 2001).

Purser, W.C.B., and Saunders, K.J., ed. *Modern Buddhism in Burma: Being an Epitome of Information Received from Missionaries, Officials & Others* (Rangoon: Christian Literature Society, Burma Branch, 1914).

Richter, Anne. *The Jewelry of Southeast Asia* (London: Thames & Hudson, 2000).

Sao Sanda. *The Moon Princess: Memories of the Shan States* (Bangkok: River Books Co. Ltd, 2008).

Sangharakshita. *Facing Mount Kanchenjunga: An English Buddhist in the Eastern Himalayas* (Birmingham: Windhorse Publications, 1991). (Also available online: http://www.sangharakshita.org/bookshelf/facing-kanchenjunga.pdf)

———. *In the Sign of the Golden Wheel: Indian Memoirs of an English Buddhist* (Birmingham: Windhorse Publications, 1996). (Also available online: http://www.sangharakshita.org/bookshelf/golden-wheel.pdf)

Saw Myat Yin. *Culture Shock! A Survival Guide to Customs and Etiquette: Myanmar* (Tarrington, New York: Marshall Cavendish Corporation, 2007).

Shway Yoe. *The Burman: His Life and Notions* (London: Macmillan and Co. Ltd, 1910).

Singer, Noel F. *Burmah: A Photographic Journey, 1855–1925* (Gartmore, Stirling, UK: Paul Strachan-Kiscadale Ltd, 1993).

Skidmore, Monique. *Karaoke Fascism: Burma and the Politics of Fear* (Philadelphia: University of Pennsylvania Press, 2004).

Stewart, A.T.Q. *The Pagoda War: Lord Dufferin and the Fall of the Kingdom of Ava, 1885–6* (Bangkok: White Lotus Press, 2003).

Prince Taw Phaya Galae. *King Thibaw: The Inside Story* (Rangoon: Thiha Yadana, 1959). Translated for the author from the Burmese into the English by Than Htay.

———. *From Yadanabon to Ratnagiri* (Yangon: Nan Devi Company, 2007). Translated for the author from the Burmese into the English by Than Htay.

Thant Myint-U. *The Making of Modern Burma* (Cambridge: Cambridge University Press, 2001).

———. *The River of Lost Footsteps: Histories of Burma* (New York: Farrar, Straus and Giroux, 2006).

Than Tun, ed. *The Royal Orders of Burma, A.D. 1598–1885,* vol. 9, A.D. 1853–1885 (Kyoto: Centre for Southeast Asian Studies, Kyoto University, 1989).

Tin Maung Kyi, Dr. *150th Anniversary of Mandalay (1859–2009)* (Mandalay: Gant Gaw Myaing Publishing House, 2008).

U Pok Ni, trans. Hla Pe. *Konmara Pya Zat. An Example of Popular Burmese Drama in the 19th Century,* vol. 1 (London: Luzac & Co. Ltd, 1952).

U Than Swe. *Records of the Royal Audiences* (Myanmar: Yarpyii Bookhouse, 2003). Translated for the author from the Burmese into the English by Than Htay. (Before the publication of this book, the *Sarphat Thu* journal carried many of its chapters as articles.)

U Thein Maung. *A Collection of Ratnagiri Articles (The Inside Story of King Thibaw's Ratnagiri Days)* (Yangon: Nay Yee Yee Publishing House, 2008). Translated for the author from the Burmese into the English by Than Htay.

Zimmer, Heinrich Robert. *Philosophies of India* (Princeton: Princeton University Press, 1974).

Interviews and Letters

Mr and Mrs Abhyankar. Personal interview with author, in Ratnagiri, on 26 November 2004.

Mr Achrekar. Gallery Assistant, Archeological Survey Office, Thebaw Palace, Ratnagiri. Personal interviews with author on 16 July 2004 and 27 November 2004.

Mr Alim, A.N. Additional Treasury Officer, Ratnagiri Treasury, Ratnagiri. Personal interview with author on 25 November 2004.

Birje, Anil. Personal interview with author, in Ratnagiri, on 16 July 2004.

Borkar, R.R. Personal interview with author, in Mumbai, on 24 June 2005.

Borkar, R.R. Letter and photographs to author, sent on 10 July 2005.

Bose, Indira. Personal interview with author, in Kalimpong, on 5 June 2005.

Chandarana, Kamal (Gulabi). Personal interviews with author, in Kalimpong, Kolkata and Ratnagiri, on 3–5 June 2005, 24–25 February 2008 and 28–29 September 2010, and telephone interviews over the years.

Daw Khin May and Daw Devi Thant Cin. Personal interviews with author, in Yangon, on 21 November 2006, 23 November 2006 and 14 February 2009, and telephone interviews over the years.

Daw Devi Thant Cin. Letters to author dated 23 October 2008 and 13 November 2005.

De, Monila. Personal interview with author, in Kalimpong, on 5 June 2005.

Dr (Mrs) Gore. Personal interviews with author, in Ratnagiri, on 20 July 2004, 25 November 2004 and 26 November 2004.

Mr Gajabhiye. Director, Directorate of Archeology & Museum, Mumbai (now retired). Personal interviews with author on 5 August 2004 and 12 April 2005.

Gandhi, Nanasahib. Personal interview with author, in Ratnagiri, on 19 July 2004.

Gijbale, Sulabha S. (Tara). Personal interviews with author, in Ratnagiri, on 27 November 2004 and 12 August 2007.

'HRH the Prince Shwebomin the Crown Prince of Burma'. Personal interview with author, in London, in mid-October 2006.

Joshi, Anil. Personal interviews with author, in Ratnagiri, on 26 November 2004 and 27 November 2004, in Mumbai, on 25 May 2006, and telephone interviews over the years.

Joshi, Anil. Letters to author sent on 14 December 2004 and 8 April 2005 and email sent on 22 January 2005.

Mr & Mrs Josse C.R. Personal interview with author, in Kalimpong, on 5 June 2005.

Mr and Mrs Kanitker. Personal interview with author, in Ratnagiri, on 26 November 2004.

Kule, Jayshree Harishchandra (Jayu). Personal interviews with author, in Mumbai, on 21 September 2007 and 11 August 2009.

Lad, Manik. Personal interview with author, in Mumbai, in early 2009.

Mr Lanjawar. Asst Director, Archeological Survey Office, Thebaw Palace, Ratnagiri. Personal interviews with author on 16 July 2004 and 24 November 2004.

Major Subba, M.K. Personal interview with author, in Kalimpong, on 5 June 2005.

Maung Lu Gyi. Personal interviews with author, in Kolkata, on 3 June 2005 and 25 February 2008, and telephone interviews over the years.

More, Malti. Personal interview with author, in Ratnagiri, on 25 November 2004 and 11 August 2007.

Mr Masurkar. Personal interview with author, in Ratnagiri, on 12 August 2007.

Mr Namchu. Personal interview with author, in Kalimpong, on 5 June 2005.

Mr Niturkar. Gallery Assistant, Archeological Survey Office, Thebaw Palace, Ratnagiri. Personal interview with author on 11 August 2007, and telephone interview in mid-March 2010.

Palande, Dhanashree. Personal interview with author, in Ratnagiri, on 17 July 2004.

Parulekar, Bapusahib. Personal interviews with author, in Ratnagiri, on 19 July 2004 and 27 November 2004.

Pawar, Chandrakant. Personal interviews with author, in Ratnagiri, on 16 July 2004, 19 July 2004, 24 November 2004, 25 November 2004, 27 November 2004, 11 August 2007, 12 August 2007 and 28–29 September 2010.

Pawar, Digambar. Personal interview with author, in Ratnagiri, on 16 July 2004.

Pawar, Urmilla. Personal interviews with author, in Ratnagiri, on 16 July 2004 and 17 July 2004.

Princess Hteik Su Phaya Gyi. Personal interview with author, in Yangon, on 26 February 2005, 23 November 2006 and 15 February 2009, and telephone interviews over the years.

Princess Hteik Su Phaya Gyi. Letters to author dated 10 March 2006, 24 February 2006, 25 January 2006, 18 January 2006, 24 July 2005, 5 June 2005, 30 May 2005, 7 May 2005 and 2 April 2005.

Prince Richard. Personal interview with author on 16 February 2009.

Prince Taw Phaya. Personal interview with author, in Pyin Oo Lwin, on 20 February 2005, 30 November 2006 and 20 February 2009, and telephone interviews over the years.

Prince Taw Phaya. Letters to author dated 22 October 2009, 22 June 2009, 25 July 2009, 8 January 2009, 4 November 2008, 12 September 2008, 19 May 2008, 5 December 2007, 29 October 2007, 9 September 2007, 1 October 2006, 24 August 2006, 9 February 2006, 28 November 2005, 10 July 2005, 22 May 2005, 21 May 2005, 6 April 2005 and 2 March 2005.

Prince Taw Phaya Galae, Personal interview with author, in Yangon, on 27 February 2005 and a few telephone interviews.

Prince Taw Phaya Galae. Letters to author dated 24 August 2005, 20 July 2005, 14 July 2005, 20 May 2005, 2 April 2005, 29 January 2005 and 8 January 2005.

Salgaonkar, S.S. Personal interviews with author, in Ratnagiri, on 17 July 2004, 19 July 2004, 24 November 2004, 27 November 2004 and 12 August 2007.

Salgaonkar, S.S. Letter to author dated 21 August 2004.

Salvi, Vijayrao. Personal interviews with author, in Ratnagiri, sent on 24 November 2004, 27 November 2004 and 12 August 2007.

Sathe, Sangeeta. Personal interview with author, in Ratnagiri, on 17 July 2004 and 12 August 2007.

Sathe, Suryakant. Personal interview with author, in Ratnagiri, on 12 August 2007.

Sawant, Manali Vilas. Personal interviews with author, in Ratnagiri, on 20 July 2004, 26 November 2004, 28 November 2004 and 11 August 2007.

Sawant, Shakuntaladevi. Personal interviews with author, in Ratnagiri, on 20 July 2004 and 28 November 2004.

Sawant, Surendra. Personal interview with author, in Ratnagiri, on 20 July 2004.

Sawant, Vilas. Personal interviews with author, in Ratnagiri, on 20 July 2004, 26 November 2004, 28 November 2004 and 11 August 2007.

Sawant, Vilas. Telephone interview with author on 22 October 2007.

Dr Shinde. Personal interview with author, in Ratnagiri, on 11 August 2007, and telephone interview on 7 August 2005.

Shirke, K.B. and Rajendra. Personal interview with author, in Ratnagiri, on 26 November 2004.

Shirke, Mohan. Personal interview with author, in Ratnagiri, on 12 August 2007 and telephone interview on 28 November 2004.

Shirke, Rajendra. Telephone interview with author on 28 November 2004.

Sitling, A.T. Personal interview with author, in Kalimpong, on 5 June 2005.

Tin Maung Aye. Personal interview with author, in Mandalay, on 19 February 2009.

Tyagi, Archana. Police Commissioner, Ratnagiri. Personal interview with author, and permission to photograph the Outram House.on 19 July 2004.

U Aung Win. Personal interview with author, in Mandalay, on 21 February 2009.

U Sein Maung Oo and Princess Tin Tin Kyi. Personal interviews with author, in Yangon, on 26 February 2005, 21 November 2006 and 15 February 2009, and telephone interview on 3 February 2005.

U Sein Maung Oo. Letters to author dated 22 June 2006, 18 May 2006, 29 January 2006, 13 November 2005, 13 October2005, 8 February 2005, 29 January2005, 19 October 2004 and 10 October 2004.

U Soe Win. Personal interview with author on 24 November 2006 and 14 February 2009, and telephone interview on 23 November 2008.

U Than Swe. Personal interviews with author, in Yangon, on 2 December 2006, 24 November 2006 and 26 February 2005, and telephone interviews over the years.

U Than Swe. Letters to author dated 12 May 2009, 20 June 2008, 8 January 2008, 30 December 2007, 2 September 2007, 7 August 2007,12 May 2007, 17 April 2007, 16 February 2007, 27 October 2005, 20 July 2005, 10 June 2005, 3 May 2005 and 1 April 2005.

Newspapers/Magazines/Bulletins/Journals

'The Ambassador Who Paid a Visit to the Second Daughter', by U Than Swe, *Yadanagiri Neetgone Yarpyi Sarpay*, May 2009. Translated for the author from the Burmese into the English by Than Htay.

'An Attractive Compound Wall for Thiba's Palace', *Tarun Bharat,* 17 July 2004. Translated for the author from the Marathi into the English by Vidula Warawdekar.

'The British "Pacification" of Burma: Order without Meaning', by Michael Aung-Thwin, *Journal of Southeast Asian Studies,* vol. 16, no. 2, September 1985.

'Burmah' (Reports Death of Royal White Elephant (?)), *The Times,* 17 December 1885.

'Burmah', *The Times,* 12 October 1885, 19 December 1885 and 28 December 1885.

'Burma's Ex-Queen Dead', *The New York Times,* 25 November 1925.

'Burma Raja', by Monila De, *The Statesman,* 13 December 2002.

'The Burmese Envoy in Paris', *The Times,* 8 December 1885.

'Burmese Princess's Death', *The Times of India,* 7 June 1947.

'Burmese Prince's Unique Challenge', *The Rangoon Mail,* 18 January 1928.

'The Burmese Regalia', *The Times,* Letter to the Editor, September 1965.

'The Burmese War', *The Times,* 1 December 1885, 2 December 1885, 4–5 December 1885 and 7 December 1885.

'The Burmese War. Occupation of Mandalay', *The Times,* 3 December 1885.

'Burmese Wedding. Thebaw's Daughter Married', *The Times of India,* 5 July 1920.

'Ceremonies Old and New in Burma', *The Illustrated Weekly of India,* 29 May 1938.

'Chief Queen Hteik Su Myat Phaya: The Final Chapter of the Donor of the Mandalay Mya Taung Monastery', by Ludu Daw Ahmar, *Myadaung Tharthanar Nittaya,* January 1983. Translated for the author from the Burmese into the English by Than Htay.

'Contemplating about Death', by Maung Moe Thu, *Kalaya Magazine,* 2006. Translated for the author from the Burmese into the English by Than Htay.

'Crown Princess Hteik Su Myat Phaya, the First Daughter of King Thibaw Passed Away', *The Hanthawaddy Daily,* 19 June 1947. Translated for the author from the Burmese into the English by Than Htay.

'Events Beyond the Sea', *The New York Times,* 1 January 1886.

'Ex-King Theebaw in Exile', *The New York Times,* 30 November 1895. (From *The London Daily News.*)

'Ex-King Theebaw. Atrocities of His Reign', *The Times,* 21 December 1916.

'Ex-King Theebaw Dead. Sketch of His Wild Reign', *The Times of India,* 19 December 1916.

'Ex-Queen of Burma. Report on Complaints', *The Times,* 12 February 1925.

'Ex-Queen Supayalat of Burma. Death from Heart Failure', *The Times of India,* 25 November 1925.

'The Fourth Daughter', by Tint Naing Toe, *The Nan Net Khin Journal*, n.d. Translated for the author from the Burmese into the English by Than Htay.

'The Fourth Princess's Explanation. Letter to Editor Dated 23/7/1931', *The Rangoon Mail*, 26 July 1931.

'Gossip from the Old World', *The New York Times*, 25 January 1885.

'Grandchild of King Thibaw Passes Away', *The Myanmar Times*, 26 June–2 July 2006.

'Heart-breaking Matters', *The Myanma Alin Daily*, 14 November 1938. Translated for the author from the Burmese into the English by Than Htay.

'Hundred Times behind the Bars', by Anil Joshi, *Lokprabha*, 14 May 2004. Translated for the author from the Marathi into the English by Aksharmaya.

'The Hidden Treasures at Mandalay, Burmah', *The Illustrated London News*, 14 April 1894.

'Interview with King Theebaw's Brother in Calcutta', *The Times of India*, 5 November 1885.

'King Theebaw's Treasures, Some of the Loot from His Mandalay Palace Exhibited', *The New York Times*, 10 October 1886. (From *The London Telegraph.*)

'Last of the Burmese Kings, Mr Noyce Reminiscences', *New Burma*, 6 December 1935.

'Latthakin, the Great Patriot', by Prince Taw Phaya Galae (Aung Zay), *Payphuhlwar Magazine*, November 1987, no. 78. Translated for the author from the Burmese into the English by Than Htay.

'Lecturer U Thet Tin Attends a Royal Audience', by U Than Swe, unpublished, courtesy U Than Swe.

'Ledi Panditta in Chief Queen's Presence', by U Than Swe, unpublished, courtesy U Than Swe.

'Letter to the Governor of Burma, from The Second Princess', by U Than Swe, *Yoak-Shin Taikabya Magazine*, no. 10, October 2005. (Reference: *Thuriya Magazine*, December 1924.) Translated for the author from the Burmese into the English by Daw Mya Mya Kin.

'Life at the Burmese Court under the Konbaung Kings', by Yi Yi, *Journal of the Burma Research Society (JBRS)*, vol. 44, no. 1, June 1961.

'Lord Dufferin's Career', *The New York Times*, 1 April 1905.

'The Lost Royal Grandeur', by Abhijeet Hegshetye, *Maharashtra Times*, 15 April 1989. Translated for the author from the Marathi into the English by Vidula Warawdekar.

'The Mandalay Gazette', *The New York Times*, 26 December 1879.

'Mindon's Heirs', *The Nation Supplement*, 26 August 1962.

'The Monarch of Mandalay', *The New York Times*, 28 March 1879.

'Oh! How I Yearn for Our Comrade Taw Taw', by Ludu Daw Ahmar, *Kalaya Magazine*, December 2006. Translated for the author from the Burmese into the English by Than Htay.

'The Passing of Burma's Ex-Queen', *The Rangoon Times*, 1926.

'The Pauper Princess Isn't Asking for Much', by Anil Joshi, *Chitralekha*, 15 January 1996. Translated for the author from the Marathi into the English by Vidula Warawdekar.

'Portrait of Our Teacher through the Flutter of Wings', by Su The Moun, *Ma Hae Thi Magazine*, August 2006. Translated for the author from the Burmese into the English by Than Htay.

'Prince Taw Phaya Galae (Aung Zae): A Noble Life and a Noble Death', by Lut Lat Soe, *Wellness Magazine*, August 2006. Translated for the author from the Burmese into the English by Than Htay.

'Prince Taw Phaya Galae (Aung Zay): An Everlasting Memory', by Nan Ei Ei Zar, *Tha Ra Phu Magazine*, August 2006. Translated for the author from the Burmese into the English by Than Htay.

'Princess Paya', *The New York Times*, 7 June 1947.

'Protest by Third Princess of Burma against Discontinuation of Her Grant of Medical Expenses', *New Burma*, 21 January 1938.

'The Queen of Burmah', *The New York Times*, 21 May 1882. (From *Fraser's Magazine*.)

'Queen Tharasein Attends a Royal Audience', by U Than Swe, unpublished, courtesy U Than Swe.

'Rare Treasures Given Back to Burma After 80 Years', *The Times*, 11 November 1964.

'The Reconstruction of Mandalay Palace: An Interim Report on Aspects of Design', by Elizabeth More, Bulletin of the SOAS, vol. 56, no. 2.

'Reported Death of Ex-King Theebaw', *The Times*, 20 December 1916.

'Royal Palace of Mandalay', *The New York Times*, 4 June 1882. (From *Fraser's Magazine*.)

'Taw Phaya Galae Passes Away', by Khin Maung Nyunt, *Maha News Journal*, 2006. Translated for the author from the Burmese into the English by Than Htay.

'The Ruler of Mandalay', *The New York Times*, 20 February 1881.

'The Second Daughter Who Made Her Home in Kalimpong', by Pyizone, *Yoke Shin Amyoutay Magazine*, 2005. Translated for the author from the Burmese into the English by Than Htay.

BIBLIOGRAPHY

'Shall We Ignore Them?' *Journalgyaw Weekly*, 29 June 1940. Translated for the author from the Burmese into the English by Than Htay.

'The Situation in Burmah', *The Times of India*, 21 December 1885.

'Some of Theebaw's Crimes', *The New York Times*, 14 May 1882 (From *The London Daily News*.)

'A Song Composed in Honour of Hteik Su Myat Phaya Lat' (anthology of poems), *Dagon Magazine*, n.d. Translated for the author from the Burmese into the English by Than Htay.

'The Story of Ashin Hteik Su Myat Phaya Lat and Khin Maung Lat', *The Myanma Alin*, n.d. Translated for the author from the Burmese into the English by Than Htay.

'The Sun-descended King', *The New York Times*, 9 April 1880.

'Theebaw and His Capital', *The New York Times*, 27 December 1885. (From *The Pall Mall Gazette*.)

'Theebaw in Exile', *The New York Times*, 17 February 1886. (From *The London Daily News*.)

'Theebaw's Gilded Palace', *The New York Times*, 27 June 1888.

'Theebaw's Wife and Baby', *The New York Times*, 25 November 1883. (From *The Times of India*.)

'Theebaw's Taxes', *The New York Times*, 21 May 1882. (Rangoon Letter to *The London Daily News*.)

'Theebaw in Rutnagherry', *The Times of India*, 19 April 1886.

'Three Burmese Queens', *The New York Times*, 20 August 1888.

'Three Hundred Carats', *The New York Times*, 3 August 1890.

'Thiba's Granddaughter, Tu Tu Alias Baisu, Has the Right to Prove Her Tenancy Rights', *Ratnabhumi*, 14 December 1987. Translated for the author from the Marathi into the English by Vidula Warawdekar.

'The Third Princess on Her Marriage Controversy. Letter to the Editor Dated June 24, 1931', *The Rangoon Mail*, n.d.

'This Is the Way King Thiba of Burma Lived in Ratnagiri', by Anil Shrikhande, *Saptahik Manohar*, 18–24 June 1978. Translated for the author from the Marathi into the English by Aksharmaya.

'Thrones of Burmese Kings', by Yi Yi (read by permission of the Burma Historical Commission at the Kanthaseinlai Society on 31 January 1960), *Journal of Burma Research Society (JBRS)*, vol. 43, no. 2, December 1960.

'Tu Tu Pawar, King Thiba's Homeless Granddaughter, to Get Land from the State', *Ratnagiri Times*, 3 August 1995. Translated for the author from the Marathi into the English by Vidula Warawdekar.

'U Chit Phwe, Daw Sein Thon Attends a Royal Audience', by U Than Swe, unpublished, courtesy U Than Swe.

r Burmah & British Interests in the East', *The Times of India*, 4 November
1885,

ity of Opposites', by Pa Ra Gu, *Kalaya Magazine*, September 2006.
Translated for the author from the Burmese into the English by
Than Htay.

'Voyage through Burma', *The Illustrated London News* Group, London, 1995.

'The War in Upper Burmah', *The Times of India*, 19 December 1885.

'Why Theebaw Lost Burmah', *The Times*, 28 March 1890. (From *The Rangoon
Gazette*.)

'Writer, Poet, History Researcher Prince Taw Phaya Galae U Aung Zae
Passes Away', by TWN, *The New Spectator Monthly Journal*, September
2006. Translated for the author from the Burmese into the
English by Than Htay.

Miscellaneous

Aung Zaw. 'Behold a New Empire', *The Irrawaddy*, October 2006, vol. 14, no.
10, http://www.irrawaddymedia.com/article.php?art_id=6426%3
E&Submit=Submit.

Barron, Cheryll. 'Burma: Feminist Utopia?' *Prospect Magazine*, issue 139, 27
October 2007, http://www.prospectmagazine.co.uk/2007/10/
burmafeministutopia/.

'Burma Last King Thibaw's Grandson Is Dead', *Democratic Voice of Burma*, 18
June 2006, http://www.dvb.no/ (DVB website)—article no longer
accessible.

'Burmese Letter to King George II Deciphered After More Than 250
Years', by Victoria Ward, *The Telegraph*, 14 January 2011, http://
www.telegraph.co.uk/news/worldnews/asia/burmamyanmar/
8259851/Burmese-letter-to-King-George-II-deciphered-after-
more-than-250-years.html.

Finlay, Kirkman. 'An Account of a Journey from Rangoon by Train and
Steamer to Mandalay Which Took Place between 21 January and
14 February 1879' (it includes the author's account of an interview
with the Kinwun Mingyi and King Thibaw and closes with an
appeal for official intervention to open up trade with Upper
Burma). A handwritten journal, SOAS Library, London, MS/380016.

Floor Plans, Thebaw Palace, Ratnagiri. Courtesy Directorate of Archeology
& Museums, Mumbai.

'The Gratuity Law for the Royal Relatives' (1951 Law no. 7), 1 October
1950. Courtesy U Than Swe. Translated for author from the
Burmese into the English by Than Htay.

Halliday, James (aka David Symington). An unpublished manuscript, Britis
Library, London, MSS EUR D 1156/10.

'Irrawaddy: Obituary: Aung Zay (1926–2006)', 20 June 2006, http://
www.burmanet.org/news/2006/06/20/irrawaddy-obituary-aung-
zay-1926-2006/#more-4455.

Khin Maung Soe. 'Burma's Tomb Raiders', *The Irrawaddy*, November 2006,
vol. 14, no. 11, http://www.irrawaddy.org/article.php?art_id=6434.

———. 'The Tragic Queen', *The Irrawaddy*, February 2007, vol. 15, no. 2,
http://www.irrawaddy.org/article.php?art_id=6872.

'King Thibaw's Grandson Is Ill', *Democratic Voice of Burma*, 13 June 2006,
http://www.dvb.no/—DVB website—article no longer accessible.

'*Mandalay in 1878–9: The Letters of James Alfred Colbeck Originally Selected and Edited
by George H. Colbeck in 1892*', SOAS Bulletin of Burma Research,
vol. 1, no. 2, Autumn 2003, http://docs.google.com/viewer?a=v&=
cache:gFhES9YPfdEJ:web.soas.ac.uk/burma/1.2%2520PDF%
2520FILES/1.2%252011%2520colbeck.pdf+James+Alfred+
Colbeck&hl=en&gl=in&pid=bl&srcid=ADGEEShb
3FGSjyRCFrVjUTNSWb6c1Ljeq8zDDF-B26LPKn7tu
UuPlZisvDTl3kykas3GR97egQE5vU68IFMInfVblBusyp
Gr1GfXE-82BK0gfDCwM9ZSw8HGgHt4uJ__SUvKho
Si9X2I&sig=AHIEtbSWh00aOwkYJW1RmcsO5GdWQkb1dg.

'Mandalay Massacres: Upper Burma during the Reign of King Theebaw',
Rangoon Gazette Press, April 1884, British Library, London, MSS
Eur E 290/18.

Never Shall We Be Enslaved. Film directed by Kyi Soe Tun. Myat Mi Khin Film
Production, 1997. Courtesy U Than Swe.

Princess Hteik Su Gyi Phaya's (Rita) letters to David Symington (aka James
Halliday), British Library, London, MSS Eur D 1156/7.

*Private Affairs by H.R.H. the Fourth Princess, Daughter of the Late H.M. King Thi Baw
and His Crowned Queen of Burma, Whose Inner Facts are Unknown to the
Public*, courtesy Prince Taw Phaya Galae.

Sladen Collection. Rough 1885 Diary kept by Colonel Sladen. British
Library, London, MSS Eur E 290/65.

Sladen Collection. Handwritten letters regarding the Nga Mauk ruby etc.
British Library, London, MSS Eur E 290/50.

'Taw Phaya Galae (Aung Zae) 1926–2006', courtesy Daw Khin May and
Daw Devi Thant Cin. Translated for the author from the Burmese
into the English by Than Htay.

Thakin Kodaw Hmaing. Poem about the death of the Queen, *Thuriya
Magazine*, December 1925. Translated for the author from the
Burmese into the English by Than Htay.

Than Than Nwe. 'Gendered Spaces: Women in Burmese Society', *Transformations*, no. 6, February 2003, http://www.transformations journal.org/journal/issue_06/pdf/nwe.pdf.

'*The Truth*', vol. 8, *A Detailed Study of the Statements Published by the Ayeyarwady Publishing House Using the Address of the Chiengmai University, Thailand.* Office of Strategic Studies Ministry of Defence (Myanmar). Translated by the New Light of Myanmar & Daw Kyi Kyi Hla, http://www.myanmar-information.net/truth/truth-8.pdf.

Numerous legal papers pertaining to Tu Tu's property in Ratnagiri. Courtesy Chandrakant Pawar.

Numerous letters, invitations, news clippings, articles, essays, diaries, photographs, etc. belonging to Latthakin and the Second Princess. Courtesy Kamal Chandarana (Gulabi).

Films (and blurbs) regarding Mandalay Palace attack/occupation during WW2: ABY99; JFU56; JFU83; JFU84; ABY81. Film and Video Archive, Imperial War Museum, London, 18 March 2009.

Thebaw Palace Ratnagiri—printout collected at Thebaw Palace.

Speeches: Aung San of Burma. From his speech, 'An Address to the Anglo-Burmans', delivered at a meeting of the Anglo-Burman Council, at the City Hall, Rangoon, on 8 December 1946, http://aungsan.com/Anglo_Burmans.htm.

Archives Consulted

National Archives of India, New Delhi.
The Maharashtra State Archives, Mumbai.
National Archives Department of Myanmar, Yangon.

INDEX

ACKNOWLEDGEMENTS

Amitav Ghosh's enthralling and evocative book, *The Glass Palace*, is what sparked my interest in the last king of Burma and his family. His story stayed with me much after I read the last page of the book, and I felt compelled to find out what happened next. My first debt of gratitude is therefore to him, for starting me off on an extraordinary journey. My friend, Neeru Nanda, pushed me to convert the interest into a book, and has been there for me every step of the way—to her I am sincerely thankful.

Descendants of King Thibaw and Queen Supayalat in India and Burma very generously shared their memories and much of their time with me, networked me with others, gave me old articles and newspaper clippings, books written by them and others, and old photographs. They were a real pleasure to meet and to get to know, and to them I am forever grateful: the First Princess's grandchildren, the late Digambar Pawar, Chandrakant Pawar (Chandu), Malti More, Sulabha Gijbale (Tara); the Second Princess's son, the late Maung Lu Gyi; the Fourth Princess's children, Princess Hteik Su Phaya Gyi, Prince Taw Phaya (a special thanks to him for the long letters he penned in response to my endless questions), and the late Prince Taw Phaya Galae. Other members of the family to whom I am grateful include: Urmilla Pawar, Jayshree Kule (Jayu), Sangeeta Sathe and Sunil Gijbale; Kamal Chandarana (Gulabi) (a special thanks to her for having accompanied me to Kalimpong, and for all the material she shared with me); Daw Khin May, Daw Devi Thant Cin, U Soe Win, Daw Naing Naing Win and Prince Richard.

There are so many others without whom this book would either not have been possible, or the journey not as meaningful and enjoyable, and to them all, named or unnamed, I would like to express my deep gratitude. These include:

Dr Thant Thaw Kaung of Myanmar Book Centre, Yangon, my first contact in Burma, not only supplied me with books and articles, but also helped connect me with one of King Thibaw's grandsons. Two wonderful gentlemen, U Sein Maung Oo and U Than Swe, amazingly well versed in the history of the Burmese royal family, very generously shared their knowledge, and gave me numerous photographs, articles and books. (A special thanks to U Than Swe for all the time and information he gave me in spite of his very busy schedule). Princess Tin Tin Kyi, Winn Myintzu, Dr Tin Maung Aye and Bay Bay (Thiri Aung) also helped me in various ways. Dr Than Htay did almost all my translations from Burmese into the English (by hand!), so neatly and carefully. Umaa Gupta and Daw Mya Mya Kin also kindly helped me with some translations.

In Ratnagiri, Anil Joshi, a journalist, was of great help, as was Dr (Mrs) Gore, Bapusahib Parulekar, Vijayrao Salvi, Rajendra Shirke, Mohan Shirke, and the late S.S. Salgaonkar. Gopal Bhaurao Sawant's daughter-in-law, the late Shakuntaladevi Sawant, his grandson, Vilas Sawant, and Vilas's wife, Manali, also generously shared information with me. Archana Tyagi, Police Commissioner (2004), permitted me to photograph her residence (Outram House). Successive assistant directors and gallery assistants at the Archeological Survey Office, Thebaw Palace, (including Mr Lanjawar, Mr Surve, Mr Achrekar and Mr Niturkar) have all been very kind and repeatedly gave me permission to wander around and photograph the property. Collectors and treasury officers in Ratnagiri have given me time over the years, and have attempted to locate the ashes of the First Princess, but very disappointingly nothing has come of it so far. I interviewed numerous people in Ratnagiri, and they were all gracious and informative and I apologize for not naming them all individually. My friend Tara Subramaniam accompanied me on most of my trips to Ratnagiri and assisted me with Marathi; her help was invaluable. Vijaya Dabholkar, Vidula Warawdekar and Aksharmaya translated for me numerous Marathi articles (and a book) into the English. Mr Gajabhiye, now ex-

Director, Directorate of Archeology and Museums, Mumbai, provided me with very useful information both about Tu Tu, whom he had personally interviewed, and about the Royal Residence (officially called Thebaw Palace) and the tombs in Ratnagiri. Mr Borkar, who had worked in Ratnagiri years ago, also shared information on Tu Tu and her family and gave me a few photographs.

Monila De, a writer in Kalimpong, was gracious and helpful. Various people in Kalimpong told me stories they had heard, let me wander through their homes, and take photographs. These were homes in which the Second Princess had stayed: the Josses (Arcadia), Mr Namchu (Panorama 2), Major Madan Subba (Panorama 1), Indira Bose (Tapoban), A.T. Sitling (Vikchu Kothi). I am particularly grateful to Mr Sitling for introducing me to the writings of Sangharakshita, the English Buddhist monk, who had known Latthakin and the Second Princess.

Sanjay Narayen introduced me to the Maharashtra State Archives— a very useful introduction as this archive holds a wealth of information on King Thibaw's years in Ratnagiri. Suprabha Agarwal, Director, Ashok Kharade (now retired) and Mr Thombre, all from the Maharashtra State Archives in Mumbai, have been extremely helpful as have all their staff. U Soe Paing, the Myanmar consul in Kolkata, helped me get permission to research in the National Archives Department of Myanmar in Yangon (and assisted me in helping Maung Lu Gyi get his mother's ashes back to Burma). The deputy director, Daw Khin Khin Mya, and her research assistants (including Latt Latt Soe), at the National Archives Department of Myanmar, were amazingly obliging, quick and efficient. The staff at the National Archives of India, New Delhi, was very cooperative, as was the staff at the British Library, London, both in the India Office Records, St Pancras, and in Newspapers, Colindale. At the British Library, I'd like to specially mention Nisha Mithani of India Office Private Papers, who kindly assisted in clearing some of my doubts, and Jackie Brown and Jovita Callueng, Permissions Assistants, who efficiently helped me get clarifications and permissions for copyright material. Joy Wheeler at the Royal Geographic Society, London, was very helpful and enabled me to view archived pictures from their collection. The Victoria and

Albert Museum, London, had held the Mandalay Regalia before it had been returned to the government of Burma in 1964, and John Clarke, Nina Appleby and Helen Persson all kindly helped me get special access to images of the Regalia. Ian Kikuchi at Imperial War Museum, London, arranged a private viewing for me of reel films of the shelling and bombing of the Golden Palace (called Fort Dufferin at the time) during the Second World War, and enthusiastically shared his views on some of them.

Dr Michael Charney, Reader in South East Asian and Imperial History at the School of Oriental and African Studies (SOAS), London, has been of tremendous help and support ever since I first called on him in 2005. Over the years he has generously shared information and his time. He has plugged me into a Burma Research Google group. He has gone through my manuscript and provided me with detailed comments. His help and insights have been absolutely invaluable. The staff at SOAS have also always been kind and helpful.

Amitav Ghosh not only took time to read my manuscript but also asked me many questions before writing a detailed review of the book on his blog; for this I will always be very grateful. I'm also very appreciative that Joseph Lelyveld took the time to provide me with his comments on the book.

Dushyant Dave, a senior advocate in the Supreme Court of India, along with Nikhil Goel and Sheela Goel, generously helped *pro bono* with the petition for special leave to appeal in the Supreme Court of India in 2005 in the case of Tu Tu's property in Ratnagiri, from which she had been forcibly evicted. Very unfortunately, too much time had lapsed since the case had been lost for it to be reconsidered, in spite of their best efforts.

Carmen Kagal, author and editor, was of tremendous support by being one of the first people to read my manuscript and provide me with valuable feedback. She, very generously, read it carefully again during the editing process. Vimla Patil, ex-editor of *Femina*, and a very senior journalist, generously shared photographs and stories of *her* research of the descendants of the Burmese royal family. Mr and Mrs Michael Lewis kindly introduced me in London to HRH the Prince Shwebomin, whose calling card reads: 'The Crown Prince of Burma'.

Tarini Kumar, a bright, young college student at Swarthmore College, USA, very efficiently helped me one summer with my footnotes, bibliography and more. Anil Mehta, Sangeeta Bhansali and Bimal Mehta, publishers and family friends, have generously helped me over the years with advice on various matters.

Arti Vakil, my friend, suggested in 2004 that I read Amitav Ghosh's *The Glass Palace*—my book would not have been written if I had not read this book. My friend Ketaki Sheth, a renowned photographer, took my photograph for the book jacket. Aurobind Patel, also a friend and an amazing graphic designer, structured the family tree for this book and was always available to bounce ideas off. My cousin Gita Simoes, a very talented artist and graphic designer, drew the peacock image used in the book, and helped me with the selection, and planned the layout of, the photographs and illustrations in this book. I am also grateful to Nishita Mehta and Avadhut Parsekar for having assisted Gita. Mazda Imaging did a great job of scanning and restoring images. My friend and lawyer, Poorvi Chotani, helped clarify a few aspects of the copyright law for me. My friends Priyadarshini and Rahul Kanodia, and Rajesh Agarwal and his team including Satyam Pandyaat Datamatics, also helped with copyright issues by providing me with categorized information. My friend, Vidya Vencatesan, ex-Honorary Secretary, Asiatic Society of Mumbai, and a professor at University of Mumbai, gave me countless letters of introduction to archives and libraries. Sastry Karra, a friend, introduced me to Burmese palace music, and has over the years generously gifted me with books and CDs. Dina Desai, also a friend, shared her ancestral collection of old Burmese postcards with me.

My friends Anita Mody, Minal Bajaj, Ranjana Salgaocar, Seema Javeri, Tara Subramaniam and Vandana Kanoria accompanied me on my first visit to Burma in 2005, and made it very special. (A warm thanks to Vandana for having stayed behind with me, and for always looking out for books and articles on Burma for me; and to Minal for having ensured I used a tape recorder for interviews, and for helping me locate Gulabi in Kolkata.) Anita, Minal, Seema and Vandana also read my manuscript (either in part or the whole), as did my brother, Vikram Malkani, and my friends Jaya Vencatesan, Neeru, Vidya, Rohita

Doshi, Durriya Kathawala, Saumya Roy and Kriti Bajaj. They all offered me valuable suggestions and great encouragement.

Rama Bijapurkar introduced me in early 2009 to Krishan Chopra at HarperCollins. Krishan was generous in extending deadlines, and was always available to provide clarifications. Debasri Rakshit, my editor at HarperCollins, has been of great help. I am also grateful to Shuka Jain, Art Director, and Amrita Chakravorty, Visualizer, at HarperCollins for their creative inputs for the cover of the book.

This whole endeavour would not have been possible without the support of my husband, Pradip Shah, and my son, Karan Shah. Karan repeatedly read my manuscript, and offered numerous insightful comments. Pradip has not only read my manuscript, but has accompanied me on some of my trips to Ratnagiri, Kolkata, Kalimpong, Yangon, Pwin Oo Lwin, Mandalay and London. He has passionately collected lithographs and rare books for me on his trips to London. Both have followed my research with great interest and have been extraordinarily understanding of my preoccupation.

To my great sorrow, neither of my parents, to whom this book is dedicated and to whom I owe so much, is alive to see it in print.

ABOUT THE AUTHOR

Sudha Shah was schooled in Mumbai and thereafter got her degree in Economics from Smith College, USA. Married and settled in Mumbai, she has one son. She has spent the last seven years researching and writing this book.